Chicago Skyscrapers
1871–1934

BORLAND BLDG.

ROOKERY BLDG.

AMERICAN TRUST BANK

CONTINENTAL & COMMERCIAL NAT. BANK BLDG.

MARQUETTE BLDG.

POST OFFICE

REPUBLIC BLDG.

GT. NORTHERN HOTEL

RAILWAY EXCHANGE BLDG.

MONADNOCK BLDG.

McCORMICK BLDG.

OLD COLONY BLDG.

CONGRESS HOTEL

BLACKSTONE HOTEL

TRANSPORTATION BLDG.

RAND McNALLY BLDG.

LA SALLE STATION

Chicago Skyscrapers
1871–1934

Thomas Leslie

University of Illinois Press
Urbana, Chicago, and Springfield

Frontispiece: Panorama of the Loop from
the roof of the Insurance Exchange, ca. 1913.
(*120 Photographic Views of Chicago*,
Rand McNally, 1915)

© 2013 by the Board of Trustees
of the University of Illinois
All rights reserved
Manufactured in the United States of America
C 5 4 3 2 1
∞ This book is printed on acid-free paper.

Library of Congress Cataloging-in-Publication Data
Leslie, Thomas, 1967–
Chicago skyscrapers, 1871–1934 / Thomas Leslie.
pages cm
Includes bibliographical references and index.
ISBN 978-0-252-03754-2 (cloth: alk. paper)
ISBN 978-0-252-09479-8 (e-book)
1. Skyscrapers—Illinois—Chicago—History.
2. Chicago (Ill.)—Buildings, structures, etc.
I. Title.
NA6232.L47   2013
720'.4830977311—dc22   2012040478

To my parents, who first showed me Chicago.

The laws of nature are exact, and the laws of nature have a good deal to say about what Chicago shall be.

—*Chicago Daily Tribune*, July 7, 1889

[T]he architect is not only an artist, but also an engineer, a man of science and a man of affairs. In these latter capacities, the architect of to-day has at his command instrumentalities and opportunities unknown to his predecessor. . . . [T]he architect is of the world as well as in it.

—*Dankmar Adler*, 1896

Contents

0.3 Chicago from the roof of the Court House, ca. 1870. (Chicago History Museum)

Preface

For half a century, Carl Condit's 1952 book, *The Rise of the Skyscraper*, and its subsequent expansion in 1964 as *The Chicago School of Architecture* have served as the definitive histories of tall building construction in Chicago during the late nineteenth and early twentieth century.[1] Condit (1914–1997), a Cincinnati native with degrees in literature and mechanical engineering, taught at Northwestern University from 1945 through 1982. His two books on the city's early skyscrapers won instant acclaim from historians, architects, and engineers alike, and his subsequent books on the city's urban development revealed broad links between Chicago's social, political, economic, and construction cultures. *The Chicago School of Architecture* was among the first required texts I read as an architecture student; it introduced me to the city and its buildings, and I have returned to it countless times for its unequaled scholarship and literary quality.

After fifty years, however, Condit's masterwork seems ripe for reappraisal (figure 0.3). His firm pronouncements about the "School's" aesthetic standards have left little room for discussion, and much scholarship on Chicago's architecture since Condit has thus studiously avoided issues of technology and its complicated influence and expression. Donald Hoffman's studies of John Wellborn Root's work, Gerald Larson's investigations into individual building structures, and books or articles by Tom Peters, Cecil Elliott, Sara Wermiel, and Donald Friedman have formed the major post-Condit forays into the technical aspects of these early skyscrapers. More common, however, has been a broader, welcome interest in examining Chicago skyscrapers as elements in the city's social and cultural life: Daniel Bluestone, Robert Bruegmann, Katerina Ruedi Ray, and Joanna Merwood-Salisbury, for instance, have all shown how technology was just one of many aspects that made skyscrapers so important to Chicago.

Faced with Condit's definitive scholarship, a new study on tall building construction in Chicago might best look to critical reception of his books to find a toehold, and reviewers have found much to critique in these now-iconic works. Condit's thesis was that the city's skyscraper architecture of the late nineteenth century presented a "techno-aesthetic synthesis" that was a precursor to both European modernism and (a point made only in his later book) the early twentieth century Prairie School.[2] Less tangible, but equally important, Condit proposed that this entire strain of innovative, tradition-cleansing, and structurally expressive architecture represented, in the words of critic Paul Sherman, the "humanism of the age of science: man's creative liberation through technology."[3] Condit's book suggested that progressive modernism in architecture was not merely a contemporary style, but actually a tradition dating back nearly a century, and that it had direct links to the technically based architecture of his day.

Other critics were less sanguine about Condit's theses. Henry Robert Kann, writing in *Technology and Culture*, praised Condit's linkage between structure and aesthetics, but found the claim of a connection between Loop skyscrapers and Prairie School houses tenuous.[4] Henry Russell-Hitchcock was unreserved in his critique of the 1952 book, which he found "indicative of critical unsophistication, if not of ignorance" for failing to consult major primary sources and mislabeling several key works with facile stylistic labels. He also felt that Condit's argument did not account for precedents dating back to mill construction in cities throughout the eastern seaboard.[5] Winston Weisman found more substantial problems in his belated review of *The Chicago School* for the *Journal of Architectural Historians* in 1967. Weisman was hardly a neutral reviewer; he had written extensively on the problematic use of the terms "Chicago School," and "skyscraper" (see chapter 9), and made a career of claiming examples in New York and elsewhere as precursors to the synthesis

that occurred in Chicago. He accused Condit of parochialism in leaving the impression that the early works of Jenney were "pioneer" structures when in fact precedents could be found in Boston, New York, and even Cincinnati.

More incisive was Weisman's frustration with Condit's biographical approach. "His decision to treat the monuments as products of individual architects or firms," Weisman noted, "rather than in chronological sequence, makes it difficult for the uninitiated to understand the *pattern of development*" [emphasis added]. This echoed an earlier concern of Hitchcock's that Condit had ignored "general lines of development," in his emphasis on individuals and firms.[6] Weisman went on to note that Condit's choice to divide the book by architect, rather than by chronology, obscured important developments, in particular the distinction between "articulated" and "curtain" walls. Condit had set up Sullivan's building for Schlesinger and Mayer as the "classic statement" of the former, and thus as the paradigmatic Chicago School building. But Weisman rightly pointed out that this negated the development of the thin, largely glass and terra-cotta curtain wall that had flourished in the city just a few years before. Weisman noted that these two themes—the expressed structural frame and the veiling skin—were almost entirely at odds with one another in architectural intent (see chapters 6 and 7),

and argued that it was meaningless to "stretch the rubric 'Chicago School' to include the vast variety of forms represented" by Condit's examples: the swelling brick facade of the Monadnock (Burnham & Root, 1891) and the glass undulations of the Reliance (D. H. Burnham & Co., 1895) to name but two.

Further, Weisman was troubled by Condit's arbitrary distinction between "the external expression of structure and function," which he had identified as a hallmark of the School, and "historical features" or ornament that Condit decried as "impure" or "frivolous." "There is no indication that the author realizes that the clientele of the period were not devotees of a pure architectural doctrine," Weisman wrote. "Condit's dogmatic position makes him appear less the critic and more the cult leader." Ornament, to any practicing architect, is what comes after most major problems have found a solution, and Condit's reliance on often-trivial additions of colonnades, cornices, or stringcourses to assess the historical importance of large blocks of steel, brick, and terra-cotta have struck many as counterproductive. Condit's efforts to cast the city's architects as father figures to the ascendant and allegedly ahistorical "school" of international style modernism obscured, for Weisman, the richer, messier histories of these structures, especially their client's tastes and desires, their precedents and influences, and—particularly important—

their actual technical conceptions. Condit, Weisman concluded, "seems to be less concerned with understanding the architecture of Chicago than with judging it on the basis of a rather arbitrary set of criteria."[7]

Weisman's critiques are particularly potent after two generations, when the stylistic rigors of midcentury skyscraper modernism that Condit valued are seen as arbitrary, just as the historical tropes of many nineteenth century skyscrapers were at the time of his book. An architectural culture that now values eclecticism and historical referents and artifacts is probably better served by a study that sees such references as mere punctuation rather than by Condit's reaction to historic ornament or the lack thereof. More importantly, however, is Weisman's concern that Condit failed to elucidate "patterns of development," in particular the inherent tension between the skyscraper as an expressed or veiled frame. At the time of Condit's writing, the frame was clearly the primary expressive motif for skyscraper architects, particularly in Chicago where immediate visual parallels could be drawn between, say, Sullivan's Schlesinger & Mayer (1899, 1902) and the Brunswick or Hartford Insurance Buildings (Skidmore, Owings, and Merrill [SOM], 1961 and 1965). Today, however, the tendency is to give primacy to the skyscraper *skin*, suppressing the frame behind for reasons both practical (environmental concerns, in partic-

ular), and aesthetic. The completion of the 1360-foot-tall Trump Tower in Chicago, also by SOM (2010), exemplifies this trend, which might better be seen in relation to the thin glass and terra-cotta skins of the Reliance or the Fisher (D. H. Burnham & Co., 1895 and 1896).

The time thus seems right to supplement Condit's masterwork with a volume that fills the lacunae noted by Weisman: first, focusing on *patterns of development* rather than *biography*; second, recognizing that Chicago's innovations often built upon examples from other cities and other disciplines; third, understanding that historic references and ornament were often deployed not in *opposition* to the expression of structure but in *support* of it; and, finally, realizing that the buildings of Condit's "School" obeyed no fixed criteria or rules, but rather sought efficiency, legibility, and continuity in an era of rapid technical and stylistic flux. This led to different formulae for construction and function based on a changing palette of materials, and thus to changes in skyscraper form, configuration, and appearance.

It is Weisman's charge to understand these structures as moments within larger "patterns of development" that offers the strongest basis for a new historiography of post-fire Chicago skyscrapers. Each of the chapters that follow examines a set of constructive developments, noting that changes in construction type—for example, Weis-

man's distinction between the articulated walls of the 1880s and the curtain walls of the 1890s—occurred alongside changes in available materials, systems, and codes, and that the appearance of a new or newly affordable material or tactic brought with it interest, investigation, and experimentation on the part of architects and builders. If these led to tangible benefits in terms of spatial efficiency, construction cost, building maintenance, or (pace Condit) marketable architectural effects, they were quickly adopted by designers and developers who sought any possible competitive advantages over their peers. Where Condit struggled to rationalize these developments within narratives of structural expression and architectural purification, parsing the structures involved in terms of their technical *causes* reveals influences that had little to do with biography or style—and that connect these buildings to much wider industrial, economic, and scientific contexts.

I use the term *cause* advisedly. It is loaded with pitfalls and potential and thus deserves careful explanation. It is too easy to see these buildings as the direct result of some impelling force—the raw push of capitalism upward, for instance, or the more benign but allegedly no less resistible force of new technologies such as steel or the elevator. This, of course, can hardly be the case; such abstract terms have no *agency* by which to raise or shape buildings. Yet it is also true that without the *motivation* of greater profits, or without the structural capabilities offered by steel or the efficient circulation of the elevator the architects, engineers, builders, and financiers of Chicago's skyscrapers would not have built them in the forms that they came to inhabit. The "hard" determinism of Condit's argument, whether intentional or not, spawned a largely deserved reaction that relied on "soft" social constructionism to investigate these buildings, but these two poles have left a productive middle ground to be explored in seeking explanations and "causes" for these buildings.

I propose that the term *cause* be understood in its strictly Aristotelean sense, or as Max Hocutt has suggested, that it be retranslated as "because" and used to show how functional, material, typological, and motive factors all enabled, contributed to, and influenced—rather than determined—skyscraper form. In the classic Aristotelean parable, the house is there "that people may live in it, but also because builders have stacked one stone upon another," and this reflects the two basic types of causation—*final* (functional), and *motive* (constructive)—that underlay Aristotle's biological investigations. As I have elsewhere suggested, it may be useful to expand Louis Sullivan's classic Chicago aphorism "form follows function" to also note that form is the less linear result of complex negotiations between construction, function, and expression,

or what Kevin Alter has called "aesthetic desires and material facts."[8] In this sense, "causes" are factors that enable, restrict, or influence the balance between required function and performance on the one hand and available materials and techniques on the other. This model does not claim agency or mechanism for any of these disembodied concepts; rather it sees the architect (or, more properly, the collective of designers, engineers, consultants, and contractors) as the orchestrator(s) of these complex and often contradictory influences. This, of course, suggests an integrative design sensibility rather than a merely compositional one that rings truer in terms of contemporary practice than heroic narratives offered by traditional histories.

In this model, designers were faced with performance requirements from their clients—primarily how to build more and more efficient floor plates, but also how to best fireproof, access, and illuminate them. They were also faced with available materials and techniques—stone, steel, brick, and glass, for instance—that offered possible solutions to these requirements alongside potential costs and complications. Brick, for example, was inexpensive, fireproof, and durable, making it ideal in some respects for skyscrapers. But it was also comparatively weak, and it could handle the loads of tall buildings only in massive, bulky piers that compromised plan efficiency. Bal-

ancing such factors, or finding ways to pair materials or techniques in order to eliminate conflicts between performance and assembly, lay in the collective wisdom of architects, engineers, builders, and clients.

Complicating even this already untidy dynamic was the role of architectural expression. Once a plan or detail had been worked out, architects and clients alike believed that this solution would have to be integrated into a coherent, overall experience—visual, formal, and/or spatial—whether conforming to the dictates of a recognizable "style" or not. This relied on the architect's sense of composition and understanding of the communicative potential of details and ornament to elucidate or to conceal structural and constructional patterns within. Much literature of the day discussed how Chicago architects eschewed "beauty" as an end and instead pursued a rigorous course of cheap, efficient designs. But even if, as the *Tribune* reported as early as 1889, "Chicago utilitarians [were] not given to making burnt-offerings to bygone ideals," it could hardly be said that appearance or composition were ignored.[9] Rather, even if ornamental programs could not be economically rationalized, it was nevertheless possible to take elements that were functional or constructional necessities—piers or columns, spandrel panels, windows, and mullions, for example—and to nudge, tailor, and punctuate them to arrive at a suitable composition. "Given conditions which would normally result in plain structures," explained the *Tribune* in 1892 at the height of the city's then-greatest building boom, "its architects have not been afraid to treat them in that manner."[10]

Montgomery Schuyler, who would return many times to the city's commercial buildings in his writings, suggested in 1891 that Burnham & Root had adopted precisely this strategy—orchestrating the functionally necessary components of a building into an aesthetically legible whole—with particular sophistication: "[T]hese buildings . . . reward their self-denial in making the design for a commercial building out of its own elements, however unpromising these may seem—in permitting the building, in a word, to impose its design upon them, and in following its indications, rather than in imposing upon the building a design derived from anything but a consideration of its own requirements."[11] This disciplined search could then be *lightly* ornamented with details that emphasized the patterns of structure and operation: "[T]he members that mark the division are carefully and successfully adjusted with reference to their place and their scale, and the treatment of the different parts is so varied as to avoid both monotony and miscellany."[12]

Efforts to refine a practical solution for a visually satisfying end were permissible expenses, as owners could no more afford an unattractive building than an overly decorative one. Schuyler praised Chicago architects for avoiding the "desire to get the better of a practical client by smuggling architecture upon him," and instead finding effective ways to gently mold and accent their client's commercial schemes toward grammatically legible designs.[13] Grammar changed, of course, as the functional and tectonic formulas of buildings changed; the solutions to a facade composed of windows in bearing brick walls were proportionally and geometrically distinct from those of windows in steel frames in particular, and while individual cleverness might be able to add some distinctive flourishes, it was inevitable that in a competitive market building designs would gravitate toward proven solutions, compositions, or arrangements. These, in turn, would suggest some architectural treatments while limiting or foreclosing on others.

This march—of gradually evolving solutions to new combinations of problems to be solved and a palette of available solutions to them—provides a developmental narrative of the kind that Weisman sought in place of Condit's biographical one. While imperfect, occasionally contradictory, and never as neat as one might prefer, arranging Chicago's tall commercial structures in terms of architecturally and constructionally distinct types proves useful in elucidating the city's skyscraper evolution from five-story mill construction at the time of the Fire to a type recognizable by 1934 as the basic template for tall building construction throughout the twentieth century. This evolution occurred in both incremental, almost unrecognizably subtle steps and in what evolutionary biologist Steven Jay Gould called "punctuated equilibrium," that is, sudden bursts of new forms or types that were quickly adopted and that sufficed for repeated iterations, until some other change in material availability, code restrictions, or functional necessity emerged. These typologies were all sensitive to their industrial, economic, and cultural contexts, and the fickle nature of the commercial rental market meant that building types were made obsolete with astonishing rapidity as new conveniences or efficiencies emerged in the market. While such an evolutionary model is limited, it was a model that was recognized even at the time, by John Root among others.[14]

A list of 330 major structures built in Chicago between the Great Fire and the Great Depression (see appendix) and an attempt to describe their technical systems (in particular, structural, foundational, and cladding) yields seven overlapping constructive *types* that dominated at various times, based on material availabilities and costs, structural techniques, code impositions, or changing functional standards (figure 0.4). The following study is thus divided into chapters that explore

0.4 Cast-iron storefronts along Lake Street, ca. 1870. (Chicago History Museum)

The overlapping dates show that this sequence was only generally chronological—daring clients pioneered improvements earlier, while the more conservative continued to build in well-tested modes even as other experiments began to prove themselves. But these overlaps also reflected the intertwined nature of the systems being considered. In particular, the separation of building structure and building skin into discrete systems—one of riveted, self-braced steel, the other of lightweight brick veneer or terra-cotta and glass—manifested itself in taller, narrower buildings and in glassier skins. These effects cannot really be separated from one another, but they merit two distinct types because they relied on distinct changes in structural engineering and in regional industry.

the technical milieu from which each type was distilled and the influence on architectural or structural composition that it suggested or encouraged. These seven material types are

- Taller masonry buildings that employed improved masonry, foundations, and fireproofing (ca. 1874–1891, chapter 2);
- Skeletal frames that offered greater plan efficiency and improved daylighting through narrower, iron-reinforced brick piers (1879–1892, chapter 3);
- Wind-braced frames that used steel to reduce spatially incfficient masonry walls and piers (1890–1897, chapter 4);
- Skins of lightweight terra-cotta and glass that exploited new wind-bracing techniques and depressed glass prices to

achieve unprecedented transparency (1895–1904, chapter 5);
- Heavier fireproof jackets around steel frames, mandated by new codes, that characterized a generation of buildings with large windows and widely spaced bulky piers (1897–1910, chapter 6);
- More solid curtain walls that reflected the ability of electric lighting and mechanical ventilation to replace thermally inefficient (and increasingly expensive) plate glass windows (1905–1918, chapter 7); and
- Towers that resulted from an explosive real estate market that challenged code restrictions on height and that took fuller advantage of powered construction and circulation (1920–1934, chapter 8).

This narrative, in addition to providing a chronology, also cuts across traditional histories based on style, in particular the notion that the Beaux-Arts somehow battled and eventually overcame the utilitarianism of the "Chicago School" (figure 0.5). Instead, such a technically based narrative demonstrates that, while mercantile classicism was latent in Chicago architecture as early as the 1892 Fair, its full flourishing occurred only after developments allowed solid skins and relatively small windows that supported its proportions and aesthetics. Indeed, the expressive Chicago Frame served as a matrix for classical ornamentation throughout its history. This assessment will show that the long-assumed antagonism between the technically conceived and expressed object—the steel frame—and the culturally situated "style" of the Beaux-Arts was in fact an intricate weaving of practical design and ornamental program.

Such a chronology does not address Weisman's other primary concern, namely, what happened in Chicago that was distinct from New York, Boston, or Philadelphia, and why this was so. Caution is in order. There is a long history of partisan debate between Chicago and New York over which city built the "first" skyscraper—a debate in which both sides are not even wrong, as the term can be defined in many equally valid ways. If we accept that the emergence of the skyscraper as a type occurred over decades, then it is perhaps more useful to consider why certain innovations occurred in one location versus another. Certainly all of these cities boasted leading examples of tall commercial buildings: by 1896 the 214-foot-tall Fiske Building and the 189-foot Ames Building marked Boston's skyline; New York could point to the 235-foot Western Union Telegraph (George B. Post, 1875), the 350-foot Pulitzer (or World) Building (George B. Post, 1890), the slightly shorter but structurally more advanced Havemeyer Building (George B. Post, 1892), or the 350-foot Manhattan Life Insurance (Kimball and Thompson, 1894) as early leaders in height. As

0.5 Times Building, ca. 1870. (Chicago History Museum)

Thomas Misa has pointed out, Chicago did not necessarily build *taller* structures, but the city did build *more* taller structures, and larger ones in terms of plan and volume, than any other city through 1890.[15] A handful of seemingly minor differences—in soil conditions, codes, and urban patterns—influenced telling distinctions between typical skyscraper construction in Chicago and elsewhere, and a culture of technical innovation and restrained, disciplined expression grew among Chicago-based architects, engineers, and builders who regularly shared their work in meetings and journals. The result, according to Schuyler, was that "undoubtedly, there is such a thing as Chicago architecture."[16]

Most apparent among these distinctions were Chicago's regular street grid

and its poor soil. The former, coupled with the city's youth, meant that developers could purchase large, rectangular lots that encouraged standard structural and circulatory systems. "In New York," noted Barr Ferree, "the custom of selling land in lots of 25 by 100 feet has given many of the office buildings an especially unhappy dimension in width," not only in terms of proportion but also in terms of functionality and, at greater heights, lateral stability.[17] In Chicago, by contrast, "builders here refuse to have anything to do with a narrow lot. They must have from forty to eighty feet of frontage."[18] Downtown land was sold by the front foot, not by the square foot, encouraging speculators to put together larger and larger plots; those along main business streets typically expanded to 100 to 150 feet of frontage.[19]

Chicago's lots thus avoided the tight, puzzle-like nesting of structure, circulation, and rental space that characterized New York and Boston buildings of the day, but Chicago's poor soil (see chapter 2) encouraged architects and engineers to divide these lots into regular point foundation grids that dealt systematically with the Loop's water-laden clay. Boston had "excellent natural foundations of clay, gravel, and sand" that presented no difficulties in constructing "a gigantic pile." Chicago's structures, however, had to sit more gingerly on the "jelly-cake" beneath, and had to be precisely calculated to avoid differential settlement. This encouraged regular, repeated column bays that surcharged the compressible soil beneath discretely and equally. As a result, not only were buildings more regular, but skeletal construction and isolated foundations—called "bridge construction" at the time—were necessities in Chicago but not in cities with firmer soil.[20]

Less distinct but still influential were the geographical confines of the Loop and Chicago's particularly progressive building code. Land prices were high in Manhattan, too, but wild swings in Chicago prices meant that speculators were keen to build more quickly to take advantage of bubbles in the local market. New York's code, however, more directly influenced that city's structural designs. By requiring wall thicknesses based on height—larger at the base

and tapering toward their tops—New York's officials assumed a type of construction known as "cage," that is, a bearing exterior wall with internal structural elements of either brick or iron. Such a system made sense in a city with bedrock foundations, but cage construction, while it occurred in Chicago during the 1880s, presented intractable difficulties on compressible soil, since its exterior masonry was inevitably heavier than the lighter iron within, and thus it settled further. By the time Chicago codified exterior wall construction in 1893, brick veneers and curtain walls were ascendant. But New York maintained its bearing-wall code for over a decade after that, negating any advantage that nonbearing curtain walls might provide in terms of space. As a result, while interior structures of New York and Chicago buildings might be similar, there was an almost inevitable difference in their exterior walls; Chicago's faced no code requirements that they be thick at the base, and thus clients and architects built exterior skins as thin and light as possible—"veneers," in the pejorative of the day.[21]

A Chicago building during the 1890s could thus be distinguished from its New York counterparts by a greater tendency toward regularity and a thinner exterior wall, but this did not account for the cultural differences between the two cities. Chicago, like any boomtown full of new money, was a place where

one's ability to hustle an extra buck or two meant far more than one's pedigree: "Here," wrote a shocked John Foster Fraser as late as 1902, "is a town where it is no disgrace to be a swindler," and the Loop developed a reputation as a business district "paying less heed to culture than to profits."[22] For many, this translated into an architectural philosophy that showed either a careless indifference to traditional styles or a bold foray into a new, utilitarian aesthetic. For the former, the "city of pig-stickers" showed its lack of manners by erecting "packing boxes with holes in them," with none of the tasteful refinement that was de rigueur in the building cultures of Boston or New York.[23]

Much of this criticism took place around the 1892–1893 World's Columbian Exposition, an event that seemed to ratify the superiority of leading New York architects, who were invited to design its more academically classical structures. Chicago architects were actually well-represented, though, and to some eastern critics the Fair's tastefulness reflected well on Chicago, showing that the city could indeed rise to a cultural occasion. "Chicago has done more for art in this country than has any other city," F. W. Fitzpatrick noted in *Inland Architect* in 1905, referring to the Exposition.[24] But this artistic expression had its place, and in a city that reveled in lack of pretense a commercial building that put on airs might seem to its hardnosed businessmen a waste of labor and expense. Just a few years after noting the city's lack of picturesqueness, Schuyler returned to compare the building cultures in New York and Chicago, and he found the plainer buildings of the latter more rigorous and thus more compelling. Influenced by the writings of M. Paul Bourget, who wrote in *Outre Mer* of Chicago's skyscrapers as "a new kind of art, an art of democracy, made by the crowd and for the crowd, an art of science," Schuyler began to assemble a utilitarian philosophy to describe the strangely satisfying aesthetics of the city's comparatively stripped-down buildings:

> There is the particular consideration that in this strictly utilitarian building the requirements are imposed with a stringency elsewhere unknown in the same degree, and very greatly to the advantage of the architecture. Elsewhere the designer of a business building commonly attempts to persuade or to hoodwink his client into sacrificing something of utility to "art," and when he succeeds, it is commonly perceptible that the sacrifice has been in vain, and that the building would have been better for its artistic purpose if it had been better for its practical purpose. . . . Commercial architecture in Chicago is long past that stage, and that it

is so is due rather to the business man than to the architect."[25]

Schuyler believed that the cost and schedule pressures brought to bear on a skyscraper project dictated simplicity, regularity, and repetition and prevented stylistic pedantry and languid detailing. The Chicago architect, in his view, was more attentive "administrator" than artist, and the results were designs that possessed little mediation between solution and expression— there was neither time nor money for stylistic detours that did not yield tangible results. Elsewhere, Schuyler suggested that this approach led architects to "the thing itself," the skyscraper noumenon presented raw and without distractions, and this was certainly overreaching, as architects did have aesthetic choices to make in the layout and detailing of even the most rigorously commercial skyscraper.[26] But these, for Schuyler, could be marshaled toward an explanation of the building's function and construction rather than simply referencing tasteful precedent. The work of a designer to clarify instead of to conceal marked for Fitzpatrick the resulting difference between Chicago's working methods and New York's:

> Chicago was not only the first city to erect tall buildings . . . but was the first to make them artistic, and is the only city today whose tall build-

ings are respectable from an artistic point of view. . . . In Chicago the architects when confronted with a tall building proposition accepted it as a new form, and something for which there was no existing precedent, and proceeded to build their structures of few architectural features, of simple lines and dignified masses. In the most part good square fronts pierced with unlabored fenestration.[27]

Where the enforced economy of lightly decorated, functionally suggestive frames spoke to the assumed honesty and thrift of the small businesses that occupied skyscrapers in the 1890s, larger companies funding headquarters projects for themselves in later decades wished to make different statements about their permanence, their worldliness, and their ability to procure and spend large amounts. But through the first years of the century, Chicago's real estate market was built on leaner, hungrier developers and on smaller, thriftier tenants, and the more ascetic, so-called "Chicago Style" of construction and composition fit that image well.

Whether this was a commercial expedient or a larger movement in architectural theory and aesthetics has been debated ever since, but the example of simpler, minimally ornamented structures certainly made Chicago's reputation as a center of architectural innovation. "No buildings of the present day have been so laughed at as the high office building of Chicago," wrote Barr Ferree in 1894, "yet in no buildings, as a rule, have the correct principles of high building design been more frankly admitted." This was due, Ferree thought, to Chicago's youth and geography—"her people are not so closely subjected," he felt, "to the influence of tradition and custom as in the East."[28] Boston architect Henry Van Brunt, writing in 1889, ascribed the burgeoning success of Chicago architecture to this lack of allegiance to tradition or fashion:

> Chicago seems to have fairly won the distinction of being the fountain-head of architectural reform in the West. . . . The dangerous liberty which the entire absence of schools, traditions, precedents, and consequently of discipline in art has conferred upon the architects of the New World, and more especially of the West, and which has given rise to all the crudeness and vulgarity of our vernacular buildings, has proved, in the hands of a few well-trained young men in Chicago a professional privilege of the most conspicuous importance—a privilege, indeed, which has not been enjoyed to the same extent in any other city in the world.[29]

Thus, while wary of Weisman's concern that Chicago seen in isolation leaves out significant developments in New York and elsewhere, even contemporary critics made a meaningful distinction between Chicago's skyscraper architecture and that of other cities. The building industry in Chicago formed its own associations, journals, and networks that functioned independently from, and in some cases in direct opposition to, those of the East Coast. Though technical knowledge and stylistic controversy flowed between the two, Chicago nourished a building culture that *was* different from New York's. Historians may disagree on exactly what separated the two, but there has long been agreement that this separate culture is worth studying, if not in isolation, than as a concentrated case of a regional development that ultimately found wide acknowledgment. There remain exceptional projects or structures that are reminders that regional building culture remained fluid. How, for example, does one parse a major Chicago building such as the 1885 Field Warehouse designed by a Boston architect? Or a significant example designed by Chicago architects but built elsewhere, such as Sullivan's 1899 Bayard Building in New York? I have generally integrated these outlying projects because the frisson they created between Chicago's building culture and that of another city often

proved productive. H. H. Richardson's Field warehouse, for instance, spurred Chicago architects to explore certain themes that influenced their work as well as later developments.

In addition to its regional focus, the following study is also temporally delimited by two events that mark the start and cessation of major construction booms in Chicago. The 1871 Fire is an unavoidable starting point, though as shown in chapter 1, the building that occurred in the fire's wake was neither as technically nor architecturally progressive as legend has it. Nonetheless, the migration of expertise and capital to the city in the early 1870s did mark an important moment in the growth of an embryonic construction industry, one that replaced a patchwork of material suppliers, jobbers, contractors, and laborers (figure 0.6). The concluding date of 1934 demands greater explanation. Condit effectively ended his history of the Chicago skyscraper in 1913, noting the final, neoclassical works of Daniel Burnham with a disparaging paragraph and then turning to the Prairie School movement that occurred in the city's hinterland. Such an abrupt transition in typology and geography is, I believe, a significant problem with Condit's work, and I have chosen to remain "downtown" longer than most historians of the Chicago School. The city's skyscrapers after 1910 were qualitatively different from those of the century's first decade, and many historians have seen them as a repudiation of the principles of earlier years. By including these I want to show that the economic, functional, and material forces that shaped the buildings of the earlier decades were linked to market conditions and available technologies that were constantly in flux, and that these changed or evolved in the generation between Sullivan's 1899 building for Schlesinger and Mayer and Graham, Anderson, Probst, and White's Wrigley Building of 1924. The former is rightly seen as an iconic statement of Chicago's values cast into architectural form, while the latter has usually met with withering historical silence. Yet, as shown in chapter 8, the city experienced massive economic, social, and cultural change in the intervening years, as did the materials and technologies available to its architects and builders. Although Wrigley codified none of the heroic struggle that has made Sullivan's career such an attractive narrative, it nevertheless encapsulated Chicago's commercial, technical, and architectural aspirations with a fidelity to functional and material contingencies just as Sullivan's building had done twenty-five years before. 1934 marked the completion of the Field Building—the last major structure in the Loop for twenty years—and while there were important connections that bridged the two decades of idle-

0.6 Construction on Webster Street, ca. 1870. (Chicago History Museum)

ness brought about by economics and war, a city devoid of major construction for twenty years seems as blank a slate and thus as worthy a chronological bracket as the acreage of ash and ruin from which the city had been rebuilt sixty-three years earlier.

The resulting study shows that Chicago in these decades was a city of laboratory-like conditions that enabled architects, engineers, and builders to learn from one another's successes and failures. The pressure exerted by the city's real estate market and its tight geographic confines combined with its access to natural resources, materials, and investment capital to create an exceptionally dynamic, energetic building climate. Architects changed their design approaches both incrementally and radically as improvements were tested and proven, and they were agile in adapting their sense of style to new materials or techniques. Out of this crucible of deadlines, tight margins and informed gambles on new techniques a tradition of commercial building emerged that, if it was not a "School," was nonetheless an approach unique to Chicago, an approach whose influence spread globally as a conceptual and aesthetic ideal (figure 0.7).

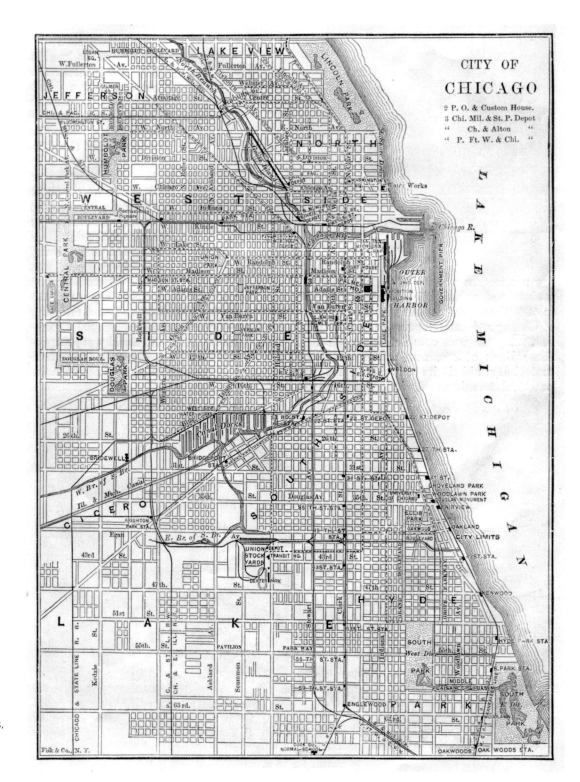

0.7 Downtown Chicago, 1884. (Augustus Allen Hays, "The Metropolis of the Prairies," *Harper's* 61, Oct. 1880, 715)

Acknowledgments

This project has enjoyed support and sustenance from several funding sources that have enabled it to persist and thrive since its inception in 2004. In particular, a Faculty Professional Development Assignment from Iowa State University, a Visiting Scholar position in the Civil and Environmental Engineering Department at Northwestern University's McCormick School of Engineering in the spring of 2010 and an extension of this time through a Sabbatical Fellowship from the American Philosophical Society in spring 2011 were vital to completing research and finishing the manuscript. I am grateful to Cal Lewis and Gregory Palermo, chairs of the Department of Architecture at Iowa State, for supporting the leave and to Dean Julio Ottino, Associate Dean Joseph Schofer, Hillary Bean, and Visiting Professor Larry Booth at Northwestern for setting up my appointment there. Mark Engelbrecht and Luis Rico-Gutierrez, as deans of Iowa State's College of Design, provided immeasurable support. I was honored to teach alongside Professor Booth, and owe him a particular debt for long and insightful conversations on architecture in Chicago. Linda Musumeci at the American Philosophical Society was exceptionally helpful in organizing their support. A Summer Stipend Award from the National Endowment for the Humanities, under their "We the People" program, enabled me to do site and archival research on the importance of plate glass to Chicago architecture in the 1890s, and a Summer Salary Grant from Iowa State's Center for Excellence in the Arts and Humanities allowed me to research and draft chapter 7, on the concealed frame. A Support Grant from the Canadian Centre for Architecture supported work to examine original construction drawings for the Monadnock Block and for the drafting of the Preface, chapter 1, and chapter 9, and I am grateful to Alexis Sornin, Genevieve Dalpé, Paul Chénier, Colin MacWhirter, and Renata Guttman for providing me access and time for this work. In the final stages of editing I also enjoyed the support of Jon Pickard and Bill Chilton, whose generous contributions to Iowa State's Department of Architecture have funded my current position as Pickard Chilton Professor in Architecture.

A visiting position at the University of Technology-Sydney in summer 2007 included time to draft significant portions of chapters 4 and 5, and I am grateful to Sandra-Kaji O'Grady for arranging a productive and enjoyable stay in Sydney. An assignment to teach in Iowa

State's Rome program in 2008 allowed time to write much of Chapter 3. Cal Lewis, Karen Bermann, Chris Kling, and Pia Schneider all provided important support during this time, and I was privileged to share a narrow writer's garret and *fatebenefratelli* status with my good friend, valued colleague, and fellow author Pete Goche.

Numerous archives and libraries played gracious host while accommodating my requests for drawings, journals, or photographs. In particular, I appreciated the assistance of the staff at the Deering and Mudd Libraries at Northwestern, the Chicago Historical Museum, the Chicago Public Library, the Ryerson and Burnham Libraries at the Art Institute of Chicago, the Crerar Library at the University of Chicago, the Architecture and campuswide libraries at the University of Illinois, the Design Reading Room and Parks Library at Iowa State (particularly Carlotta Guittierez), the Howard County, Indiana, Historical Society, the Elwood and Kokomo, Indiana, public libraries, and the Stan Mohr Local History Collection in Kokomo. The generous access allowed by HABS also aided in the production of new drawings throughout.

I was fortunate to meet and to rely upon many in the Chicago preservation and architectural communities who provided me with access to buildings, documents, or background knowledge. Gunny Harboe, Mary Brush, Anne Sullivan, and Bob Score were generous with information and ideas and provided access or contacts that proved invaluable, and the Western Great Lakes Chapter of the Association of Preservation Technology provided opportunities to test the ideas in this book in front of a knowledgeable crowd. Bill Donnell, the owner of the Monadnock Building, allowed me access to important areas of his building, as did my high school classmate Michael Blossom, who by coincidence owns two excellent boutiques on its ground floor. The Chicago Architecture Foundation assisted with access and contacts, and allowed me to present much of this work as part of their Docent Enrichment Program in 2010—I have never had such a knowledgeable or enthusiastic audience, and many of the questions they raised have helped me to clarify key points of this study. Rebecca Dixon was important in making this connection, and Pris Mims and Claudia Winkler were helpful in making connections to the Foundation's staff and community. Jackson Metcalf, Heather Weed, Kim Clawson, and Len Koroski were all generous in speaking to me about various preservation projects on which they had been involved.

Many colleagues have reviewed portions of this study or have been willing sounding boards as I've presented one idea or another to them. In particular, Jason Alread, Rob Whitehead, Leah Rudolphi, and Kevin Dong have been "go-to" sources of critique and knowledge. Don Friedman has been a constant source and fact-checker on whom I have relied since presenting aspects of this research in 2006. Brian Bowen, Anat Geva, John Ochsendorf, and Marvin Levine have also been valued colleagues in our work organizing the Construction History Society of America. Editors at *Technology and Culture*, the *Journal of Architectural Education*, the *Journal of Illinois History, Construction History*, and the *Journal of the Society of Architectural Historians* have all worked with me to make parts of this project into viable journal articles, and I am particularly grateful to Ted Cavanagh, Tom Peters, David Brownlee, and George Dodds for their assistance on these articles, as well as the anonymous readers who made productive and often pointed suggestions. Ryan Risse, Ryan Gauquie, and Shaghayegh Missaghi provided invaluable assistance in the construction of digital models, which not only provide stunning glimpses of these buildings' construction, but also reveal important new details and connections. While I have relied on the patient critique and advice of all of these colleagues, I take full responsibility for any errors or omissions in the text.

Finally, family members and lifelong friends have joined in this adventure in all kinds of ways, whether they know it or not. Ellen Mills and Russell Manthy shared my enthusiasm for local culture and cuisine, alongside architecture, and the Goys and Quinns always offered their homes as research base camps. Kathy Leslie put up with near constant conference travel and winter research trips. Most importantly, my two children have been faithful companions for long walks in the Loop and longer editing sessions in our local coffee shops. Doing our homework together has been my greatest joy this last year, and it is to Olivia and Calvin that I owe the most profound thanks.

Chicago Skyscrapers
1871–1934

Chapter 1
October 1871

Peter Bonnett Wight was one of many entrepreneurs and builders who went to Chicago following the Great Fire.[1] Frustrated by a stalled career in New York and seeking to leverage connections he had made during an earlier sojourn to the city in 1858, Wight and a young, talented colleague took up with builders Asher Carter (d. ca. 1890) and William H. Drake (n.d.). Carter, Drake, and Wight would design more than fifty buildings over the next two years, almost all of them four-story mercantile structures in the burned district; Wight's fellow traveler, John Wellborn Root (1850–1891), became the firm's chief draftsman. Within a year, Wight had also hired the feckless son of a local wholesaler as a favor. Edward Burnham's son, Daniel Hudson Burnham (1846–1912), had worked briefly in the office of Chicago architect William Le Baron Jenney (1832–1907), whose military engineering expertise in the Civil War had translated to the larger structures being demanded by the growing city. Burnham and Root became fast friends, and they would soon leave Wight's firm to set up their own practice, counting on Wight's mentorship and consulting expertise throughout their careers.[2]

The city that Wight and Root found in ruins had been a boomtown over the previous decades. As William Cronon has shown in *Nature's Metropolis*, Chicago's location at the near-confluence of two immense waterborne trade routes guaranteed that it would attract traders and speculators.[3] The slow, shallow Chicago River entered Lake Michigan along a sandbar that created a natural harbor, and the river's headwaters a few miles to the southwest were within portaging distance of the Des Plaines River, which fed the Illinois and eventually the Mississippi. Since fur-trad-

> **Chicago must have been burned down, and *I am going there.***
>
> —Peter Bonnett Wight (1838–1925), quoted by Sarah Bradford Landau,
> *P. B. Wight: Architect, Contractor, and Critic, 1838–1925.*

ing days, the proximity of the Mississippi watershed to the Great Lakes made Chicago a stopping point for nearly all goods heading east or south from the great plains. The completion of the Illinois and Michigan Canal in 1848 meant that goods could be carried by boat from New Orleans to New York without a perilous ocean voyage, but only if they passed through the increasingly mercantile city. Goods were transferred from shallow-keeled riverboats to lake boats at Chicago, providing a guaranteed market for labor, provisioning, shipbuilding, and shoreside leisure. The city attracted a reputation for its rapacious commercial market and its culture of vice and corruption.[4]

Beginning with the Chicago and Galena Railroad of 1848, railroads were rapidly concentrated in the region. Lake Michigan forced all railroads between the plains and the East Coast around its southern tip.[5] As tendrils of rail connections reached the city from the east, entrepreneurs extended the city's road and rail connection into agricultural and logging territory to the west and north. The Michigan Southern and Northern Indiana Railroads provided the city's first connection to the east in 1852, while routes west extended to the Pacific by 1869.[6] These systems shared Chicago as a terminus. Goods were unloaded and reloaded there, and layovers provided opportunities for trading and speculation. A new class of financier moved to the city to wager

on future prices, making spectacular gains and losses in markets that sprung up first on the banks of the river and later moved to more salubrious environments downtown.

The prospect of fortunes to be made in Chicago led to migration and investment. Chicago's population grew explosively throughout the nineteenth century, reaching over 300,000 by 1871. Many of these were laborers, but a growing proportion were engaged in finance. These businesses demanded office space that was cost effective and well located. Deals were struck and relationships nurtured in person, and proximity to other traders became more important than proximity to the goods being traded. The peninsula between the Chicago River's south branch and the Lake became the business and social center of the city. Businesses directly related to river trade—warehouses, grain elevators, provisioning shops, and dens of vice occupied Water Street, a congested artery that ran alongside the river. The city's commercial district focused on Lake Street, one block inland from the chaos and filth of Water Street. The lakefront along Wabash Street and Michigan Avenue was lined with higher-end residences, leaving the inland core of the peninsula for the businesses of trading, government, and more respectable lodging and entertainment. This district's streets were raised and paved between 1855 and

1858, providing improved sanitation to what would become the most prestigious and important district in Chicago.

Investment in what would later be called the Loop was rapid—indeed, explosive. Yet another class of speculators, those gambling on real estate, moved their money to the city and built structures for the growing ranks of traders, financiers, and other businessmen. Like the hardware purveyors of the California Gold Rush in the 1840s, these speculators insulated themselves from the volatility of the actual agricultural markets, relying only on the futures trade itself to ensure that their investments could be rented. Eastern capital was so interested in Chicago, however, that its real estate became an intensely volatile market on its own. Boundaries created by the river and lake and a dense network of rail yards to the south exerted a natural pressure on renters and thus investors.[7] This band of iron and water around the Loop left a fixed quantity of land, and a cycle of rabid speculation and climbing prices fed on itself throughout the century, slowed only by the Panic of 1857 and the depression of 1873–1879.[8] Around 1882, local press reported that it had become necessary for developers to "materially increase the number of stories" available in order to maximize return on exceptionally high land costs. Speculation fed on itself as individual neighborhoods within the Loop attracted interest; the opening of South Dearborn Street to a new rail station in 1885 had immediate consequences for the neighborhood now known as Printer's Row, while the Board of Trade's move to the foot of LaSalle Street in 1884 intensified building and investment in neighboring blocks.[9]

Speculation was the engine that drove Chicago's building culture. Financiers demanded efficient, lettable floors stacked to the greatest feasible heights, multiplying the dimensions of their sites as many times as possible. There were formidable limits, however, to the heights that could be achieved with available materials on the city's muddy, clay soil. If the speculative engine provided a voracious appetite for more floor area and greater height, the limited mechanisms by which such height could be achieved held even the most ambitious projects to six or seven stories. The average pre-fire commercial block in Chicago was just five.

Most apparent was the lack of efficient access to these upper floors, despite significant advances in elevatoring in the 1850s. While elevators conveyed freight and passengers in shops beginning with the Haughwout Store in New York (1854), they remained exotic novelties in office structures, where they broke down regularly and required constant maintenance. They were also slow and noisy and required full time attendance by trained operators. Moreover, the provision of a single slow cab—or, occasionally, a pair—failed to provide effective service at the be-

ginning and end of the business day, when they were swamped with passengers. Rather than extending the reach of early skyscrapers, elevators through the 1870s played only an adjunct role to grand staircases that still provided the primary access to most of a typical building's leased floors.

TRADITIONAL MATERIALS: STONE, BRICK, AND CAST IRON

Alongside inefficient elevators, skyscrapers in the post-fire era were limited by their materials, too. Timber—despite its low strength and combustibility—remained a widely used, economical material throughout the 1850s and 1860s. As the nation's leading lumber market, Chicago had easy access to the best forests of Wisconsin and Minnesota, and its builders were able to purchase at wholesale prices from incoming freight. But pressure to build cheaply and quickly also encouraged the use of shoddier wood. Mill construction, which relied on heavy oak for columns and girders that resisted fire by charring, was often replaced by framing made of smaller, more flammable pine. The city recognized that, collectively, it was building a tinderbox, but individually builders continued to risk conflagration by building cheaply. The city government mandated three "fire districts" in the 1860s that banned such construction, but these restrictions were universally ignored and "immediate profits" were placed above "future security."[10]

Builders and owners who sought greater security against fire could turn to local granite, limestone, and sandstone that was convenient for building fronts, foundations, and even bearing walls. These stones varied in strength, weathering qualities, and costs, and thus found use in a variety of circumstances. Granite and limestone generally offered the best crushing strength; granite provided an average of about 750 tons per square foot and limestone around 625.[11] Sandstone was weaker at around 200 tons per square foot, but this relatively low performance also promised greater ease of cutting and workability. In addition to strength, however, architects and builders had to consider weathering, and it was here that granite was worth its price.[12] While published reports suggested lifetimes of as low as 5 years for sandstone and 20–40 years for limestone, granite provided up to 75 years, and some published reports suggested a reliable working life of 200 years for better specimens.[13]

Geologically, Chicago sits atop a bed of limestone, and this was the major product of quarries within canal or road travel from the city; sandstone could be found further afield, and granite further still. Granite was expensive for Chicago builders, and its use was restricted to either street-level surfaces or to particularly high-end buildings. It was rarely used in the 1870s and only began to see widespread use in Chicago with the more expensive construction that occurred in the mid-1880s.[14] By the late 1880s, midwestern stone quarries were supplying Chicago with granite from Missouri, Wisconsin, and Minnesota, but the bulk of the city's quality granite came from New England, particularly from Maine, which had long-established quarrying and cutting operations that guaranteed workmanship and composition.[15] The same stone that had built Boston in the eighteenth century thus aided in the construction of many Chicago structures as well. Sandstone was available somewhat closer to hand, particularly from Berea, Amherst, and Sunbury in Ohio, from Le Grand, Iowa, and from Vert Island on the northern edge of Lake Superior, which produced a sandstone of remarkable strength and quality that could easily be shipped by lake.[16]

Locally, the Des Plaines River basin offered extensive supplies of limestone that was convenient to downtown but that varied considerably in quality.[17] These quarries' relationship to the Illinois and Michigan canal was no accident; it was excavations for this transportation link in the 1840s that revealed a bed of workable, drab limestone that gained a bright yellow hue when exposed to air.[18] The stone was quarried around Lemont and used almost at once, in a house on West Water street in 1849 and then by John Van Osdel (1811–1891) for the Tremont House and Courthouse in 1850–1851.[19] Thirty firms quarried and cut local limestone in Chicago by 1859.[20]

Lemont was briefly renamed Athens and its limestone was called Athenian or Joliet "marble," but this nomenclature fooled no one; the stone from Chicago's local quarries was strong but it discolored easily and had remarkably poor weathering qualities. Some quarries at Lemont were contaminated with naturally occurring petroleum, which appeared only after installation. The porous stone also absorbed Chicago's smoke and pollution, rendering its original yellow a dull gray or even black.[21] Worse, however, was the Lemont's tendency to erode and disintegrate when exposed to the acidic air that accompanied Chicago's pollution and smoke. Limestone that was sawn for ashlar fronts proved particularly susceptible to these corrosive effects, but carved, ornamental stone was also affected. This poor performance was exacerbated when Lemont's quarries associated in 1890, forcing builders to accept inferior stone from a pool, rather than by inspection, and by 1891 locally produced limestone was confined to foundations and paving.[22]

But all building stone is vulnerable to water infiltration and pollution. It was simply a matter of time and maintenance before a stone cornice, for example, might succumb to the constant freeze-thaw cycles of Chicago's climate. Less permeable stone such as granite offered greater resistance but no guarantees against microscopic flaws that permitted water and ice to

gain leverage. Granite, too, was vulnerable to acidic atmospheres.[23] Over time, stone's fire resistance also proved elusive; water embedded or trapped in limestone or sandstone turned to steam in the heat of a fire, leading to explosive spalling. Even granite contained trace amounts of fluid embedded in its quartz crystals that could explode in hot fires.[24] On the whole, sandstone, despite its relatively weak structural performance, emerged as the most fire-resistive of the three and this gradually ensured its use for structural walls (figure 1.1).

Chicago came to be known as a city of steel, but well into the 1880s it remained a city of brick, which eliminated some of stone's drawbacks but offered problems of its own. The clay soil that made foundations such a problem proved to be a generous provider of strong, fire-resistant building material for the city, and the first post-fire technical developments to influence the city's tall construction involved brick and terra-cotta. A well-made masonry wall could support ten tons per square foot, but this could be compromised by lack of skill, neglect, or other attempts to save time or money.[25] Mortar presented cost-saving opportunities for poor-quality lime or excess water, both of which compromised the brick bond. Bricklaying presented another conflict between quality, time, and budget. Masons knew when to "lay bricks solid and true" and when their employers' profits demanded faster, sloppier work.

Mortar was also sensitive to freezing, leading to the "pernicious practice of covering mortar beds and foundations in winter with manure" that offered further opportunities for adulteration and imperfect setting. The image of the bricklayer quickly hoisting and laying brick while surrounded by steaming piles of manure-warmed mortar suggests that masonry, for all its advantages, was not a precisely engineered material. It was impossible to calculate precisely the strength of a masonry pier or wall given these variables, and masonry design and calculation remained entrenched in rule-of-thumb methods. Bricklayers and hod-carriers also faced appalling, dangerous conditions, and the emergence of bricklayers' unions had important effects on Chicago construction as demands for higher pay and better working conditions led to paralyzing strikes.[26]

The quasimedieval conditions of bricklaying matched those of brick manufacture. Clay fields had to be tended by the back-breaking labor of turning and spading a layer buried under two feet of soil. Raw clay was then taken to large pits, where fresh water was added to achieve a workable consistency. The resulting "mud" was then stirred until uniform. "Mud-wheelers" next took barrows of the mixture to sanded tables, where brickmakers rolled out rough quantities and forced them into a mold, slicing off the excess with piano wire. Wet bricks were allowed to air dry before being

1.1 Bowen Building, 62–74 E. Randolph, W. W. Boyington, 1872. (Photo by the author)

stacked into kilns where a constantly stoked fire made the bricks monolithic and water-resistant.[27]

At the time of the Fire brickmaking remained an antiquated industry, but progress in manufacturing came over the next decades. Horsepower was first used to mold brick in Philadelphia in 1835, but the process was increasingly automated after 1870 with lever- and steam-powered machines that could turn out four thousand "finely shaped"

1.2 Lake-Franklin Block (late 1870s). (Photo by the author)

unrest in the masonry industries cast a shadow over the material; to use brick in Chicago was, henceforth, to gamble with the possibility of a strike.[30]

Cast iron showed great promise in combining the fire resistance of brick with the light weight and labor-savings of timber. It was first imported to Chicago in the 1850s, and the New York factory of Daniel Badger and James Bogardus was contracted in 1856 to construct several commercial buildings on Lake Street in Chicago designed by architect John M. Van Osdel (1811–1891) (figures 1.2, 1.3). Cast iron required metallurgical knowledge and refined fabrication techniques, particularly to achieve complex or hollow shapes, but the ability to mass-produce structural or facade elements using a single mold and minimal labor made it a near-perfect material for Chicago's overextended building climate.

Badger and Bogardus began constructing cast-iron fronts in New York in 1842.[31] Chicago's cast-iron buildings were thus not at the forefront of the material's development, but they contributed important lessons for local architects about the material's potential to replace or supplement masonry. The first use of iron beams to replace timber occurred in the 1860s, and early attempts to replace wood joist floors with corrugated iron arches extended these early structural applications. Most architectural iron in Chicago, however, was used on building fronts, where it took

bricks per hour. Reconstruction after 1871 brought brickmakers from Philadelphia to Chicago, and a decade after the fire Chicago boasted over two hundred brickmaking enterprises.[28] But alongside the growth of the city's brick manufacturers lay aggrieved makers and masons. Angry about low wages and the loss of jobs that came with the new machinery, these trades staged an epic series of strikes from 1882 to 1884 that impacted building construction, exhausted local supplies, and raised prices.[29] The lingering threat of labor the place of brick on storefronts and thereby allowed larger show windows and entrances. It was also used for window lintels, enabling longer spans and, again, larger openings.

Chicago's iron industry benefited from nearby sources of iron ore in Michigan and Minnesota—both convenient by lake—and coal deposits in southern Illinois that were accessible by rail. The first dedicated architectural iron foundry in the city was opened by Fred Letz in 1843, and this was supplemented by the Union Foundry, which subsequently became the city's major iron producer and fabricator, in 1852. Chicago proved a major consumer of both ornamental and structural iron, and competition from outside sources kept local prices low.

FOUNDATIONS

Chicago's soil was a hurdle to tall construction regardless of building type. Chicago rested upon a hundred-foot-thick layer of waterlogged clay that frustrated attempts to build on bedrock below.[32] The upper stratum of this jelly-like material above the level of the lake was dry, and it provided fragile resistance, though common wisdom at the time suggested that piercing this *hardpan* would allow the liquid beneath to bubble up and engulf any careless excavation.[33] While the hardpan formed a reasonably thick layer—between two and ten feet according to most accounts—it varied consider-

1.3 Berghoff Restaurant, facade, ca. 1872. (Photo by the author)

ably in composition, and experience proved that even this tough clay layer could support only three thousand pounds per square foot, or less than 10 percent the capacity of bedrock.[34] While it was solid, this hardpan compressed when loaded, which had to be accounted for by painstakingly estimating the weight of the proposed structure and translating this into a predicted deflection. Burnham's most trusted en-

gineer, E. C. Shankland (1854–1924), suggested that clay loaded to 3,000 or 3,500 pounds per square foot would sink "between 6 and 12 inches"—not, perhaps, an impressive distance for a building of 100 feet or more, but absolutely crucial when planning the level of the ground floor.[35] A contemporary of Shankland's, William Sooy-Smith (1830–1916), noted that settlement occurred in two phases. The combined action of physical compaction and the displacement of any entrained water under loading produced a small, rapid settlement, but gradual compression also occurred over a period of years. Crucially, Smith noted that this longer term action was unpredictable and not necessarily uniform.[36] Settlement could be mastered only through high precision in calculating a building's dead load, estimating its effect on the soil, and constructing the initial floors high enough that, after sinking, they would align with the street level. Foundations for houses and small commercial structures were traditionally built of rubble stone resting on soil.[37] This worked fine for small buildings, although cracking and uneven settlement were frequent.[38] As buildings reached five and six stories, however, settlement led to more systemic structural failures, and in the post-fire years the inadequacy of rubble walls for taller buildings became apparent.[39] Timber construction could afford the deformations and settlements that came with the resulting settlement because it was relatively flexible. Masonry, however, could not. "Chicago," the *New York Times* gloated in 1891, "is practically afloat."[40]

The deep layer of fluid clay beneath the hardpan had two important consequences. First, deep basements could not be built in any structure that rested on the hardpan, since (according to conventional wisdom) excavating into this layer would disturb the fragile crust.

Buildings constructed on hardpan were therefore limited to one shallow basement. Second, it meant that architects and engineers had to work within the bearing capacity of the hardpan until a feasible method of drilling to bedrock emerged. This spurred development of a type of floating foundation unique to Chicago, but it also meant that a structure's weight had to be carefully considered (figures 1.4–1.6). A structure that eschewed masonry in favor of lighter iron or steel could, theoretically, be built higher on the same soil.[41] Concerns regarding weight did not exist in New York or Boston, where foundations could be placed directly on bedrock.

The combination of speculative building, poor soil, and easily available wood, brick, and cast iron created two distinct typologies in Chicago commercial construction by the time of the fire. Speculative developments that required private offices, daylight, and some measure of elevational appeal were typically built of brick walls and lumber floors. Brick on the front elevation was often supplemented by stone, cast iron, or terra-cotta, but the interiors of these buildings, because of the closed layout of offices, were rarely anything but masonry. Loft or store buildings, on the other hand, required larger clear spans uninterrupted by walls. Layouts were often subject to change, which further mitigated against walls of structural masonry and favored cast iron and heavy timber.

The desire to open street-level storefronts to better light and visibility meant that even brick facades were often replaced by thin cast-iron columns and lintels at their ground floors. These modest buildings showed that planar structures of masonry-walled buildings could be replaced by linear, skeletal systems of metal. These structures did so, of course, on the smallest possible scale, with a facade of usually only twenty-five to forty feet wide, and often for only a single story. In a few cases, however, the linear metal members of the ground floor were extended through the upper floors in ornamental cast-iron window frames and columns that opened up the entire facade to the proportions of iron, rather than the more solid ones of brick. These buildings were derided as flimsy, but they offered tangible benefits in daylighting, smaller foundations, and more rapid construction.

OCTOBER 9, 1871

"There was much grace and beauty, but little solidity" to Chicago in 1871, noted the *Tribune* a year after the Great Fire. "Even the grander edifices which adorned the chief thoroughfares were, in many instances, a delusion and a snare."[42] Wood buildings fed the fire with easily combustible, sappy pine, but even limestone, sandstone, and granite disintegrated or exploded in the heat. Brick buildings proved vulnerable, too, since they contained wood windows, interior ornament, and framing, all of which burst into flame as the fire's heat reached inside. Mortar burned or disintegrated, leaving even massive brick walls to collapse, particularly as falling timbers pried apart walls in which they were embedded. Most surprising to many, iron showed itself spectacularly incapable of resisting fire. It softened under flame-driven temperatures and slowly sagged to destruction, or it cracked under the thermal stress induced by firefighters' well-intentioned streams of water. This vulnerability was highlighted by a discovery of an architectural hardware store at Randolph and State. The building itself had been fully consumed by the fire, but its iron contents had melted and congealed into a twenty-five-ton ingot in the store's former basement.[43]

Among the grand myths of Chicago's history is that fireproofed metal skeletons emerged in the fire's aftermath as owners, chastened by the devastation, rebuilt. But like many cities faced with similar catastrophes, Chicago actually set about reconstructing that which had been there before. The *Tribune* resumed publication on October 11th and published a cable from the Liverpool and London and Globe insurance company to the effect that they would honor all claims from the city despite their estimated $3,000,000 liability. Other insurance companies, keen to show that they, too, would remain solvent despite the scale of the disaster, followed suit. The

1.4 Delaware Block, 36 W. Randolph, Wheelock and Thomas, 1874 (extended later). (Photo by the author)

1.5 Commercial block, corner of Dearborn and Monroe Streets, ca. 1879 (demolished, 1881). (Contemporary lithograph, collection of the author)

1.6 Commercial block, State Street, ca. 1880 (demolished). (Contemporary photograph, collection of the author)

1.7 Nixon Block, corner of LaSalle and Monroe Streets, Otto Matz, 1872 (demolished, 1889). (Art Institute of Chicago)

permanent wooden buildings in March 1872 after a winter of rapid construction. Despite restrictions within the fire boundary, shanties and lumber structures were allowed to remain as long as necessary, and indeed some shacks remained in place for years . Those who built of masonry, like hotelier Potter Palmer (1826–1902), were in the minority, despite efforts by the city's brick industry to expand to meet the demands of the vigorous reconstruction.

A handful of structures in the burned district survived the fire, including the Lind Block on the river at Randolph Street, spared by a fluke of wind, and the five-story Nixon Block on the northeast corner of Monroe and LaSalle Streets (figure 1.7). Designed by Otto Matz, the Nixon's survival was hailed as miraculous, but in fact it embodied a principle that would come to define Chicago structures in their defense against fire. Its main structural elements included masonry walls, iron girders, and arched brick floors, and Matz specified that all structural iron elements were to be encased in a thick, heavy jacket of plaster of paris.[45] Incomplete at the time of the Fire, this iron, brick, and plaster hybrid survived, even as timber construction materials being stored within burned fiercely. Nixon quickly completed work on the building after the fire, and it became a headquarters for the city's leading architects—including Matz—as they worked to rebuild.[46] It also became an example of success-

city's mercantile and capitalist character emerged undaunted.[44] W. D. Kerfoot, a developer who would become one of the city's leading promoters and wealthiest citizens, erected a sign amid the ruins of his former office that came to stand for the city's dedication to rebuilding. "All gone but wife, children, and energy," it read, and it

came to symbolize Chicago's stoic, collaborative character. As it became clear that the city would be rebuilt quickly, laborers from across the country began to arrive. With winter approaching, many businesses erected shanties of scantling lumber that allowed them to open just days after the fire, and many businesses reopened in ful fireproofing that was both emulated and improved upon.

Another major fire in 1874 destroyed the area bounded by Polk, Adams, Wabash, and Franklin Streets. While it did less damage than the 1871 fire, it inspired more serious reform, leading to the city's first comprehensive fire code.[47] The former "fire districts" were expanded to include the city's corporate limits, and construction type was tied strictly to building height; the taller the structure, the more stringent the material requirements. Scantling construction was banned, and thick masonry construction was required for party walls to prevent fire from spreading to adjacent structures. Masonry was encouraged for all exterior walls, with thicknesses prescribed for various heights and exceptions made only for windows and storefronts, which now had to comply with their own material requirements. The 1874 code set the baseline against which all construction or architectural experiments would be compared over the next twenty years. It proposed a typical commercial structure that was entirely supported by masonry with exceptions made for well-protected iron. But it relied on thick bearing walls into which windows were spanned by bearing lintels. Iron or oak posts might support these walls on the street front or frame projecting bay windows above. But the code's assumption—one that carried through most commercial construction in the 1880s—

was that Chicago's tall buildings were to be constructed of fireproof brick.

POST-FIRE COMMERCIAL BLOCKS

Chicago grew faster than any American city through the depression-scarred 1870s, but it was spectacularly susceptible to cycles of boom and bust. Its population reached half a million by 1880, nearly doubling in size since the Fire. This would have been remarkable for any city in the country, but these years were known throughout Chicago as the "hard times," and concerns about the city's continued dynamism tempered speculation. The national economy stabilized around 1880, and speculators began building in earnest in the city again by 1881. In 1879 just under 1100 new buildings were constructed in the city, but in 1883 there were over 4000.[48] The city's building code, developed in the conservative years of the depression, came under increasing pressure as the motive to build higher returned with new investment (figures 1.8, 1.9).

If the typical post-fire, high-end commercial building in Chicago was a five-story masonry structure with heavily plastered timber or iron floor systems, narrow windows, and circulation by stairs or a slow, rickety elevator, the typical building of the late-1880s was something else entirely: reaching ten or eleven stories, it employed iron not only for floor systems but for columns and piers as well, and its elevations illustrated the demand for more daylight

1.8 Portland Block, corner of Dearborn and Washington Streets, William Le Baron Jenney, 1872 (demolished, 1933). (Chicago History Museum)

and ventilation set against the need for structurally sufficient walls. Elevators were more reliable, and occupants of the upper floors, while they might still occasionally stroll down eight or nine flights of stairs, no longer hesitated to board a safe, comfortable cab for their typical journey. These upper floors, too, reversed the long-standing maxim that lower floors guaranteed higher rents. The views, clear air, and separation from the noise and dust of the street below made higher offices more desirable, which accelerated the drive for height.

CHICAGO BLDGS.
S-16.12
CARBUTT, PHOTOGRAPHER,
VIEWS OF CHICAGO,
56. Honroe Block, Dearborn and Monroe St.

1.9 Honore Block, corner of Dearborn and Adams, C. M. Palmer, 1872 (demolished, 1894). (Chicago History Museum)

The emergence of the tall skyscraper was gradual, and the convergence of Chicago skyscrapers toward remarkably similar composition, proportions, and even detail occurred in several loosely defined steps between the end of the "hard times" around 1879 and the flourishing of what was called the "Chicago Style" or "Chicago Construction" of the late 1880s. The unusually challenging conditions of Chicago building—the geographic pressure of the Loop, the economic pressure of its overheated market, the problems of its soil and the availability of a refined though limited palette of materials—all proved to be generative rather than restrictive. John Wellborn Root of Burnham & Root and Dankmar Adler (1844–1900) of Adler & Sullivan wrote directly of their influences in the 1890s, explaining how visually coherent, expressive designs could be coaxed from this intimidating brew of economic and technical forces.[49] Both writers emphasized the active roles of designers, engineers, and builders in finding and refining these solutions. Neither believed that pressures on a design determined the outcome. Rather, they emphasized that design was patient trial and error in pursuit of discovery. Others—notably Adler's partner Louis Henri Sullivan (1856–1924)—would make bolder claims for the genius of the individual architect in corralling such diverse requirements, materials, and methods into legible architectural creations. Root and Adler, however, made gentler claims for their work, insisting that attentiveness and persistence were necessary before any moment of architectural creation could occur. Individual taste and creativity could come only after integrated solutions were found to the huge variety of issues in a commercial building of any scale.[50]

Both Root and Adler wrote that the genesis of the new type was in its "conditions," which Adler described as "human greed and . . . man's desire for gain" ennobled by "professional ingenuity and skill."[51] Root saw these engines of capitalism as simply "commercial conditions without precedent" that pushed buildings in New York, Boston, Chicago, and elsewhere "heavenward nine, ten, twelve, and sixteen stories." For Root, the hallmark of the architectural responses to these conditions was a complex layering of structure, circulation, rental space, services, and enclosure that had to be coaxed into an efficient, desirable commercial office building. This, he felt, distinguished the skyscraper from all that had come before it. Rather than cloaking this complexity behind skins of false simplicity or monumentality, Root challenged his readers to seek "the frankest possible acceptance of every requirement of modern life," even though that would eliminate easy stylistic tropes. Indeed, Root believed that style must emerge out of "working out . . . ends by the best means at hand," rather than self-consciously.[52]

One must start somewhere, and for both Root and Adler the key to the skyscraper was a plan that efficiently achieved all functional desiderata. Planning was the key to a skyscraper's economic viability, and architects were charged with finding a way to rent every square foot that could be wrung out of a site's footprint and vertical extension. Root believed that the essential problem was providing every rented space with adequate daylight, while Adler believed that daylighting was just one of many problems to be solved. Adler agreed, however, that office height and depth were determined by the maximum daylighting distance from any window—eleven-foot ceiling heights and twenty-four-foot office-suite depths were near-absolute rules for adequate sunlight, though these heights had to be greater on lower levels where sun might be cut off by surrounding structures. Root showed how an iterative process of arranging office blocks around street access and internal light courts could eventually provide a most efficient solution. But Adler went further in his prescription; the next step for him involved finding a reliable and repeatable module about which the building's circulation, structure, and aesthetics might coalesce. He saw not only structural benefits to this alignment, but also fabricational advantages:

> With uniform beam lengths there will be uniformity of column loads and, consequently, of column sections, followed again by uniformity of connections at all panel points, and, hence, that frequent repetition of individual parts and details

so favourable to rapid and economical work in the processes of mill, shop and erection. . . . The same advantages accrue in connection with internal fittings, such as doors, windows, plumbing and steam fixtures and pipes, wardrobe closets, vaults, etc., etc. If terra cotta is used for an external facing material, the repetitions of detail will reduce cost and expedite progress.[53]

Root, though not addressing the importance of the module as clearly, made a related case for accepting the rigorous diagram of functional and circulatory efficiency and material expediency as the basis for a skyscraper's design. By resolving "architectural designs into their essential elements," he wrote, the underlying structure would "absolutely dictate the general departure of external forms" and influence "all architectural detail." If the essential components of the tall commercial block were, as Adler gently claimed, an efficient stacking of space with regard to daylight, circulation, and structure, this strengthened Root's belief that such a structure had little use for "profusion[s] of delicate ornament," and that, rather, every external element should be both enduring against the elements and "wrought into the simplest forms." The pressures of economics, fabrication, and construction all had the effect of stripping architectural preten-

sions from the frame and enclosure of the skyscraper. What remained was a structural and functional grid wrapped around daylighting apertures, regular in its march across the site and relentless in its utility and economical expression.

Much would be made of the seemingly sublime power of Chicago's real estate market to streamline architecture of its stylistic baggage, but neither Root nor Adler believed that the result should be inartistic—it had to "possess a distinctive charm of external presentation."[54] Often this meant simply adjusting small details in the cladding, or designing mullions, spandrels, or other elements to support a consistent ornamental theme. At this level, the architect had room to maneuver and to tease a coherent visual experience out of metal, masonry, and timber . To Root and Adler, however, this application of style had to occur after the basic bones of a design had been located and fixed.

In the 1890s Root and Adler were writing in the midst of technical developments that pushed Chicago construction above sixteen stories. No structure of the 1870s rose to even half this height, however; and none possessed the efficient modularity or even the skeletal iron structure that both designers saw as the key to the tall commercial building. The structures built in the aftermath of the 1871 fire had more in common with mill buildings of the eighteenth century than they did

1.10 Central Music Hall, corner of State and Randolph, Burling and Adler, 1879 (demolished, 1901). (Chicago History Museum)

with the structures that would replace them just ten or fifteen years later. The rationalized, modular conception that Root and Adler both described could emerge only with developments in iron and terra-cotta that allowed architects and engineers to see their structures as thin networks of linear iron members rather than heavy masses of masonry.

The first step from Chicago's vernacular commercial building toward a distinctive, technically coherent sky-scraper style came with Adler's largest commission yet. Opened in December 1879, the Central Music Hall was the first major performance space built in Chicago since the 1871 fire (figure 1.10). The Hall marked the end of the Depression and the return of the city to a place of cultural prominence, but to the writers of Industrial Chicago, an encyclopedic account of the city's building activities since the Fire, it also represented a break with traditional ways of building and with the small scale of the city's commercial architecture. It provided an auditorium of 2,500 seats, with retail storefronts on State and Randolph streets and, above, rental offices to subsidize the Hall. These offices were described as "particularly light and airy," while the performance space had the finest acoustics in the West, an achievement that cemented Adler's reputation as an outstanding acoustic designer.

The Central Music Hall's exterior was constructed of Lemont Limestone and red granite, traditional materials that showed glancing signs of a new talent in Adler's office. Louis Henri Sullivan was hired by Adler as the Hall's design was nearing completion. Educated at MIT and at the École des Beaux-Arts, Sullivan had proved himself in the offices of Philadelphian Frank Furness and Chicago architects Johnston and Edelman and William Le Baron Jenney. Adler & Sullivan's design showed not only a break in style and conception with older, less ambitious work, but also a new level of spatial and constructive quality that proved marketable. The Central Music Hall set a standard by which the next decade of commercial architecture in the city would be judged.[55] The jump from the Hall's eight stories to the seventeen or twenty stories that marked the skyscrapers of the 1890s came about only with new materials and structural techniques, and these began with the clay that underlay the city itself.

Chapter 2

"Built Mostly of Itself": Chicago and Clay, 1874–1891

Timber, stone, and cast iron seemed to be natural materials for Chicago's commercial architecture, but they all proved susceptible to fire and were eventually relegated to ornamental purposes. These materials were all readily available to Chicago's market, but the local brick industry made fire-resistant masonry construction even more economical. By 1890, brickmaking had evolved from an artisanal into a fully industrialized process. Investment in clay-bearing pits, machinery, and expertise led to consolidation and better-capitalized brick companies, and Chicago took over from Philadelphia and St. Louis as the center of American brickmaking.[1]

Traditional masonry did not meet the new functional demands of the city's shops, offices, and warehouses when it came to floors, however. To construct a fireproof floor of brick re-quired labor-intensive arch construction that spanned short distances from wall to wall. Longer-spanning wrought-iron girders offered a more functional span, but these were vulnerable to fire. Mill construction had employed brick arches in the eighteenth century, but their fire performance was still limited by timber or iron supports. With the conflagrations of the 1870s, however, insurance companies and city governments began to mandate more fire-resistive construction. The development of a lightweight, fireproof floor system that eliminated the weight of masonry and the vulnerability of wood and iron marked the first step in the development of a new constructive type, and because of Chicago's concentration of builders and entrepreneurs and the need for light construction on its fragile soil, the city became an important center for experiments in fire-protected iron construction. Masonry skyscrapers of the 1870s and 1880s looked much the same as those from previous decades. But because they were constructed with new fireproof clay floor structures and built of new, mechanically produced bricks they were taller, lighter, and safer than their immediate predecessors were.

TERRA-COTTA AS CLADDING AND FIREPROOFING

Terra-cotta offered a combination of brick's inexpensive production and stone's ornamental possibilities. Made of finer clays containing more water than brick, terra-cotta could be molded into complex forms with more relief and detail. It could also be made in large, thin panels that saved time and labor. Terra-cotta's firing process was similar to brick's, but it required precision and care to prevent cracking, particularly with large, thin elements. Clay shrank during firing, so molds had to be carefully oversized. As the clay industries around Chicago grew more sophisticated, these precise fabricational requirements were more readily met and terra-cotta became one of the city's major building industries. Beginning with Sanford Loring's Chicago Terra Cotta Company in 1866, manufacturers drew on the city's clay deposits and growing expertise in brickmaking to produce larger, more detailed, and lighter products, including John Brunkhorst's Northwestern Terra Cotta Company, which formed an important center of intensive development and innovation throughout the 1880s and 1890s.[2]

As welcome as terra-cotta was for ornamental purposes, its use as a fireproofing material was a more important development.[3] The rapid development of terra-cotta tiles tied to and protecting metal framing members eventually proved a decisive solution to the vexing problem of structural integrity during fire, but as cast-iron fronts were replaced in post-fire Chicago by brick or stone, the iron and timber structures behind them remained unchanged. Repeated failures spawned debate over whether iron could ever be adequately protected, or whether it ought to be disqualified entirely for structural uses.[4] As early as 1873, an editorial in *Manufacturer and Builder* called for hybrid constructions of iron columns surrounded by protective brick piers—a formula that

negated iron's weight- and space-saving benefits.[5] But even brick presented an imperfect solution, because workmanship in bricklaying was critical to the material's fire-resistance, and here again speed and cost operated directly against the performance of masonry. "That bricks resist fire far better than anything else is beyond question," noted *Architectural Record* in 1895, "but a brick wall is quite another thing."[6]

While terra-cotta shared some of brick's problems with workmanship and joinery, it offered a serviceable, compact level of fire protection whose economy and efficiency were honed by testing and experiment. In England by 1850, brick arches spanning between iron beams were supplemented with hollow, oval-shaped clay pots to reduce the floor's dead weight . These pots did not protect the beams themselves, but they showed the way toward lighter weight and greater fire resistance. This type of floor structure was used in the Cooper Union building, constructed in New York in 1854.[7] An 1871 patent by George Johnson and Balthasar Kreischer proposed adding dovetailed grooves along the edges and tops of similar hollow pots, protecting exposed beam flanges within and accommodating wooden nailing strips for flooring above.[8] Kreischer patented a system that replicated the ovoid shape of the hollow pots, but in three sections, solving a persistent cracking problem in larger elements.[9] The New

York Post Office, finished in 1872, used a similar system that provided a flat ceiling surface for plastering but that required a wood or iron substructure between the upper, curved surface of the pots and the flat floor above.[10] Finally, in October 1872, Johnson and William Freeborn patented a system of angled terra-cotta blocks that formed a flat arch between beams. This eliminated the ovoid form of the pots and provided flat surfaces for plaster ceilings and nailing for floors.[11] The survival of Chicago's Nixon Building through the 1871 fire gave local credibility to the idea of fireproofed iron construction, and the publicity garnered by its survival swayed public and professional opinion toward iron and clay hybrids. New York's fireproofing experts, particularly Johnson and Wight, were quick to set up new companies in Chicago in the wake of the fire.[12]

These entrepreneurs made improvements in four areas: understanding the distinction between *incombustible* and *fire-resistant* construction; finding ways to contain and compartmentalize fires inside and out; fireproofing metal columns in addition to beams; and improving existing terra-cotta floor systems. The distinction between *incombustible* and *fire- resistant* structures reflected a growing awareness that an iron or timber structure itself was only part of the fire problem. Wooden trim, wall studs, flooring, doors, and furnishings were all part of any office building, and they all offered fuel for a developing fire.[13] Employing hollow terra-cotta tile walls and partitions, eliminating wood in favor of stone or mosaic tile in corridors, and relying on porous, nailable terra-cotta "lumber" for trim in offices all helped to reduce fuel load. Closely related to the issue of fuel load was that of fire spread and compartmentation. Walls of brick or hollow tile were gradually understood as important barriers to flame spread.[14] Because of their tendency to accelerate fires by acting as chimneys, elevator and mechanical shafts came in for particular attention. These required fireproof materials, but they also needed protection at each floor to keep out fire-heated air. Windows that allowed daylight and air into offices were also open to flames from adjacent buildings. Solid masonry party walls between buildings that extended all the way to their sites' boundaries were required after 1871, and codes demanded separation or shutters for any openings in these important barriers. Terra-cotta fireproofing for columns had to carefully balance a tight fit with the need for air spaces that insulated the iron within. Round columns were typically clad in segmental shells, while columns of more elaborate shape were usually boxed in, leaving voids that could be used for pipes or cables.[15] Terra-cotta was continually reengineered during the 1880s and 1890s to increase strength, to reduce heat transmission, and to offer more pliability for

ease of shaping; block profiles were improved to save weight and to reduce the number of separate shapes required to produce an effective system. Manufacturers added internal webs that increased strength while creating multiple layers of air spaces and insulation, and they later developed floor tiles that spanned directly between beams, rather than relying on flat arches of individual blocks, allowing tiles cut to custom lengths and thus greater flexibility in floor layouts.[16] These improvements along with rigorous fire and strength testing meant that terra-cotta flooring became an efficient, reliable method of construction within a generation of its initial application.[17]

New York could boast earlier instances of fire-resistant terra-cotta construction, but Chicago became a strong competitor in terms of manufacturers and installations through the 1880s.[18] Jenney's Portland Block of 1872 represented the first use of hollow tile flooring in Chicago, and by 1880 such systems saw regular use in the city. In particular, nine buildings completed between 1880 and 1884 used terra-cotta arches, and according to Wight the nine most significant structures built in the boom of 1884–1885—the new Board of Trade, Home Insurance, Royal Insurance, Opera House, Gaff, Mallers, Insurance Exchange, Traders, and Parker—all used either his own flooring system or that of the rival Pioneer Fireproofing Company.[19]

Pioneer produced the first comprehensive catalogue of standard elements in 1885, which featured a widely read primer on terra-cotta fireproofing of all types.[20] A third major fireproofing company, Illinois Terra-Cotta Lumber grew out of factory construction in Pullman on the city's south side. The presence of three competitive but cooperative fireproofing leaders in the city gave the industry influence in the building codes that developed between 1874 through 1903. Terra-cotta fireproofing was eventually favored by the Chicago code over plaster and even, for a time, brick.[21] Such systems were supplemented by the strategic use of fire-resistant finishes in corridors, staircases, and elevator shafts, and by escape systems, all of which accompanied a dramatic reduction in fatal skyscraper fires through the 1890s.[22] Fireproofing costs fell as systems proved themselves and manufacture improved, shrinking from 15 percent of a typical construction budget in the 1880s to under 4 percent by 1904, a premium covered by insurance savings alone.[23]

Early fire-protected iron-framed buildings achieved modest increases in height over all-masonry structures. Wrapping iron columns and girders with terra-cotta jackets saved owners floor space that would otherwise have gone toward larger brick piers, though masonry was still the primary material for exterior walls. The result—jacketed iron structures inside surrounded by bearing masonry walls outside—was called "cage" construction in New York. The skyscrapers built in Chicago's building boom of 1884–1886 all deployed this hybrid strategy of metal frame and masonry wall. Masonry walls were also necessary for wind-bracing metal structures, since standard connections between iron members could not provide the required rigidity (see chapter 4). Much of this masonry construction occurred along lot lines, where codes demanded fire-resistant party walls. Brick thus served the triple duty of picking up girder loads at exterior edges, stiffening the building against wind, and serving as a barrier against fire from neighboring structures. Such hybrid structures—strong but loose iron skeletons surrounded and braced by a carapace of punched masonry—characterized the city's skyscrapers until the late 1880s.

Skyscrapers supported, braced, and clad with masonry were made stronger and more economical by the rise of a pressed-brick industry in Chicago. The improved structural performance of pressed bricks allowed piers and walls to carry additional floors with less bearing area. This extended the reach of masonry construction beyond the old limit of six or seven floors. The "stiff-clay" method extruded a drier, stiffer mud that could be cut into lengths rather than pressed in a mold, yielding a denser brick with visible grain and greater strength. A variant of this process was hydraulic pressing, which further densified bricks for even better structural performance. The enhanced strength of hydraulic pressing came with a smoother surface and less shrinkage.[24] The St. Louis Hydraulic Pressed Brick Company led innovation in the Midwest, but its product cost nearly four times the average Chicago common brick.[25] Such a price differential spurred regional development, however, and the Chicago Anderson Pressed Brick Company began marketing hydraulic pressed brick locally in 1882. Following its use in the well-regarded Calumet Club, designed by Burnham & Root in 1884, pressed brick grew "from a fashion . . . into a permanent style" among builders and architects.[26] New pressed-brick companies entered the Chicago market in the late 1880s, including the La Salle Pressed Brick Company and Hinchliff and Owen, which supplied the millions of bricks needed to construct the town and factories of Pullman. Pressed brick became the material of choice for structural and finish masonry, and commercial construction in the city jumped from an average of five or six stories to ten or more.[27]

CLAY AND IRON BUILDINGS

Cage construction and pressed brick led to a remarkable doubling of skyscraper height in the mid-1880s, but they also influenced the appearance and configuration of the higher towers. Brick was cheaper and stronger when deployed in planar walls, and structures of the 1880s tended toward simplicity and regularity compared to the more eclectic buildings of the 1870s. Economies of scale in iron production further encouraged regular interior planning, standard girder lengths, and repetitive bay layouts—all saving fabrication time and expense. Architects found a natural allegiance between the massive walls that were a key element of the then-popular Romanesque revival style and the orderly imposition of economic demands.

After eight years of residential commissions, Burnham & Root made their commercial debut in 1881 with a seven-story version of this formula. The Grannis Block was a speculative venture by Boston financier Sheppard Brooks, and like Burling and Adler's Central Music Hall it demonstrated that solid construction and minimal decoration could provide attractive, profitable office space (figure 2.1). The Grannis had a banking hall that ran the depth of the site, and a seven-story office block that occupied its street front, leaving the rear of the site over the banking hall open.[28] This arrangement defined a typology in Burnham & Root's work, trading rentable volume in the center of the lot for daylight. Between the offices and banking hall a glass-topped lobby and staircase wrapped around a single open-mesh, hydraulic elevator. The Grannis was supported on cast-iron columns with wrought-iron girders, but its floors were built with wooden joists rather than with the terra-cotta floor arches; P. B. Wight was contracted to encase the columns and girders, but the timber floors were just thinly plastered.[29] Even so, the *Chicago Daily* noted that the Block's "solidity of construction" matched its pragmatic but disciplined exterior.[30] The Grannis facade was vaguely Romanesque, with a slightly pronounced center bay emphasizing one of five ranks of paired windows. It was briefly one of the most popular addresses in Chicago, rented at its opening "entirely to the best class of tenants." Burnham & Root themselves moved from temporary offices on Washington Street into half of the building's top floor.[31]

The Grannis's quick demise, however, proved to be a decisive moment in Chicago's adoption of more robust fireproofing schemes. On the evening of February 19, 1885, just four years after opening, the Grannis was consumed by a spectacular fire that stunned the city's architects and engineers. No definitive cause was ever established, but the rapidity of the fire's spread highlighted the inadvisability of using timber floor construction in tall buildings.[32] Wight's system around the columns had worked; these cast-iron elements were pulled from the rubble intact. But the column protection was worthless when the beams and floors around them burned and collapsed. E. V. Johnson, sensing opportunity for his Pioneer Fireproofing Company, accused Burnham and Wight of "unbusi-

2.1 Grannis Block, 21–29 N. Dearborn, Burnham & Root, 1881 (destroyed, 1885). (Art Institute of Chicago)

nesslike recklessness" for using plaster and lath rather than hollow tile to protect the floors.[33] *Inland Architect* noted that "the sentiment in favor of fireproofing has set so strong that it is doubtful if in the future any office building will be constructed otherwise," and it further decried the combination of wooden

stairs with an open elevator shaft, a dangerous adjacency of open vertical space and available fuel. Burnham & Root were nearly wiped out by the fire. Root had taken many of the firm's watercolors earlier that day for a lecture and these were the only office records to survive. Burnham himself had a nar-

2.2 Montauk Block, 64–70 W. Monroe, Burnham & Root, 1882 (demolished, 1902). (From Randall and Randall, *History of the Development of Building Construction in Chicago*)

ing.[35] The Brooks brothers placed a singular emphasis on functional performance, but correspondence with their local agent, Owen Aldis, also showed their interest in how perception played a role in a building's marketability.[36] Burnham & Root's solution combined exterior masonry bearing walls with an internal structure of cast- and wrought-iron columns. But here the columns supported floors of lightweight hollow tile, not lumber.[37] Designed and installed by Wight, the Montauk's fireproofing was the first use of "thin-wall" hollow tiles and the first-floor system in Chicago to be entirely of terra-cotta.[38] Wight was also contracted to clad the columns and to construct hollow tile partitions, giving the Montauk the best claim yet to fireproof construction in Chicago (figure 2.3).[39] This hollow tile construction saved weight, too, and thus it also marked for Wight "the era of very light floor construction."[40]

These innovations were part of a building envelope that reflected a far more conservative approach. Brooks had requested a "plain structure of face brick," and the scale and structural demands on such a tall brick structure left very little room for Root's compositional skill. Like the Grannis or even the Nixon before it, the Montauk employed narrow windows between broad, flat brick piers (figure 2.4). Each window was recessed slightly and capped by a shallow arch that supported the spandrel above. Root organized the elevation

row escape, running down the wooden staircase with as many drawings as he could carry as flames shot up through the adjacent elevator cage.[34]

By the time of the Grannis conflagration, however, Burnham & Root's next project for Peter and Sheppard Brooks had already set new standards for fireproofing. At ten stories the Montauk (1882) was Chicago's tallest (figure 2.2). It powerfully demonstrated the potential for pressed brick cage construction to achieve greater height (and profits) than older styles of build-

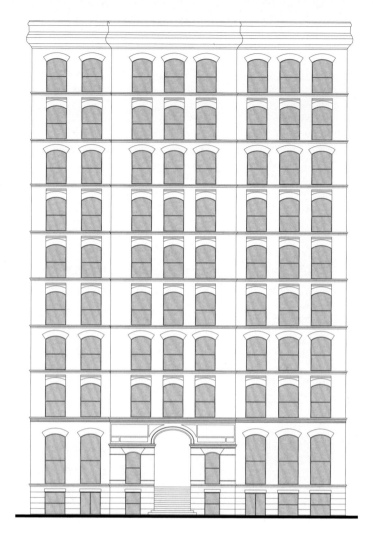

2.3 Montauk Block, Monroe Street elevation. (Drawing by the author)

2.4 Montauk Block, plan. (Drawing by the author)

using horizontal stringcourses, a common trope in contemporary New York skyscrapers intended to mitigate unfashionably "tall" proportions, but this was, even in Root's own opinion, unsuccessful.[41] To provide sunlit, rentable space in the basement, the Montauk's lower stories incorporated a half-story arrangement that required a steep entry stair. Root specified hydraulic pressed brick from St. Louis, which en-

abled the walls to carry the unprecedented weight of ten stories, and he did so in a specially formulated, dark red color to resist the city's smoke and grime. The Northwestern Terra Cotta Works provided matching colors for the roundels, stringcourses, and other ornamentation, but the effect was no doubt too consistent; the entire building, according to the Tribune, appearing "as an enormous brick set on end."[42]

The Montauk's thrifty interiors focused on light and convenience. Brooks noted in a March 1881 letter to Aldis that "the building throughout is to be for use and not for ornament," and he specifically requested that such niceties as cabinetry to hide unsightly plumbing in toilet rooms be eliminated to save costs.[43] Presciently, the one service that Brooks was willing to spend on was electricity; he suggested that wires be

2.5 Chicago, Burlington, and Quincy Railroad Building, Franklin and Adams, Burnham & Root, 1883 (demolished, 1926). (Art Institute of Chicago)

installed for future electric lights, to go alongside specified gas fixtures.[44] The Montauk included a large, glazed central court that held the main staircase and twin elevators provided by William Hale. Light and views from high above Monroe Street made up for the spartan accommodations, and the Montauk's upper offices proved popular, supporting the growing view that offices above the grime and noise of the street could command higher rents.[45]

Like the Grannis, the Montauk's fireproofing was soon tested, but here

Wight's more complete installation fared significantly better. On December 30, 1883, a fire engulfed the Crozier Building, which abutted the Montauk on the west and north. Fearing the worst, firefighters entered the Montauk and found that the building's masonry and terra-cotta had prevented the fire from spreading. One company even set its hoses up in the Montauk's upper stories, helping to extinguish the Crozier fire four hours after its ignition.[46] This robust performance publicly demonstrated the fire resistance of Wight's

terra-cotta and of brick construction; Aldis wrote Brooks to point out that the Montauk's survival was "a triumph for fireproofing," and Burnham & Root took this performance to heart, moving their office into the Montauk after the destruction of the Grannis Block.[47]

In the wake of the Montauk's commercial and technical success, Burnham & Root received three commissions for office blocks of similar scale. None exceeded the Montauk's height, but collectively they represent a plateau of stylistic and technical achievement for cage construction in Chicago. All three resembled the Montauk visually, with wide brick piers; narrower, stacked windows; and an attempt to make compositional sense of the resulting pierced masonry planes. The first of these, the 1883 Chicago, Burlington, and Quincy Railroad General Office Building, struck a balance between planning, daylighting, and ventilation with a central light court, 55 by 63 feet in plan, covered by an iron and glass skylight 120 feet above the open basement level (figure 2.5). Floors opened to a gallery facing into this court, providing light and ventilation to each office from two sides. On the exterior, a combination of stone and deep-red St. Louis pressed brick were combined in elevations that were "somewhat Romanesque," following the Montauk's formula of fitting the largest possible windows between structurally sized brick piers. Inside, the floors were sup-

2.6 Counselman Block, 238–240 S. LaSalle, Burnham & Root, 1884 (demolished, 1920). (Chicago History Museum)

2.7 Calumet Block, 111–117 S. LaSalle, Burnham & Root, 1884 (demolished, 1913). (From *120 Photographic Views of Downtown Chicago*, Rand McNally, 1909)

ported on iron girders protected by terra-cotta tiles.[48]

The Counselman and the Calumet repeated the Montauk's formula almost exactly, with a similar strategy of brick bearing walls pierced by arched windows (figures 2.6, 2.7). Root experimented with sillcourses, panels, friezes, and cornices in these two buildings, but was unable to reconcile the vertical proportions with the Romanesque's conceit of heavy, bearing stone. Their facades showed the balance between structure, lighting, and material economy playing out on Burnham & Root's drawing boards; the brick piers—particularly at the building's corners—were larger than structurally necessary. Subsequent plate glass renovations to the Counselman's street level replaced these corner elements with much narrower brick columns, showing that the original proportions were significantly oversized. There was, of course, a stylistic rationale for this: the Romanesque demanded a sense of visual solidity, but the expense of plate glass remained a limiting factor, too, and it seems clear that the balance of structure, cladding, and material economics led to decisions about proportion and aperture size that could not be traced directly to one factor or another.[49]

A more rigorous balance between structure and daylight came in one of the most noted Chicago buildings of the late 1880s, the Opera House at Clark and Washington, completed in 1885 (figure 2.8). Many critics of the day claimed that Chicago separated business and culture, housing the former in plain, "dry-goods boxes" while grudgingly providing for the latter with hackneyed copies of eastern precedents. But this criticism ignored the Central Music Hall and the Opera House, both of which subsidized cultural facilities with integral commercial blocks. Adler's Central Music Hall had served as the home for Opera during the early 1880s, but despite its ideal acoustics and architectural achievement it offered nothing like the intimacy or the

2.8 Opera House Block, corner of Clark and Washington Streets, Cobb and Frost, 1885. (Art Institute of Chicago)

exclusivity of a purpose-built opera theater.[50] In 1883 a private syndicate began work to an ambitious schedule that foresaw a two-thousand-seat theater wrapped in a block of high-quality commercial space.

With a construction cost of five hundred thousand dollars, the Opera House was one of the largest building projects yet undertaken in Chicago. Originally planned for nine stories, it was soon extended to ten, making it one of the four tallest buildings in the city. It was also one of the largest, with 180 feet of frontage on Clark and 107 on Washington.[51] For such a large, complex project the syndicate chose an unlikely pair of architects: Henry Ives Cobb (1859–1931) and Charles S. Frost (1856–1931), then just twenty-five and twenty-eight years old, respectively. Both were easterners—Cobb from suburban Boston, Frost from Lewiston, Maine, and they had been classmates at the Massachusetts Institute of Technology. The two had moved to Chicago in 1881 to design the Union Club for Cobb's brother, and within a year, the retail magnate Potter Palmer selected them to design his mansion on North Lake Shore Drive. They received several other large residential commissions between 1882 to 1884, and these social connections led to their selection by the Opera.[52]

The combination of naturally illuminated commercial and retail space with a long-span theater led Cobb &

Frost to an L-shaped office scheme around a light court above the theater. Entries on Clark and Washington tunneled under the office block to the auditorium behind. The building's elevations showed the clear influence of Burnham & Root's contemporary work. Bearing brick piers were arrayed across both fronts with pairs of double-hung windows between; at the eighth and tenth stories these piers were tied together with lines of arches. Short corner towers recalled Richardson's ornament, while a prominent central bay on the longer Clark street facade echoed the Montauk. Cobb & Frost specified Anderson Pressed Brick with custom moldings and terra-cotta that matched the brick's red-brown color, another of Root's trademarks.

While praised for its "plain, massive, and harmonious" exteriors, the Opera House's radical lower stories shocked current taste.[53] With sturdy, rusticated bases, Burnham & Root's commercial structures emphasized the bearing qualities of their masonry walls. By contrast, Cobb & Frost's design emphasized wide commercial storefronts and light-gathering second-floor windows. The brick piers above these floors were wider than the cast-iron piers of the first story—recalling the combination of brick storefronts with cast-iron bases of the 1850s and 1860s but on a far larger scale.[54] Particularly at the corners, Cobb & Frost's willingness to es-

chew traditional notions of visual "sufficiency" revealed that iron in the lower floors offered substantial spatial savings of iron over masonry.

Concerned about their architects' lack of experience on such a large project, the syndicate signed a construction contract with Clark and Fuller, a Boston firm that had opened a Chicago branch in 1881. Clark and Fuller were given wide supervisory and contractual power to negotiate with suppliers and subcontractors.[55] "General contracting" would prove controversial in the coming decades, as it transferred lucrative supervision duties from architect to builder. George A. Fuller (1851–1900) became its chief proponent after the Opera House was completed. The general contracting scheme worked well, in that the office section was completed by May 1885, a month ahead of schedule and just ten months after ground was broken.[56] The Opera House also won praise for construction quality. The *Tribune* quoted an anonymous real estate agent who compared the yet-unfinished building with its neighbors, the Court House and City Hall, both in advanced stages of deterioration. To "Washington Street," the Opera House's straightforward aesthetics and fine workmanship were tributes to the greater level of care and craftsmanship that now marked the best Chicago construction; its solidity and straightforward aesthetics distinguished it from

more slipshod, overly decorative buildings of the previous decade.[57]

The Opera House had a short life; it was demolished in 1912 to make way for Burnham's Conway Building. Its legacy was twofold. First, it provided a template for future development of mixed-use structures, in particular those that combined theater functions with office rentals. The building's second and more lasting legacy was the high standard it set for office accommodations. It was among the first to deliver luxury alongside light, height, and convenience. Unlike the Montauk, the Opera House provided intentionally high finish and construction quality, representing a new level of thoughtfulness and care in planning, designing, and execution that proved convincing in marketing the building to tenants.

The same agent who praised the Opera House for the *Tribune* also noted three buildings around the new Board of Trade Building that exemplified the new emphasis on quality and simplicity. The Mallers, designed by John J. Flanders (d. 1914), was at twelve stories briefly the tallest in the city despite a footprint of only 38 by 60 feet. These dimensions spurred Flanders to increase rental area by pushing offices into bay windows that gained light and "borrowed" space above the sidewalk. These elements required the bending strength of wrought-iron beams and the laissez-faire attitude of building officials to the commandeering of city air space. Here, Flanders used these bays both as elevational devices and to disguise the thickness of masonry bearing walls behind.

Flanking the Mallers on LaSalle and Jackson, the Royal Insurance by Boyington and the Gaff by Steven Shipman (1825–1905) condensed exterior masonry walls into vertical piers that maximized window area. The Royal Insurance's elevations—in granite on Jackson Street and brick on the narrower Quincy Street—wove vertical and horizontal structure together and filled the resulting voids with French plate glass, a straightforward interpretation of the iron grid within, but framed by arcades of arched openings at the second-floor and attic levels. Its use of electric lighting throughout made it one of Chicago's more prestigious office structures. Shipman, on the other hand, treated the Gaff's masonry elevations as masses punched by double-story windows, each with a terra-cotta spandrel dividing them, and with stringcourses splitting the facade into two-story layers. The Gaff was influenced by the Montauk—Shipman treated its exterior walls as a structural masses into which openings were punched. Boyington took a different tack with the Royal Insurance, refining the wall into a grid of spanning and bearing elements and filling the resulting spaces with as much plate glass as possible, a conception that would be carried forward in more

resolutely skeletal masonry and iron frames. The Mallers, on the other hand, treated the glass cladding as an applied system in its bay windows, an approach that would form the conceptual basis for the curtain wall buildings of the 1890s.

Architect Solon Spencer Beman's (1853–1914) building for the Studebaker Company (1886) on south Michigan Avenue followed a similar approach, providing daytime illumination for showrooms by condensing the front facade into a grid of structural stone and masonry. Between these solid elements Beman designed lights of plate glass, notably in bay windows on the third and fourth floors that ran nearly floor to ceiling and column to column. The result, as the *Tribune* described it, was that "the crowning glory of the building is light! Every floor is flooded with it."[58] Like the Opera House, these lower stories required even more glazing than the office floors above, but Beman answered criticism of that building's insubstantial lower levels with a deftly conceived set of arches and wide piers. Like Boyington at the Royal Insurance, Beman realized that the planar nature of the masonry bearing wall could be distilled into a more concentrated system of spanning lintels and bearing piers, aligned with—and thereby expressive of—the columnar grids of iron within.

Even as these tectonic experiments in more framelike exterior elements were being built, however, three firm re-

statements of traditional bearing wall aesthetics were built in the Loop. The Field Warehouse, Boston architect H. H. Richardson's largest project in Chicago, was the headquarters for the massive wholesale empire of merchant Marshall Field (1834–1906) (figures 2.9, 2.10). As James O'Gorman noted in 1978, the Field was a mélange of old and new; it grafted a load-bearing red sandstone and granite exterior to an interior structure of fire-protected iron on its lower floors and heavy, slow-burning timber above.[59] Richardson divided the half-block structure into three fire compartments, separated by heavy masonry walls that also served as wind-resisting shear walls.[60] The Field Warehouse was thus the largest example in Chicago of cage construction. Unfamiliar with local foundation lore, Richardson's design proved the difficulty of designing such a structure on Chicago soil, as the heavier exterior settled further than the lighter structure within, leading to a well-documented problem with crowning floors.[61] Like the Opera House, Field desired a building that contained "nothing cheap or flimsy," and the march of stone across the Warehouse's facades—thirteen identical bays on Adams Street and seven on Wells and Franklin—gave his mercantile empire an image that was "fitted for a fort as well for commerce."[62] But this stone was aided by iron as well. Richardson designed the building with no light court in the center and relied on the windows between these massive stone piers for all of the building's daylighting. To achieve this, each of the broad windows at the first through fourth stories was spanned by concealed iron lintels in the stonework above, and the resulting broad apertures—wider, indeed, than any other bearing wall windows of the era—were filled with enormous double-hung glass lights.[63]

The Field Warehouse was thus a summative statement of the possibilities and the limits of fenestrated bearing masonry. "Simplicity," wrote Montgomery Schuyler of its elevations, "could scarcely go further," and this willingness to let planning and construction speak through a language of appropriate and subordinate ornament and detail influenced major Chicago projects to come. Most emphatically, Adler & Sullivan's Auditorium Building repeated the Field Warehouse's formula of fenestrated bearing wall and iron-supported interiors (figure 2.11). Planned as a massive investment in the city's cultural life led by Ferdinand Peck and a syndicate of leading businessmen, the Auditorium borrowed the Opera House's financial formula, combining a six-thousand-seat theater with office space and a first-class hotel.[64] Adler faced enormous structural challenges and he responded with a rigorous separation of the program into a narrow band of simple bearing structure containing the hotel and office structure that wrapped around the long-span structure of the

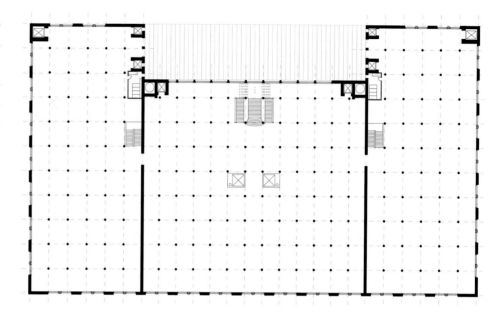

2.9 Marshall Field Warehouse, Adams Street between Wells and Franklin, H. H. Richardson, 1887 (demolished, 1930), plan. (Drawing by the author)

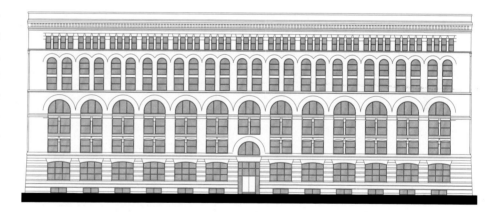

2.10 Marshall Field Warehouse, Adams Street between Wells and Franklin, H. H. Richardson, 1887 (demolished, 1930), Adams Street elevation. (Drawing by the author)

theater. This commercial "wrapper" was a step backward in terms of structural engineering; it relied on parallel bearing walls with wrought-iron girders and occasional cast-iron columns to support each floor.[65] These bearing walls were rendered, in their final scheme, as a simple stone block, clearly influenced by Richardson's warehouse nearby, with a heavily rusticated three-story base, four stories of arched windows, a light cornice and emphasized corner piers.

2.11 Auditorium Building, Michigan Avenue at Congress Boulevard, Adler and Sullivan, 1889.
(From *120 Photographic Views of Downtown Chicago*, Rand McNally, 1909)

Behind this business block, however, lay one of the most complex networks of bridgelike structural iron ever installed in a building. Determined to squeeze every cubic foot of rental space possible out of the block, the syndicate demanded additional hotel accommodations above the already daring trusswork that spanned the theater. Adler relied on engineering consultation from the Carnegie Company, which supplied structural shapes and bridge trusses.[66]

Like the Field Warehouse the Auditorium's foundations suffered from differential loading, although Adler had accurately calculated the capacity beneath the structure's bearing walls. The building's signature tower, which contained hydraulic tanks for stage machinery and additional office space, was extended by two floors late in design. Although Adler had planned for the weight of the original design, superimposing the estimated dead load on the soil with pig iron to ensure accurate settlement during construction, the added height caused the clay under the tower to compress further than that under the hotel and office building, creating a twenty-inch drop between street level and the Auditorium's main lobby, which sat beneath the Tower.[67] This proved the accuracy of calculating for the clay soil's compressibility, but it also showed the limits and inflexibility of floating foundations.[68]

Despite its settlement, the Auditorium's tower, at 225 feet (275 feet to the summit of a small observatory later built on top) was the tallest building in Chicago, just one of the project's many superlatives. At 361 by 161 feet, its footprint was larger than any commercial building in the city other than the Field Warehouse, and with a height of 144 feet its commercial wings were among the most imposing structures in the Loop. An estimated 17,000,000 bricks backed up the bearing stonework, while the interior boasted fireproof terracotta lumber for much of its interior furnishings. The office and hotel block's narrow proportions allowed thorough daylighting, but the Auditorium also contained the most extensive electric lighting installation of any building in the country, with over 10,000 lights, nearly half of them in the theater alone.[69]

The Auditorium's reception was mixed. While *Inland Architect* praised the acoustics, sight lines, and circulation of its main theater, others criticized its regularity and simplicity.[70] New York critic Barr Ferree admitted that "the conditions under which the building was erected were such that no other plan could have been followed," but thought that the structure aptly fit the "packing box" barb that was directed at much Chicago architecture.[71] Montgomery Schuyler noted the commercial exigencies of the project, suggesting that it be critiqued on its own terms because "th[e] exterior appears and must be judged only as a 'business block.'"[72] The building's aesthetics, particularly Sullivan's ornamental accents in the hotel lobby and the auditorium itself, would come to stand on their own, but the assessment of engineer Corydon Purdy (1867–1944) a generation later was that the choice of bearing walls for the commercial wings negated much of its technical achievement.[73]

A similar judgment has traditionally been applied to the best-known of Chicago's masonry skyscrapers, the sixteen-story Monadnock, stretching south on Dearborn from Jackson Street on a narrow lot left over after the southern extension of Dearborn was completed in 1884 (figures 2.12, 2.13).[74] The acknowledged masterpiece of John Root, who according to Donald Hoffmann spent more hours on its design than on any other, the Monadnock was in Burnham & Root's office from 1884.[75] Root's initial scheme anticipated a masonry and iron structure, with its exterior walls refined into wide piers and visually tied together by a mix of stringcourses and column capitals. Brooks delayed action on the project, however, and when it was revived in the late 1880s the scheme evolved into a starker, more streamlined essay in expressed brickwork and interior iron structure. Much of this was due to pressure from Brooks, who with the success of the Grannis and Montauk Blocks

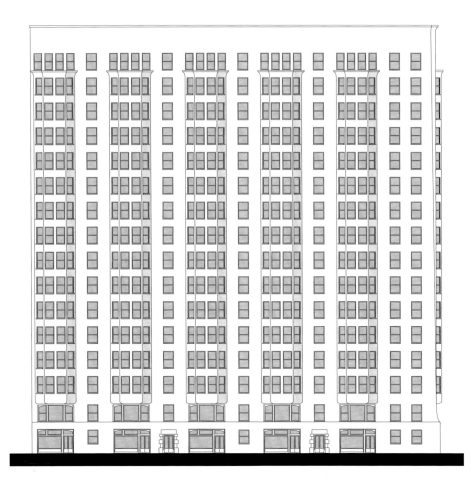

2.12 Monadnock Building, Dearborn Street between Van Buren and Jackson, Burnham & Root, 1891, Dearborn Street elevation. (Drawing by the author)

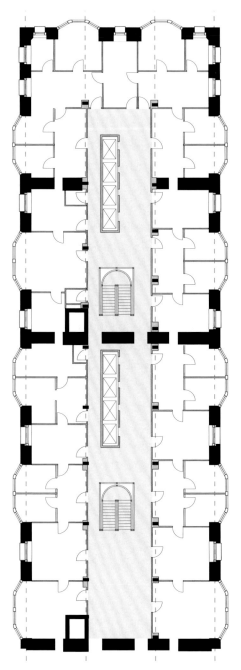

2.13 Monadnock Building, plan. (Drawing by the author)

behind him suspected that ornament presented costly maintenance and cleaning issues that negated any marketing value. When work on the project picked up in 1889, descriptions suggested that the Monadnock would carry on in the vein of the more skeletal buildings of the late 1880s (see chapter 3). Letters between Brooks and his agent, Owen Aldis, speak of "a building of steel columns and girders and beams, with all floors laterally trussed . . . cross walls of masonry every 40 to 50 feet . . . outside all steel," and the *Daily Tribune* reported in July 1889 that the 200-foot building was to be supported by "steel columns."[76]

The design that was built in 1890–1891 was strikingly different from this early scheme, however. As published in *Inland Architect* in 1890, the Monadnock's final design was a resolutely masonry exterior that showed no signs of tenuous steel work within, but it was a cage structure in that it incorporated two rows of steel columns between its two exterior bearing walls (figures 2.14, 2.15). Root's design focused on articulating the exterior masonry walls in section and elevation. Along Dearborn and Federal Place, the Monadnock's offices were pushed out from their masonry support with brick-clad bay windows, forming an undulating, fabriclike surface. In section, Root detailed the building's base and cornice along with the tops and bottoms of these bay windows in curved brick, making the massive brick walls spread outward in their lower stories to match a thick, granite-accented base. At the top, the building's famous cornice was curved outward, with no break lines or stringcourses, while the building's corners were chamfered from a sharp corner at the base to a round one at the top. In Hoffman's words, ornament was "not so much discarded from the building as absorbed into its very walls."[77] *Brickbuilder* described the masonry work as "one of the most skilful [*sic*] pieces of work on the part of both brickmaker and contractor to be found in this country."[78] Indiana-based Anderson Pressed Brick was responsible for the custom-molded brick that allowed Root such a free hand, and George Fuller and Co. supplied the masons who achieved the tight masonry joints, all of which are testament to the rise of a sophisticated, integrated industry.

Such masonry detailing and expression belied the amount of steel actu-

2.14 Monadnock Building, view from north. (Chicago History Museum)

ally in the structure, however, and the massive appearance of the Monadnock's elevations disguised the fact that the building was really a hybrid of metal and brick. Steel was used exten-

sively in the foundations, with I-beams for "grillage" footings described further in chapter 3, and as Hoffman and Condit have both noted, the building relies on steel girders with deep con-

2.15 Monadnock Building, view from northeast. (Contemporary postcard, collection of the author)

carry the dead weight of the masonry above, was what captured critics' and architects' attention. Even Barr Ferree, who had so roundly critiqued Chicago's Auditorium, was forced to admit that the Monadnock had more "dignity and strength . . . impressiveness and power" than the "riotous" designs dotting New York's skyline.[80] Montgomery Schuyler, perhaps unaware of the Monadnock's concealed ironwork, christened the building's quietly expressive masonry as "the thing itself." Some local critics, however, saw in its "stupendous" bulk a threat to sunlight and air, and the Monadnock would become a key exhibit in the pressure for height restrictions in the early 1890s (figures 2.16, 2.17).[81]

The legacy of the Monadnock was that the tenets of masonry construction, both technically and aesthetically, had limits that could only be overcome with newer materials and structural techniques. While Root was fully capable of drawing coherent and engaging expression out of the tall, attenuated proportions of the building's masonry mass, there was far more occurring behind the smoothly curved brick walls than his expression could faithfully represent. The Monadnock was a "masonry skyscraper" par excellence, but it required steel foundations, braces, and cantilevers to supplement, reinforce, and even replace masonry as a structural material at its record-breaking height.[82] Although narrow, deep windows on its ground floor were considered critical

nections that rigidly connect the long masonry walls on Dearborn and Federal Place with its thick masonry cross-walls, making it a precursor to the moment-framed skyscrapers of the mid-1890s (see chapter 4).[79] The building's bay windows, which showed up only in the final, 1890 scheme, relied for their support entirely on steel brackets cantilevered from the interior frame, similar to the "veneered" buildings discussed in chapter 5. Yet Root's monolithic composition, particularly the swelling of the Monadnock's base to reflect and

2.16 Monadnock Building, view from south prior to construction of second phase, showing masonry cross wall. (Chicago History Museum)

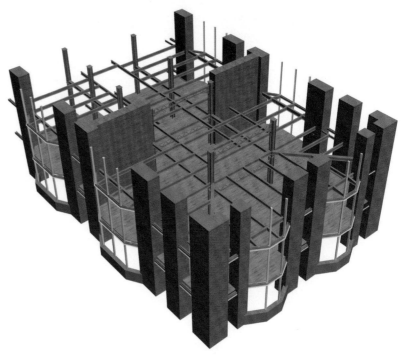

2.17 Monadnock Building, digital reconstruction showing brick and steel construction. (Shagayegh Missaghi and Ryan Gauquie)

flaws in the bearing-wall conception, its steel-framed, cantilevered bay windows matched other experiments such as Flanders's Mallers Building or the more radical Tacoma (see chapter 5) in pushing office space beyond the building line.[83] It was also among the earliest Chicago buildings to be wired for electric light, though its fixtures were also designed to support the cheaper and, at the time, still popular option of illuminating gas.[84] Finally, the Monadnock experienced the same settlement problems as the Auditorium and the Field Warehouse, demonstrating the problems in-

herent in combining light and heavy construction on compressible soil.[85] Subsequent Chicago skyscrapers showed a disinclination on the part of engineers to combine dense bearing masonry and lighter metal framing on the same ground; instead, they sought ways to make steel do both the bearing and stabilizing work of brick.

As the last experiments in cage construction in the city, the Monadnock and the 1892 Woman's Temple proved the limits of the clay and iron tower in Chicago. Foundation problems faced any building with heavy construction;

the continued high cost of lighting and the need for visibility discouraged thick, heavy walls with small, punched windows; and the structural limitations of brick meant that purely bearing masonry structures could go no higher than the Monadnock's sixteen stories. Perhaps more damning, the immense scale of the Monadnock's brick piers on its lower floors was alarming to developers who were keen to squeeze more rentable area and daylight from their plans.[86] When the Brooks family extended the Monadnock in 1892, they hired Holabird & Roche to continue the basic plan of the original building, keeping the original structure's bay windows but thinning the brick piers and, in the final phase, reinforcing them with steel columns. While the extension suffered from detailing that seemed hackneyed next to Root's smooth, undulating surfaces, the Monadnock extension was a more expressive statement of the metal structure within and a suggestion that Root's design marked the end of a structural typology. Future buildings in Chicago would rely less on massive planes of walls and piers like those in the Monadnock and more on narrower lines of discrete skeletal columns and girders hinted at by the Studebaker. The Monadnock's cantilevered bay windows and the metal skeleton that supported its interior were more efficient structural techniques that would dominate the 1890s, and that were already occurring in skyscraper experiments throughout the Loop by the time of the Monadnock's construction. These skeletal frames were encouraged by the need for daylight in offices, and they emerged first as a new technique in masonry construction, then as hybrids of brick and iron, and finally as self-supporting, self-braced, and more lightly clad steel skeletons.

Iron structures protected by terra-cotta offered hope against conflagration, but they also enabled interiors that were more spatially efficient and better illuminated than pure masonry structures. Masonry's low compressive strength made for large, space-consuming piers that congested floor plans, especially on lower levels where owners typically desired more open retail spaces. It also meant thick, solid exterior walls that restricted natural light. Iron offered solutions to both problems. It required less cross-sectional area than brick or stone for a given load, which allowed smaller interior columns and thus more open and flexible floors. But architects began to recognize that it could also take some—or even all—of the loads carried by exterior walls. For centuries, brick walls had performed key structural duties and had been treated as massive, planar elements, inside of which lighter structures could form more delicate, skeletal counterparts. But the application of fireproofed iron to building exteriors provoked a wholesale change in the conception of exterior walls, building on the examples of nascent skeletal structures in cast-iron storefronts and facades. If exterior bearing walls could be reconfigured in much the same way as interior structures—if their loads, too, could be organized and channeled into skeletal, iron grids—then they could be more porous, with larger apertures that were restricted only by the bearing capacities of iron rather than brick. Like the more efficient floor plates inside, structure would take up far less space in such elevations, leaving more room for windows. The emergence of the skeleton frame can be understood as the migration of fireproofed iron to the edges of the building, bringing with

> **Experience has demonstrated that all spaces within the enclosure of four walls which are not well lighted by sunshine, or at least direct daylight, are in office buildings non-productive.**
>
> —John Wellborn Root, "A Great Architectural Problem," 1890

it the efficiency and the constructive logic of this new hybrid construction. It also brought with it unprecedented aesthetic opportunities.

PRECONDITIONS: LIGHTING

John Root's "Great Architectural Problem" noted that illumination was the fundamental issue facing Chicago's commercial architects, even more than weight or foundation capacity.[1] While advances had been made in interior lighting through the 1880s, daylighting remained the most widespread solution to illuminating commercial interiors through the early twentieth century. Candles and oil lamps remained in use, though by the time of Root's essay in 1890 they were supplemented by illuminating gas, which doubled brightness to about eight candlepower.[2] Electricity became available in Chicago in the mid-1880s, but the very real possibility of electrocution—often described in lurid news reports—and the high cost of generating equipment made it an expensive and risky luxury until the turn of the century.

The inefficiencies of oil and gas lighting were compounded by the inherent dangers of open flame; in 1884, the majority of fire fighting calls in Chicago involved overturned or exploding oil lamps.[3] Illuminating gas, usually manufactured from coal, presented a partial solution through fixed wall- or ceiling-mounted lamps. In 1850 the Chicago Gas Light and Coke Company built a network of pipes, gasometers, and distilling plants to provide public lighting along Lake Street and they enjoyed a monopoly over illuminating gas throughout the city. The quality of its gas was variable, however, and its prices were extortionate until the People's Gas Company provided much-needed competition in 1885.[4] People's Gas offered a cheaper, cleaner product, but claims by each company about dangers in the others' gas meant that by the 1890s gas lighting had earned a reputation in Chicago as "decadent" and archaic. There were, however, few alternatives to gas or oil.[5] John Barrett demonstrated an "unsteady but very powerful" electric arc light at Chicago's Water Tower in 1878, and Edison's 1882 installation of a central generating plant in New York aroused Chicago's expectations for electrification. Chicago illuminated the streets and tunnels around City Hall with $42,000 worth of Edison lamps and dynamos in 1885, but they took two years to install, and this delay was seized upon by gas interests as evidence that electricity was a mere novelty.[6] Incompetent contractors and faulty work abounded, particularly where inferior wiring could be concealed behind plaster.[7]

More importantly, electricity was expensive to install, provide, and maintain. Edison's preference for direct current systems brought problems of distribution because it was ineffective beyond six hundred feet, requiring a full generating plant for each building.[8] Such plants included dynamos, wiring, and fixtures, along with incandescent lamps that came with lifetimes measured in weeks. Clients thus had to match the initial expense of such installations with annual costs for fuel, maintenance, and lamp replacement, which meant that electric lighting was 20–30 percent more expensive than gas.[9] Luxury developments that did employ full electric lighting plants in the 1880s—hotels, social and business clubs, department stores, and higher-end office buildings—provided fixtures and current parsimoniously.[10] Standard practice provided two or three sixteen-candlepower lights in each office space, which was enough for ambient illumination but hardly a usable level for fine tasks such as bookkeeping.[11] Alternating current and central utilities eventually removed the costs of dynamos from individual lighting systems, but electric lighting was not a viable replacement for sunlight in office interiors until after 1900, and Root's view that daylight was the best solution to the problem of the tall office building was shared among commercial architects.[12] The received wisdom on window sizes in 1890, as Root summarized, had sellled on story heights of ten and a half feet, sills just two feet from the floor, and lintels six inches from the ceiling. Windows less than six feet in width were not thought to be effective.[13] Such proportions were hardly achievable in bearing masonry walls, and space-wasting light courts remained necessities in larger buildings.

FOUNDATIONS

On October 18, 1891, the *New York Times* printed the following: **"**Who shall restrain the great layer of jelly in Chicago's cake? Who can say when it will be released, to be mixed with the sluggish sewage of the river, and then to fill the streets and pour in at the windows while the thin upper crust sinks to its ultimate resting place on the lower clay?"[14]

While daylighting pressed designers to condense or eliminate brick walls above ground, foundation issues mitigated against heavy exterior walls, especially those paired with lighter interior structures. Given the flexible, compressible muck of Chicago's clay soil, embarrassing foundation failures under the Auditorium, the Field Warehouse, and the Monadnock demonstrated that differential settlement between masonry and iron construction was inevitable.[15] Owners and engineers invested in extensive borings to establish safe bearing loads under all parts of the Loop, but designs for these foundations atop this wet clay remained as much art as science.[16]

Through the mid-1880s, one promising solution to laying foundations in the Loop was to drive timber piles into the clay until they met sufficient resistance through either bearing on hardpan—a crust of dried clay about twenty feet below the Loop—or friction with the surrounding soil.[17] Rules of thumb suggested that individual piles could carry between 40,000 and 50,000 pounds if they reached hardpan, but this demanded precise placement. In practice, piling proved difficult and unreliable. Piles could be shifted, moved, or even sheared off. Grain elevators along the river relied on this system because piles were the only solution to building in the riverfront's saturated soil, but most of the Loop had been raised above the water table in the 1850s, and piles exposed to cycles of dry and wet environments were prone to rot.[18] Worse, improperly engineered or placed piles led to a record of failure in downtown foundations—in particular under the Cook County Courthouse—that frightened off developers and engineers alike.

Another method for providing bearing on poor soil was to float the structure on a thick mat of concrete, spreading column loads over the entire ground area of the building. This approach required no deep excavations or even piling, but it relied on the assumption that the mat would settle monolithically. The Government Building, constructed in 1879, relied on a continuous mat foundation, as did City Hall and the tower of W. W. Boyington's Board of Trade, both built in 1885. But the mats under all three buildings broke apart, causing differential settlement, leaning walls, and cracked interior finishes that led to the eventual demolition of all three structures.[19]

In 1873, architect and builder Frederick Baumann proposed a system of "isolated piers" that would allow engineers to quantify individual column loads and provide pads to spread these loads over precisely calibrated areas.[20] To spread column loads Baumann proposed pyramids of stone, brick, and concrete that matched the dimensions of the column's base plate above to the estimated required area of soil below.[21] By 1885, so-called "pyramidal footings" ensured proper bearing with limited quantities of expensive cut stone, but the pyramids took up valuable space below grade; Montgomery Schuyler noted in 1891 that their use had practically eliminated the basement in Chicago business buildings altogether.[22] In some cases a usable basement floor could be squeezed in under a raised entry level, as at the Montauk, but this made storefront leases difficult. Mechanical systems for heat and elevatoring also began to compete with these pyramids for basement space.[23] By the mid-1880s, experiments with iron rails replaced pyramids with flat sandwiches of metal and concrete. Iron's bending capacity allowed foundation pads to work as cantilevers in reverse, spreading the point loads of columns without the volume required by pyramids of stone. Basements could now be opened up above, rather than around, these foundations. Iron also represented substantial savings in labor and weight over cut stone, and there was no shortage of railway iron in Chicago.[24] Bent, twisted, or flawed iron that was useless for rails could be repurposed at a substantial discount for building foundations.

Iron- and steel-reinforced grillage foundations were tried in the mid- to late 1880s. They employed layers of iron rails in alternating directions surrounded by a matrix of protective concrete. Such grills were about three feet thick, which allowed reasonable basement space between the hardpan and the street. Daniel Burnham credited P. B. Wight with engineering the first grillage foundation, which was installed to repair H. H. Richardson's American Express Building, and Wight also consulted on the Montauk's foundations.[25] At ten stories, the geometry needed to distribute even the lightened loads of hollow terra-cotta floors meant that the Montauk's pyramidal foundations were as tall as the basement itself, which Wight noted was thus "largely sacrificed for this purpose."[26] This explained the Montauk's awkward, split-level ground floor, with commercial space both one-half story above and below grade. The stone-filled basement was then located beneath this half-basement, as far down as builders dared go. But to make room for a large boiler, Wight suggested embedding railway iron in the concrete layers that underlay the pyramids. This meant that the pyramids could rise from a smaller footprint, while the composite concrete and iron

pad below could spread the load over a large area of soil. This was a crucial step toward developing the full grillage foundation, though in Wight's words, it merely gave "very large offsets to the concrete" rather than fully overcoming the problem of weak soil beneath.[27]

Grillage foundations based on principles espoused by Baumann and Wight contributed to the burst of tall construction that led up to the 1892 Columbian Exposition. Even the twenty-one-story Masonic Temple (1892) rested on networks of steel beams and rails that spread its enormous weight over the shallow hardpan. But isolated pier substructures also suggested refinements in the way building superstructures were conceived; their isolated pads were most effective when paired with isolated piers or columns above. The efficiencies of this foundation type extended to exterior walls too. If exterior walls were reconceived as systems of piers, they, too, could be supported on isolated pads, allowing them to be precisely balanced with the lighter iron structures within. The bedrock of New York and Boston allowed large exterior walls to be easily translated into linear foundations, but Baumann's isolated pier system resolved these linear elements into point loads, condensing large masonry planes into grids of vertically and horizontally segregated structures that left space for far larger windows.

There was, therefore, a particular urgency in Chicago to develop a skel-

etal approach not just to skyscrapers' internal structures but to their external structures as well. In addition to allowing larger windows, distilling walls into piers and columns provided tangible benefits for foundations, suggesting a fuller translation of cage structures into skeletal structures than occurred in other cities. This development was fraught with technical and compositional problems, because massive exterior walls had long served multiple structural purposes and defined the appearance and perceived solidity of tall buildings. The resolution of monolithic exterior walls into grids of discrete elements provided more attenuated proportions and thus demanded new stylistic approaches.

AESTHETICS

Should this programmatic ideal of wider openings and narrower solid panels be decorated in familiar styles? Or should the new proportions and functions be celebrated? The *Brickbuilder* suggested in 1894 that the continuation of older forms on such radically redefined structures was absurd.[28] Thomas Hastings, of Carrere and Hastings and the chief architect of the New York Public Library, thought that a new resolution of structures into skeletal frames augured a new approach to architectural expression: "I cannot imagine a more natural and beautiful solution than to treat these iron and steel constructions with curtain-walls, by honestly showing the iron or steel on the facade, with a filling-in of terra-cotta, brick or faience, with projections constructed in apparent iron and terra-cotta."[29]

This view was not universally shared. Barr Ferree had, by this time, already dismissed the entire philosophy of expressed structure, suggesting that the industrial iron and steel that supported skyscrapers was more tastefully concealed.[30] For Ferree, the freedom offered by minimal steel columns and girders simply allowed a broader palette of stylistic options than large brick surfaces. Structure did not *need* to be expressed—it could serve as a matrix or armature upon which any style might be "hung." "The possibilities of the [skeletal] system are immeasurable," agreed *Industrial Chicago* in 1891. "It may revel in the Renaissance, boast of the majesty of the Romanesque, or dwell with the ascetic in the monastic Gothic."[31] But only the most luxurious developments could afford to sacrifice window size for classic or Romanesque proportions; speculative offices in particular forced architects to respond to a far lighter structural matrix that did not immediately suggest such massive appearances.

In addition to their skeletal proportions, skyscrapers' heights presented problems for historicism; if no academically acceptable piece of architecture had been built to such tall ratios before, what stylistic rules were to govern? Some articulation was clearly called for, though, as the pejorative labeling of earlier buildings as "dry goods boxes" made clear.[32] To make sense of the vertical proportions of these towers, there were essentially two choices: one could divide the building into horizontal bands as Root had done with the Montauk, or one could provide articulation that ran vertically, emphasizing height. These carried with them implied styles—the former suggested the plinths, entablatures, and friezes of classicism, the latter the fluting of the gothic—and they came to represent two schools of thought that were, for a time, representative of regional preferences.

Many Chicago towers experimented with horizontal divisions, but what seemed unique to Chicago was a broad willingness to admit what critic Montgomery Schuyler called the "facts of the case," and to derive architectural expression from a more vertically oriented, gridded structure. Chicago architects were often credited with subordinating architectural treatment to the economics of building massing and construction, in particular the verticality and repetition that the program for a speculative office building required. P. B. Wight, writing years later in the *Architectural Record*, suggested precisely this approach: "In the earlier Chicago skyscrapers the steel skeletons were generally filled in with brick or terra-cotta walls and carried little ornament. The New York architects tried to give them 'style.' . . . The Chicago architects did not fall into this error. . . .

Instead of using strong horizontal lines, except at the top and the bottom, they accepted the situation and made the vertical lines more prominent."[33]

But the questions of style—of vertical versus horizontal or of ornament versus structural expression—only highlighted larger issues about the nature of the skyscraper as an experiential object. Commentators frequently noted that the Chicago's skyscrapers aspired to aesthetic and conceptual rigor that the heavily ornamented or stylized skyscrapers of other cities lacked. "A dry goods box may, by the addition of a certain amount and quality of ornament, be changed into a beautiful ornamental chest," according to the *Chicago Daily* in 1892, but "all the ornament in the world, no matter how applied, will not make the Chicago office building a whit more useful, nor will it bring to its owners a penny more of income."[34]

In other words, the skyscraper was a problem to be solved first, after which the resulting arrangement of structure, function, circulation, and cladding could be ornamented in whatever way its mass and components suggested. Speaking of the work of Burnham & Root, which he found particularly rigorous in this regard, Montgomery Schuyler noted that their frankly diagrammatic facades and straightforward detailing, without any "incongruous preciousness," had its distinct, almost ascetic charms: "[T]hese buildings, by far the most successful and impressive of the

3.1 First Leiter Store, corner of Wells and Monroe, William Le Baron Jenney, 1879 (demolished, 1970). (Art Institute of Chicago)

from anything but a consideration of its own requirements."[35]

This is not to say that such a rigorous approach was universal; "it is by no means to be inferred," said Schuyler, "that Chicago does not contain 'elevator buildings' as disunited and absurd and restless as those of any other American town."[36] William Le Baron Jenney in particular was taken to task by critics for his confusing and often arbitrary compositions. But in the work of Sullivan, Burnham & Root, and Holabird & Roche, the ideal of a lightly ornamented, clearly presented solution to the balance of function and structure inherent in the tall office building reached a point of high refinement, one where ornament played a supporting, not an obscuring role. These architects recognized the appeal of a straightforward presentation of technical principles. Ornament was seen not as the "crime" that the avant-garde of coming decades would decry, but rather as a useful emphasis for basic compositional principles derived from economic and functional factors. Ornament here served to enhance the visual continuities, rhythms, and proportions of a properly solved architectural problem, rather than to conceal, as Ferree suggested, the skyscraper's aesthetically difficult realities.

SKELETON FRAME BUILDINGS

The five-story building erected by William Le Baron Jenney for dry-goods

business buildings of Chicago, [do] not merely attest the skill of their architects, but reward their self-denial in making the design for a commercial building out of its own elements, however unpromising these may seem—in permitting the building, in a word, to impose its design upon them, and in following its indications, rather than in imposing upon the building a design derived

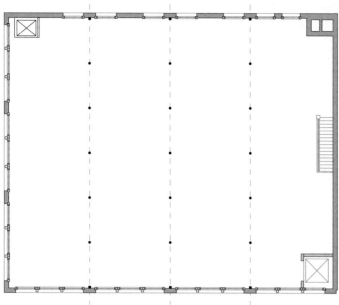

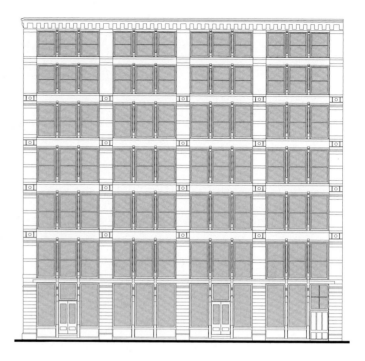

3.2 First Leiter Store, plan. (Drawing by the author)

3.3 First Leiter Store, elevation. (Drawing by the author)

merchant Levi Z. Leiter at Wells and Madison has traditionally been considered Chicago's earliest skeletal exterior, though it was only a tentative step (figure 3.1). The building served as a shop and storehouse, and light was of paramount concern, especially given the shallow corner lot. Jenney worked to reduce the exterior of the building as much as possible by supplementing traditional brick piers with iron columns. The Leiter lot, 82 by 102 feet, was not large enough for a light court, and on the north and west sides party and alley walls required significant fire protection. Jenney placed stairs, two elevators, toilets, and plumbing chases against these solid walls, freeing the

street fronts on Wells and Monroe. He then divided the plan into four structural bays, with timber girders spanning the short dimension from west to east (figures 3.2, 3.3). Timber was still seen as a reliable choice for beams and floors in 1879 despite improvements in fireproofed iron, but it sacrificed depth. Iron girders would have been able to carry the heavy floor loads with more slender beams.

Supporting each girder were five cast-iron columns that borrowed connection details from mill construction. At the east and west walls, a rectangular cast-iron column carried the end of each girder, but these columns were also tied to masonry piers. Iron lin-

tels carried brick stringcourses and sills across window openings at each level, and these were also supported by a combination of brick pier and iron column. On the south, Monroe Street facade, where no spanning girders required support, Jenney did away with cast-iron columns altogether. The four brick piers that formed this elevation were backed up with more brick, all of which supported an embedded girder at each floor.

The supplemental iron reduced these piers' weight and size, and the resulting elevations showed Jenney's nascent understanding of the exterior wall as a grid rather than solid plane. Hybrids of iron and masonry existed by

3.4 Home Insurance Building, corner of LaSalle and Adams, William Le Baron Jenney, 1885 (demolished, 1931).
(Art Institute of Chicago)

this point mostly as separate systems—in Viollet-le-Duc's influential *Entretiens*, for example, they were shown as separate systems for support (masonry) and span (iron). At the Leiter, however, iron and brick were amalgamated—they shared the same loads and there was no clear distinction about how loads were split. Its structural advance was thus only the small step of making brick piers stronger, and thus smaller in plan, but the architectural consequences were important. Jenney filled the large voids between the now-slimmer brick piers with as much glass as economy allowed, in large double-hung windows that ran nearly floor to ceiling, with only low spandrels at floor level.

The Leiter's grid of undersized brick piers and minimal spandrels may have inspired Frederick Baumann to supplement his theory of isolated pier foundations with an 1884 pamphlet proposing "concealed iron construction of tall buildings."[37] Widely circulated, the pamphlet called for a "rigid *skeleton or hull of iron*" to be erected separately from an enclosing skin of "stone, terra cotta, or brick," the latter to be fully supported by the former. While offering few details on connections between the two systems, Baumann recognized that by concentrating structural loads on a skeletal iron frame the exterior structure could be radically reduced: "LIGHT—the most indispensable desideratum with a building," he suggested, would thus be "procured even in the lowest, most valuable stories, where otherwise the necessarily broad piers would be a hindrance." Presciently, he called for stiff connections between girders and columns to "impart firmness to the structure," but his preferred technique, riveting, was not possible in a brittle material like cast iron. Nevertheless, he suggested that a clad frame would enable faster construction, and that above eight stories the savings in masonry would pay for the extra costs of an iron structure. "Were it possible to clothe them with proper elegance, and were they proof against neighborhood fires," his pamphlet claimed, skeletal iron structures would maximize "convenience, *secureness and light*; all this, of course, combined with a shine of elegance."[38] Baumann would design two buildings that employed the skeletal ideal—the Conkey (later Franklin) on South Dearborn in 1887 and the Chamber of Commerce at LaSalle and Washington in 1890. Other architects, however, explored his idea more thoroughly, liberated by the skeleton's spatial and constructional efficiency while struggling with its more tenuous proportions and the bulkier masonry fireproofing that concealed its presence.

Earliest among these was Jenney's Home Insurance Building, which was in design as Baumann's pamphlet was circulating (figure 3.4). While the building has been the subject of debate as the "first skeleton frame," its structure was only a small improvement over the Leiter's system and it remained a crucial step away from Baumann's skeletal formula. The Home Insurance Company of New York enjoyed an excellent reputation in Chicago for its "prompt and full payment" following the 1871 fire, and by 1883 the company decided to locate a regional headquarters in the Loop.[39] The company purchased a corner lot, 138 by 96 feet, at Adams and LaSalle and selected its architect by competition, a controversial method at the time.[40] Jenney's design called for an eight-story building (later extended to nine) of pressed brick and stone with a raised basement and first floor—similar to the Montauk—with lettable office floors around a light court (figure 3.5). For the upper floors, the building committee instructed Jenney to design for the "maximum number of well-lighted small offices." Jenney recalled later that they in fact suggested iron's potential to achieve this, requesting a study of "the method of construction that would satisfy the requirements for stability and for small piers." This directive was matched by the foundation-driven need for less dead weight in the floors above, and in fact Jenney's writings at the time focused more on the weight-saving potential of iron than on its skeletal possibilities.[41]

"When coupled with the condition of a very compressible soil, carrying only a light load per square foot," he wrote, the requirement for daylight "necessitated a different method

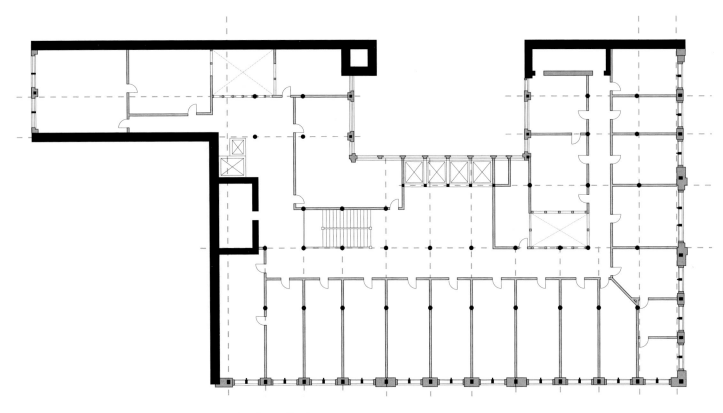

3.5 Home Insurance Building, plan. (Drawing by the author)

of construction from those in general use," and it was this method that made the Home Insurance so influential.[42] Jenney laid out a standard frame of iron columns and girders for the building's interior, fireproofed by terra-cotta covering. At the lot lines, however, he was obliged to use solid masonry to satisfy City inspectors. These walls were load-bearing brick, but for the two street fronts he proposed a new integration of brick and metal. To reduce width and bulk, each masonry pier contained within it an iron column that took at least some of the floor loading. In itself this was not new; iron columns wrapped in masonry had been used by

George Post at the Poultry Exchange in New York (1884), suggested by Viollet-le-Duc and employed even by Jenney himself on a modest scale in two structures in Indianapolis.[43] For the greater height of the Home Insurance, however, Jenney knew that on warm days iron would expand more than brick. The columns would then absorb the entire load of the structure and tear the iron girders away from the brick skin.[44] He thus detailed (or claimed to have detailed) the masonry skin so that each level was carried on iron lintels that framed into columns, leaving the brick to support only its own weight. As the column expanded it would lift not

only the interior structure but the exterior skin as well, preventing differential movement. But to what extent this system of masonry skin supported on each floor was actually realized is uncertain, and it was contradicted by Jenney's own writings. At the time of the Home Insurance's construction, Jenney wrote of the resulting exterior elements as hybrid structures and described the iron as reinforcing rather than independently load-bearing: "[A] square iron column was built into each of the piers in the street fronts," he wrote, downplaying the importance of the iron and leaving its exact bearing status unclear (figure 3.6).[45]

Jenney later stated that only the masonry *between* piers, or the top and bottom framing of the building's windows, was actually carried by iron structure and that the masonry surrounding the column itself was self-supporting (figures 3.7, 3.8).[46] Further evidence for this interpretation comes from details of the cast-iron lintels themselves, which were not bolted to the columns but simply rested on cast lugs.[47] Jenney also selected hard-burned structural brick rather than cheaper face brick for the piers and required that joints within the brick piers be filled and packed with high-cement mortar, noting that this could support higher structural loads than standard construction.[48] Collectively, these details make the case that the Home Insurance's brick piers bore substantial load, because there would otherwise have been no reason for the extra expense.

There was no confusion about how the building handled wind loads. Like all of its tall contemporaries it relied entirely on masonry. Charles Strobel, assessing the building's claims to structural innovation in 1896, suggested that the masonry lot line walls "were of sufficient thickness to perform the double duty of carrying their own weight and of staying the building."[49] Jenney attempted to create a stiff metal frame by clamping all joints between columns and girders so that "any movement [would] be transported entirely across the building," and he included large iron hoops

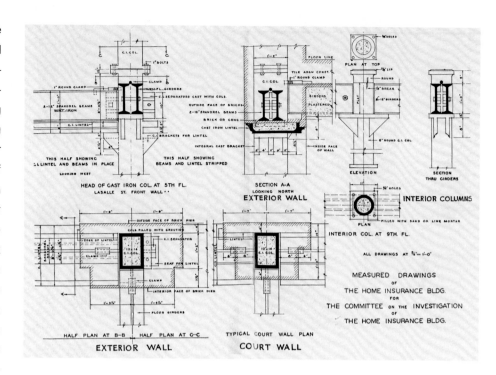

3.6 Home Insurance Building, structural details. (From Field Report)

to belt the brick structure together. But these were not sufficient to brace the building on their own.[50] Any opportunity for creating as stiff a frame as Baumann had suggested was lost by Jenney's decision to attach the girders to the columns only with single bolts, relying on bent rods to fix these joints for erection purposes.[51] Larson and Geraniotis suggest that this detail arose to allow for wide site tolerances, and it could provide little if any resistance to rotation caused by wind. Indeed, the cast-iron lintels were notched to allow the frame to rotate without crushing surrounding brick.[52] The Home Insurance's foundations were also decidedly conservative, with stone pyramids rather than steel

grillage.[53] A final, surprisingly traditional detail lay in the load-bearing granite of the lower two stories. The Home Insurance could, however, boast Chicago's first architectural use of steel (in place of wrought iron). This substitution was proposed by the Carnegie mills, which had supplied the structural iron for the project and were keen to see their new, Bessemer-mill product employed in a high-profile building.[54]

Jenney's elevations for the Home Insurance reflected its mixed structure of stone, iron, and brick and its combination of tradition and experiment. Though its skeletal nature was reflected in an underlying grid of brick and terracotta lines, Jenney reverted to tradi-

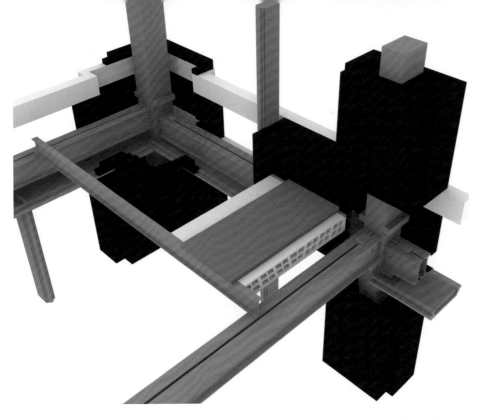

3.7 Home Insurance Building, digital reconstruction showing internal structure. (Ryan Risse)

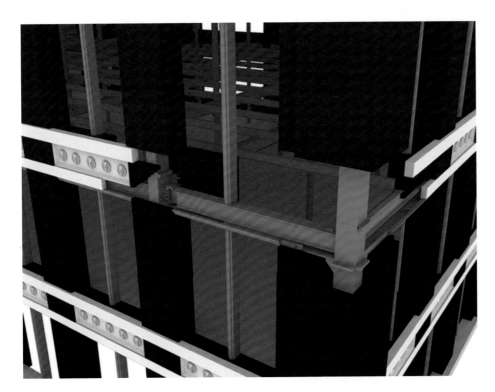

3.8 Home Insurance Building, digital reconstruction showing external wall. (Ryan Risse)

tional masonry forms to embellish and ornament the facades. Corner piers, for example, were much thicker than intermediate ones, giving the illusion of greater load-bearing capacity when, in fact, corners carried only half the floor load of other external piers. A profusion of stringcourses, arches, and pilaster capitals also confused the building's expression. Never accomplished at composition, Jenney seemed intent on disguising the stark proportions and simple repetitions of the metal and brick structure.

The Home Insurance was hailed for its size, but its reception as a "first skyscraper" came only long after its completion. In the 1890s a debate emerged regarding the first use of skeletal framing; Jenney was championed by Chicago interests over New York's George Post, whose 1884 Poultry Exchange also featured a hybrid construction of iron and brick. Never fully resolved—or really resolvable—the debate was revived in the early 1930s when the Home Insurance was demolished to make way for the Field Building. At that time, a team of architects and engineers led by Thomas Tallmadge examined the iron structure and concluded that "the Home Insurance Building was the first high building to utilize as the *basic* principle of its design the method known as skeleton construction," a carefully nuanced conclusion.[55]

A more thorough assessment, however, was offered in an independent report commissioned by the Western Society of Engineers. This committee of architects and engineers based its conclusions on five criteria for "modern steel skeleton construction":

1. "We find the steel skeleton was self-supporting.
2. Structural members were provided for supporting the masonry, but on account of the size of the piers it is probable the load was divided between the columns and the piers.
3. The wind load was carried by the masonry as the steelwork was not designed to take wind bending.
4. The masonry work could not be started at an upper floor without providing temporary support for the eight inches of masonry in front of the cast-iron columns.
5. The walls were not of the curtain type but were . . . of the ordinary bearing type. It is apparent that the designer of this building was reluctant to give up the known strength and security of heavy masonry walls and piers for the untried curtain walls and steel wind bracing of the modern skeleton building."[56]

In fact it would be a decade before new materials and new bracing techniques produced a Chicago tower

3.9 Jewelers Building, 15–19 South Wabash, Adler and Sullivan, 1882. (Photograph by the author)

meeting all of these criteria (figures 3.9, 3.10).[57]

Further experiments in the potential for hybrid structures of iron and brick came in the early work of Adler & Sullivan. Often seen as less mature preludes to their more synthetic work of the 1890s, five major buildings executed between 1880 and 1884—the Borden, Rothschild, Jewelers, Revell, Troescher, and Ryerson—demonstrated their developing interest in expressive skeletal masonry structures. Where Burnham & Root had struggled to rec-

oncile the narrow proportions of even unreinforced pressed brick against traditional massive proportions (the oversized corners on the Counselman, for example), Adler & Sullivan enthusiastically explored the more attenuated proportions of structural brick and cast iron. While none of these works recognized the possibilities of fully iron-reinforced piers, each combined iron with masonry to arrive at elevations that were less massive than most of their contemporaries and that proposed skeletal exteriors that approached the

3.10 McVickers Theatre, Adler and Sullivan, 1879 (demolished). (Art Institute of Chicago)

the beginnings of a vertical system."[58] In practice, this meant treating each brick pier as an isolated structural element, rather than as part of a wall, allowing Sullivan to distinguish formally and tectonically between elements of the facade that were load-bearing and those that were simply there to close in the building. This suggested that the compositional possibilities of bearing, spanning, and enclosing elements on elevations were untapped, and vast.

Adler & Sullivan adopted two important strategies to organize exterior walls into expressive hierarchical grids of structure and cladding . First, where other buildings of the time aligned brick piers parallel with the main elevation, presenting the widest possible face of solid masonry to the exterior, Adler & Sullivan tended to align their piers perpendicular to the facade, taking more depth but leaving more open space on their elevations. The result was the dissolution of the "wall" into a line of independent supports similar to the effect at the Leiter Store; Sullivan's "vertical system" refined wide piers into discrete, attenuated, and more vertical elements. Sullivan claimed that the idea of discrete vertical elements was directly related to the independent pier principle of foundations that had recently been set forth by Frederick Baumann.[59] But a more intriguing possibility offered by the "skeletization" of the facade lay, for Sullivan, *between* these piers, for if the wall was dissolved into a series of linear, ver-

narrow proportions of interior columns and girders.

Sullivan, reflecting on this early period, agreed with Jenney and Root that "the immediate problem" in each of them "was increased daylight, the maximum of daylight." This led, he said, to the use of increasingly slender piers, "tending toward" if not always achieving "a masonry and iron combination, tical elements, the architect now had free reign to fill the open spaces between these verticals with spandrels and glazing that could play a larger role in the facade's appearance and expression. Sullivan had options before him that suggested a hierarchy of materials (masonry, cast iron, terra-cotta, and glass) expressive of the skin's hierarchy of functions (structure, span, enclosure, and daylighting).

A punched masonry wall consists necessarily of two components—a wall and an opening—but the skeletal frame offered three—piers, openings, and horizontal bands that separated openings and concealed floor edges. This horizontal spandrel was only incidentally structural. It had to support the mullions and glass of the windows immediately above it, but if the girders inside were properly placed and connected to the columns, the spandrel itself bore no floor weight. It was, rather, carried by the floor structure itself, and thus presented a new and challenging condition: a solid but nonstructural exterior element.[60] How, Sullivan must have wondered, was this to be properly expressed? Should it be of the same material as the piers? Or should it relate to the windows themselves? Should it be of brick? Or of iron? And, should it occur in plane with the exterior piers, or should it be set back to reflect its secondary structural importance? Finally, what relationships should these spandrels have to one another?

3.11 Revell Block, corner of Wabash and Adams, Adler and Sullivan, 1883 (demolished, 1960). (Art Institute of Chicago)

Should they form horizontal bands that overlapped the vertical piers, adding a dialectical horizontality to the facades? Or should they be secondary, with the piers passing by them with little or no acknowledgement of their subsidiary duties? Jenney had made tentative explorations of these possibilities in the Leiter Store, where shallow spandrels were set back slightly from the face of the supporting piers. But Adler & Sullivan investigated this new conception with encyclopedic zeal.

The six-story Borden Block (1880) was their first commercial collaboration, and its elevations reveal the beginnings of this exploration (figures 3.11–3.13).[61] The site offered two roughly equal frontages that Sullivan divided into six bays each, leaving an almost square grid on each. Pressed brick reduced the area of the vertical piers, though Sullivan did

3.12 Borden Block, 50–56 W. Randolph, Adler and Sullivan, 1880 (demolished, 1916). (Art Institute of Chicago)

3.13 Rothschild Building, 210–212 W. Monroe, Adler and Sullivan, 1881 (demolished, 1972). (Art Institute of Chicago)

not yet turn these piers perpendicular to the facade. The openings between piers were correspondingly large, however, and filled with double-hung lights separated by cast-iron mullions and spanned by cast-iron lintels.[62] At the ground and second floor, the piers were supported by cast-iron columns that further opened the facade. The Borden boasted isolated foundations, and this seems to have influenced Sullivan's understanding of the wall as a set of piers rather than a structural plane.[63]

The partnership's Jewelers Building (1882) and store for E. Rothschild & Brothers (1884) each furthered the Borden's tentative explorations. In both cases structural elements were delineated with continuous vertical piers, and the glass and solid elements in between, covering the edges of floor plates, were rendered in different materials and with more tenuous proportions, creating a visual hierarchy that organized these elevations in demarcated zones of brick, iron, and glass. Sullivan developed these as woven systems of structure, aperture, and enclosure, with iron reserved for mullions and nonstructural spandrels, while the major vertical elements of the facade were more robust brick and stone. Sullivan's ornamental flourishes highlighted joints be-

3.14 Ryerson Building, 16–20 E. Randolph, Adler and Sullivan, 1884 (demolished, 1939). (Art Institute of Chicago)

3.15 Troescher Building, 15 S. Wacker Drive, Adler and Sullivan, 1884 (demolished, 1978). (Art Institute of Chicago)

tween materials and systems with subtle inflections that telegraphed the distinctions in function and material throughout the facade.

Martin Ryerson commissioned three other speculative buildings from the firm (figures 3.14, 3.15). The Revell (originally the Gage, 1883), the Troescher (1884), and the Ryerson (1884) all continued this system of structurally hierarchical articulation, with pronounced vertical elements marking the positions and rough proportions of columns behind, recessed iron or terra-cotta coverings for spandrels, and windows whose planes were set back from all of these. The Revell was commissioned at the same time as the Jewelers, but was finished a year afterward and on a grander scale. Its interior structure was all iron, fireproofed by P. B. Wight, and its exterior matched the formula of the earlier structure, with brick and stone piers forming the elevational frame, filled by spandrels and windows of cast iron and plate glass. Here, Sullivan found a more cogent stratification, dividing the first two stories with stringcourses while allowing the office rental floors an unimpeded vertical run of three stories, with a less obvious division at the top story. This tripartite division matched that of the Jewelers, acknowledging that the first two floors held retail or retail-related functions in contrast to the offices on the third and higher floors and foreshadowing his claim for functional expression that would garner wide acclaim.[64] The cast-iron window bays and spandrels show another of Sullivan's preoccupations, a willingness to let the repetitive nature of such structures define his facades. Within the bays themselves, central fixed panes and two flanking, double-hung units combined ventilation and light gathering into elements that presaged the "Chicago Windows" of the 1890s and early 1900s.

The Troescher and Ryerson buildings represented opposing poles of ornamental restraint and exuberance, but in each case simple internal loft structures formed the compositional basis for their elevations, and the structure in each served as a set of regulating grids. The six-story Ryerson on East Randolph consisted of three structural bays on a party wall lot, and Sullivan adopted the regular pattern of the structure behind as a rigorous basis for an elaborate elevation. Underneath its profusion of decoration lay a remarkable facade, with angled windows making each vertical bay project slightly from the back of its surrounding columns, again drawing a legible distinction between bearing and carried elements. The Troescher was a more sober integration of structure and skin, with the structure afforded more room and with windows recessed further into the elevation, dif-

ferentiating between solid and void. It had the most skeletal appearance of any Chicago building to that time, and it made clear the possibilities for both daylighting and for a new formal expression of the patterns and systems within. Sullivan attenuated the column facings to their dimensional limit, providing the largest possible openings for cast-iron and glass window bays that ran from the second story to the attic. As David Van Zanten has observed, this gave Sullivan a new architectural element to consider—the attenuated column as opposed to the wider brick pier -and newly expansive windows between.[65] Despite ornament that many critics found excessive, Thomas Tallmadge later claimed that here Adler & Sullivan "trembled on the edge" of the skeletal frame, reducing the external structure to minimal vertical supports while grasping that this development required a newly attenuated system of visual articulation.[66]

These five structures by Adler & Sullivan present a tantalizing foreshadowing of three key construction types to come: the skeleton frame buildings of the late 1880s that adopted the hierarchy of expression and the attenuated proportions of the Troescher; the curtain wall buildings of the 1890s that followed the idea pursued in the Ryerson (see chapter 5); and the structural grids of the early 1900s that picked up on the more neutral infill panels of the Revell (see chapter 6). These experiments all

explored the aesthetic and conceptual shifts suggested and in some cases demanded by new materials (pressed brick in particular) and by new demands for efficiency (especially daylighting). Their exterior walls remained of bearing masonry, but Adler & Sullivan exploited the revelatory strength of pressed brick to achieve thinner proportions, and by turning masonry walls into articulated piers they found skeletal possibilities even in brick facades. They also recognized that the new composites of brick and iron posed key questions: was the tall building a structure infilled? Or a structure clad? What of the structure was worth expressing, or adopting as the basis for an elevation? Was the real drama of the skyscraper its vertical reach, or should the horizontal bands of spandrels play an equal or supporting role? These tentative experiments offered no definitive answers but rather models that Adler & Sullivan would refine extensively during the next decade.

A trio of similarly scaled office buildings by Burnham & Root done in 1885 and 1886 showed the clear influence of Adler & Sullivan by condensing masonry walls into articulated piers and spandrels, though these were tempered—many critics believed compromised—by Root's stylistic allegiance to the commercial Romanesque style (figure 3.16). The First Insurance Exchange on LaSalle St. (1885), the Rialto annex to the Board of Trade (1886), and the headquarters for the Phoenix Fire Insurance Company on West Jackson Street (1886) wrapped or applied Root's now-trademark ornament around increasingly legible structural grids, matching larger windows with articulated brick piers. This approach was similar to Adler & Sullivan's, but without the key step of turning the piers perpendicular to the street and thus into a set of discrete structural and visual elements (figures 3.17, 3.18). Root instead continued to think of these piers as condensed elements of exterior bearing wall, a decision that emphasized mass and continuity over articulation.

The Insurance Exchange of 1885 was built of bearing masonry walls and timber joists fireproofed by Wight's terra-cotta system.[67] It featured St. Louis hydraulic-pressed brick, which had become the norm for structural masonry in Chicago, but it also included for the first time a type of soft ornamental brick that allowed much finer, more detailed carved ornament. Root used this quality to express the brick exterior as continuous, flat verticals broken only by four narrow bands of cornices and horizontal projections. The Rialto (1886) was a nine-story structure connected by a bridge to Boyington's recent Board of Trade building, with a full block of frontage on Van Buren between Pacific and Sherman. It adopted an H-shaped plan above its first floor, a scheme "planned with special reference to light and air."[68] It was also noted for being an

3.16 Rialto Building, corner of LaSalle and Van Buren Streets, Burnham & Root, 1886 (demolished, 1940). (Art Institute of Chicago)

"early high iron and steel" structure, and though little evidence of its framing or detailing survives, it was Burnham & Root's first foray into metal-reinforced brick piers, though its much thicker corner piers show that Root's struggle to balance structural logic with compositional desire continued.[69] The Phoenix Building also included a well-documented metal skeleton, in particular its rear wall, which P. B. Wight described as "a complete skeleton construction with enameled brick on the outside and a hollow tile wall on the inside . . . each . . . supported on its own system of horizontal beams."[70] Here the nascent development of the Home Insurance Building—a masonry wall

3.17 Insurance Exchange, corner of LaSalle and Adams Streets, Burnham & Root, 1885 (demolished, 1912). (Art Institute of Chicago)

3.18 Phoenix Building, 111. W. Jackson Street, Burnham & Root, 1887 (demolished, 1957). (Art Institute of Chicago)

that was carried, rather than one that did the carrying—was realized more clearly. The Phoenix was an essay in the proportions and rhythms of reinforced brick. It featured a regular march of accented brick piers, with bay windows at each end cantilevered from these piers' front plane.[71] It also featured the highest level yet of office accommodations and services in Chicago, including five elevators by W. E. Hale—"among the best in the city"—and lighting provided by windows that "flooded" the interiors.

These three Burnham & Root buildings, all constructed in the immediate aftermath of the Home Insurance and of Adler & Sullivan's experiments, show that Root's developing aesthetic was profoundly influenced by the tentative emergence of the skeletal frame in these other works. The difference in proportions, rhythms, and structural articulation between the Insurance Exchange, the Rialto, and the Phoenix, and earlier Root-designed buildings such as the Montauk or the Grannis Block, was important. The 1885–1886 buildings all featured narrower brick piers, wider openings, and rhythm and surface modeling that was derived from the march of regular columnar elements rather than from the articulation of a planar masonry wall. Hybrids of masonry and iron, they were also hybrids of a Richardsonian ideal of mass and a new gridded linearity; brick piers were sculpted out of and into the exterior "wall," and unlike the Field Warehouse, the vertical nature of the brick and iron piers came to dominate the tectonic and compositional aspects of the exterior.

Both P. B. Wight and, later, Donald Hoffmann suggested the importance of this moment in developing an integrated approach to frame design and expression.[72] While occasionally masked beneath ornament that seems in hindsight distracting, the buildings of Sullivan and Root began to grapple with the architectural implications of gridded frames. As building exteriors moved from bearing, planar elements to skeletal elevations, these two architects in particular began to reconsider traditional expressions of such facades and their components. While others sought to mitigate lighter proportions with clas-

sical allusions, the ornamental programs of Sullivan and Root sought an expression of joinery, revealing or emphasizing hierarchies and patterns among such prosaic constructive elements as piers, spandrels, and apertures.

In Burnham & Root's case, integration of structure, planning, and expression found its supreme expression in the Rookery, which in scale and quality was Chicago's most impressive building yet (figures 3.19, 3.20). Named for the makeshift City Hall that it replaced, the Rookery was developed by a syndicate that included Burnham, Owen Aldis, and elevator manufacturer William Hale.[73] With this group of builders, financiers, and designers, the Rookery became Chicago's center of architectural, contracting, engineering, and subcontracting expertise. It was intended to be the most luxurious commercial structure in Chicago and its size alone guaranteed it considerable attention.[74] Beyond sheer scale, however, Burnham & Root sought to provide comfortable, well-finished surroundings, with granite and dark brick and terra-cotta on the exterior, and marble, glass, and gold on the interior. Even the alleys adjacent to the building were paved with smooth asphalt to suppress the noise from trucks.[75]

The Rookery's lot was 178 by 177 feet, and at ten stories it was nearly a cube. While these proportions gave Root a solid, regular volume to articulate, they required careful planning

to ensure daylight and air throughout. Burnham & Root thus went back to the light court model of the Chicago, Burlington, and Quincy Railroad headquarters, carving a void into the site's otherwise dark center. But they improved on the efficiency of the earlier plan by laying out double-loaded, racetrack corridors on each floor, so that one rank of offices looked outside, and the other in to the light court. The court, 75 feet square, was finished in glazed enameled brick to reflect and diffuse sunlight to the lower floors. At its base a glass and wrought-iron skylight enclosed the lower two stories, creating a light-drenched lobby finished throughout in white marble. The "Great Architectural Problem" of daylighting here found its purest solution yet, as the brilliant white walls of the court made even the building's inner reaches, in the words of *Industrial Chicago*, "a thing of light." (figures 3.21, 3.22)[76]

The bright light court contrasted sharply with the exterior. Granite on the street level supported facades of brick and terra-cotta above, rendered in wide piers that separated individual office windows. These were shaped and ornamented to break the large elevations into vertical and horizontal bands. The structure was again a hybrid; the exterior wall was a mix of structural pressed brick and large loops of iron that bound the piers to one another.[77] Within, a central line of iron columns and girders supported beams

3.19 Rookery Building, LaSalle Street between Adams and Quincy Streets, Burnham & Root, 1888. (Drawing by the author)

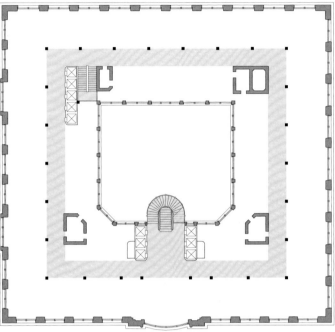

3.20 Rookery Building, plan. (Drawing by the author)

that spanned from the exterior and light court walls. There was no relation, however, between the positions of these columns and those of the exterior piers; rather, piers and spandrels were designed to accept crossbeams wherever the contingent logic of the interior planning demanded. More organized frames of later decades would align girders with piers and columns to more directly channel gravity loads, and the Rookery's almost random arrangement shows an incomplete integration of the frame as an architectural element. The office and service arrangements are inefficient and casual when compared to the more rigorous arrangements that Burnham would design over the next decade.

The Rookery's frame was a gravity-resistant system only; like the Home Insurance, it was supported against lateral forces by a system of belts and hoop-steel that loosely tied iron elements to the mass of the exterior brick walls. Connections between beams, girders, and columns were made with comparatively loose iron straps. But the Rookery's masonry walls were reinforced to create a stiff hybrid frame that combined the strength of iron with the rigidity of brick. "Nowhere is the masonry left to tie itself," noted *Engineering and Building Record* of the Rookery's structure. "Everywhere it is helped out by iron, and all the members of the building are so thoroughly tied together that it would seem almost impossible for any breaks or structural defects to show themselves."[78] The presence of four large masonry vaults in the interior corners of each floor also helped to brace the building against wind. Columns and girders were connected by cast lugs bolted to girder webs, and they were protected by standard fireproofing elements of terra-cotta flat arches, plaster ceilings, and cement floors by the Pioneer Company.[79] The Rookery's overall structure can thus be usefully compared with that of the Home Insurance: both featured piers that were composites of iron and brick; both relied on a combination of reinforced iron joints and large swaths of masonry for their wind bracing; and both featured elevations that expressed neither the bulk of masonry nor the attenuated lines of metal, instead offering measured steps away from the spatial and daylighting limitations of bearing masonry though not yet exploiting the full potential of the all-metal frame.

The Rookery did offer some novel technical features. Burnham & Root specified grillage foundations throughout, the first thorough application of the technique that Wight had recommended as an expedient under the Montauk. Its light court and the lower stories of its two alley walls also presented a clear contrast with its composite exterior skin. In the "quest for light," Root designed curtain walls for these two areas—exterior walls that were carried by the structure and that offered no support to the floors inside. The light court's extensive glazing was seen as a novel contrast to the building's more public facades by *Engineering and Building Record*, who noted that these walls were "not made of masonry, but . . . built up of a frame-work of iron, entirely self supporting, and tied to the floor of each story."[80] This was a recipe for innovations to come. The

3.21 Rookery Building, view from northwest. (Contemporary postcard, collection of the author)

reduction of an elevation's solid elements to nearly the dimensions of the iron itself, the resulting maximization of daylight and space, and the structural separation of skin and frame all anticipated developments of the 1890s that the Rookery's bearing masonry exterior could not yet address. Bearing no

3.22 Rookery Building, view from southwest showing Quincy Street elevation. (Photograph by the author)

THE LUDINGTON·CHICAGO
W. L. B. JENNEY. ARCHITECTS.
W. B. MUNDIE.

3.23 Ludington Building, corner of Wabash and 11th Streets, William Le Baron Jenney, 1891. (Art Institute of Chicago)

load, the light court walls required no fireproofing, which permitted unusually slender verticals and thus particularly large expanses of window.[81] On the alley walls, the effect of the towering mass of brick sitting on two stories of lightweight iron and glass presented a less settled appearance than the unbroken, massive solidity of the two major street front elevations, but Root had few precedents to work from, and the need for daylight in these heavily shadowed walls clearly outweighed his concern for a traditional appearance.

The integration of masonry and iron found an entirely different expression in the post–Home Insurance work of Jenney, which directly explored the transformation of exterior walls into networks of spanning and bearing lines. The Ludington and the Second Leiter Store, both completed in 1891 at the corner of Wabash and 11th Streets and on the block between State, Congress, and Van Buren, respectively, carried the nascent logic of the Home Insurance to more coherent structural and compositional ends (figures 3.23, 3.24). Jen-

ney was a better stylist when faced with tighter constraints, and these structures were both designed to be rapidly built, unpretentious buildings—the Ludington for light manufacture, the Leiter as a lower-end retail emporium. In both, Jenney sought to resolve exterior walls into grids that reflected both structural and constructional logic, though he was less concerned with the articulated distinction between column and spandrel and more concerned with expressing the hierarchy of vertical elements—that is, the difference between

3.24 Second Leiter Store, State Street between Congress and Van Buren, William Le Baron Jenney, 1891. (Contemporary postcard, collection of the author)

column and mullion. Given limits to the size of plate glass lights at the time, this was an important consideration, because no manufacturer could supply single panes to match the scale of the structural voids obtainable with metal frames. Architects were thus faced with somehow dividing these apertures, and Jenney developed an approach that ordered vertical elements according to both structural and visual logic. At the Ludington, he used spandrel panels as an intermediary to bring column cladding forward and to push simple mullions back; this highlighted the importance of the structural elements and offered a regularity to the facade that was aided by a simple program of cast-iron and terra-cotta ornament. Faced with a much longer block at the Leiter Store, Jenney blurred the distinction between column and mullion, emphasizing every other structural element in the facade and dividing windows into varying groups of lights depending on their level above the street. Critics have claimed ever since that this approach led to more confusion than expression, however, and the stark lines of the simpler Ludington offered a more articulate model; by reducing the number of facade elements to a logical minimum, its structural and cladding hierarchies were immediately apparent.

These framed buildings all show an attempt to "skeletize" exterior walls and structures to match the spatial efficiencies of iron columns and girders within. Where interior structures had benefited from such attenuated proportions since early mill construction, reducing the outer wall to similar proportions of solid and void presented technical and architectural conundrums. Exterior walls had formed gravity and lateral bracing systems for generations and turning these elements into skel-

etal frames sacrificed considerable rigidity against wind; this was an easier sacrifice for loft buildings wedged between sturdy party walls, but not for freestanding buildings like the Rookery. Despite the push for daylight noted by Jenney, Root, and others, there were material limits to transparency; glass still had to be installed in relatively small lights, and brick's inherent mass meant it could not hew as closely to underlying metal structures as daylighting or skeletal composition might demand. But faced with the need to funnel loads into discrete foundations, Chicago's architects and engineers also recognized the advantages of regular, superstructures that provided easy transitions to isolated piers below. As exterior walls became more skeletal in response to lighting requirements and the enabling opportunities offered by iron reinforcing or structure, architects and engineers discovered both fabricational and planning benefits to aligning girders, columns, piers, and foundations with

one another. While "piers" in the walls of Richardson's Field Warehouse were supported by linear foundations and bore no relation to the structure within, the Leiter Store, the Ludington, and the Home Insurance showed the benefits of such alignment and integration. By treating structure, elevation, and substructure as participants in an overall system with a shared, rigorous planning grid, these buildings demonstrated efficiencies in construction and functionality, and new architectural possibilities of aligning space planning and exterior composition with structural design. Jenney's buildings—the Second Leiter and the Ludington in particular—carried this gridded alignment of structure, elevation, and space even further, but two technical developments—internal wind bracing and new facade materials—would match this rigor with a further liberation of the exterior from its structural duties, enabling the more lightweight, transparent skins that marked Chicago construction in the mid-1890s.

Fireproofed iron brought greater planning efficiency, more effective daylighting, and new forms of expression, but brick remained an important structural component in Chicago skyscrapers well into the 1890s. Despite its formidable strength, cast iron was a troublesome material to fabricate and erect, making it impossible to construct an iron frame stiff enough to resist wind in addition to gravity. Iron's rise to new heights in Chicago was thus accompanied by brick walls that continued to brace tall buildings against wind even as they relinquished much of their responsibility for gravity loads. This lingering reliance on spatially inefficient masonry eventually found a material solution as steel offered important fabricational benefits over cast iron and improved structural performance over wrought iron. Steel frames could be made stiffer, and therefore wind-resistant, in ways that iron frames could not, and this had two important effects: first, the elimination of cast- and wrought iron as structural elements, and, second, the relegation of brick to a cladding and fireproofing role in commercial construction after 1895.[1]

CAST IRON, WROUGHT IRON, STEEL

As late as 1890, iron enjoyed significant advantages over steel in both reputation and cost. Wrought and cast iron had been used extensively since the late eighteenth century, particularly as incombustible materials in mill construction. *Wrought* and *cast* referred to the methods of production, but also to iron's variable composition. Cast iron was closer to raw pig iron in its high carbon content. It was a strong but brittle material that could be worked or shaped only by melting. Wrought iron, on the other hand, relied on time and labor-intensive puddling to remove carbon. This resulted in a loss of strength, but also—critically—an increase in ductility at relatively cool temperatures, which meant it could easily be hammered or rolled into useful shapes.

Together, these two forms of iron had been used in tall building construction since the 1851 Crystal Palace. Cast iron was stronger than wrought iron in compression, but it was vulnerable to flaws and internal stresses that resulted from the casting process. Since these were largely undetectable and could cause catastrophic failure in tension or bending, its structural use was limited almost entirely to compressive applications, where a flawed column would fail only to the extent of the imperfection. Tensile or bending members were made of wrought iron because its composition could be more definitively established and it was therefore more reliable.

Steel's carbon content was similar to wrought iron but more carefully balanced to achieve a combination of ductility and strength. Wrought iron was made by pounding or floating out excess carbon but the Bessemer process, developed in the early 1850s, produced steel by blasting carbon out of molten ore with air and a limestone flux and then adding back the proper percentage of carbon in carefully measured amounts. The result of this precision in carbon content was a material that was workable and reliable in tension like wrought iron but that had nearly the compressive strength of cast iron. These qualities were desirable for tools, weapons, and cutting implements (all traditional uses for steel), but structural elements did not require sharp edges, and the ductility necessary for rolling structural shapes was a natural property of wrought iron, which was already widely used. The structural performance of steel was better than wrought iron, to be sure—between 10 and 30 percent depending on the application. But this was not enough to inspire a wholesale move away from wrought iron, with its proven record and lower price. And steel posed no immediate challenge to the use of cast iron for columns, where statically ideal cylindrical shapes could be manufactured at the time only by casting.

Nevertheless, the replacement of cast and wrought iron by steel took less than a decade, from the first publicized use of steel in building construction in the Home Insurance Building in 1885 to the definitive pronouncement by *Engineering Record* in 1895 that cast iron "could not be recommended" for structural purposes.[2] What occurred in the intervening decade paired the scientific development of steel into a reliable and calculable product with the realization that its unique combination of strength and ductility allowed it to contribute to wind bracing in ways that cast and wrought iron could not. Steel's high strength and superior workability enabled engineers to design self-supporting metal frames that resisted gravity and lateral loading and that needed no further assistance from masonry shear walls. Just as iron had eliminated the need for gravity-resisting elements made of brick, so steel eliminated the remaining need for masonry elements that would resist wind. Freed entirely from the massive walls that iron frames needed to resist wind, steel alone could fulfill the skeletal frame's promise of thoroughly light and open structures that occupied negligible floor and sectional space.

THE NEED FOR BRACING

Before the late nineteenth century, wind bracing had rarely been more than a minor consideration in structural calculations—the dead weight of brick or stone construction could absorb all but the most severe wind forces. However, the lighter weight of skeletal buildings, their increased height, and the unreliable nature of iron connections brought this issue to the fore. Chicago's tall building designers of the 1880s were among the first to recognize this problem and to solve it with dedicated lateral-resistant systems. The Home Insurance Building and the Rookery, for example, both relied on masonry walls set at right angles to one another to stay themselves against wind.

The problems presented by wind in tall building construction were threefold. First, as buildings were built ever higher in proportion to their base they effectively became vertical cantilevers with a distributed load of wind over their entire surface. Higher buildings presented more difficult problems because their increased area of exposed wall gathered wind load while increasing the length of the lever arm by which wind could pry the building from its foundations. Lighter, taller walls reduced a skyscraper's resistance to wind while offering more surface area for that wind to push against.

Second, the internal stresses induced by such resistance could be formidable. If columns were too small, or splices too weak, a building could theoretically be sheared from its foundations.[3] This problem was compounded by ground-level floors that required large, open spaces. Engineers had to find ways to collect wind forces and channel them through a network of structure that maneuvered around and between openings. Bending presented additional problems. In absorbing the internal leverage of the wind acting on the building face, columns on the leeward side of the frame would be compressed, while those on the windward side would be stretched. These loadings added complexity to the calculations required to engineer the frame. Columns that bore the compressive effects of a sudden gust might well be pushed beyond their capacity by the compressive loads from the floors above.

Finally, wind added unpredictable loads from unknowable directions to the connections between structural members. Effective design of column and beam connections involved detailed analysis, complex math, and an understanding of load distribution and material behavior that did not exist in the 1880s. Concerns about the performance of connections were not merely theoretical. In December 1879, the Firth of Tay Bridge in Scotland collapsed in winds that were well within its claimed structural limits. A subsequent investigation concluded that the bridge failed through a combination of poorly designed and manufactured connections. The geometry of the bridge's supports created huge tensile loads on its diagonal, cast-iron bracing members. These members were connected by bolts placed through holes that had been imperfectly cast and aligned. Over time, repeated loads stretched the cast iron of the bridge so much that

emergency shims had to be inserted to remove slackness from its frame. Excess motion caused by the stretched elements and loose connections created additional dynamic loads on cast tension rods and their connections to the frames, which ultimately failed and led to the structure's demise.[4] This disaster showed that connections not only needed to be strong, but that they also needed to be tight, as slackness could lead to unexpected and dangerous dynamic loads that would further stress structural elements, creating a vicious cycle with deadly consequences.

At the largest scale, the overall shape and section of buildings remained important to wind resistance, and rules of thumb told engineers and architects when proportions began to approach dangerous limits. Edward C. Shankland (1854–1924), who engineered Burnham's tallest buildings of the 1890s, suggested that a building's height could exceed its base by a factor of between four and six without requiring special frame design, while other experts suggested that a safe proportion was only three to one.[5] Lest they be constrained by these primitive rules of thumb, engineers and architects had to find ways to channel and resist lateral forces in the new lightweight frames. Masonry walls, which had been used in buildings such as the Tacoma to absorb loads from wind, reached their peak efficiency in relatively short buildings. In the late 1880s

buildings had grown "so high that it does not appear possible that the masonry walls, after considering their own crushing weight, can have much efficiency left for the purposes of bracing the frame," according to engineer H. H. Quimby.[6] The thick masonry walls of the Monadnock and the Woman's Temple had touched the practical limits of masonry bracing, as shown by their walls of cyclopean thickness that settled with alarming unevenness.

As new heights made masonry walls less and less efficient, the metal frame gained recognition as a viable system for channeling wind forces. There were few architectural precedents, but the world of bridge engineering, where large iron and steel cantilevers were common, showed the way.[7] Railroad bridges used the triangular geometry of trusses to achieve cantilevers and single spans with far less weight than traditional masonry arch bridges, and by standing trusses on end engineers had a valid model for designing skyscrapers for wind loads. Engineered trusses could be used in place of masonry walls to absorb lateral loads, eliminating substantial weight.

Although the principle of designing building frames as vertical bridges made sense, the mechanics of wind loads were poorly understood, and engineers could not agree on design criteria. Wind effects had become noticeable in tall buildings, and a popular (though unproven) urban myth of the mid-1890s suggested that pendulum clocks on upper stories occasionally ground to a halt because of wind-induced sway.[8] Collapses of small buildings due to wind were not uncommon, although architecture fortunately experienced no skyscraper disaster on the scale of the Tay Bridge. Skepticism about the performance of tall buildings nevertheless became a serious issue within the design professions. Engineers were uneasy when faced with the problem of wind since there were few ways to measure it accurately or to understand its complex effects on buildings. Measurements of wind effects on buildings produced wildly divergent and surprising results—showing, for example, that wind deflected by skyscraper walls often had as much vertical as horizontal force, and that the eddies created by wind on leeward facades created negative pressure that was capable of pulling out windows.[9] As early theories of wind loading and bracing took shape, the most puzzling aspect seemed to be the continued stability of buildings that were apparently constructed without regard to lateral stability. This robustness was eventually attributed to the minimal but widely spread stiffness of hollow tile partitions, but even after this contributing effect was identified, engineers were frustrated by their inability to accurately calculate it.[10]

Wind pressure did not lend itself to laboratory analysis. Instead, the profession had to rely on direct observation and a best guess for turning this into an estimate for design loads. Such an empirical approach implied grave unknowns. A five-minute gust of eighty-five miles per hour—the highest sustained wind speed in Chicago—was recorded at Burnham and Shankland's private observatory atop the Monadnock.[11] But was this the maximum wind that Chicago might ever experience? To what extent were engineers and designers to assume the worst imaginable storm, and for what wind velocity should they design? By 1885, engineers developed mathematical tools to approximate wind speed into average pressure. Velocities of sixty miles per hour translated, roughly, to pressures of eighteen pounds per square foot, while a wind of eighty-four miles per hour created pressures around thirty-five pounds per square foot.[12] H. H. Quimby, who assembled the most comprehensive study of wind measurements and techniques for resistance in 1891–1892, recommended a horizontal design load of forty pounds per square foot for all buildings, but other engineers (including Shankland), less conservative and concerned with the implications of this figure for the weight of their structures, argued for design loads of thirty or thirty-five pounds per square foot.[13] Both Chicago and New York incorporated these lower figures into their building codes in the 1890s, while Boston and Philadelphia made no reference to

wind loads at that time. The continued survival of tall structures through windstorms in all four cities suggests that the lower figure was not unsafe and the inherent stiffness of internal construction must have provided more wind resistance than had been assumed.[14]

Quimby, undeterred, noted that proper wind bracing was insurance against storms of unforeseen ferocity, and his view—if not his suggested loading value—was widely shared through the 1890s. Wind bracing became an important part of structural frames in Chicago's real estate boom of 1890–1891, and it took three forms. Each system relied on metal rather than masonry, which eliminated weight, and allowed plans and facades that were more open than the masonry systems of the previous decade. Each also depended upon increasingly precise standards in manufacture, because perfect alignment was understood as critical to avoiding the slackness that had doomed the Tay Bridge. Frame-based wind-bracing schemes added members or connections to make building structures act as cantilevered, vertical trusses. In order of increasing complexity, these schemes included rod or sway bracing, knee braces, and portal frames. More spatially efficient systems, especially lattice or plate girders, improved on these by the mid-1890s (figures 4.1–4.3).[15]

Of these structural systems, rod or sway bracing was closest to actual

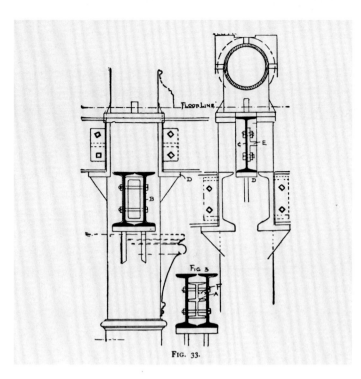

4.1 Typical cast-iron structural connections. (William H. Birkmire, *Skeleton Construction in Buildings*, New York, Wiley & Sons, 1894, 51)

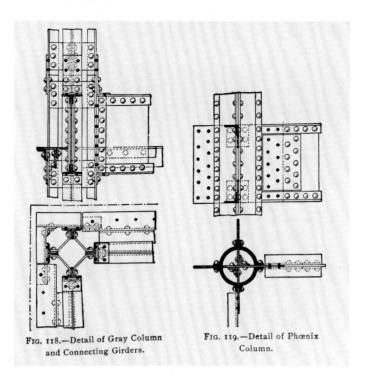

4.2 Typical riveted steel structural connections. (Freitag, *Architectural Engineering*, 215)

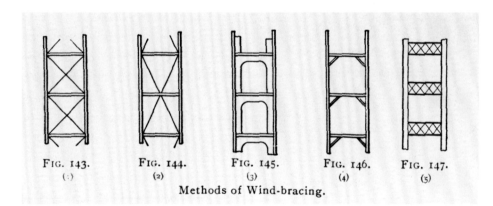

4.3 Methods of wind bracing. (Freitag, *Architectural Engineering*, 258)

bridge construction. It employed diagonal members set within the building frame and connected at intersections of columns and girders. This cross bracing triangulated each panel, ensuring that any wind that might deflect the vertical truss would be unable to change the shape of these triangular panels without stretching the metal tension rods. Thus, the tensile strength of wrought iron or steel could be directly deployed against lateral loads. Over multiple stories, these rods had to connect to one another—the tensile loads they absorbed had to be transferred to similar triangulated panels in stories below, and continuously to the foundation. Buildings braced by sway-rods typically had two or more dedicated vertical planes on which, at every level, rods connected to columns and girders. These planes of metal bracing took the place of masonry shear walls, and sway bracing occupied a plan width of a few inches at most instead of the foot or more that brick required to be effective. Diagonal braces could actually be built inside partition walls, but they often conflicted with doors, corridors, and open retail or banking halls. Rods were often extended over two stories

4.4 Manhattan Building, 431 S. Dearborn Street. William Le Baron Jenney, 1890. (Art Institute of Chicago)

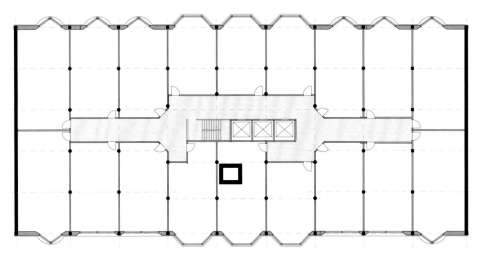

4.5 Manhattan Building, plan. (Drawing by the author)

or offset using a secondary set of structural elements to provide greater opportunities for such openings, but these came at the expense of efficiency and constructability. Sway-rods were typically the most economical solution to wind bracing as well as the lightest, but the problems of planning openings—particularly at ground level where open space was most highly valued—complicated or occasionally prevented their use.[16]

The earliest extensive use of sway-rods in Chicago was Jenney's 1890 Manhattan building (figures 4.4, 4.5). At sixteen stories it was the tallest office structure in the city until the completion of the Monadnock, yet it sat on a narrow lot between Dearborn and Plymouth Court, making it far narrower than any recommended base-to-height ratio. Jenney's solution placed planes of diagonal cross bracing in the building's short dimension at regular intervals and relied on the length of the lot to brace it in its long direction. While the building's sway bracing gained Jenney and the Manhattan credit for an almost uniquely lightweight system, analysis by Harry Weese in the 1970s showed that much of the cross bracing had actually been removed over time by shop and office tenants seeking to expand—with little apparent effect on the building's stability. A later building by Jenney, the 1894 New York Life Company on LaSalle Street, offered an explanation for the Manhattan's survival without these elements. Jenney's engineering was conservative, and he designed on the assumption that the Manhattan's structural frame alone would carry all wind loads on the structure. But this intentionally ignored the significant contribution of hollow tile partitions. With New York Life, Jenney explained that his design for the frame relied on *both* rigid connections and the latent resistance in these partition walls. The Manhattan, like all office buildings of the era, contained numerous tile partition walls in its east-west direction, and these walls turned out to be sufficient to carry the wind loads on the structure.[17]

Sway-rod wind bracing was also adopted for two other well-known Chicago buildings of 1891–92: the thirteen-story Venetian, designed by John Holabird (1854–1923) and Martin Roche (1853–1927), and the more celebrated twenty-one-story Masonic Temple by Burnham & Root (figures 4.6–4.10). Both buildings had narrow, rectangular floor plans whose proportions offered an adequate footprint to resist wind loading in one direction, but they required additional bracing parallel to their shorter sides. The Venetian employed a system that relied primarily on diagonal bracing concealed within four continuous partition walls. These were located strategically to allow greater flexibility in planning, and the connections between sway-rods were shifted to a separate system of struts beneath each floor, enabling more convenient

4.6 Venetian Building, 15 E. Washington, Holabird and Roche, 1892 (demolished, 1957). (Chicago History Museum)

door placement. At the second floor, the bracing was interrupted in favor of a portal frame system (see below) that spanned the width of a banking hall. These structural gymnastics proved

the possible integration of such bracing with open floor plans, but they required much more material to bridge such voids.[18] The Masonic Temple was the ultimate example of diagonal sway-

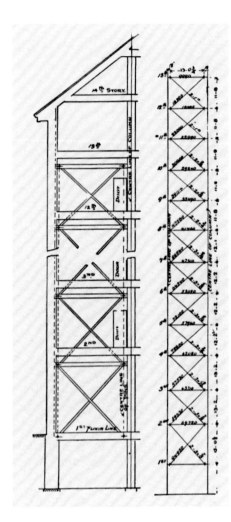

4.7 Venetian Building, sections showing wind bracing scheme. (Birkmire, *Skeleton Construction*, 176)

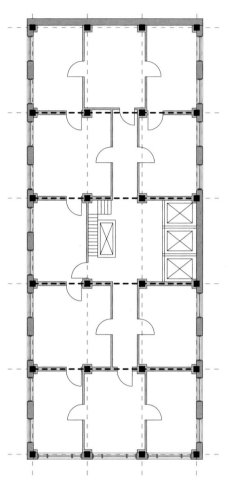

4.8 Venetian Building, plan showing wind bracing scheme. (Drawing by the author)

to triangulate their connection, instead of triangulating a whole panel with tie rods. This strategy was borrowed from the stiff connections between decks and hulls in ship construction. By fixing the connection between girder and column, designers assured that bending loads in one would be transferred to the other, effectively recruiting the cross section of one member to assist in resisting the load on another and forcing both elements to resist gravity and wind loads in tandem. This removed barriers from floor plans, since there was no need to sacrifice whole panels to structure. However, these braces took up headroom near the columns, and they added more iron or steel to building structures than did sway-rods, meaning extra weight and material expense. Architectural solutions to their difficult geometry included coved ceilings, corridors placed away from these restrictions, and large column heads that concealed short diagonal braces. A similar approach lay in expanding such braces until they blurred the connection between girder and column into an arch, or portal frame. These systems can almost be read as steel walls with holes cut through them, rather than spidery skeletons with wind bracing attached.

The best-known example of portal framing was Holabird & Roche's Old Colony Building (1893), a 212-foot tower constructed, like the Manhattan, on a narrow block between Dearborn and

rods' potential, using single-, double-, and triple-story panels to brace its record-breaking 273-foot height along two partition lines that were integrated into the plan. Like the Venetian, the Masonic Temple's sway-rods, "similar to those in an iron pier of a railway viaduct" according to Edward Shankland,

were connected to a secondary system of horizontal struts located beneath the floors that allowed doors to be placed nearer to column lines.[19]

A common alternative to full diagonal sway bracing was knee bracing, in which shorter diagonal members were placed between columns and girders

4.9 Masonic Temple, corner of Randolph and State Streets, Burnham & Root, 1892 (demolished, 1939). (*120 Photographic View of Chicago*, Rand McNally, 1912)

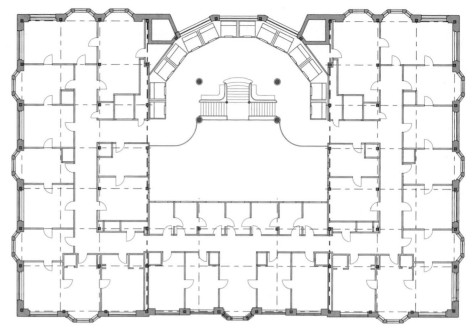

4.10 Masonic Temple, plan. (Drawing by the author)

Plymouth Place (figures 4.11–4.13). Like the Venetian and the Masonic Temple, its plan was a narrow rectangle deep enough in the north-south direction to resist wind loads but requiring added strength in its shorter, east-west direction.[20] The building's engineer, Corydon Purdy, originally specified a system of offset tie rods, but this was changed late in the design process after a dispute with the steel supplier. Wrought-iron columns were substituted for steel, and Purdy was forced to change the structural design.[21] He devised a system of elliptical iron arches that engaged both beams and columns and that used deep iron webs to reinforce structural joints between framing members. The arches provided needed stiffness in the building's short direction, but they were heavy, and they reduced ceiling height in their corners. Holabird & Roche designed coved plaster ceilings in the affected offices, but the wasted volume, extra weight, and expense of the Old Colony's portal system reflected the drawbacks of this approach.[22] Jenney used similar but shorter braces in the 1892 Isabella Building, but even this revised system interfered with ceiling heights where the knee braces attached to columns.[23] Although numerous examples of knee-braced and portal-framed buildings were constructed (including Holabird & Roche's 1893 southern extension to the Monadnock), the consensus by the mid-1890s was that the weight of metal they required, coupled with the requirement for exacting fabrication and erection, made them uneconomical. Their use faded quickly.[24]

Such inefficiencies were eliminated by the lattice girder, one of the key innovations in tall building construction to emerge from Chicago in the 1890s

4.11 Old Colony Building, Dearborn Street between Van Buren and Jackson, Holabird and Roche, 1894. (*120 Photographic View of Chicago*, Rand McNally, 1912)

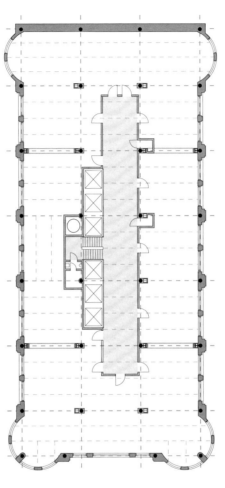

4.12 Old Colony Building, plan. (Drawing by the author)

or portal frames. But a stiffer frame offered extraordinary flexibility in plan and section—indeed, it opened up the sections and elevations of these buildings entirely.

The girder in question had to be deep enough to provide contact area for rigid connections to columns, and it was often composed of paired angles for flanges and an open, latticed grid to save weight. Columns in this system were also oversized to help absorb bending, with wide flanges on all four sides to match the oversized girders that could be connected to form a rigid joint. When multiplied throughout the frame, these stiff joints acted collectively. Instead of relying on individual truss panels, the entire frame could absorb and direct wind loads through multiple load paths to the foundation. Shankland termed this the *table leg principle*, drawing an analogy between the carpentry joints connecting tabletops and legs and his own development, though his principle worked over multiple stories and in three dimensions.[25] Each "table" in plate girder buildings was rigidly connected to adjoining tables above and below, and while the result was a distribution of lateral stresses too complex to compute mathematically, the multiple load paths and sharing of loads across and through the building frame provided a comfortable redundancy. Floor plans and sections were entirely unencumbered by lateral bracing in this system,

(figure 4.14). This principle, later more accurately called the *moment frame*, stemmed from the realization that an accumulation of many small, rigid elements could provide the same stiffness as a few large planes of trusses, essentially adapting Jenney's realization that many small tile partitions could collec-

tively brace an entire building. Edward Shankland proposed that the stiffening function of a knee brace might, with the right materials, be accomplished within the joints between columns and beams themselves. This approach required greater precision in fabrication and assembly than either sway-rods

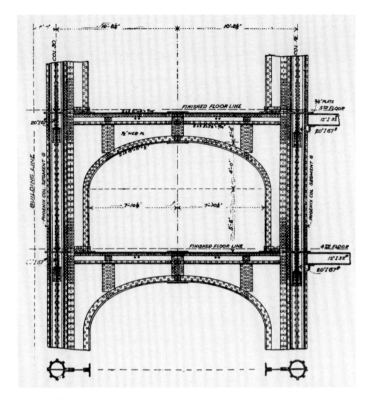

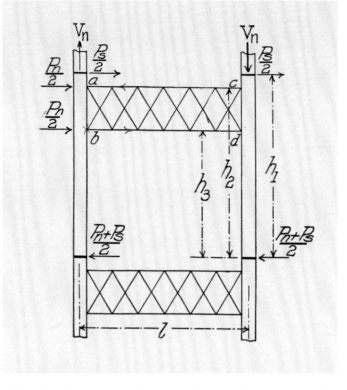

4.13 Old Colony Building, typical portal frame. (Birkmire, *Skeleton Construction*, 199)

4.14 Lattice girder theory. (Freitag, *Architectural Engineering*, 276)

making them more efficient. Girders, columns, floors, and partitions could all be recruited to the task of lateral bracing; though each element might need added depth or thickness, the overall building maintained the openness that became the functional and architectural hallmark of commercial construction in Chicago.

Fully operational lattice or plate girders came into use in tall building construction by the mid-1890s, but sway-rods, knee braces, and portal frames were common during the boom years of 1890–1894.[26] Quimby and engineer J.

P. Snow, however, recognized the advantages of the stiff frame as early as 1892, and there is evidence that stiffer connections between beams and columns played significant roles in skyscraper engineering—intentionally or not—well before the pure lattice girder became common.[27] "If architects and architectural engineers would use built sections of plates and angle irons for their large girders, instead of the conventional rolled beams," Snow noted, "they could make much more efficient connections with their columns than is usual in ordinary building construc-

tion."[28] Even though most buildings of the early 1890s employed the additional insurance of sway-rods or braces, therefore, engineers already recognized the potential advantages of stiffening the frames . But these more spatially efficient solutions required material qualities that could not be achieved in traditional forms of iron.

CAST IRON, STEEL, BOLTS, AND RIVETS: THE QUEST FOR STIFFNESS

Achieving stiffness within skeletal metal frames was difficult, requiring careful attention to design, fabrication, and

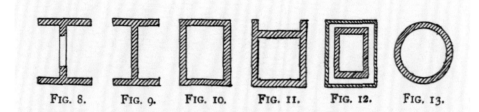

FIG. 8.   FIG. 9.   FIG. 10.   FIG. 11.   FIG. 12.   FIG. 13.

4.15 Typical cast-iron column shapes. (Birkmire, *Skeleton Construction*, 21)

assembly. To ensure that girders and columns could act together as a stiff frame, they had to be constructed with exquisite concern for precision and tight connections. Structural steel allowed solutions to these problems that were not available in cast iron, and this was the arena in which steel proved its abilities to support taller, stiffer, and more efficient skyscrapers.

Cast iron is inherently limited by brittleness. It is not ductile enough to allow drilling, nor could iron members be fabricated with sufficient accuracy to allow precision bolting or riveting on site. Erectors had to contend with columns that were often slightly out of plumb, dimensionally inaccurate, or slightly twisted because of the casting and cooling processes—and because of the material's brittleness, such flaws could not be corrected by drilling or cutting. Connections between cast-iron columns and floor beams were usually made with pins and oversized cast holes that allowed for this wide tolerance, but these resulted in loose joints and the resulting structures thus re-

quired additional bracing systems, usually of masonry.[29] Loosely pinned connections were further compromised by imperfections in columns themselves. Cast-iron columns were limited by the casting process to one story, and they sat atop one another, requiring that their mating surfaces be accurately machined. If connecting faces were slightly out of plumb, the bearing surfaces between them could be reduced to a slender edge, stressing the iron beyond its limit.[30]

Cast-iron columns were available through the late 1890s in four configurations: hollow cylinders or rectangles, cruciforms, and "H-shapes" (figure 4.15). While hollow castings made more efficient use of material, the crosses and H-sections offered better opportunities to connect girder loads directly to the column's center. Hollow section columns could not be fully inspected, and unseen variations in the thickness of the shapes' walls could dramatically reduce their capacity.[31] A worrying record of failure dogged the use of cast iron columns in the 1890s, and as steel

became affordable engineers began to favor it in structural applications.

Connections between columns and girders were just as problematic. Lugs or shelves cast into the column were the most effective method of transferring girder loads into the column, but there was no good way to make a reliably fixed connection between the two. Bolt holes had to be cast larger than the bolts for placement, which allowed movement between structural elements. The brittleness of cast iron meant that bolts could not be tightened fully in the field without risking cracking and fracture. The slight inaccuracies that were inherent in cast-iron fabrication were disastrous for bolted connections. A small variation in the shape of a bolt hole, for example, would allow connected members to slip, and even a very small amount of motion could be multiplied by repeated dynamic loading.[32] Just as critically, the bolt might bear against only a portion of the metal at the edge of its hole, transferring a full load to only a fraction of the cross-sectional area designed for it. As a result, "drilled holes and turned bolts" were, according to *Engineering News*, "scarcely feasible" in cast-iron construction.[33]

Riveting, another means of field connection, seemed to offer a solution. But this was again discouraged by cast iron's brittleness. Riveting consisted of heating metal plugs to the point of pliability, inserting them into predrilled holes in two metal plates, and then hammering both sides, filling the hole completely with metal and, once cool, holding two pieces together with a durable mechanical connection. Riveting was used to connect wrought iron before 1850, and its strengths and potential flaws were rigorously examined by the British engineer and contractor William Fairbairn as early as 1872. The major advantage of riveting lay in the compression of the soft, hot rivet metal within the joint, which would completely fill a drilled hole, guaranteeing full bearing of the rivet on both elements. As the rivet cooled, it also shrank, further tightening the joint. Properly done, a riveted connection offered remarkable stiffness, reliability, and speed. But given the brittle nature of cast iron, hammering and riveting could cause catastrophic failure on the construction site, and thus riveting was not possible in cast-iron skyscraper construction either.

Steel, by contrast, had nearly the ductility of wrought iron. Rolled, thin plates could be punched or drilled easily and accurately, and even greater precision could be achieved by reaming, in which slightly undersized, punched holes were redrilled with a larger bit in the shop or field. Engineers could specify slightly undersized holes in steel members. Once in place, temporary bolts would hold members together, and these undersized rivet holes would be redrilled to a consistent, straight profile, after which the riveting

gang would begin work. The perfect alignment of the holes guaranteed that each rivet would absorb a predictable percentage of the total load, and that the entire cross section of each rivet would be recruited. Steel offered an additional advantage, in that thin, reliably dimensioned steel plates and angles offered readily available elements for making simple riveted connections in the field. Lugs and shelves were replaced by fabricated steel connectors, which could be prepunched and reamed either in the factory or in the field to ensure a tight fit.[34]

As early as 1891, riveted connections using drilled and reamed holes had become standard in steel building structures. George Fuller noted that this technique made structures "more solid," while Jenney praised the technique's scientific basis:

The columns [in Chicago construction] were at first of cast iron with ingenious devices to tie the beams rigidly to the columns. As soon as riveted steel columns of a proper quality could be manufactured, their superior advantages at once brought them into use, which has now become general. All column connections are now made with hot rivets. The metal for the work is all tested, and the workmanship inspected at the mills by professional inspectors. The same science, and the same superin-

tendence is required in calculating and erecting one of these high buildings as in a steel railroad bridge of the first order.[35]

The considerable superiority of riveting was sufficient for the *Engineering News* to declare in 1897 that cast iron was no longer a suitable material for structures, and that in fact it had not been one for some time. "The architects of Chicago seem to have reached practically that conclusion," it noted, "while those of New York remained unconvinced."[36] In addition to its reliability, riveting proved to be affordable and rapid. By 1904, the average riveting gang of five men (one tending a small furnace, two to toss and catch the hot rivet, and one each manning the riveting hammer and backstop) could place and hammer over two hundred rivets in a nine-hour day, with an average cost per rivet under ten cents.[37]

As reliable as riveted connections became, they were only as secure as the members they joined, and intense experimentation and innovation was needed to create efficient, reliable columns in skyscrapers of the 1890s. Columns played a key role in providing stiffness in all types of wind-resistant frames, but they were particularly critical to the development of the steel moment frame in mid-decade. By 1890, considerable theoretical effort had gone into understanding the structural behavior of columns, particularly their hybrid performance when stressed both by gravity and wind. William Burr, in his 1888 book *Elasticity and Resistance of Materials*, codified basic column theory by analyzing the column's bending behavior as a beam that might be loaded in any direction at any time. While the material in a metal beam had to be concentrated at its top and bottom to provide a resisting lever against bending, a metal column had to be shaped to resist bending in all directions—or at least in as many directions as possible. This theory favored hollow round shapes, which placed all of their material at their perimeter. However, closed columns presented unique fabricational and constructional problems. Not every foundry was equipped to cast or roll hollow shapes with precision, and inspecting, connecting, or fireproofing these shapes was difficult.

Hollow columns also entailed significant eccentric loading, presenting performance and design issues. Column theory assumed a consistent application of loading across the column's section. Under ordinary circumstances—for example, a beam resting atop an evenly planed column top—this was a reasonable assumption. However, beams that framed into the side of a hollow shape transferred load to the column section asymmetrically. This was a particular problem for columns at building perimeters, where girders engaged columns on only the inside face.

These off-center loads added bending to the columns' compressive loads.[38] The combined effects of these bending and compressive stresses created incalculable static conditions. Rather than developing theories of eccentric loading, handbooks of the day simply advised designers to bring girder loads to the centerlines of columns as efficiently as possible.[39] This erased the theoretical advantages of hollow shapes, and the struggle to reconcile ideal performance with the need to minimize eccentric loading troubled column design for a generation.

STEEL COLUMNS

Writing in 1896, William Le Baron Jenney argued that the switch from cast-iron to steel columns was the most crucial development in the realization of the tall metal frame: "Since the Home Insurance Building, the most important improvement that has been made in . . . Chicago construction . . . was the introduction of steel-riveted columns, which are now made cheaply and in all respects thoroughly satisfactory. All the assembling at the building is done with hot steel rivets; increased rigidity is secured, as well as a material reduction of the weight of the columns."[40]

Steel's ductility, workability, and reliable strength permitted columns whose shapes were better able to balance ideal static geometry with fabrication and assembly. The rolling process pressed air bubbles out of the soft material, providing a more reliable product, and it produced thin shapes, which made drilling more precise. Rolled sections also permitted longer column lengths than could be provided by casting, and making columns continuous over multiple stories reduced a critical source of slackness in building frames. However, columns could not readily be fabricated or transported in lengths greater than two or three stories. Therefore, columns in tall buildings, no matter how rigid, had to be spliced together, and each column was only as strong as the splice itself (figures 4.16, 4.17). Riveting these splices in the field guaranteed tight, monolithic connections that were crucial to providing stiffness throughout building frames. Columns were staggered in construction so that splices in adjacent columns occurred on alternate floors, which avoided concentrations of potentially weak connections on one story, and erectors convinced engineers to locate splices just above finished floor levels, usually twelve to twenty-four inches clear, enabling floor beams to firmly position column ends.[41]

Manufacturers began to produce specialized, rolled steel sections for columns by 1890, balancing ideal cross sections with reliable surfaces for connections and splices. The Phoenix column, manufactured by the Phoenix Iron works near Philadelphia, was assembled from curved plates into riveted, circular elements with straight flanges at its edges. While steel Phoenix columns could be drilled and planed to exacting dimensions, their curved surfaces made connections, particularly stiff moment connections, difficult. Phoenix tried several solutions, including cross-plates sandwiched between the column's segments. These provided steel tabs for attachments and provided continuity between girders framing into opposite sides of the column.[42] Such cross-plates, however, added weight nearer the less efficient center of the column section, which reduced the columns' efficiency. Curved surfaces also made splices difficult, and it gradually fell from use in buildings around the turn of the century.

By 1892, strong connections between beams and columns received as much attention as ideal structural shapes. Engineer W. H. Breithaupt noted in the *Engineering Record* that "there is practically little or no difference in unit strength among the various sections in use. The one therefore which best admits of connections is the one in general to be preferred."[43] Given standard dimensions for plates and angles, it was relatively simple to design columns by building up thickness at the column perimeter and connecting these with thinner webs, similar to beam and girder design. This distributed material toward the column's edges—approaching if not equaling

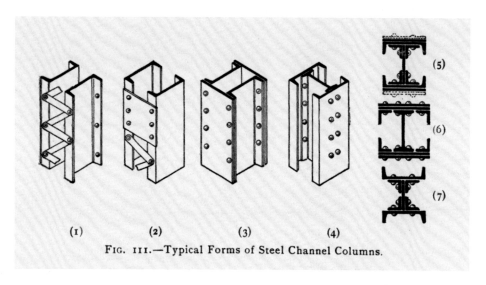

FIG. 111.—Typical Forms of Steel Channel Columns.

4.16 Riveted steel column shapes. (Freitag, *Architectural Engineering*, 196)

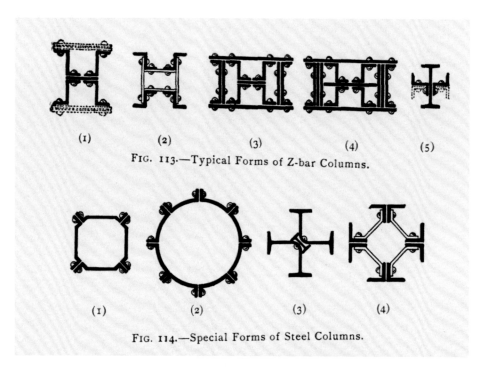

FIG. 113.—Typical Forms of Z-bar Columns.

FIG. 114.—Special Forms of Steel Columns.

4.17 Typical steel column shapes. (Freitag, *Architectural Engineering*, 199)

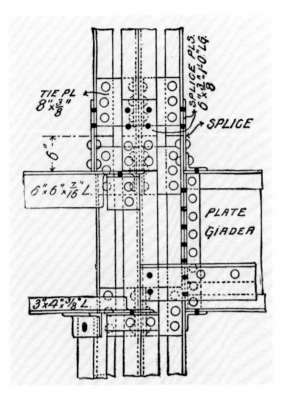

4.18 Typical riveted splice/girder connection. (Freitag, *Architectural Engineering*, 222)

the excellent theoretical performance of Phoenix shapes—but with the advantage of flat, easily riveted surfaces on all four sides. Latticed webs replaced planes of steel with lighter trusswork, eliminating weight from columns and permitting inspection of their interior surfaces for workmanship and corrosion. Most popular in Chicago were H-shaped or box sections assembled from rolled Z-bars, which were easy to produce. Z-shapes could form a variety of complex sections. In conjunction

with cover plates of varying sizes they provided a consistent chassis for columns that could be reliably spliced to the full height of a building and supplemented on lower floors by cover plates, tuning the column's cross section to its load at each level.[44]

The idea of a central chassis to which cover plates of steel could be attached formed the basis for patented column shapes that saw wide use in more technically advanced buildings of the mid-1890s. The Larimer column deployed two I-beams, each bent at ninety degrees at the center of their web, forming a cruciform section that behaved like two I-beams perpendicular to one another. The Gray column bettered the Larimer, however, with a more efficient deployment of steel angles and a chassis of flat steel bars holding them in place. The angles were placed back-to-back in four pairs, each pair forming the vertex of a square cruciform shape. Bent steel bars were riveted to adjacent pairs of angles at regular vertical intervals, forming a central diamond lattice for a web. Nearly all column material was thus located at the edge of an inscribed square. Even the bent steel bars occurred only intermittently, leaving no material whatsoever on or near the column's center, where it would be least efficient. The flat surfaces of the angles offered convenient locations for bolting or riveting, and the hollow form allowed continu-

ous vertical runs for pipes and cables.[45] Perhaps most importantly, the angles' thicknesses and depths could be easily adjusted within the overall dimensions of the column's square plan. Its performance could thus be tuned to its location in the building, with lighter angles used in upper stories where loading was lower, and heavier, deeper angles used near the base where loading was greater. These variations could all be made within the same column footprint, which made splices simpler and fireproofing more regular (figure 4.18). The Gray did require extensive shop riveting for its fabrication, and the intermittent nature of its internal bracing meant that it was susceptible to localized eccentric loading.[46] Despite its relatively high cost, however, the Gray provided the best balance between ideal static behavior and expedient assembly on site. It was the column of choice in the late 1890s, and was used through the 1930s, when it was superseded by specially rolled steel sections that approached its efficiency while eliminating its shop and field riveting.[47]

CONCLUSIONS

Steel's suitability for trussed, braced, and—eventually—moment frames spawned a major shift in structural design for tall buildings. Riveted steel elements provided stiffness that had heretofore been available only in heavy, labor- and space-intensive masonry walls. The benefits of this shift from masonry to steel included quicker construction, more open floor plates, and lighter foundation loads. Not coincidentally, the wholesale change from brick to steel also reduced Chicago's dependence on strike-prone brickmakers and bricklayers. But as important as steel's impact on skyscraper construction and structure was, it also influenced the composition and proportioning of exterior elevations. It took some time for architects to fully recognize that the withdrawal of a building's structure from its exterior walls left skyscraper elevations open to experiment; manufacturers, too, were only gradually able to develop new materials that could replace masonry as affordable, effective cladding. But by the mid-1890s, skyscrapers' exterior walls had shed not only their structural responsibilities, but also their heavy composition and construction. With the loss of their bearing and stabilizing functions, exterior walls were reconceived as environmental enclosures—thinner, lighter, more transparent envelopes that were hung outside of the new steel frames. Derisively termed "veneered" buildings, the less pejorative term "curtain wall" soon came to define these lightly clad buildings of the 1890s, replacing the traditional punched mass with a skinned frame. By 1896, *Inland Architect* would claim, with some justification, that "walls" (meaning, in their view, masonry walls) had been eliminated from the skyscraper altogether, while critics debated the aesthetic impact of a development that stood against decades of monumental appearances. As important as the braced frame was to reaching greater and greater heights, its immediately visible legacy was that it freed exterior walls from their heaviest structural demands and allowed them to be rethought as cladding rather than structure.

Chapter 5
Glass and Light: "Veneers" and Curtain Walls, 1889–1904

The self-braced frame offered benefits in spatial efficiency, building weight, and flexible planning. Freed from the bulk of masonry bearing or shear walls, wind-resistant steel frames largely fulfilled the promise of the metal skeleton on their interiors. Outside, however, the reduction of exterior walls to environmental enclosures offered a tectonic and stylistic conundrum. The continuing charge to build light in order to reduce foundation loads implied that exterior walls might now be seen as the simplest and thinnest possible coverings engineered to take up as little floor space and to add as little weight as possible. But designers were still limited by a palette of regionally available and affordable materials, and even stripped of its structural role brick remained Chicago's most readily available cladding. This meant that skyscraper skins continued to be relatively thick and heavy, and they continued to rely upon strike-prone manufacturing and on-site labor. Architects and owners were undoubtedly primed for any opportunity to rid their projects of such cumbersome material and troublesome production, but it was not until after two major material developments that more functional, lightweight, and cost-effective materials superseded masonry cladding around 1895. The development of the lightweight, thin "curtain wall" in the mid-1890s occurred in two phases: the reduction of the exterior skyscraper wall from a bearing or shear-resistant element to a masonry veneer, and the subsequent refinement of this veneer to a thin, largely transparent and very lightweight curtain of glass and enameled terra-cotta.[1]

"VENEERED" BUILDINGS

"This entire question of exterior walls," noted New York engineer, architect, and author William Birkmire (1860–1924), "narrows itself down to the fact that a satisfactory covering is simply needed for the great steel frame."[2] So great were the capabilities of steel framing compared with masonry that exterior skins not only lost their carrying role, but they became reliant themselves on the frame behind for their own support—the *Daily Tribune* noted of the Great Northern Hotel in 1891 that its brick exterior was "not even expected to carry its own weight."[3] This carrying capacity of the metal frame was not new—Bogardus had recognized the potential for such an inversion of traditional roles for skin and structure as early as 1850—but its deployment on such a large scale was a dramatic change from a generation of structural masonry elevations in Chicago and elsewhere.[4]

In some measure, the flourishing of lightweight skins supported by rigid steel frames was uniquely permitted by Chicago's codes. New York building codes did not, until 1892, allow non–load-bearing exterior walls, and even with the passage of such an amendment, New York remained far more conservative than Chicago in permitting thin masonry veneers hung from steel frames, assuming a bearing function for all exterior walls and requiring them to thicken toward the building's base. In New York, every fifty feet of height required an additional four inches of brick in addition to a twelve-inch minimum, so that a building two hundred feet tall would require, at its base, twenty-four-inch-thick walls.[5]

By minimizing the required thickness of masonry walls, Chicago's code helped architects and engineers solve the problems that continued to plague tall buildings on its poor soil. At 90 pounds per cubic foot for hollow brick and up to 140 pounds for pressed, the reduction of masonry envelopes from deep structural walls to thin veneers had immediate benefits. The six-foot walls of the Monadnock's first story, for instance, weighed nearly a ton per running foot. Replacing this with a twelve-inch-thick wall of nonstructural hollow tile would have eliminated some 95 percent of the first-floor walls' dead weight.

Other advantages of veneered skins included dramatic savings in space. In addition, light construction enabled more efficient bay windows, since their veneered brick walls imparted less load than structural walls on cantilevered floor beams. Oriels both increased floor space and brought additional light inside. Any construction that enabled deeper, lighter, more transparent bays thus had multiple benefits.[6] Non-bearing masonry also allowed efficiency in construction, because the assembly of a building skin no longer had to proceed from the base up. Lower stories contained most of a typical skyscraper's custom ornament, and these special brick and terra-cotta elements had to be designed and manufactured separately from the repetitive ornament that typically decorated upper floors. As simpler, mass-produced elements were often finished first, such veneered construction allowed builders to start the exterior wall of a building in midair, hanging it from the steel frame beginning at the third or fourth story and working upward. This also left the street level open for deliveries and material movement and saved the often-fragile and expensive street-level ornament from damage during construction. The appearance of a building taking shape in midair drew considerable notice: "to the general public," noted Birkmire, "the effect of seeing a building enclosed from the fourth and fifth sto-

ries upward while the lower stories are still left open is somewhat surprising."[7]

Such radical construction techniques alarmed experts and the public alike. Chicago held hearings in 1891 on whether such seemingly fragile constructions were sufficient to ensure public safety, which the New York Times reported upon with partisan relish. "In these Chicago buildings," it stated, "the walls are merely thin veneer and are tied to the metal frame."[8] Chicago Fire Chief Denis Swenie testified publicly that exterior terra-cotta fireproofing would "not be effective" in a conflagration. Others believed that wind and weathering would "loosen this veneering" and send it catapulting to the sidewalks below.[9] Swenie eventually became one of the leading figures behind Chicago's more progressive building codes, but his remarks resonated with those concerned that, in the race for profit, the thin walls of veneered buildings sacrificed sensible methods. Even the term veneered implied a false, cheap process.[10]

Despite these concerns, masonry veneers began to appear on Chicago skyscrapers in the late 1880s as the metal frame became commonplace. While Jenney and Burnham & Root made modest experiments with iron and steel hybrids, the young firm of Holabird & Roche executed three buildings that definitively separated internal iron frames from exter-

5.1 Tacoma Building, corner of LaSalle and Madison Streets, Holabird and Roche, 1889 (demolished, 1929). (Contemporary postcard, collection of the author)

nal skins of masonry, terra-cotta, and glass (figure 5.1). William Holabird and Martin Roche were former employees of Jenney who formed their own firm between 1880 and 1881. Their work through the mid-decade was mostly residential and landscape design, but in 1884 they won an informal competition sponsored by Wirt D. Walker for a building on a small lot at the corner of LaSalle and Madison. The size of the lot did not permit a tall enough building to make the investment worthwhile, in Walker's opinion, and he resolved this by purchasing a neighboring lot to the north and asking Holabird & Roche to redesign their scheme to take advantage of the larger footprint. The resulting plan was typical for a corner site; Holabird & Roche left the rear corner open above the second floor to serve as a light shaft and wrapped a double-loaded corridor around this void. Reliant on heavy masonry walls at the ends of the plan and additional cross-walls on either side of a central elevator bank for wind bracing, the structure reached thirteen stories, or 165 feet, and Walker christened the building *Tacoma* in the erroneous belief that it was a Pontiac word for "tallest" (figure 5.2).

The Tacoma's masonry walls, however, were set perpendicular rather than parallel to their adjacent street facades, and therein lay the building's radical innovation. By removing bearing and bracing masonry from

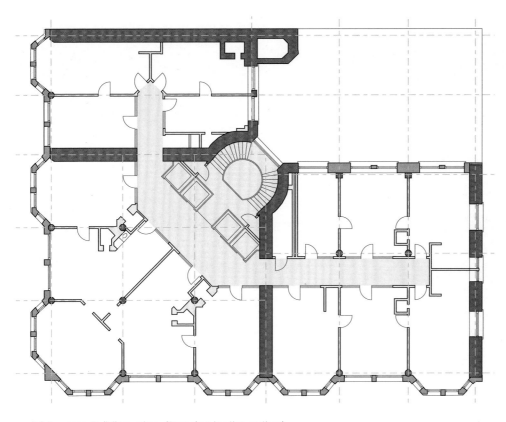

5.2 Tacoma Building, plan. (Drawing by the author)

the building's street frontages, Hola-bird & Roche freed these elevations from structural constraints and opened them to as much glass and light as economically feasible. Brick was still used to form spandrel panels and to back up terra-cotta elements, but it no longer took up the majority of the street elevations. Holabird & Roche draftsman Edward Renwick (1860–1941) later recalled that this scheme had been a last-minute option, inspired by Sanford Loring, president of the Chicago Terra Cotta Company. Loring, according to

Renwick, proposed tying terra-cotta cladding elements directly to a metal frame rather than embedding them within masonry walls. This saved about two hundred and sixty square feet per floor, since terra-cotta's manufacturing dimensions allowed thinner facade elements such as spandrels and mullions.[11] Rather than relying on a convenient dimension for bricklayers, Loring's suggested system also meant that facade elements could be as narrow or as thin as functionally necessary. Holabird & Roche made the Tacoma's of-

fice windows eight feet, three inches high, with sills just nineteen inches off the floor, pushing lightweight bays beyond the building line in oriels that ran from the second floor to the building's cornice (figures 5.3, 5.4).[12] Each bay was hung from the building frame on a lightweight network of cantilevered wrought-iron girders and cast-iron vertical supports.[13] Floors and skins were supported by separate lintels of wrought and cast iron, respectively, reflecting the greater bending loads of the interior system.

The result was a facade unlike anything in Chicago. With tall ranks of projecting bay windows, the Tacoma presented an undulating skin of glass and razor-thin terra-cotta that was highlighted by a vitrinelike corner, where bays nudged against one another, making the terra-cotta–clad pier on the corner seem more an incident in an otherwise crystalline skin than an element of bearing structure. The *Tribune* noted this impressive coalescence of function and radical appearance: "Each front of the building bulges with bay windows," its reporter wrote, "adding many square feet to the rentable floor space. The building will not contain a single dark room or corner."[14] *Industrial Chicago* made much of the building's tectonic innovation, noting that it was the first large-scale realization of a "screen wall, supported at each story, using iron and steel for carrying

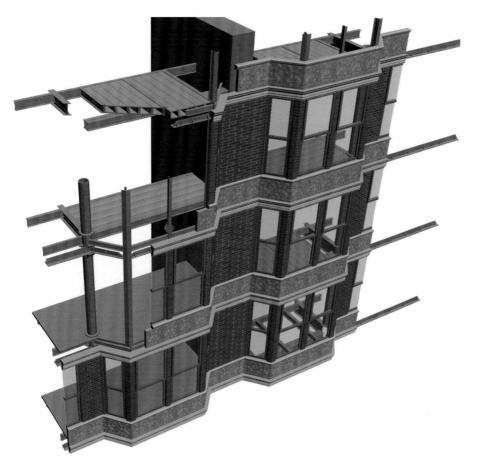

5.3 Tacoma Building, digital reconstruction of curtain wall. (Shagayegh Missaghi and Ryan Gauquie)

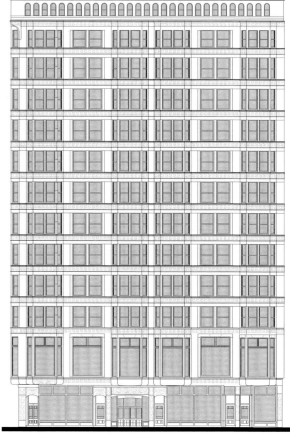

5.4 Tacoma Building, Madison Street elevation. (Drawing by the author)

all weights," a notable distinction from the external masonry and iron walls of the Home Insurance and Rookery.[15]

But the Tacoma was not a pure frame. For all the innovation of its envelope, the heavy brick walls it relied upon for lateral stability offset much of its skin's spatial efficiency. Holabird & Roche's structural development was simply to take the bearing and lateral functions of exterior masonry and turn them inward, gaining light, transparency, and a remarkable elevation at the expense of internal planning. While there were elements of the Tacoma's frame that kept pace with current innovations—a late change from wrought-iron girders marked the first use in Chicago of Bessemer steel in a building structure, matching the achievement of the Home Insurance, and Holabird & Roche specified riveted wrought iron to a far greater extent than in any previous building to create rigid floor diaphragms—the Tacoma's masonry bracing walls meant that the structure remained a hybrid of skeletal metal and massive brick.[16]

While the effect of the gossamer skin impressed many, it was also unnerving to a city used to massive brick skyscrapers. "Many people," the *Tribune* reported, "have an idea that it is a mere shell set up on pins, and that if two wide-awake blizzards should ever happen to meet in Chicago it would come down with a great flop from its high perch." But the paper carefully noted the structural sleight-of-hand at work. Because of its largely hidden masonry walls, the *Tribune* went on, "the Tacoma is not really a light structure."[17] Public and critical uneasiness, however, led Holabird & Roche to abandon such a visually lightweight approach for their next downtown buildings, the Caxton and Pontiac (figures 5.5, 5.6). These two buildings also featured cantilevered bay windows, but had significantly greater surfaces of nonstructural brick veneer than the glassy Tacoma. The Caxton, completed in 1890 for Boston financier Brian Lathrop, was for a narrow site between Dearborn and Fourth Street (now Federal). Because of its small site, party walls on its north and south ends provided all of its lateral resistance. Inside, the building's structure was entirely of steel, and Holabird & Roche refined the plan to take advantage of the resulting absence of masonry walls. Four column lines divided the lot from north to south, embedding columns within partition walls on the interior, and between three vertical bay windows on each street facade. While these bays featured large double-hung windows, they were set within a brick border that spanned the two outer bays, giving the illusion of bearing masonry and concealing entirely the proportions of the steel frame behind. The Caxton thus had the unique distinction of presenting the most rigorous, regular struc-

tural plan of any downtown building to date—and of concealing it. Nevertheless, its regular bay windows gave some hint that the orderly nature of the metal structure within held compositional possibilities, an integration of rationalized structure and appearance that would become Holabird & Roche's trademark.

The clearest example of a veneered building was Holabird & Roche's Pontiac, constructed at the corner of Dearborn and Harrison in 1891 for Peter and Shepherd Brooks (figures 5.7, 5.8). Its genesis was particularly lengthy; it was originally planned as a five-story loft building for printers and ended up as a fourteen-story commercial office building. While the Pontiac's frame was all riveted steel, it nevertheless employed the same hybrid structural system as the Tacoma, with a party wall at its north end and an additional masonry cross-wall in the lot's shorter direction, echoing the Brooks's tendency toward conservative structural solutions.[18] Again, the heavy nature of this system was concealed on the elevations, where Holabird & Roche pushed the light- and space-gathering capacity of bay windows to their practical limits. On each office floor, the Pontiac provided four cantilevered oriels that spanned two column bays, gaining more floor space than the single-bay projections of the Tacoma. The skins of these double bays ran entirely in front of their supporting columns, concealing them from the street and again emphasizing the tectonic separation between

5.5 Caxton Building, 508 S. Dearborn, Holabird and Roche, 1890 (demolished, 1947). (Art Institute of Chicago)

frame and cladding. All of these projections were faced with brick, again giving the illusion of a comfortably heavy structure. Such an expression summed up the ambiguities inherent in the veneered principle, though the scale of the Pontiac's cantilevered bays showed the way toward a more provocative expression, one in which the skin's light, nonstructural essence would be further exploited.

5.6 Pontiac Building, corner of Dearborn and Harrison Streets, Holabird and Roche, 1891. (*120 Photographic View of Chicago*, Rand McNally, 1909)

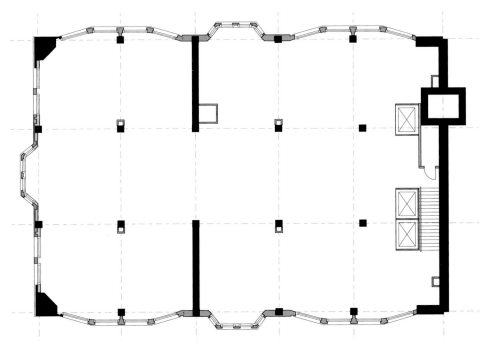

5.7 Pontiac Building, plan. (Drawing by the author)

THE CURTAIN WALL—A NEW TYPE

The veneered buildings of the early 1890s thus adopted advanced structural techniques while relying on traditional materials for their exteriors, albeit deployed in a new configuration. Visually these provided a comforting solidity, even as they offered consider-

able savings in dead weight and floor space. But by the mid-1890s, a dramatic change occurred in the composition of the typical Chicago skin: whereas earlier buildings featured elevations of chiefly masonry, buildings of the mid-1890s had elevations that were mostly glass. Both veneered and curtain-walled buildings relied on riveted steel frames for their lateral stability, and these structural systems were improved incrementally over the next two decades. But improvements in building facades were rapid and dramatic in this era. Architects and engineers found greater spatial and illuminatory efficiency in two developments in cladding materials: the first of these,

exterior-grade, glazed terra-cotta, enabled lightweight cladding that offered more compact outside walls than brick; the second, the economical production of plate glass within Chicago's economic orbit, allowed larger, affordable windows.

The results of these related developments were buildings with exceptionally light cladding that hung, curtainlike, from self-braced frames. These buildings offered little confusion about whether the skin played a role in the structure's stability, and the exterior membranes on such buildings appeared to contemporary eyes as fragile, gossamer drapes compared to the heavy masonry skins of buildings only a year or two earlier.

In the most extreme cases, these buildings' frames were pulled in from the exterior edge. Terra-cotta thus no longer had to clad relatively wide sections of steel columns and girders—it had only to disguise and protect smaller steel mullions and subframes. This allowed slender terra-cotta elements on the exterior, spawning a search for a new style to adequately organize the narrow proportions and open elevations allowed by these materials. As the steel frame itself became self-supporting, the building skin shed its structural role and its solid conception, and the innovative separation of structure and cladding proposed by the Tacoma became a standard feature in Chicago skyscrapers for a few brief years.

PRECONDITIONS—
ENAMELED TERRA-COTTA

Terra-cotta was familiar to Chicago builders throughout the 1870s and 1880s but, like the limestone and sandstone it was intended to replace, terra-cotta was vulnerable to freeze-thaw cycles and impossible to keep clean in Chicago's smoky, sooty atmosphere. As manufacturers produced denser and less porous products, however, terra-cotta gained favor for ornamental uses. This evolution was accelerated by the Northwestern Terra Cotta Company, which experimented with admixtures to engineer dense but pliable clays that could precisely follow molds while offering a surface resistant to water and

pollution. Other smaller but equally innovative terra-cotta firms followed suit, including Lake View Terra Cotta and Brick and the Illinois Terra Cotta Lumber Company, both of which supplied both fireproofing and ornamental work. The steady business of the former allowed investment and experimentation in the latter.[19]

Northwestern announced its first glazed terra-cotta product in 1884.[20] Glazing created a water and pollution-resistant shell for terra-cotta, but it had significant costs and flaws. Glazes were painted on by hand, and they created brittle surfaces. Cracks due to mistakes in application, thermal expansion, or careless handling provided opportunities for water infiltration. Builders and owners were skeptical and initially reluctant to employ Northwestern's product in quantity, and it was not until Burnham & Root's Rand McNally Building of 1889 that it was used extensively.[21] In 1892 a St. Louis skyscraper featured a fully terra-cotta front, and by 1894 more than a dozen buildings in Chicago employed enameled terra-cotta in significant quantities. Many of these were standard brick facades with larger terra-cotta panels, such as the Columbus Memorial (W. W. Boyington, 1892), but the example of the Rand McNally's success inspired facades and cladding that eliminated brick altogether. Skeleton frame buildings by Jenney including the Ludington and Isabella used the material to clad exterior steel columns;

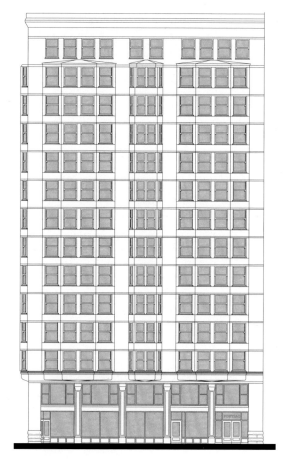

5.8 Pontiac Building, elevation.
(Drawing by the author)

buildings by Holabird & Roche—the Venetian in particular—combined glazed terra-cotta with brick to achieve ornamental effects across broad surfaces.

Terra-cotta, when waterproofed, offered solutions to brick's ongoing problems of weathering, weight, and labor. The molding process allowed easy customization. Hollow sections for exterior terra-cotta that had enabled reliable fireproofing also aided in waterproofing, as any moisture that penetrated between terra-cotta blocks could be wicked away by these voids.[22] Because of its porous nature, terra-cotta weighed roughly half as much as brick, and about 40 percent as much as marble or granite. But because terra-cotta was made in hollow sections, it was even lighter for a comparable area of wall.[23] With advances in production led by Northwestern, enameled terra-cotta eventually cost less per square foot than brick or stone.[24] Perhaps more importantly, on the job site it could be wired to steel frames and grouted in place instead of hand-laid, saving time and labor.

Enameled terra-cotta's greatest advantage from a design perspective, however, was its pliability. It could be molded into tighter configurations than standard brick, and it could be extruded with great precision. Like porous terra-cotta that could be fabricated to cling tightly to steel on fireproof interiors, enameled terra-cotta could more closely jacket exterior steel members. Details and ornament could thus better adhere to steel's taut proportions, allowing more attenuated facade elements than permitted by masonry's bulk. Architects and critics of the time recognized a new potential for building skins that more expressively telegraphed the skeletal nature of the supporting structure. Writer G. Twose, expounding on the new use of terra-cotta in the *Brickbuilder*, believed that it would eventually "assume forms de-

termined by and identified with the constructional principles of the steel it envelopes, clinging round the column and the beam as the flesh covers the bone."[25] Twose suggested the linearity of the Gothic as an appropriate model for steel's tenuous proportions, and this ideal would be realized with remarkable success in the curtain-walled structures of the mid-1890s.

PRECONDITIONS—PLATE GLASS

Thinly framed elevations also allowed larger windows that filled the spaces between more attenuated elevational elements, but fulfilling this functional requirement required glass far larger than anything yet seen in skyscraper construction. Despite its technologically advanced reputation, glass was mostly handcrafted by blowing or spinning until well into the twentieth century. These methods produced panes limited in thickness by the strength of the glass-spinner or -blower, and with inherent optical flaws. For domestic and small-scale commercial installations, these sufficed.[26] But for larger commercial buildings, the limitations in traditionally produced glass meant that windows of any scale had to be pieced together from small lights. Visual distortions in handcrafted glass were also a functional disadvantage in shop windows and a distraction in high-class offices.

Plate glass, on the other hand, could be made thick enough to cover

large areas in single lights, and it could be polished until it was flawless, though these benefits came at a significant cost (figure 5.9).[27] Polished plate glass was made by melting large pots of silica and pouring it on to large casting tables where it was gradually cooled. The resulting "rough plate" was solid and free of internal flaws or air bubbles, but its surfaces had to be ground and polished to achieve its renowned surface, processes that wasted half of the material and that could take twelve hours.[28] Although some architectural situations required polished plate's flawless finish—mirrors and storefront windows, for example—the expense involved in fueling its energy-intensive production limited its wider use; polished plate glass cost 76 cents per square foot in 1880, compared to less than five cents for hand-made "window glass."[29] These high prices created an attractive market, and major factories for plate glass were built between 1881 and 1883 at Crystal City, Missouri, and Creighton, Pennsylvania.[30] Western Pennsylvania had newly discovered reservoirs of natural gas that promised a cleaner atmosphere within its furnaces, could be tapped for little or no cost, and required no labor to maintain. Because of gas-based production American plate glass could compete with French and English imports in quality and cost for the first time.[31]

The discovery of natural gas near Findlay, Ohio, in 1886 set off a brief flurry of investment there, but geologists soon recognized that this was only the tip of a vast underground reservoir that crossed north-central Indiana. This set off a speculative frenzy in the agricultural towns of Indiana's "Gas Belt," centered between Kokomo and Anderson. By far the largest operation to take advantage of generous fuel and land deals offered by Indiana towns was Diamond Plate Glass, founded by two Akron, Ohio, industrialists, Col. A. L. Conger and Monroe Seiberling, who raised capital from Ohio and, critically, Chicago (figures 5.10, 5.11).[32] To recruit the company, the city of Kokomo gave Conger and Seiberling nineteen acres with direct rail connections to downtown Chicago.[33] Their company aggressively hired skilled craftsmen from Pittsburgh and St. Louis plants, and they constructed the most sophisticated plate glass plant in the world between May 1888 and July 1889.[34] After nearly a year of commissioning and tuning, the plant produced fifty-five hundred square feet of high-quality glass per day by mid-1890.[35] The market in Chicago was so promising that Diamond Plate Glass began constructing a second, even larger plant on the same rail line in Elwood, Indiana, a few miles to the south, covering fourteen acres and employing over one thousand by 1893.[36] Diamond Plate's massive operations were able to undercut other manufacturers, sparking a major slide in plate glass prices throughout the United

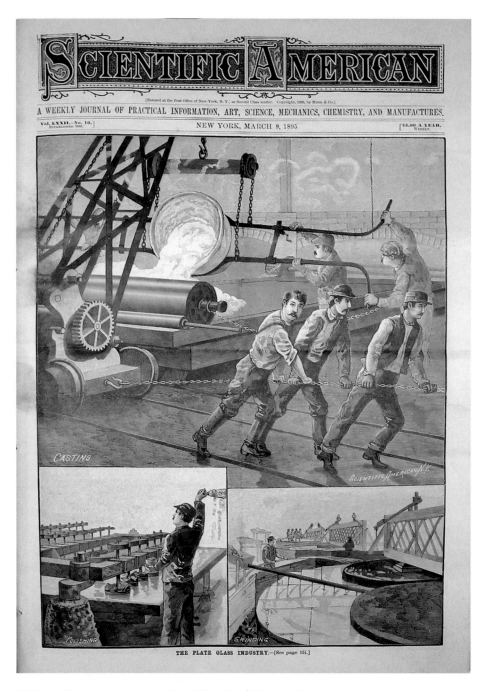

5.9 Plate Glass manufacture in the 1890s. (*Scientific American*)

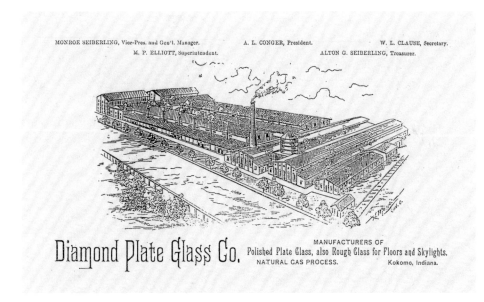

5.10 Diamond Plate Glass Co., Kokomo, Indiana, ca. 1892.
(Kokomo Public Library, Stan Mohr Collection)

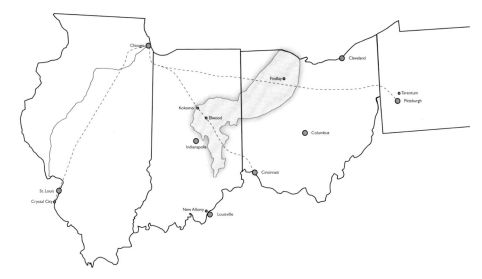

5.11 Indiana Gas Belt and "Pan Handle" rail line. (Drawing by the author)

States but also producing rapid technical advances, including record-breaking window sizes.

Larger glass sizes reduced labor-intensive framing and puttying on job sites, and Chicago architects and builders quickly took advantage of Diamond Plate's technical superiority to the Crystal City and Pittsburgh plants. Kokomo's connections to Chicago provided the basis for a unique relationship, and the presence of investors and customers in the Loop was significant enough that Diamond Plate was actually incorporated in Illinois—not Indiana.[37] Diamond Plate's board meetings were held in Chicago, and the result was a set of intimate commercial and business links with Chicago's network of builders, jobbers, and warehouses. George Kimball's wholesale glass business handled the vast majority of plate glass in Chicago from a warehouse on the corner of Wabash and Congress, and while he had held an exclusive arrangement with Crystal City he was swayed by the proximity and lower cost of Indiana glass. He not only represented Diamond Plate to contractors and jobbers, but also played a key role in the company's management.

The rapid expansion of the Indiana plants after 1890 was, however, tempered by some difficult realities. The dangers of handling large sheets and the combustible nature of glass furnaces led to accidents and large fires at Elwood and Kokomo.[38] In the summer of 1890, a strike at the Kokomo plant highlighted that the company's immense profits had not benefited workers.[39] Equally alarming, however, was the effect of the two new plants on plate glass prices nationwide. As the massive plants at Kokomo and Elwood reached working capacity, there were ominous indications of overproduction. Prices that had steadily dropped with advances in manufacturing technology began to reflect unhealthy imbalances of supply and demand. Internal competition between Pittsburgh, St Louis, and Indiana plants added downward pressure on costs. By 1893, the country was immersed in a major economic crisis and building activity was depressed nationwide, but stocks of plate glass were at an all-time high after three years of Indiana production. Every plate glass factory in the country voluntarily shut down in June 1893 in a vain attempt to support prices, but by the end of 1894 it became clear that individual factories would not be able to survive on increasingly narrow margins.[40] Diamond Plate made a desperate move to keep control of the industry in December 1894, but by spring, the company had collapsed and Pittsburgh Plate Glass announced that it had taken over the factories at Kokomo, Elwood, and Crystal City, tripling its capital stock.[41] Prices remained depressed, however—a disaster for the industry but an unexpected boon to developers and architects looking for ways to provide more and more daylight to commercial interiors.

CURTAIN WALL BUILDINGS

The introduction of enameled terracotta and inexpensive plate glass allowed architects of the mid-1890s to design skins in which solid (if lightweight) veneers could be replaced by largely transparent "curtains." The enameled terra-cotta in curtain walls could hew much more tightly to the steel frame behind than brick, and the resulting windows could be much larger. The innovations of the Tacoma building could, by the mid-1890s be matched with gains in internal efficiency brought about by the self-braced, riveted steel frame. Faced with continuing pressure to provide daylight to offices, and offered the new combination of curtain wall construction and a glut of plate glass in local warehouses, Chicago architects responded with vigor, adopting what Dankmar Adler called a "rage for large plate-glass surfaces" in the brief period of the glass industry's greatest distress.[42] Reporting on this "new kind of construction" during the comparatively lean middle years of the decade, the local press noted that "economy induced the liberal use of plate glass, this material being cheaper than brick."[43]

This, of course, suggested a radically different formula than even the light skeletal frames of a few years before. Critic G. Twose summarized the revolutionary development brought about by large windows and tight terra-cotta jackets on traditional skyscraper function and aesthetics: "The demand for light in office buildings has reduced the [skeleton frame] to a minimum of spandrel and mullion, so that the mere elemental protection of the steel framework which it envelops, but which in turn supports it, is the sole duty left to be performed in these modern monuments."[44]

Twose defined a new type: the tall commercial block as a grid of skeletal members with infill, reliant on masonry for neither wind bracing nor environmental enclosure. Twose's realization that this skeletal evolution was now taking place on the exterior suggested that the grid appeared now in a slightly different form than it had in the 1880s. Twose's use of "spandrel" and "mullion" in place of "beam" and "column" declared a striking independence for the exterior wall that rejected the integration of earlier, skeletally expressed frames.

Other evidence that the exterior wall had shed its strict adherence to the frame can be found in debates about this generation of buildings in the popular and professional press. Franklin Head, writing in the *New England Magazine*, contrasted for his lay readers the "dark and gloomy . . . building of twenty years ago" with Chicago sky-scrapers of the 1890s. "The latter idea," he wrote, "is to make the walls as thin as is consistent with safety, the windows large and numerous, and the interior as light and airy as possible."[45] Professional critics, however, took a more cautious view. The lightening of the skin and the reduction of solid members to minimal linear elements presented a compositional problem, and there was considerable debate as to what the appropriate aesthetic and ornamental response to these new forms should be. New York critic Barr Ferree pondered in *Scribner's* in 1894 whether beauty could not instead be imparted by designing skyscraper facades to utterly disguise the tenuous proportions of steel columns and girders. "A pier," he felt, "is not deceitful if it contain a steel core that performs the greater part of the work. . . . [W]e need not concern ourselves with an imaginary idea that, unless we exhibit every portion of their construction we are committing a grievous error."[46]

But other critics of the early 1890s took veneered architecture to task for not recognizing the expressive potential of the newly available steel and glass, and this balance between composition and expression formed the basis for a provocative debate at the 1896 Annual Convention of the American Institute of Architects.[47] Recognizing the inevitable economics of glass and steel, J. W. Yost pleaded for ornamen-tal programs and compositional strategies that celebrated the gridded forms that these materials suggested, proposing a philosophy that focused on the dialogue between void and solid in a largely transparent elevation: "If steel construction is the master, plate glass is the faithful servant. The great strength of steel has a tendency to reduce the solids and increase the voids, to reduce the thickness of walls, and decrease the depth of shadows. The character of posts and lintels is such as to induce the use of straight lines, and the same influence is exerted by the difficulty of using curves in the windows filled with plate glass. The influence of these characteristics would be in the direction of angularity of style."[48]

Several Chicago buildings bore out precisely Yost's aesthetic proposal—that the ornamental programs of such buildings be confined to expressing the tenuous, linear nature of the steel skeleton, and that the voids filled by plate glass be celebrated as important compositional elements in their own right. "Angularity of style" became, in the hands of Chicago architects, a subtle neo-Gothic decorative program, highlighting the vertical reaches of steel columns with fluted terra-cotta coverings that consciously pushed solid spandrels back behind these expressed, visually delicate piers. This was in line with another of Yost's proposals, namely "a tendency to decrease ponderosity of structure," meaning the elimination of masonry as not only material but also as an ideal for composition.

While Yost's prescription seems remarkably progressive, foretelling twentieth-century modernism's odes to transparency and lightness, it was not universally accepted. In response to his paper, both George Post and Dankmar Adler noted dissatisfaction with the functional performance and the aesthetic consequences of the "steel cage and plate glass epidemic."[49] Post believed that the urge for daylight was unwarranted: "Why make the entire side of an office plate-glass," he wondered, "when the first act of the tenant would be to cover up the glass with blue shades?" Adler, for his part, believed that the responses to steel and glass built to that time did not go far enough. Inspired by Sullivan's recent publication in *Lippincott's* of "The Tall Building Artistically Considered," he called for the wholesale reconsideration of architectural composition based not only on changes of function, but also of materials and environment. Ornament—or "style"—in this view was a task that came after a balanced solution had been worked out between the needs of space and daylight and the availabilities of material and construction: "Steel pillars and steel beams occupy so little space that in order to enclose structures of which they are the essential supporting parts, they must be furnished with a filling if a space inclosing structure is to be erected, and steel posts and beams to be adequately protected against possible attacks of fire must receive bulky fire-protective coverings. In these fillings and coverings we obtain media for artistic treatment which may be handled solely with reference to the desire to adapt 'form' to 'function.'"[50]

The ultimate expression of these "fillings and coverings" occurred in the handful of Loop skyscrapers built in the depression years of the mid-1890s. Two of these, the Reliance and Fisher, were notable for their use of E. C. Shankland's lattice girders, but they received much greater notoriety at the time for their glass and terra-cotta skins (figures 5.12, 5.13).

The Reliance emerged from unpromising circumstances. Elevator engineer and contractor William E. Hale hired Burnham & Root to design a fourteen-story tower for the southwest corner of State and Washington Streets in 1890, but he was frustrated by tenants who held multiyear leases in the existing building. To commence work (and, perhaps, to encourage the tenants to move along), George Fuller began by jacking up the upper four floors of the old First National Bank Building and removing its foundations and first floor while tenants above remained "undisturbed." By the time leases ran out in 1894, however, Root's death and a discouraging economy had shelved plans for the original tower. Hale instead asked Burnham to reconceive

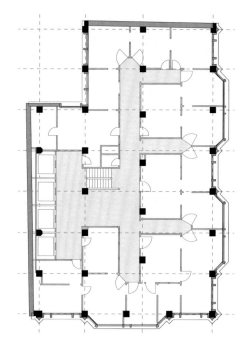

5.12 Reliance Building, corner of State and Washington Streets, Burnham & Root/ D. H. Burnham & Co., 1891, 1895, plan. (Drawing by the author)

the building as a home for doctors needing consultation and examination rooms downtown, a program similar to that of Boyington's Columbus Memorial Building across State Street.[51] This revived program brought with it a pressing need for daylight, both to aid in examination and to project a hygienic image to tenants and their patients. Hale pressed for "ample light in each office" as a primary concern.[52] Following Root's death, Burnham hired a new design partner, Charles Bowler Atwood (1849–1895), and their design took advantage of plate glass' implosive pricing, with elevations designed around

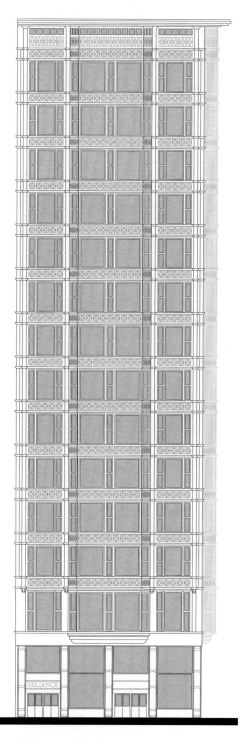

5.13 Reliance Building, elevation from State Street. (Drawing by the author)

5.14 Reliance Building, view from northeast.
(*120 Photographic View of Chicago*,
Rand McNally, 1909)

5.15 Reliance Building, construction view. (J. K. Freitag)

massive lights of glass over seven-and-a-half-feet square set in projecting bay windows that also included double-hung windows on both sides. The resulting elevations were nearly 90 percent glass, with the remainder composed of thin, white, enameled terra-cotta in a nominally Gothic style, the first Chicago use of such brilliant coloration and, given its claims of cleanliness, an appropriate application for a medically themed building (figure 5.14).[53]

This skin was not only bright and transparent; it was also cantilevered from the Reliance's self-braced steel frame in broad double-bays, entirely veiling the building's steel structure. Atwood was forced to work with the foundations from the earlier project, which divided the State Street elevation into four bays and left a column line on the center. The double bay may thus have been a trope to avoid leaving a pronounced vertical down the center of this elevation. Such a double-bay was not unprecedented—the Pontiac featured double-width oriels, too. But in combination with its transparency and tenuous terra-cotta lines, the Reliance had an entirely different relationship between structure and skin. Where the skin and structure of earlier veneered buildings had been integrated into reinforced piers, the Reliance suggested

that these two systems might be productively separated (figures 5.15–5.17).

The Reliance curtain wall attracted wide attention and concern. *Scientific American* noted that its windows had been made "as large as the situation of the columns would allow."[54] Atwood's choice of a nominally Gothic ornamental program emphasized the building's vertical proportions, but it upset critics who believed that "a building should not only *be* firm and strong, but it should *seem* so." Barr Ferree, writing for *Inland Architect*, referred to it as "scarcely more than a huge house of glass divided by horizontal and vertical lines of white enameled brick," while the *Architectural Record* dismissed the lower floors' "plate glass foundations" as visually "insufficient."[55] Twenty years later, former Burnham employee A. N. Rebori offered a more nuanced critique, writ-

5.16 Reliance Building, construction view. (J. K. Freitag)

5.17 Reliance Building, view of construction site with Columbus Memorial Building. (Chicago History Museum)

ing that the Reliance was not "an artistic solution of the problem, but only a statement of it," and this has been the Reliance's greatest conceptual legacy: the boldest reduction yet of a building skin to its cladding function with no illusion of structural capacity or purpose attached (figures 5.18, 5.19).[56]

The Reliance, though, was not the most thorough statement of the braced frame's liberating effect on building skins. While its State and Washington Street facades posed the possibility of the skin as a lightweight, nonstructural envelope, it occupied a corner lot, and thus despite its thorough wind bracing

fully half of the Reliance's perimeter walls were constructed of thick masonry. Its immediate successor, the Fisher Building, surpassed it in thoroughly rejecting masonry for structural *and* cladding purposes (figures 5.20, 5.21). Set on the Van Buren Street end of the narrow block between Dearborn and Plymouth Court, the Fisher's only neighbor was a short, four-story building to the north. Developed by paper bag magnate Lucius Fisher to exploit advance knowledge of height restrictions planned for the 1893 code, the Fisher was permitted at 235 feet, and after a two-year delay it was constructed in 1895–1896. When

it opened it was the fourth tallest building in the city (figures 5.22, 5.23).

In addition to a sophisticated wind-bracing system that used moment connections and riveted steel, the Fisher featured an exterior entirely of terra-cotta and glass; the owner of the building to the north refused to sign a party wall contract, and Atwood thus had to provide a fireproof curtain wall, not a masonry party wall, on the shared lot line.[57] On its main facades the Fisher featured orange-yellow terra-cotta wrapped around the Gray columns of Shankland's structure with narrow spandrel panels at each floor. This facade

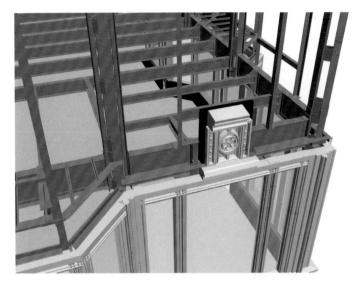

5.18 Reliance Building, digital reconstruction showing corner detail. (Ryan Risse)

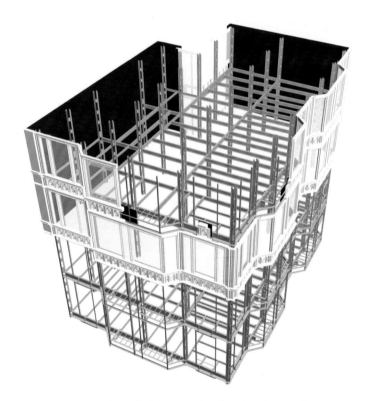

5.19 Reliance Building, digital reconstruction showing relation between steel frame and curtain wall. (Ryan Risse)

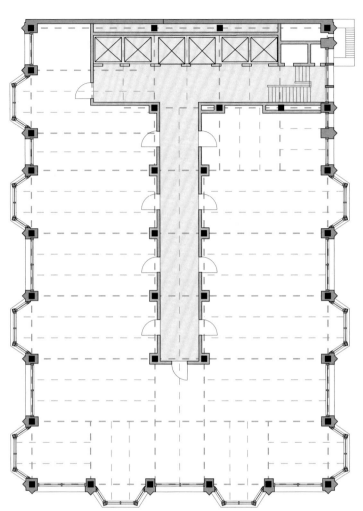

5.20 Fisher Building, corner of Dearborn and Van Buren Streets, D. H. Burnham & Co., 1896, plan. (Drawing by the author)

5.21 Fisher Building, elevation from Plymouth Court.
(Drawing by the author)

5.22 Fisher Building, construction view. (J. K. Freitag)

5.23 Fisher Building, construction view.
(J. K. Freitag)

was over 70 percent plate glass, deployed in alternating single-bay oriels and flat panels. These lights were slightly smaller than those at the Reliance, and Atwood chose double-hung windows, rather than larger fixed lights, throughout. This reflected the needs of the Fish-

er's business clientele, in contrast to the Reliance's medical tenants, but its effect was no less impressive from the outside. *Inland* celebrated the Fisher and its lightweight construction with a special issue, claiming that it represented a definitive break with traditional masonry construction: "In the evolution of the modern office building there is nothing more wonderful than that the fact should have been accomplished of erecting a building literally without walls. . . . here, for what we believe to be the first time in human experience, one of the highest commercial buildings in the world has been erected almost without any bricks."[58]

Inland's editors recognized that this involved the elimination of brick both as a structural material, which the Reliance had already accomplished, and as a cladding material, which was something new. Owners and contractors may well have rejoiced at the opportunity to dodge the labor troubles that had plagued brickmaking and bricklaying, but *Inland* implied that there were new architectural possibilities as well. The Fisher shared the Reliance's critical reception—*American Architect and Building News*, ever keen to find an excuse to put Chicago architecture in its place, called it "twenty-one stories of perfect and complete unrest," and others found Atwood's jesting neo-Gothic ornament unscholarly.[59] Its height made it an example for those who wished to maintain limita-

tions on tall construction, too.[60] But *Inland*'s judgment suggests that the Fisher should occupy a more important place in skyscraper history than it has typically enjoyed. Its elevations, fussier and slightly less transparent than the Reliance's, have never impressed historians like the earlier building, but its open site allowed it both a more complete terra-cotta-and-glass envelope and a better organized structural layout. The Fisher's structurally separate but architecturally integrated braced frame and glazed envelope constituted the clearest statement yet of an architecture based on the logic and rhythms of steel construction and glazed cladding (figure 5.24).

Although the Reliance and the Fisher most clearly exemplified this combination, two related buildings of the era are worth noting. Atwood's design for the extension of the Great Northern Hotel, just north of the Fisher along Jackson Street, featured an office block and hotel with terra-cotta-and-glass bay windows repeating the proportions and lines of the Fisher (figure 5.25). Its structure, however, was complicated by the requirement of a large theater at the ground level; thus, in addition to being fully self-braced, the extension's steel structure was also partly cantilevered over the space of the theater below. Solon S. Beman's Second Studebaker Building, on Wabash south of Congress, was a simple loft structure hemmed in by two party walls, but its

5.24 Fisher Building, view from southwest. (Chicago History Museum)

5.25 Great Northern Theater Office Building, Jackson Street between Dearborn and State, D. H. Burnham & Co., 1896 (demolished, ca. 1960). (Contemporary postcard, collection of the author)

main facade was a remarkable combination of glass and cast iron that at roughly 95 percent glass surpassed even the Reliance in transparency (figures 5.26. 5.27).[61]

It has always been tempting to see these curtain-wall structures as precursors of their twentieth-century counterparts, but these experiments were not as prescient as they might appear. For Burnham, the experiment was momentary and quickly abandoned. It was only in the 1920s that scholars and ar-

5.26 Second Studebaker Building, 629 S. Wabash, S. S. Beman, 1896, view from Wabash Street. (Contemporary postcard, collection of the author)

chitects saw in hindsight the foreshadowing of a new aesthetic in buildings like the Reliance. Burnham abandoned this formulation as soon as it became problematic, first because of revisions

to the Chicago Building Code (see chapter 6) and then because of higher plate glass prices and lower electricity costs. To construct a "building without walls" in 1896, however, was an important achievement. By positing a skin that was draped over the frame rather than integrated with it, Burnham and Atwood were able to achieve buildings with significantly improved performance relative to structures of only a year or two before, with more glass, lower foundation loads, and more easily achieved height. At the same time, this formulation required a new approach to skyscraper aesthetics, and Atwood rose to this challenge with programs of airy detail, proportions, and even color. Atwood's emphasis on verticality, line and plane, and repetition of ornamental elements reflected developments in steel frames, enameled terra-cotta cladding, and plate glass. While the neo-Gothic proportions of the Reliance and the Fisher would quickly be eclipsed by a code- and materials-driven return to bulk and mass, they offered an alternative interpretation of the steel frame as a light, glassy constructive type, one that built upon the development of the wind-braced frame's separation of skin and structure.

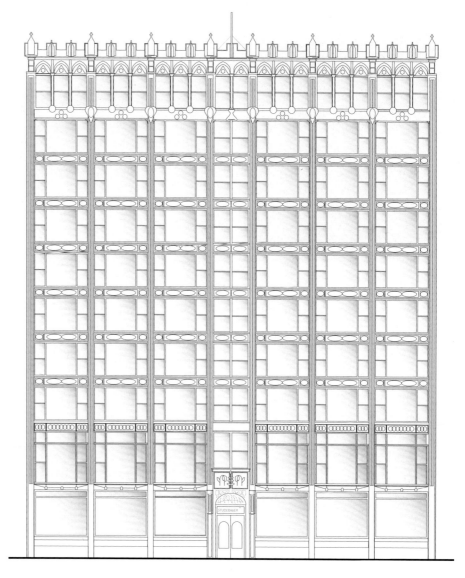

5.27 Second Studebaker Building, Wabash Street elevation. (Drawing by the author)

Chapter 6
Steel, Clay, and Glass: The Expressed Frame, 1897–1910

The synthesis of self-braced frame and curtain wall demonstrated by the Reliance and Fisher buildings was remarkably short-lived in Chicago. Only a few similar buildings were erected due to the depressed national economy of the mid- to late 1890s and Chicago's long real estate lull after the 1892–1893 Columbian Exposition. But as building resumed toward the end of the decade, a new typology, that of a more thickly jacketed steel frame with inset, usually tripartite windows, defined the city's commercial architecture. This formula became the city's architectural signature, with terms like "Chicago construction," the "Chicago window," and the "Chicago frame" finding their way into critical discussions. The emergence of this new type—the tectonic opposite of the curtain wall in that the frame again came to prominence in building elevations—was based upon the same set of material and economic pressures as the curtain wall, but it resulted from an important development in Chicago's building code that legislated against the glassy, lightweight skins of the mid-decade.

1893 CODE'S EFFECT ON HEIGHT AND FACADE COMPOSITION

The 1893 Chicago Building Ordinance ended the laissez faire attitude that had dominated the city's approach to building in the 1870s and 1880s. It featured an intensive focus on building safety, producing regulations that were progressive in their prescriptions for building envelopes but onerous in their limits on height. Since the completion of the Montauk, two objections to skyscrapers had gained traction in political circles: tall buildings increased fire problems, and their bulk deprived neighboring lots and streets of sunlight and fresh air. These were, no doubt, real concerns, but they tended to be voiced by aldermen with interests outside the Loop, who benefited from a greater spread of high land values. The height limit set in 1893—130 feet or ten stories—was widely blamed for contributing to a dearth of construction in the middle of that decade; the few skyscrapers that were constructed in 1895–1896 were mostly permitted before this restriction took effect. Limits were raised to 155 feet in 1896 but were reduced to 130 feet in 1898. They were raised again to 180 feet in 1901, and as Chicago began to emerge from the depression the City responded to pleas from developers by raising the limit to 260 feet in 1902.[1]

In addition to limiting height, the 1893 code also carried stringent new mandates for construction. Particularly influential was Section 111, which limited the size of bay windows to fifteen feet in width and three feet of projection over the property line. Bays were also restricted to one every twenty feet of frontage, and were prohibited from being within five feet of one another. Fireproofing regulations after 1893 also demanded eight inches of jacketing material, whether of brick or terra-cotta. Collectively, these rules discouraged further experimentation with bay windows like those of the Reliance, instead favoring large, flat windows set into brick-jacketed steel frames. Curtain walls were further limited by Section 135, which stipulated walls of increasing thickness for higher buildings whether load-bearing or not. While this was less onerous than New York's code, the advantage that Chicago's architects had enjoyed disappeared with the ordinance; exterior walls for any building ten stories or higher were required to be twenty-eight inches thick at the lowest stories, eliminating the advantage of veneered or curtain-wall construction. By 1903, window frames were also required to be of incombustible construction, eliminating wood in favor of cast iron or steel.[2]

The Fisher and Reliance were permitted prior to the adoption and enforcement of the new ordinance, but the results of limitations on bay windows were evident immediately in three projects permitted and built after its provisions took effect. Adler & Sullivan's Stock Exchange (1894), D. H. Burnham

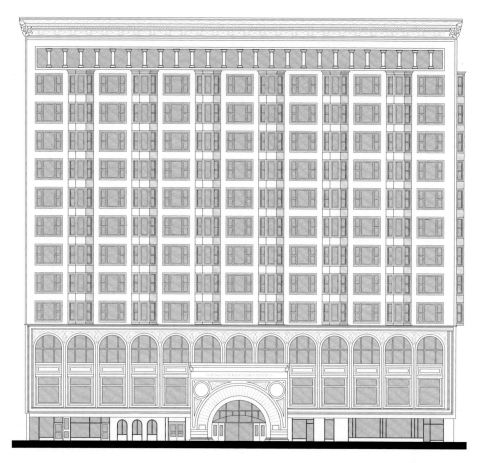

6.1 Chicago Stock Exchange, 30 N. LaSalle Street, Adler and Sullivan, 1894 (demolished, 1972), LaSalle Street elevation. (Drawing by the author)

& Co.'s Railway Exchange (1904) and Holabird & Roche's Chicago Savings Bank (1905) all deployed bay windows but with dramatically different results from those of the veneered era (figures 6.1–6.5). The Stock Exchange, a project to fund a new trading room through the provision of office space for traders and associated businesses, alternated bay windows with flat, tripartite windows in a hybrid elevation that emphasized verticality—a theme that Sullivan would

soon propose as the skyscraper's most basic expression.[3] Although the effect added a rich modeling to otherwise simple elevations, the bay windows paradoxically offered less glass surface than the tripartite window surrounding them because of the new, stringent limitations on size and fireproofing. Holabird & Roche's Chicago Savings Bank, built a decade later, followed this formula on its longer, northern elevation, with broad tripartite windows separat-

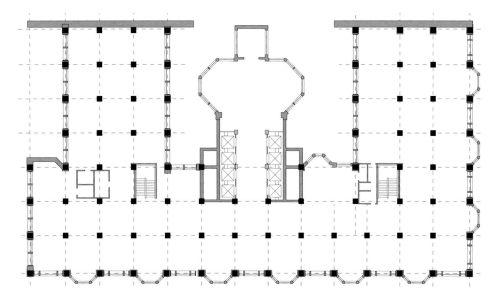

6.2 Chicago Stock Exchange, plan. (Drawing by the author)

ing code-limited bays of windows set within heavy terra-cotta mullions. Views were certainly the reason behind the narrow bay windows of the Railway Exchange, however, which was designed and partially financed by Burnham. The Michigan Avenue location offered broad views over the developing Grant Park, which alone suggested opening up offices to vistas of the improving lakefront. These bays combined glazed terra-cotta from Northwestern with ordinance-limited plate glass windows; unlike the Chicago Savings Bank or the Stock Exchange, however, they alternated with simple double-hung windows. With a heavy classical interior, the Railway Exchange was an odd hybrid of monumental and tenuous; despite its relative solidity compared to

the firm's earlier Fisher Building, for instance, it drew criticism for the narrow proportions of its exterior.[4] These three buildings collectively announced the end of the bay window in Chicago's skyscrapers, proving their limited utility when restricted in scale and composition and demonstrating the problems of spacing them to meet the new code.

CHANGES IN REGIONAL INDUSTRY—STEEL AND GLASS

The 1893 ordinance's effects were paralleled by developments in material availability. By 1900, Chicago's steel industry had largely phased out rail production to focus on structural products. Carnegie's Pittsburgh mills continued to be formidable competitors, but they had the disadvantages of

distance and a reputation for uneven quality. Illinois Steel in turn developed its own sources of iron ore and took advantage of the Great Lakes' shipping routes to reduce material costs. With improvements at Calumet Harbor and the Chicago Sanitary and Ship Canal, the southern edge of the city attracted new iron and steel companies. Mergers around 1900 saw Illinois Steel absorbed by U.S. Steel, which combined mills into larger, more efficient operations, and while labor suffered under the new monopoly's drive for efficiency, builders benefited from new economies of scale, particularly after the construction of the mammoth Gary Works in 1906. U.S. Steel's monopoly crushed much of its competition, but small firms were also spurred on by its fixed prices, finding ways to undercut it.[5] This regional competition forced U.S. Steel to keep its products and services of higher quality and its prices lower in Chicago than in other, less competitive markets, and steel in Chicago went from an exotic, experimental structural material in the 1880s to a cheap, reliable, and eventually ubiquitous one by 1900.

Even as the Chicago's steel industry enjoyed robust growth, however, Indiana's glass industry continued to suffer crashing prices that were only partially arrested by the combination of most U.S. glass factories by Pittsburgh Plate Glass in 1895. Pittsburgh Plate tried desperately to raise profits through a nationwide strategy that eliminated local jobbers such as George Kimball and sought to limit regional fluctuations in price and demand.[6] They also took advantage of new fabrication techniques, including the continuous annealing lehr, bending and beveling machinery, and vacuum-held polishing tables. A massive reconstruction and refitting of the Kokomo plant occurred between 1908 and 1910, increasing its capacity.[7] These improvements led to lower prices, improved quality, and healthier margins; by 1905, single lights of up to twelve by fifteen feet were commercially practicable, and the labor they saved on site was considerable.[8] Large windows thus remained viable, cost-effective elements, and although the Chicago Building Code prevented their deployment in curtainlike veneers, large plate glass windows enjoyed a renewed life in a new configuration, set into rather than wrapping fireproofed steel frames.

FIRE PERFORMANCE

Fireproofing and life safety enjoyed industrywide standardization between 1895 and 1910. Evidence from building fires and testing showed that terracotta fireproofing was effective, and it became a well-understood, well-tested system as products converged toward one another.[9] Testing by government and industry officials provided reliable, empirically derived data while new materials such as mineral wool and asbestos assisted with both compartmen-

6.3 Chicago Stock Exchange, view from northeast. (Contemporary postcard, collection of the author)

talization and reduced fuel loading.[10] Catastrophic fires still marred Chicago and other cities—the disastrous Iroquois Theater fire in 1903 was only the worst of several Loop fires during the de-

cade and conflagrations in Philadelphia and Baltimore also reinforced the ongoing need for comprehensive fireproofing. The survival of terra-cotta–protected steel structures in these blazes

6.4 Railway Exchange Building, corner of Michigan Avenue and Jackson Boulevard, D. H. Burnham & Co., 1904, view from southeast. (Contemporary postcard, collection of the author)

6.5 Chicago Savings Bank, corner of State and Madison Streets, Holabird and Roche, 1905, view from northeast. (Photograph by the author)

highlighted their performance, but gruesome deaths and damage within immaculately preserved steel frames revealed imperfections in compartmentalization, means of exit, and durability.

The Baltimore fire of 1904 revealed that reinforced concrete also provided robust resistance to fire and heat, and concrete floor and structural systems slowly gained market share over the

next two decades.[11] The success of concrete as a fireproof flooring system was set against its considerable weight penalties, though, throughout the 1900s and 1910s. Chicago began to accept concrete floors in lieu of terracotta between 1903 and 1910. Concrete had always served as a topping for hollow-tile arches, forming a level surface and receiving wooden nailing boards for timber flooring. Floor systems began to incorporate greater and greater depths of structural concrete as its fire resistance was proven, until terra-cotta was reduced to weight-saving pans or eliminated entirely in steel-reinforced floor systems. Concrete systems allowed flat ceilings between columns, and pulling columns in from the edges of outside walls allowed thin, cantilevered slab edges at building exteriors, offering greater opportunities for light and air.[12] Concrete's relatively low strength compared to steel, however, meant that it was a spatially inefficient material for skyscraper columns. Most concrete construction of this era therefore relied on steel column sections, though these were sometimes encased in a thick layer of protective concrete that replaced terra-cotta as fireproofing and that served as a minor structural adjunct. Concrete was also used to provide fireproof enclosures around elevator and stair shafts, and these were often woven into floor plates with steel reinforcing to provide lateral resistance as well.

Even with its strong allegiance to steel, Chicago constructed more concrete buildings in the first decade of the twentieth century than any other city. Most of these were low-rise factory buildings, but a handful of taller structures—notably the Born Building by Holabird & Roche on South Wells (1908)—pressed the advantages of the material as a fireproof structural system. Concrete was handicapped in Chicago by the lack of extensive deposits of minerals necessary for cement production, but Lemont limestones and sandstones,

along with recycled slags and cinders from the region's steel industry proved to be excellent aggregates when protected by a concrete matrix. If Chicago was not quite entering a "new stone age," as the *Tribune* suggested, and if optimistic dreams for one-hundred-story concrete skyscrapers would not materialize for another century, the material found widespread local applications in bridges, sewers, canals, and roads, and in residential towers after World War I.

CAISSON FOUNDATIONS

Concrete's greatest architectural contribution in Chicago, however, lay underground.[13] In a letter to the *Chicago Economist* in 1891, Dankmar Adler noted that while the spread foundations that characterized the city's substructures were "extremely ingenious," they were also "entirely insufficient for the ultimate development of the requirements of the tallest business buildings."[14] Few shared Jenney's confidence in floating buildings on large steel and concrete grilles, and even his own writings revealed doubts about the system he championed; in 1889 he advised that tie-rods in iron frames be made tight, not only to aid in resisting wind loads, but also to support columns in tension should their foundation pads fail.[15] In fact, failures of spread foundations were common. The Auditorium's tower was only the most visible, and buildings such as the Masonic Temple, the Unity, and the Fisher all leaned over

neighboring streets and structures. "Absolutely perpendicular walls in the Chicago skyscrapers are few," noted the *Tribune* as late as 1901, "the floating foundations of most of them . . . have tended to throw the building out of a perpendicular."[16] Foundation failures frequently involved neighboring structures, and here the politics and economics of close quarters added to calls for a better system. Buildings such as the Manhattan had pioneered cantilevered foundations, in which loads at the edges of a lot could be tied back to interior columns to avoid party wall disputes. But these systems were complex and expensive, and they heightened concerns about differential loading as interior columns were asked to carry even more load.

By the mid-1890s, successful foundations had been achieved using other means. The 1892 Owings Building, for instance, had used a thick concrete mat like the one that had failed so dramatically under the Post Office and County Courthouse buildings, but it used a grillage of railroad iron embedded within the concrete that resisted bending and forced the mat to settle monolithically. The Auditorium's tower had also relied on just such a reinforced concrete pad, and while its settlement was excessive, it occurred in one piece, without breaking up.[17] Pile foundations had been employed in the Art Institute (1893), the Public Library (1897), and, most dramatically, at the

Schiller Building (1892), where the concentrated loads that resulted from an office "bridge" over the theater were too great to have been borne by isolated pads.[18] Adler publicly stated his preference for these piles, noting their long record of success in riverfront warehouses and grain elevators.[19]

The Schiller Building spurred other reintroductions of what Adler termed the "long neglected and undervalued pile foundation."[20] In 1892, Gen. William Sooy Smith (1830–1916), who had consulted with Adler on the foundations of the Auditorium's tower, pointed out the continuing problems with settlement in isolated pier foundations and made the case for piles resting on deeper, more robust strata. In addition to a more secure foundation, he noted, such a system permitted deeper basements beneath the hardpan that formed a lower limit for foundations of the day.[21] Sooy Smith estimated that a single pile resting on deep hardpan could support between 60,000 and 80,000 pounds. Perching a tall office building atop a bundle of fifty-foot tree trunks seemed implausible, but in fluid soil such as Chicago's, pile foundations had a particular advantage. The hydrostatic pressure of the city's waterlogged clay both stabilized and supported such needlelike elements. Friction between clay and timber provided a robust resistance to gravity, while the stiff clay-braced piles along their lengths, eliminated buckling

and bending problems that typically plagued long, narrow columns. Nine major downtown buildings used piles by 1900, including Schlesinger & Mayer and Marshall Field's.[22]

As ideal as piles proved to be in Chicago soil, Sooy Smith believed that even they could be bettered by caissons, or poured concrete piles that rested directly on bedrock.[23] Pressurized caissons had been used throughout the late 1800s in bridge construction, but open wells sufficed for smaller skyscraper caissons. Contractors could simply dig a round hole of sufficient cross section, reinforced with walls to resist the hydrostatic pressure of the surrounding, fluid soil. Digging through hardpan was difficult, but it was easier than trying to drive piles lhrough it. Oncc excavated to bedrock, the well could be filled with concrete and rubble, forming a long, soil-braced column that had great compressive strength and an even more solid footing than piles on hardpan. A brick caisson that stabilized Kansas City's new municipal building on the edge of a bluff in 1890 offered a useful precedent for Chicago.[24]

Sooy Smith unsuccessfully proposed such a system to Burnham & Root for the Masonic Temple, but the Stock Exchange, where a difficult party wall arrangement demanded independent support, was the first Chicago skyscraper to have true caisson foundations. Here, workers dug seven deep

wells through hardpan and clay and surrounded them with wooden lagging. Once the wells reached bedrock they were filled with concrete. The resulting columns simply bypassed the spread foundations of the neighboring structure, preserving it while supporting the much heavier Stock Exchange.[25] Once proven, caissons took over from both floating and pile foundations, and as their reputation became more and more secure they became almost self-perpetuating. If a neighbor was going to install new caissons, it made sense to secure one's own building by the same method first, before digging started next door. Caissons, like piling, also allowed deeper basements that penetrated the top hardpan layer. With deeper excavations, equipment such as dynamos, motors, and boilers could be banished to a second basement level, leaving the first basement available for rental.[26] Chicago's first subbasement, in the 1905 Tribune Building by Holabird & Roche, accommodaled large printing presses, isolating their vibrations from the floors and walls of the building around them.[27]

With the availability of such reliable foundations, limitations to height based on Chicago's weak soil disappeared, as did incentives to make buildings lighter. Architects and engineers of the 1880s and 1890s had to keep the weight of their hardpan-supported structures under three or four thousand pounds per square foot of site area, but by the early 1900s they could design for bearing on bedrock, which has up to ten times the capacity of hardpan. This had two notable effects. First, pressure on the City to relax height restrictions grew as one more technical obstacle to taller construction was overcome. The City responded with a gradual easing of height limits, and with a more forgiving eye toward construction that exploited a loophole in the ordinance that allowed unoccupied "spires and towers." Second, the discipline of regular massing that carefully balanced floating foundations had instilled was swept away. With caissons on noncompressible bedrock, architects no longer needed to worry about placing vastly different loads in close proximity to one another on compressible clay. Engineers could now avoid the type of foundation failure that had marred the Auditorium's tower, for instance, by supporting both heavy towers and lighter, lower blocks on deeper, incompressible rock, allowing great flexibility in massing. Richard Schmidt's 1903 Montgomery Ward building on Michigan Avenue, which featured a 394-foot tower supported on deep piles, was the first structure to take full advantage of the ordinance's tower loophole and the new possibilities for different loads across a building's footprint. Restrictions on volume and area, however, made towers and spires a rare exception to the far more common flat-topped sky-

scraper block that became ubiquitous in the Loop during the first decade of the century.

THE SKYSCRAPER TYPE: STANDARDIZATION

While structure, glazing, and foundations continued to evolve from 1895–1910, the dominant theme of these years was the standardization of a skyscraper formula. Steel framing, wind bracing, fireproofing, and terra-cotta cladding all experienced incremental rather than revolutionary changes in these fifteen years, and these elements coalesced into a recognizable set of structural, functional, and architectural characteristics. Several publications celebrated the turn of the century with a stock-taking of the skyscraper type, concluding that techniques for planning, engineering, and constructing tall commercial buildings had become standardized. *Inland Architect* issued an encyclopedic assessment of current skyscraper technology in a special commemorative issue in 1900.[28] This issue was preceded by several handbooks for designing and building skyscrapers. *Skeleton Construction in Building* by William Birkmire (1860–1924) first appeared in 1894, and was updated and supplemented by his more widely ranging *Planning and Construction of High Office Buildings* in 1898.[29] Joseph Kendall Freitag (1869–1931) published *Architectural En-*

gineering in 1895 and *The Fireproofing of Steel Buildings* in 1896.[30]

With the opportunity to experiment iteratively and with an increasingly codified body of knowledge, Chicago architects developed a skyscraper type of widely spaced, masonry-jacketed steel frames filled with broad windows and accentuated by flat cornices and elaborate street levels. These characteristics have come to be seen as the embodiment of a mythical "Chicago School." Individual expression was typically limited to a few subtle choices in detailing, and the differences between even the most visually distinct buildings of the era are often wholly ascribable to a few ornamental elements.

The normalization of the skyscraper was not just an architectural or engineering phenomenon, it also became a fixture in urban culture. The skyscraper fascinated the general population not only for its technical achievement and its transformation of daily routines, but also as a barometer of the nineteenth-century American city's ambitions, difficulties, and challenges.[31] It certainly spawned ambiguous responses in Chicago, which began to celebrate itself as the skyscraper's birthplace. Debates over height, stability, and solidity persisted even as skyscrapers proved their resistance to fire, wind, and uncertain soils. Opponents marshaled arguments based on safety, daylight, sanitation, and aesthetics in attempts to influence restrictions on height and construction. While arguments based on fire safety waned in the face of fireproof buildings' record of the 1890s, skyscrapers' effects on their neighboring streets and smaller structures gained more traction. The loudest appeals came from agitated property owners and civic benefactors, who argued that developers' quests for light and air came, inevitably, at the expense of others. "What will happen in the building world," asked one *Tribune* editor, "when every street in Chicago is lined with skyscrapers and the whole situation becomes, as a matter of fact, unceasing, relentless warfare for possession of the light of day?"[32]

Sanitation and hygiene sparked reactions to tall buildings based on concerns for the cleansing effects of wind and light. As one Alderman complained, "the meridian sun of an August day fails to reach the pavement, and snow-drifts will not melt until July." Dearborn Street, with the Monadnock, Old Colony, Fisher, and Manhattan in close proximity, became a rallying cry for skyscraper opponents. Some critics argued that they blocked healthy winds, leaving streets to fester in stagnant, disease-ridden air. Others cringed at the concentration of thousands of occupants in narrow confines, stacked up in rooms where the "disinfecting qualities" of direct sunlight were blocked by neighboring towers.[33]

Less objectively, the ornamental restraint that to later eyes appeared pro-totypically modern still seemed to many critics a philistine lack of taste. The comparison of Chicago buildings to "perforated dry-goods boxes" remained a common jab in the 1890s.[34] Among architects and clients, however, there was a growing appreciation for the inherent appeal of a quietly expressive framed building. Attempts to decorate these structures to match prevailing taste occasionally resulted in professional ridicule, making a more sober acceptance of the basic forms and compositions offered by the steel frame a viable alternative. Both the Owings (1890), designed by Henry Ives Cobb for mercurial real estate baron F. P. Owings, and the Columbus Memorial (1893), the last work of W. W. Boyington, were criticized for their unrestrained ornament.[35] The pressure exerted by owners to reduce expensive decoration was occasionally recognized as a negative benefit, preventing flights of ornamental excess and resulting in buildings that carried their own expressive nobility.[36] In 1902 the *Tribune* noted this gradual acceptance; "plain buildings" prevailed and would likely influence future work, and architects had begun "doing nothing more noticeable than to attempt to be plain." The result was that Chicago's buildings were "prevalent but in no sense distinctive."[37]

EXPRESSED FRAMES

But *could* more distinctive skyscrapers be coaxed out of the plain facts from which they were conceived and realized? Three distinct approaches to this question were posed by architects of the era: Louis Sullivan sought philosophical justification for his designs in a quasi-organic adherence to functional forms; Holabird & Roche took a less deliberate approach by simply refining the proportions and elements left from their solution to the problem of planning; and Burnham found ways to decorate the resulting frame in the popular language and details of academic classicism. All of these approaches came in for praise and criticism, and all represented commercially acceptable strategies for making raw "plain buildings" distinctive enough to satisfy public tastes on their clients' budgets.

Sullivan's approach was best known from the publication of "The Tall Building Artistically Considered" in *Lippincott's* magazine in March 1896. This essay featured his aphorism "form follows function," but it also contained a formula for skyscraper design in which massing, fenestration, and ornament were to be marshaled for the purpose of achieving an efficient disposition of spaces, but also for making such a solution legible. While his famous aphorism suggested a utilitarian disregard for anything compositional, in fact Sullivan was interested in the aesthetic presentation of the problem's solution, not just in the solution itself.[38]

Sullivan began by identifying the primary functional elements of a modern office building that echoed the textbooks of the era:

> Wanted—First, A story below ground, containing boilers, engines of various sorts, etc.—in short, the plant for power, heating, lighting, etc. Second, a ground floor, so-called, devoted to stores, banks, or other establishments requiring large area, ample spacing, ample light, and great freedom of access. Third, A second story readily accessible by stairways—this space usually in large subdivisions, with corresponding liberality in structural spacing and in expanse of glass and breadth, of external openings. Fourth, Above this an indefinite number of stories of offices piled tier upon tier, one tier just like another tier, one office just like all the other offices—an office being similar to a cell in a honeycomb, merely a compartment, nothing more. Fifth and last, At the top of this pile is placed a space, or a story that, as related to the life and usefulness of the structure, is purely physiological in its nature, namely, the attic. In this the circulatory system completes itself and makes its grand turn, ascending and descending. Finally, or at the beginning rather, there must be on the ground floor a main aperture or entrance common to all the occupants or patrons of the building.[39]

This suggested two compositional approaches. First, the office floors formed a design problem all their own; their dimensions and proportions were given by rental and anthropomorphic requirements, which in turn dictated the best structural spacing. Windows were to fill the resulting void to the extent possible; Sullivan did not directly reference John Root's "Great Architectural Problem," but it was clear that the key problem of filling the space between columns and girders was a problem of aperture, not of solid elements. Eschewing arbitrary ornament, Sullivan's most important suggestion was that the designer embrace the repetitive nature of these offices as the basis for their visual expression, all of which should "*look* alike because they *are* all alike." Second, where this system was inflected by other functions or conditions—the base levels and the attic—Sullivan felt that the expression should change to reflect these. The first floor should acknowledge the need to provide an entrance and possibly retail storefronts, modifying the relentless grid above. The attic, too, should represent that it needed no light-gathering windows and (less convincingly, to many) that it should somehow terminate the many tiers of office space below.

Sullivan thus argued for both unselfconscious acceptance of the conditions facing the architect and their more intentional orchestration into efficient and expository designs. He argued for "a thoroughly sound, logical, coherent expression of the conditions" that was "innocent" and "logical," yet he admitted that "some gift for form in detail, some feeling for form purely and simply as form, some love for that," was necessary to give the resulting logical statement "charm of sentiment."[40] This was hardly an aggressive statement of unrelenting pragmatism; form *followed* function, but it was, in Sullivan's view, not *determined* by it. Dankmar Adler, responding to Sullivan's publication in an invited panel discussion at the 1896 AIA Convention, noted that new materials added an additional variable to the equation. Steel and plate glass in particular, he felt, had influenced form to an even greater extent than commercial functions—which had really remained largely unchanged during the skyscraper era. "The materials of which buildings are erected," he noted, "always affect the designs to a greater or less extent," negotiating between function, construction, and aesthetic aspiration.[41]

Adler & Sullivan's buildings of this era demonstrated this interplay between functional solution, material realization, and individual expression. Beginning with the much-heralded 1890 Wainwright Building in St. Louis, Sullivan's designs—or, perhaps, Sullivan's sculpting and refinement of Adler's engineering solutions—integrated the nascent formula of repetitive office cells with broader first stories and heavy, terminating attics. Their designs of the early 1890s all deployed floors of offices in regular ranks of single windows, separated by brick piers that expressed the mechanical repetition of these cells and their structure throughout. In line with his dictum that a skyscraper "must be every inch a proud and soaring thing," Sullivan detailed windows and piers to emphasize vertical proportions; the windows and their intervening solid spandrels were set back from the plane of the vertical piers, resulting in facades that, on first glance, appear as giant screens of alternating light and shadow in vertical stripes. All of this vertical drama was contained, however, by base stories that were detailed as plain, ashlar blocks to permit larger storefront windows and attic stories of round windows and heavy, overhanging cornices.

While the essential functions of all building elements were thus clearly legible, Adler's response showed a significant shortcoming in Sullivan's strict functionalist claims. The brick piers that divided each office window from the next in their work of the early 1890s were not all structural—as is evident from the double-width windows at the first-floor level of the Wainwright or the 1894 Guaranty Building in Buffalo. In fact, as Joseph Siry has pointed out, only every other pier carried floor loads, meaning that fully half of the piers carried only the cladding itself.[42] These piers "look the same" even

though they are manifestly "not the same." The proportioning of these facades thus came in part from a sense of visual balance, and the difference in size between brick pier and supporting steel column, as revealed in contemporary construction photographs, was so great that some questioned whether the frame was being expressed as accurately—or as adequately—as the repetitive office cells were. Sullivan's later work—especially the Gage facade (1899) and the Schlesinger & Mayer buildings (1900 and 1904)—show stricter adherence to the material proportions and structural systems behind terra-cotta skyscraper skins.

These later projects came well after Adler's critique and, perhaps more tellingly, after several examples of more thoroughly expressive integrations of structure, function, cladding, and composition by Holabird & Roche. That firm had, by the time of Sullivan's essay, developed a reputation for efficiency in planning and execution, but it also began to attract more refined higher-end commercial commissions. In 1891 the Brooks family hired Holabird & Roche to extend Burnham & Root's Monadnock Building for the length of Dearborn between Jackson and Adams. They responded with a more articulate version of Root's dialogue between oriel window and massive brick wall. The extension featured a dramatic departure in structural technique from Root's bearing masonry walls,

with its northern half completed in tight pressed-brick piers, its southern half with steel reinforcement. It has never been clear what led to the change, but both new wings omitted Root's elegant but expensive curved brick at the cornice and base, opting instead for a combination of expressed pier and recessed oriel, the former delineated with terracotta edges that terminated in arched windows at the penultimate story. The result was a more efficient floor plate and a facade divided into legible zones of structure and aperture rather than a monolithic mass.[43]

This combination of expressed pier and recessed oriel was not, however, repeated in Holabird & Roche's later work. Cheap glass, the need for expansive daylighting, and the strictures of the 1893 Code all put pressures on the dimensions of the typical steel-framed facade, expanding apertures and compressing solid, terra-cotta or brick elements into tight wrappers around steel columns and girders behind. Like Sullivan, Roche believed that skyscrapers' elevations should represent the nature of the steel structure within. By 1893, Roche had replaced the oriels of the Monadnock extension with simpler planes of flat plate glass, more closely adhering to Yost's suggestion of a dialogue between positive and negative elevational space. He also, critically, added dedicated spandrel panels that allowed him to render an entire facade as either a pattern of vertical striations or a more neutral grid of columns and girders. The windows occupying the interstices of these frames were refined into so-called Chicago windows, with large fixed lights, usually square, flanked by double-hung units. Together these elements opened the offices behind to both daylight and ventilation, but they also formed a secondary grid of vertical mullions that Roche used as a foil to the larger structural grids of these facades.

In the twenty years after the Monadnock Extension, Holabird & Roche produced over a dozen Loop buildings that deployed this formula in energetic displays of subtle elaborations. All included five basic elements: first, an internal steel structure that informed the basic layout of the main elevations; second, vertical facade elements of brick or terra-cotta that telegraphed the position of the columns within; third, horizontal spandrel elements of brick, cast iron, or terra-cotta, positioned relative to the plane of the verticals; fourth, tripartite windows with a fixed center light and flanking double-hung units; and, fifth, compositionally inspired top and base elements that framed the skeletal facades between, similar to Sullivan's approach. While Holabird & Roche relied almost exclusively on these elements, each of their buildings deployed them in different proportions and positions, sometimes aligning the spandrels with the verticals, sometimes setting them back, and more rarely setting them prominently forward, finding

possibilities for articulated facades that relied entirely on this sense of layered cross-graining. Mullions between fixed and movable windows created tartan-like secondary grids, compositions of heavy and light layers in which each element's visual weight echoed the distinctions and hierarchies between structure and cladding.

The Venetian and the Marquette were the first of Holabird & Roche's works to combine these elements into a cogent formula, and even in these early expressed frames the variations in minute positioning and detail were notable. Roche divided the Venetian's narrow street front into three equal bays of simple piers and spandrels, plainly expressed. From the tenth floor up, however, Roche detailed the facade in an ersatz Moorish theme that aligned, loosely, with the building's name, while a gabled roof at the top completed the facade with eaves that mimicked a continuous cornice. Inside, the structure was noted for its cross-braced wind system (see chapter 4), but Roche chose not to show this system on the facades. In contrast to its effusive top, the main body of the Venetian's elevation represented a first step toward the stark frame and window composition for which Holabird & Roche would become widely known.

The Marquette (1895) was a synthesis of Holabird & Roche's developing formula with a sense of mass and classical allusion (figures 6.6, 6.7). A preliminary scheme, designed in haste to beat anticipated code changes in 1891, was similar in concept to the Tacoma and Monadnock Extension (figure 6.8), with heavy masonry cross-walls and an undulating skin of round and angled oriels. By the time the Brooks Estate committed to construction in 1893, however, wind-braced steel connections had been largely proven and bay windows had come under criticism as potential hazards. While such concerns did not stop Burnham from including bay windows in their contemporary Fisher and Reliance buildings, these seem to have convinced the more conservative Brooks estate, and the Marquette eliminated bay windows in favor of massive tripartite windows that gave the same exposure while receding inside the perceived solidity of the surrounding piers. Claimed as a "second Rookery," the Marquette was laid out in three wings around a central light court. Its main facades along Dearborn and Adams were rendered in heavy brown brick and terra-cotta marshaled into a strict grid of solid piers and recessed spandrels that explicitly referenced the underlying grid of steel girders and Z-bar columns engineered by Purdy and Henderson.[44] At the base, even larger plate glass windows opened to street level retail, while a three-columned entrance on Dearborn (now demolished) married classical quotations to the proportions and locations of the structural grid within.[45] At the top, a two-story

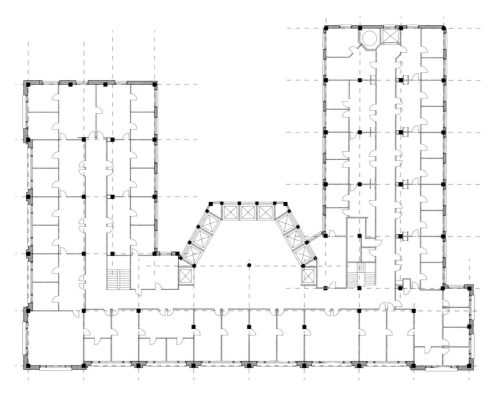

6.6 Marquette Building, corner of Adams and Dearborn Streets, Holabird and Roche, 1895, plan. (Drawing by the author)

6.7 Marquette Building, view from southeast. (*120 Photographic Views of Chicago*, Rand McNally, 1909)

6.8 (opposite) Monadnock Block, southern half of Dearborn Street between Jackson and Van Buren, Holabird and Roche, 1893, view from southeast. (*120 Photographic Views of Chicago*, Rand McNally, 1909)

attic capped the gridded elevations, and the entire composition was held beneath a deep cornice that echoed the main entrance in its classical detail. These ornamental details at its top and base, however, were fixed to a matrix that was so faithful to the proportions and disposition of the steel frame as to offend critics; the *American Architect* complained that the first-floor windows were so large that the "exterior wall . . . can scarcely be said to exist" and described the elevations in scathing detail: "the building is almost devoid of architectural interest on the exterior," it reported, "there seems to be a hopeless settling down to the idea that a large office-building must be a huge box pierced with holes at regular intervals."[46] The *Chicago Daily* was more succinct. Despite the displays of classical elements, it explained to its readers that "the office building is for revenue only, and no consideration of architectural effect can be allowed to interfere."[47]

Similar criticism was leveled at Holabird & Roche's 1894 Champlain Building (figure 6.9). The elevations of the Champlain, according to D. Everett Waid of *Brickbuilder*, "are a dead white terra cotta, with such an effect that the first syllable of 'Champlain' has been replaced with a word usually represented by a blank. The building is offensively plain to incite such profanity."[48] Indeed, the Champlain eschewed not only the ornament, but also the articulation of

6.9 Champlain Building, corner of State and Madison Streets, Holabird and Roche, 1894 (demolished, 1916), view from southeast. (*120 Photographic Views of Chicago*, Rand McNally, 1909)

6.10 Mandel Brothers Store, corner of Wabash and Madison Streets, Holabird and Roche, 1900. (Contemporary postcard, collection of the author)

the Marquette, with the only relief in the facades being a very small setback of the spandrel panels from its vertical piers. Its window mullions were rendered in dark cast iron, leaving the stark white grid of terra-cotta as the building's primary image. The *Chicago Economist* also complained about the facade's stark appearance, but it recognized a welcome efficiency for developers and codified the tripartite window that was now becoming a ubiquitous feature of Holabird & Roche's work: "[T]he purpose of the Trustees was to erect a building not only highly attractive, but affording the most abundant light to its occupants, and to that end as much glass as possible would be used. The windows will occupy the entire distance between the stories save the small amount of space required for the mullions. . . . On each side of this large plate will be a smaller window, say two or three feet wide, provided for the purpose of ventilation."[49]

Holabird & Roche addressed the issue of their "offensively plain" elevations in three ways: in their department store designs Roche opted for a decorated frame, applying classical devices to plain white terra-cotta grids (notably the 1900 Mandel Brothers Store and its 1905 extension, the 1905 Boston Store (figures 6.10, 6.11), and the 1912 Rothschild/Goldblatt's Store); on less distinguished loft and office buildings, such as the Williams (1898), the McCormick/ Gage (1899), and the Kresge (1905), Roche compressed the building's expression into more densely packed articulations of piers, spandrels, and windows; finally, on higher-end commercial blocks such as the Republic (1905), somewhere between the mercantile tastes of the department stores and the utilitarian needs of the lofts, he found compromises that blended limited classical ornament with detailed elaborations of the structure and cladding inside (figures 6.12–6.14).

Even with applied elements such as a three-story colonnade of Corinthian columns at its top, the Boston Store and its brethren came across to many—including Montgomery Schuyler (writing as Franz Winkler) as "revoltingly simple." Built in phases (and eventually replacing the Champlain Building), the Boston presented a block-long terra-cotta grid containing enormous show windows—and little else. "The front," Schuyler reported, "is a mere sash frame with huge square panes . . . the architectural embodiment of the 'Chicago Idea' in commercial architecture. . . . [T]he essentials are all supplied and evidently only the essentials."[50] An attic colonnade, later much critiqued by Condit and others, formed an offering of sorts to mercantile tastes for more stately fronts, but this was a single moment of ornamental relief in an otherwise relentless grid. A more elaborate take on this approach informed the Mandel Brothers Store, across State Street, where Roche employed arcaded windows for the building's top three stories. The "facts of the case" in Schuyler's words, were thus modified by a "*suggestio falsi*" that leavened—in his view unsuccessfully—"the appearance of grim reality" that he felt marked the firm's work.[51]

Roche's approach to basic loft structures was less ornamental. Beginning with the Williams Building of 1897,

6.11 Boston Store, Madison Street between Dearborn and State, Holabird and Roche, 1905. (Contemporary postcard, collection of the author)

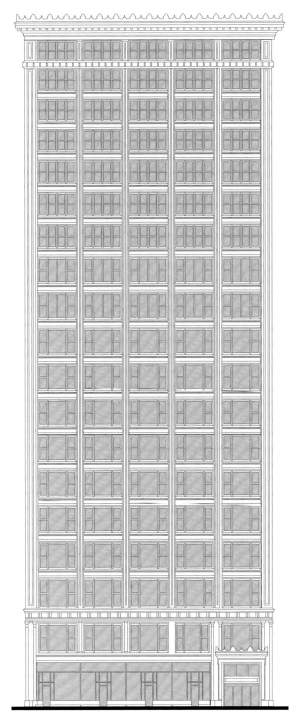

6.12 Republic Building, 209 S. State Street, Holabird and Roche, 1905 (demolished, 1961), elevation. (Drawing by the author)

these buildings formed an ongoing essay in the articulated frame, and the firm experimented tirelessly with understated detailing that gently emphasized either vertical or horizontal proportions (figures 6.15–6.17). Changing the position of a brick course or two to delineate hierarchy within a facade demanded little in the way of construction time or cost—certainly less than the commissioning of large, custom-fabricated ornamental pieces—and it took up less depth in the exterior wall. A terra-cotta system that employed fine variations in position was also relatively easy to design and manufacture. These delicate maneuvers of masonry planes thus stood in for the more emphatic attempts to coax identity and visual interest out of the department store blocks and were eventually seen as more architecturally successful. In the Wil-

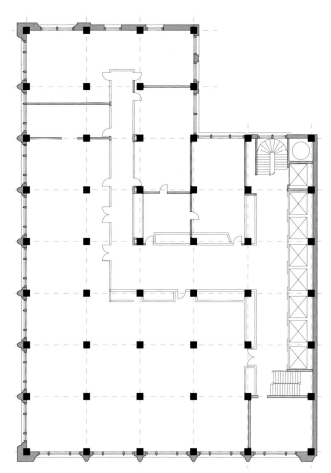

6.13 Republic Building, plan. (Drawing by the author)

liams, brick cladding around the piers was simply set one course forward of the brick spandrels, which in turn were topped by a sill emphasized by dentil-like bricks turned outward beneath it.[52] The result was a facade of surprising richness, undulating between the layers of window, spandrel, and pier.

Miniscule but still legible detailing was furthered in the terra-cotta facade of the Ayer Building on Wabash, built to provide commercial space that could be quickly reconfigured for changing clients.[53] Constructed on the site of a building that burned in 1898, the owners rejected any suggestion that the front windows be constricted to prevent exposure to possible exterior fires. "The building is an open confession," wrote P. B. Wight in *Brickbuilder*, "that where the fenestration calls for the greatest possible amount of daylight, the risk of fire from such exposure must be accepted."[54] While terra-cotta fireproofing was now required to have the same overall dimension as brick, it could be fabricated with finer detail, and Roche used this malleability to add layers of articulation to the resulting facade. The windows themselves were divided into center lights of 155 by 100 inches and broad sidelights of double-hung windows, each pane measuring four feet square, all set just 27 inches above the floors. These enormous tripartite windows were framed with terra-cotta rendered in sparkling white with ornamental piping, reveals, and linework that

6.14 Republic Building, view from northeast. (Contemporary postcard, collection of the author)

created a layered elevation, expressing a hierarchy of bearing, spanning, and enclosing elements by their positions in the depth of the facade and their relative thicknesses. The Ayer certainly offered technical advances—its south party wall was supported on caissons, for instance, and its enormous windows were good indications of the sophisticated plate glass being produced in Indiana. Roche modeled these advances into an elevation that was expressive and engaging though based on nothing more than structural

6.15 Williams Building, 205 W. Monroe, Holabird and Roche, 1898, detail of elevation. (Photograph by the author)

6.16 Gage Group, 18–30 S. Michigan Avenue, Holabird and Roche, 1899, detail of elevation. (Photograph by the author)

proportions and positions within. Wight speculated that its richness was largely due to the facade's sophisticated relationship of horizontal voids and vertical lines, seeing it as evidence that "simplicity and refinement of detail" could arise from the dialogues between solid and void, support and span, or enclosure and transparency.

Holabird & Roche's later loft buildings—the McCormick (Gage) Group on Michigan Avenue, the Kresge Building on State Street just south of the Reliance, and the McNeil Building of 1911—followed the Williams and Ayer in wrapping steel structures with either brick or terra-cotta, providing minimal spandrels set back in elevation from the fireproof column coverings, and filling the remaining voids with glass lights divided by cast-iron or terra-cotta mul-

lions. The Gage Group was highlighted by Louis Sullivan's commission for one of the three facades, which he articulated in a related fashion, eschewing Holabird & Roche's tripartite windows for ranks of double-hung units and cladding the two columns on his front elevation with flourishing organic capitals.

Much of Holabird & Roche's work negotiated between the branding of department stores and the utilitarian aspirations of loft developers. Many of these projects blended strict expression of structural and cladding necessities with ornamental programs and compositional tropes that elevated the "dry goods box" to something commercially palatable. Aesthetics mattered to tenants and customers, making appearance a functional requirement alongside lighting and circulation. The

Republic Building was a particularly good example of a skin that was intended to allow "the maximum amount possible of window space in proportion to masonry," but that made concessions to popular taste with heavy classical detailing of enameled terra-cotta. Its deep cornice and wide corner piers contrasted with its facade's skeletal appearance and its first-floor storefronts, which spanned the entire front with plate glass windows. The Republic's upper stories were also exemplary instances of the developing style of expressed piers, tripartite windows, and inset spandrels here decorated with classical ornament. In other buildings that involved corporate identity—the Oliver Typewriter headquarters on Dearborn, for instance—a nuanced blend of wide windows and expressed structure shared space with ornamental panels of cast iron and terra-cotta that were not overtly referential. Perhaps the most thorough of these integrations came with the Brooks Building of 1910, which owed debts to the Republic Building, to Sullivan's treatment of the Gage facade, and to the Ayer Building's elaboration of its piers as piped, Gothic elements standing in front of the facade's other components. Although the large center lights of their earlier work were replaced at the Brooks with double-hung windows, the effect of the pier articulation and the development of the spandrel panels with deep sills produced a deeply modeled facade.

Holabird & Roche's expressive elevational formula was matched by Sullivan's final major work in the Loop, for Schlesinger & Mayer (later Carson, Pirie, Scott), which he executed in three phases between 1899 and 1904 (figures 6.18–6.20). Here, Sullivan managed to exemplify, subvert, and extend the language of the expressed frame that was emerging as a standard approach to the commercial block in Chicago. The project began as a nine-story infill on Madison Street, three bays wide, rendered in a plain terra-cotta grid. Sullivan went against the instinctive verticality he had promoted in *The Tall Office Building Artistically Considered*; instead, he added subtle horizontal piping across the terra-cotta grid at the sill levels and drew rich details for the inte-

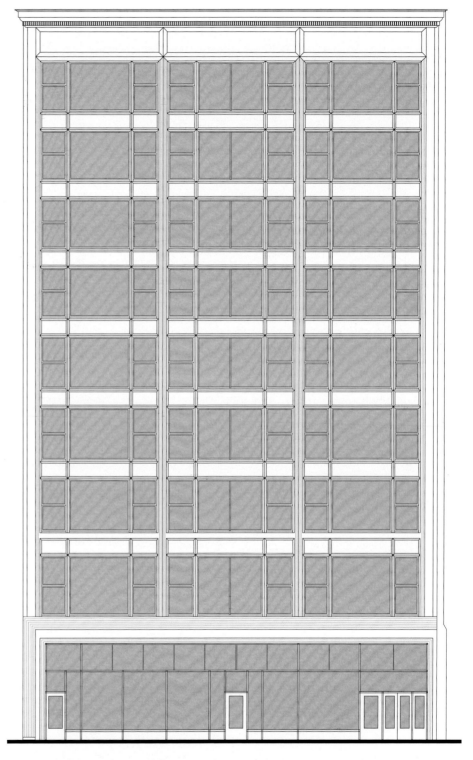

6.17 Ayer/M'Clurg Building, 218 S. Wabash, Holabird and Roche, 1900, Wabash Street elevation. (Drawing by the author)

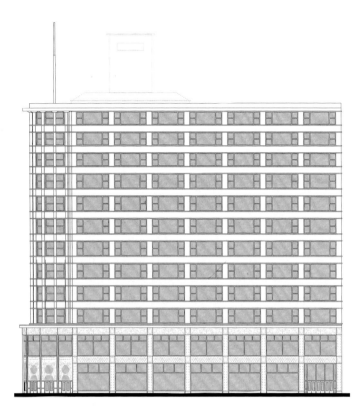

6.18 Schlesinger & Mayer Department Store, corner of State and Madison Streets, Louis H. Sullivan, 1899–1902. (Drawing by the author)

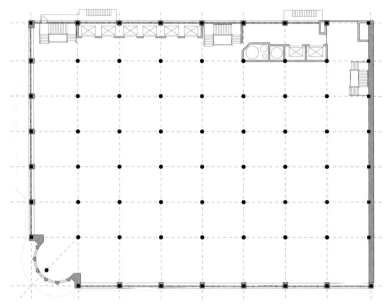

6.19 Schlesinger & Mayer Department Store, plan. (Drawing by the author)

rior surfaces of the window frames, setting tripartite windows within a planar, neutrally grained grid. Even at this early stage Schlesinger & Mayer had plans for the full quarter block and Sullivan was certainly anticipating the broad horizontal reach of the future State Street facade. He included the germ of an ornamental idea that, as the store grew larger, could expand with it. This also informed the two base stories and the attic, a recessed story underneath a cornice of classical proportions, both of which were decorated in Sullivan's botanical ornament.[55]

It was the eventual expansion of Schlesinger & Mayer's operations that produced the refined statement of function, structure, and construction for which the building became known. Begun in a rush over the winter of 1902–1903, the second phase involved digging new caisson foundations while the existing corner store remained in operation, a feat that merited its own coverage in the architectural press.[56] Work was so hurried that proper steelwork could not be found and cast-iron columns were substituted to enable the project to proceed. The scale of the building was also increased from nine to twelve stories when code restrictions on height were loosened between the two projects.[57] Pressed for time, Sulli-

van opted for simplicity. The resulting plan pushed services and circulation to the east wall of the first building, leaving a regular grid of columns supporting steel girders and arched tile floors. On the exterior, the horizontal windows of the original were continued, broken by a corner element that offered a vertical accent and access to the corner of State and Madison—the "busiest corner in the world."[58] When the city denied permission to continue the bay window storefronts of the original

6.20 (opposite) Schlesinger & Mayer Department Store, detail of Madison Street elevation. (Photograph by the author)

6.21 Stewart Building, corner of State and Washington Streets, D. H. Burnham & Co., 1897. (*120 Photographic Views of Chicago*, Rand McNally, 1909)

jection at the top that distinguished it from the terra-cotta above.[59] The attic's windows and round columns were also explicitly compositional. The result was a contrast between the grid of jacketed structure—detailed to emphasize the windows within but defined by twin requirements of structure and light—and three elements that framed this grid: base, attic, and corner rotunda. Ornament was treated as decoration; piers were dressed to "attract the eye" at street level and at the cornice, but not between.

In contrast to Holabird & Roche and Sullivan, Burnham's office took the trabeated nature of the steel frame as a call for more robust programs of Beaux-Arts classicism (figures 6.21, 6.22). The first clear statement of these principles can be found in the Stewart Building, across the street from the Reliance. This was Burnham's first large office building in the Loop after Atwood's death (the Illinois Trust Bank at LaSalle and Jackson, finished in 1896, covered only two stories), which alone might explain its more conservative style. However, the Stewart was also the first of Burnham's office buildings to be permitted under the 1893 Code, and its solidity can also be seen as a response to that code's restrictions on bay windows and emphasis on thicker fireproofing, similar to Holabird & Roche's work at the Marquette. While the design was described as "light and airy . . . so arranged that every suite of offices has outside light," this was ac-

building's base, Sullivan instead specified enormous plate glass windows at the street level, but continued the cast-ironwork framing that contrasted with the terra-cotta above—blossom-

ing, Harriett Monroe suggested, "into a profusion of delicate ornament justified by the purpose of the structure," adhering tightly to the proportions of the piers behind, but with a horizontal pro-

6.22 Silversmith Building, 10 S. Wabash, D. H. Burnham & Co., 1897. (Photograph by the author)

complished in a very manner than at Reliance or Fisher.[60] The Stewart represents the burgeoning idea in Burnham's office that the structural frame could serve as a substrate for an applied program of Beaux-Arts ornament. Over the next decade the economic formula

of these skins would change to allow stricter adherence to classical precedent, but as long as large windows demanded thinner piers, such styling was limited to the selection of ornamental elements attached to an otherwise neutral frame (see chapter 7).[61]

The structural frame inspired other Chicago architects of the time to similar responses: extensions of the lightly ornamented, jacketed, and expressed frame with broad infill windows can be found in the Foundation Hall building by E. R. Krause (1859–1935) on South

Michigan Ave. (1904) and the concrete structures of Richard Schmidt (1866–1959), particularly the sprawling Montgomery Ward Warehouse on the north branch of the Chicago River (1907) and the Dwight Building (1911). Schmidt also authored two rare attempts to merge residentially inspired Prairie School detailing to the expressed frame, notably in the Grommes and Ulrich Building (1901) and the Chapin and Gore Building (1904). Ultimately, however, the expressed frame was most widely seen beginning around 1908 as an underlying matrix for classically derived imagery, in line with Burnham's experiment at the Stewart. Many historians have seen these as an unworthy coda to the heroic expressed frame buildings of 1895 to 1910, but the gradual infiltration of Chicago architecture by the Beaux-Arts was a logical extension of trabeated expression and the further evolution of lighting technologies. While Condit effectively ended his discussion of the Chicago skyscraper around 1908, the next generation of Beaux-Arts skyscrapers is worth study, because it continued the trend of technically proficient, functionally based building structures and skins. Now, however, the influence of technologies within the city's new code restrictions suggested different proportions for windows and cladding, and architects responded with decorative programs that employed the more solid surfaces of this later generation's functionally based skins. The expressed frame would gradually be diffused into an ornamented mass as new solutions to Root's "great architectural problem" emerged.

Chapter 7
Steel, Light, and Style: The Concealed Frame, 1905–1918

The expressed frame defined Chicago's commercial architecture for nearly fifteen years. But like the curtain wall and other types before it, it was surpassed by a new tectonic formula as material and performance technologies evolved. The type's large windows and gridded facades faded in importance after 1910, and in their place came building elevations of remarkable solidity—overtly classical in appearance and detail, with small windows and vast expanses of cut, trimmed, and elaborately ornamented stone and terra-cotta. To many historians, these buildings were not worthy of the name "Chicago School." Yet these solid skins and concealed frames were also the result of specific technical vectors— new technologies, newly available materials, and continuing pressures for efficiency in both construction and operation. That these vectors now implied

a rigid frame clad with a curtain wall composed primarily of solid elements instead of glass, and with smaller windows that responded to a different set of lighting criteria, suggests that architects of this era were no less responsive to the technical, economic, and functional criteria than they were a decade or two earlier. The state of skyscraper art showed a profound and sudden shift during the era, transforming the expressed grids and broad windows of "Chicago construction" into something nearly the opposite.

STEEL, GLASS, AND TERRA-COTTA— CHANGING CONDITIONS

Steel's growing affordability alongside encouraging economic news rebuilt momentum in real estate between 1900–1910. After the market bottomed out around 1898, Chicago built more high-end skyscrapers each year for a

decade. By 1910 inexpensive building materials, agreements between labor and capital, well-organized design and construction regimes, and continued improvements in construction meant that commercial real estate was, once again, enormously profitable. Tenants gradually abandoned older buildings with slower elevators, smaller offices, and darker corridors for newer, more efficient buildings. "Old Chicago is being torn down," one journalist reported in 1910, "and new Chicago erected in its place."[1] The Calumet, first Insurance Exchange (at LaSalle and Adams), Rand-McNally, and the Opera House—all major achievements in the 1880s—were demolished between 1910 and 1913. They were replaced by buildings aimed at tenants seeking greater efficiency, comfort, and pretense. Chicago exhibited a new and "very encouraging tendency on the part of builders . . . to construct a more attractive and ornamental type of structure," according to the city's Building Commissioner in 1910. "I can now suggest to a man who is putting up a building in Chicago," said one anonymous architect in 1910, "that by adding 3 or 10 or even 13 per cent to the cost he can make something that will be a distinct credit to the city, although it will not bring in a cent more rental, and he will listen to me. A few years ago he would not."[2]

Popular tastes and civic pride merged with fantasies of antiquity during this era, influenced but hardly determined by distant recollections of the 1892 Columbian Exposition. Classicism was given a prolonged life by the impact of the French Ecole des Beaux-Arts on American education and tastes, but such tendencies were stymied in commercial architecture by the ongoing need for daylighting, which continued to require large apertures. The slender proportions of light-gathering curtain walls combined with the high cost of ornamental elements such as columns and archways mitigated against classicism's full flowering in the generation after the Fair, though a latent tendency toward the Beaux-Arts emerged between 1892 and 1910 in hotels, banks, and clubs—all building types that had different functional and economic strictures than commercial construction. This tendency failed to thrive in commercial architecture, however, until lighting technologies and material

availabilities changed in its favor. The expressed frame's demise came alongside changes in glass prices and availability, frustration with the environmental penalties for large windows, and the replacement of daylight by electric illumination. Collectively, these factors influenced a new conception of the frame/skin dialogue that had been so richly explored by architects in the previous decade.

The midwestern plate glass boom that had influenced the curtain walls of the 1890s and the large tripartite windows of the 1900s ended as quickly as it had begun. Pittsburg's takeover of Diamond Plate Glass in 1895 began a slow easing of the material's price collapse. Automated polishing and continuous annealing kept prices low even as the glut eased, but the Indiana industry was dealt a fatal blow at the turn of the century when the gas field under Indiana and Ohio ran out and gas wells began backfilling with ground water. Factories deserted central Indiana, leaving for the state's eastern coal belt, but Pittsburg Plate maintained the factories at Kokomo and Elwood, using coal gas that was piped from Chicago through gas lines that had once run the other direction.[3]

Troubles in Indiana were matched by the growing effect of the glass monopoly on prices nationwide. 1902 marked the bottom for the glass market, after which Pittsburg Plate was able to slowly stabilize prices and manage

competition effectively. Glass remained affordable through World War I, but the spike in prices throughout the building industry during the war hit glass particularly hard, and the cost of a square foot of polished plate climbed back up to a historic high in 1920. The rise in energy costs around the war more directly affected glass prices than steel, brick, or concrete, and plate glass went from being a luxury material in 1890, to being "cheaper than bricks" around 1895, to again being expensive enough to warrant careful rationing in 1918.

An increase in glass prices alone might explain the tendency toward more opaque building skins, but alongside these prices lay environmental penalties inherent in single-layered plate glass that encouraged architects to look for alternative lighting solutions. Glass conducted heat as well as transmitting light, a major inconvenience during Chicago's cold winters and hot summers. Office workers bundled up in colder months —the fingerless gloves of the bookkeeper were just one stereotype to emerge from the popular press of the day—but the bigger problem was summer.[4] Awnings sprouting from Chicago skyscrapers demonstrated that direct sunlight made office environments unbearable. Ventilation combined with shading devices could mitigate summer heat, but without air-conditioning, lighting and interior environmental control remained a zero-sum struggle. The more daylight an office had, the more vulnerable it was to temperature swings during winters and summers.

Complaints about heat and glare from large, east-facing windows in the 1897 Public Library were the most public example of the dilemma that faced all builders.[5] Though later generations would see the glass skins of the 1890s as prophetic, Chicago architects of the early twentieth century considered them environmental mistakes. Speaking in 1931 regarding the appearance of the Glass House by brothers George and William Keck (1895–1980 and 1908–1995) at the Century of Progress Exposition, John Holabird remarked that glass walls had been explored in the mid-1890s but then sensibly abandoned by Chicago's skyscraper architects. Architect George C. Nimmons (1865–1947) agreed, weighing the perceived advantages of all-glass skins against some rather stern realities. "If our walls were entirely of glass," he believed, it would lead to "structures which are almost impossible to keep warm in winter and cool in summer or which let in such a glare of sunlight that it's unpleasant for the occupants."[6]

After midcentury, efficient air-conditioning and insulated glass would eventually remove the thermal penalties that came with large windows, but Holabird and Nimmons represented common sense in 1930s Chicago. Without environmental control the architectural ideal of glass walls presented formidable challenges in hot or cold

weather.[7] Indeed, the Simonds Saw and Steel Building at Fitchburg, Massachusetts, of 1930 gained national press for eliminating natural light entirely, instead "embodying radically advanced ideas for scientific creation of artificial lighting, ventilation, and other working conditions."[8]

Faced with rising glass prices and environmental penalties, however, Chicago architects and developers at the turn of the century had few alternatives to windows and light courts until an economical alternative to daylighting presented itself. But the effectiveness and affordability of artificial lighting as an alternative to daylighting occurred rapidly in the city between 1908 and 1912. Although Chicago buildings had been wired for electric light since the early 1890s, three developments transformed this luxury service into a ubiquitous presence: first, electric rates and service policies underwent a dramatic transformation in Chicago; second, electric distribution and provision made gains in efficiency and reliability; and third, the global application of better-performing filaments between the 1908 GEM Lamp and the 1912 "Mazda" tungsten lamp meant that bulbs and fixtures became more reliable, more efficient, and more cost-effective than earlier carbon-filaments. These technical advances had immediate impacts on costs. The price of an incandescent bulb dropped from $1.10 in 1908 to $0.30 in 1914, while the cost

of electricity to illuminate that bulb for an hour dropped from two cents to a penny over the same period.[9] The effects of dropping prices were immediately apparent in commercial applications; the *Tribune* noted in 1910 that stores had begun illuminating both display windows and sidewalks even after closing time.[10] Offices also adopted greater levels of electric lighting, evidenced by the increase in recommended levels from three footcandles per work surface to ten or more.[11] By World War I, electric lighting had transformed office interiors. Smaller windows remained important primarily for *qualities* of light—views in particular. But the need for environmentally inefficient, costly plate glass windows to illuminate interiors passed with the realization of the affordable, reliable tungsten light bulb and cheap electricity to power it.[12]

THE CONCEALED FRAME

The functional and material influences on skyscraper skins in 1912 were, therefore, very different from those of fifteen years earlier. The abandonment of the aesthetically and conceptually compelling system of piers, spandrels, and windows developed by an earlier generation was seen as a tragedy only in hindsight, a judgment that has largely come through the interpretations of Frank Lloyd Wright and Sigfried Giedion. In Giedion's narrative the "School" that "strove to break through to pure forms, forms which would unite construction and architecture in an identical expression," was frustrated by the rise of mercantile classicism and the infestation of Chicago's honest striving by an invading Beaux-Arts influence.[13] There are numerous problems with this narrative, of course, in particular the gap between the popular reception of the Fair's aesthetics in the early 1890s and the appearance of the classical skyscraper in Chicago—perhaps the 1897 Stewart Building, by Burnham, though this remained an isolated example in Chicago until the Edison of 1907. If classicism was such a popular choice, this lag suggests that there were practical reasons why it could not be realized right away. And the long gap until neoclassical skyscrapers became the *norm*, rather than isolated examples—around 1911—leaves nearly two decades between the stylistic ideal claimed by Giedion and its wholesale adoption.

In Root's "Great Architectural Problem," design came about through an understanding of lighting and structural requirements, *after* which decisions were made about ornament and expression. We might ask whether the Beaux-Arts buildings that Giedion et al. lamented did not follow the same logic. Faced with a lighting equation that favored broad expanses of solid surface interrupted by smaller windows, the tension between solid and void that Yost and Twose had embraced in the 1890s disappeared. In its place lay a conundrum: how to treat a curtain wall that

was no longer mostly glass. The massive qualities of the Beaux-Arts found a proportionally agreeable matrix in these new, functionally derived skins.

These technical developments did not, alone, give rise to the classicization of the Chicago skyscraper; there were strong stylistic influences on local architecture in this direction, and these influences enjoyed a wide popular following. Classical themes emerged very quickly in civic buildings and in building programs "in which the limitations imposed upon an architect are by no means so stringent as those in business buildings," according to Montgomery Schuyler.[14] Neither electrification nor building codes nor a classical revival alone were enough to inform the Chicago Beaux-Arts skyscraper on its own. Rather, the combined push of material conditions and pull of aesthetic desire influenced the symmetrical compositions, massive solid appearances, and antique ornamental choices for these buildings, eventually precipitating a dominant design formula that would inform skyscrapers for a generation.

The Beaux-Arts method combined a rational approach to programming with a hierarchy of architectural expression and a palette of acceptable aesthetic choices. It preached neither willful composition nor strict functionalism, instead seeking a balance of programmatic solutions and structures within ordering principles borrowed from ancient examples. This approach, though,

could easily devolve into facile classical allusion. Perhaps the most colorful description of this was elaborated by Theodore Wells Piestch in 1899, in an article entitled "What the Beaux-Arts Training Means to the Architect" that placed the "French" method squarely between the poles of Italian facadism and British expressionism:

> [T]he architecture of Italy, France, and England have been humorously compared to the heads of three bald men. The first, an Italian, finding himself bald, dons a wig. The illusion is complete. . . . [R]eference here is had to many Italian buildings whose facades are mere *placages*.
>
> The second, the Frenchman, wishing to obviate the glare of a denuded cranium, deftly combs the longer hair from either side together. . . . There is an analogy here with French architectural composition in that we often find a part of the whole subordinated and sacrificed to the general harmony of the ensemble.
>
> The Englishman goes to no such painstaking. As he boldly shows his bald picked scalp to the world, so in building you will never find him hesitate to disclose with unblushing unconcern all the architectural family secrets of the interior, and stamp them with blunt frankness on the elevation.[15]

Frederick Baumann suggested that Chicago's traditions had followed precisely this "English school" in its emphasis on structural articulation, but an "English" emphasis on articulation was more work than the French habit of "contriving to cover."[16]

Finding a ready-made Roman solution that rationalized functional or material contradictions proved to be an expedient way of designing, and an understandably popular one in the time-strapped offices of many American architects. At its best, Beaux-Arts methodology could produce a Boston Public Library (1887–98), rich in allusions and spatial experience, but bland copying informed countless pastiches of typologies, facades, and elements that made it, in Montgomery Schuyler's words, "one of the greatest labor-saving inventions ever."[17] This repetitive, formulaic classicism is what Giedion and others found most offensive in the Beaux-Arts influence, even though it represented a dilution of the *Ecole*'s actual principles—of the clear *esquisse* and its disciplined resolution into supporting details and components.[18]

Such a combination of ornament and logic seemed a Chicago trait to critic Henry M. Hyde, who saw skyscrapers' combination of "utility" and "some degree of dignity, if not beauty" as fertile territory for the French method. In fact, Hyde noted, by 1901 there were numerous Chicago buildings that "stood for Beauty" according to

the Beaux-Arts system: the Art Institute (1893), the Illinois Trust and Savings Bank (1896), the Chicago National Bank (1902), the Illinois Theater (1900), the Federal Building (under construction, but complete by 1905), the Crerar Library (1898) and the Field Columbian Museum (planned at the time, but not completed until 1912) all represented for Hyde the tendency toward the "saner and simpler ideals" of the Beaux-Arts in the city.[19]

This list demonstrates the influence of the Beaux-Arts on Chicago architecture, but it is most notable for what it leaves out. The Art Institute, the Crerar Library, and the Field Museum were all low-rise cultural buildings; the Illinois Theater was a four-story auditorium, and the Federal Building was a monumental civic structure. The two commercial buildings mentioned by Hyde, the Illinois Trust and the Chicago National, were banks *without* office blocks above; the Illinois Trust two stories, Chicago National three. Thus, as late as 1901, Hyde could not find a skyscraper worth mentioning in his list of classical buildings in Chicago. While there were, by this point, office blocks that deployed classical ornament or flourishes—the Marquette, for instance—they would not have fulfilled his requirement for a thorough sense of "monumentality," being in his words mere "attractiveness combined with utility." The expressed frames that took over around this time, as shown in chapter 6, occasionally adopted elements

of classical language but their proper proportioning was limited by the large windows that competed for elevational space. Hyde felt that a truly Beaux-Arts structure, one that possessed the *character* of the classic and not merely its trappings, had to offer some measure of solidity. This was possible only in buildings that could eschew daylight, either for programmatic or economic reasons. Two- or three-story banks could be illuminated with skylights if their banking halls extended the full height of the building; hotels and clubs could afford the maintenance and service costs associated with artificial light during the day. But commercial buildings required vast quantities of daylight until about 1910, and thus the commercial skyscraper frustrated initial efforts to instantiate the solidity and monumental ideals of the Beaux-Arts character. In the words of A. N. Rebori (1886–1966), who had worked for Burnham and who would become one of the city's most ardent classicists: "It requires . . . but a casual study of the structural conditions upon which modern construction is dependent, to realize that the laws of Vignola were not drawn to solve such problems as those with which the designer starts out to illustrate them. Surely the difficulties are not lessened when classical detail is employed, for the moulding and ornaments, increasing with the module of measure, tend to sacrifice the space in the facade that is needed for light and air."[20]

Rebori implied that Burnham compromised by treating his early classical skyscrapers as more pretentiously ornamented versions of the expressed frame. Assuming that such ornament did not significantly impact lighting or construction cost, "the modern businessman," stated Rebori, "was not adverse to the expenditure of large sums of money for the assumed appearance of his building," since "attractiveness in general design add[ed] materially to the revenue productiveness of his enterprise."[21]

P. B. Wight noted that Burnham & Co.'s buildings in the years between the Stewart (1897) and Continental Bank (1913) adopted greater and greater solidity in response to Charles Jenkins's critique of the Reliance Building's flimsy "plate-glass foundations."[22] This reaction, said Wight, led to the Burnham's preference for more bulky piers, belying the narrower proportions of the steel within them. "[Burnham] seems to have satisfied the demands of his clients for big windows by building his main piers far apart," combining daylight and visual mass in wider, less structurally efficient bays, Rebori noted.[23] These more massive piers were merged with flush spandrels into flat grids, removing the articulation, vertical expression, and visual hierarchy that had defined the expressed frame. The solid elements of Burnham's facades merged into a single, unified block, more closely matching the visual proportions of the Beaux-Arts' compositional imperatives.

Burnham's friendship with Charles Follen McKim during the planning of the Columbian Exposition marked the flowering of his personal interest in classicism. But the Beaux-Arts also influenced the office through the group of partners that emerged after Atwood's death in 1896. Ernest R. Graham (1866–1936), a native of Lowell, Michigan, had come to Burnham's firm in 1888 with degrees from Coe College and Notre Dame, but little architectural training. He was assistant director of works during the Fair's construction and a trustworthy foil to the increasingly erratic Atwood.[24] After Atwood died and engineer E. C. Shankland retired in 1898, Burnham made Graham his sole partner. Graham acted as an organizer, manager, and marketing force, an arrangement that lasted ten years until, flush with work and with a staff approaching 200, Burnham and Graham promoted three other longtime employees—Peirce Anderson (1870–1924), Edward Probst (1870–1942), and H. J. White (1870–1936)—to partnership.[25] White and Probst rose through the drafting department and managed production of drawings and contracts.[26] Anderson had trained originally as an electrical engineer but went to Paris in the late 1890s to study at the *Ecole* on Burnham's suggestion, returning to Chicago and the lead design position in the firm in 1899. Anderson's design lieutenants were Peter Weber (1864–1923) and Frederick Dinkelberg (1862–1935). Born to a wealthy family in Lancaster, Pennsylvania, in 1859, Dinkelberg graduated from the Pennsylvania Academy of Fine Arts and joined Burnham's firm in 1892, designing several last minute pavilions for the Exposition.[27] Dinkelberg supported Anderson in championing the Beaux-Arts method, writing a neoclassical manifesto in *Inland Architect* in 1908.[28] He was credited with the interior of the Railway Exchange (1904) and the Flatiron Building (1907), two early examples of robust classicism in the firm's work, as well as the Conway Building (1912), which showed the style in full flower in the office during Burnham's final days.[29]

Burnham's partners integrated classical aesthetics and the structural frame using increasingly solid elevations and classical proportioning. This aesthetic was aided by the further development of enameled terra-cotta, which allowed facades in the white, cream, and buff palettes that French taste—if not archaeological evidence—demanded. While it had served well for the Reliance's neo-Gothic ornament, enameled terra-cotta also found a natural partner in the gleaming, classical aesthetics that marked Burnham & Co.'s work through its last decade.

CLASSICAL LANGUAGE AND THE FRAME: MERCHANT'S LOAN AND MARSHALL FIELD'S

Classicism in Chicago skyscrapers had begun with seeds of academic ornament that decorated the trabeated nature of the skyscraper frame with the details—if not the correct proportions—of Beaux-Arts classicism. Two buildings commissioned by Marshall Field and designed by Burnham & Co. show the opportunities and difficulties in matching classical ornament and expressed frame. Merchant's Loan and Trust (1901) and Marshall Field's rebuilt State Street store (1902, with later additions) were conceived as frames with applied ornament. Arguably this was a conceptual fit, since architectural mythology described typical classical ornament as arising from trabeated wood, and later stone, frames.

A key moment in matching classical aesthetics and the steel frame came with Burnham's commission for Merchant's Loan and Trust, Chicago's oldest bank (figures 7.1, 7.2). Marshall Field, one of the bank's directors, offered to construct a new building, using his own funds, on land at Clark and Adams that he owned and to lease the building to the bank. Field's parcel was a rectangle with one hundred feet of frontage on Clark and one hundred and eighty feet on Adams. Burnham carved a light well out of the northern edge of this lot, leaving a broad U-shape to distribute the offices. The bank was to oc-

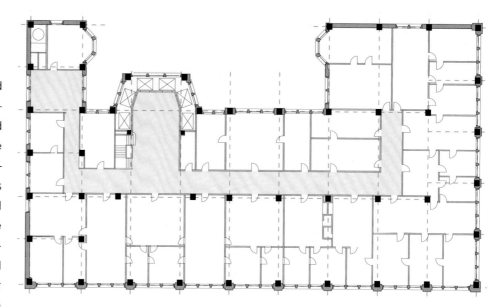

7.1 Merchant's Loan and Trust Building, corner of Clark and Adams Streets, D. H. Burnham & Co., 1901, plan. (Drawing by the author)

cupy the entire second floor, reached by a monumental stair and indicated from the street by enormous, almost square windows. The remainder of the plan called for railroad offices on the ground level and ten stories above "as lofty as the present building law will admit."[30] The banking hall was a feast of classically detailed marble, lighting, and furnishings, and while office tenants enjoyed slightly less elaborate finishes their accommodations were as rationally planned and as commodious as the banking hall. *Inland Architect* described the offices in terms that show the continuing need for daylight: "every office is an outside room. Those on the south side front on Adams street, on the east on Clark street, on the north and west on the open courts, which in-

sure a perpetual easement of light and air. There is not a dark room in the building. There are no dark corners or inaccessible offices."[31]

Merchant's Loan provided huge window openings for offices, double-hung in triple sets rather than in combinations of fixed and double-hung lights. The bulk of the facade was thus similar to contemporary work by Holabird & Roche, but Merchant's Loan was the beginning of the classical tide that would define Burnham's late commercial work. While its general appearance was "severely plain," in keeping with the utilitarian ethic of the day, its facades picked up opportunities for classical references where they could. The steel frame was wrapped with terra-cotta fireproofing and a granite veneer;

7.2 Merchant's Loan and Trust Building, view from southeast. (Contemporary postcard, collection of the author)

windows and spandrels were then set back, leaving the oversized verticals to run continuously from the third to tenth floors. Granite was also used for mullions between windows instead of cast iron, further emphasizing the vertical grain and making the windows appear as if they were carved from a stone mass.

Aside from these subtle articulations, however, Merchant's Loan carried nearly all of its classical allusions at the base, top, and corners. The base was rendered in granite pilasters that supported a frieze and architrave, and the capitals atop the pilasters were clearly Tuscan. The cornice was classical, too, and its corners, like those of Burnham & Root's earlier masonry buildings or Sullivan's more recent work, were overemphasized to add visual weight. Set against the plain but articulated grid of the main office floors, however, these devices all demonstrate the transitional nature of Merchant's Loan—a rigorously planned building in which opportunities for linking the structural discipline of its plan and elevation within a Beaux-Arts composition were tentatively but thoughtfully explored. Such an assessment came out in *Inland*'s coverage: "To plan columns and cornices and swelling fronts with a view to the impressiveness of exterior is, and doubtless should be, the waking dream of the true lover of architecture. But to construct an enduring and dignified pile at the intersection of two leading thoroughfares in a great city, with both exterior and interior of harmonious and appropriate design, with ornament subordinated to utility and with every detail drawn to the line of commercial advantage—that is the hard technical task of the twentieth-century architect."[32]

This is supported by the later analysis of Rebori, who described the stripped classicism of Merchant's Loan as a key moment in the firm's development: "The architects do not subordinate the economic efficiency and productiveness of this building to any exterior effect, nor do they subject convenience in any degree to the exigencies of mere appearance. They simply present a solution of the problem in which classic details are successfully adapted to the needs of a building devoted to strictly commercial functions."[33]

Marshall Field also employed Burnham for the reconstruction of his flagship retail store on State Street between 1900 and 1907, with similar results (figure 7.3). By 1890, Field's occupied the entire frontage of State between Washington and Randolph, in storefronts, mid-rise buildings, and an Atwood-designed building at Washington and Wabash constructed in anticipation of the 1892 Fair. Atwood's annex was the Loop's strongest example yet of monumental classicism applied to a commercial structure. But it had been a failure because of its dim interiors, and there was no suggestion that it might form the basis for the larger project. Instead, Burnham took a systematic approach that resulted in an exterior similar to Merchant's Loan: a granite-clad frame designed around functional, light-gathering apertures, articulated with stone mullions to heighten the sense of mass and classical elements at the base (particularly around the entry), top, and corners. The result was a stone-clad frame that emphasized unity and mass rather than articulation and tension, but that remained every bit as functional as the terra-cotta or brick and cast-iron facades of other expressed frame buildings. Inside, a sumptuous full-height interior court provided lighting, similar to the banking hall of Merchant's Loan yet extending for multiple stories.

The second and third phases of Field's expansion also relied on light courts and large windows. Even in 1905, the *Tribune* reported that a key feature of the building was that "exterior construction affords the largest amount of light possible," although this was supplemented by electricity.[34] While subsequent phases "conformed in outward appearance" to the first, changes on the interior reflected rapid developments in retail and construction technology. The 1906–1907 extension, which replaced Field's original building at State and Washington, contained a second, even more elaborate atrium, topped by a Tiffany glass ceil-

7.3 Marshall Field & Co. Store, State Street between Washington and Randolph Streets, D. H. Burnham & Co., 1902 + additions. (*120 Photographic Views of Chicago*, Rand McNally, 1909)

ing claimed to be the world's largest. Field, who died in January 1906, never saw his store as a unified building, but by 1914 his empire had rebuilt the entire city block, offering over a million and a half square feet of retail space at a total cost of over two million dollars. The result was a mass of trabeated granite that struck a balance between classical expression and functionality. Burn-

7.4 First National Bank Building, corner of Dearborn and Monroe Streets, D. H. Burnham & Co., 1903, view from southeast. (Contemporary postcard, collection of the author)

MASS VERSUS FRAME: FIRST NATIONAL BANK AND COMMERCIAL NATIONAL BANK

Burnham's First National Bank of 1903 and Commercial National Bank of 1907 were important transitional steps from articulated frame to solid mass. Given the success of Merchant's Loan and Trust, it is no surprise that other financial institutions now used Burnham to deploy the same combination of efficient planning and ornament that referenced solidity, tradition, and conservative taste. First National Bank had a long history in Chicago and a twenty-year tenancy in a post-fire building at the corner of Dearborn and Monroe.[35] Burnham's involvement began with a small project to overhaul and expand this building in 1899, but as rental rates continued to recover after the depression the bank contemplated a larger venture. With explicit references to Burnham's building for Merchant's Loan, the bank announced in December 1901 that it would construct "an office building to exceed in size and outlay any structure in the West," investing somewhere between four and five million dollars to provide a combination of banking, administrative, and speculative office space. This was the most ambitious commercial construction project in Chicago since the Auditorium. It occupied two-thirds of the half-block along Monroe between Dearborn and Clark and rose to seventeen stories. The footprint—two hundred feet on Dearborn

and over two hundred and thirty feet on Monroe, including the site of Burnham & Root's Montauk Block—was large even by Chicago standards, and the real estate transaction completing the site was the largest in Chicago history.[36]

First National's plan was developed around a full light court and divided into eleven bays on Monroe and nine along Dearborn (figures 7.4, 7.5). This translated to a long U-shaped block of regular bays and a service bay of elevators and toilet rooms enclosing the western end of the light court. A racetrack corridor provided access to offices on each floor and connected the elevator banks with an entry on Dearborn. Offices were thus arrayed along the three major open fronts, with just a few focused on the light court.[37] First National's exterior was similar to Merchant's Loan and Marshall Field's, with a shaft of office floors rendered in a classically articulated frame. Designer Peirce Anderson took the additional step of setting spandrel panels flush with the vertical piers while pulling back stone mullions from the resulting plane. This emphasized the building's punched stone mass. But these were subtle distinctions compared to the treatment of the base and cornice. Where Merchant's Loan and Marshall Field's both punctuated a rigorous grid of structural expression with subsidiary classical ornament, First National took the additional step of incorporating purely compositional arcades at both the banking

ham's replacement of cast-iron mullions with stone, as at Merchant's Loan, represented a subtle hint toward more monumental compositions. But aside from this there was little to distinguish Burnham's expressed frames from those of Holabird & Roche—or even Sullivan—save for the appearance of applied cornices, entries, and stringcourses that telegraphed a more classically derived composition.

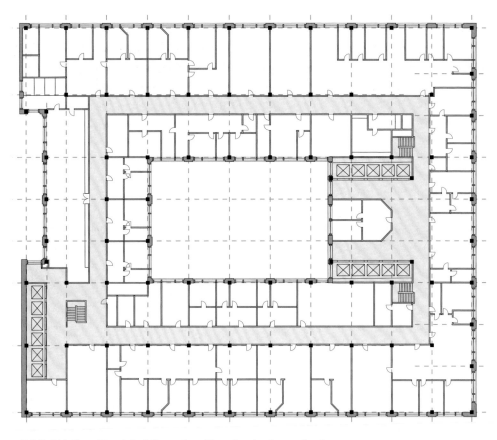

7.5 First National Bank Building, plan. (Drawing by the author)

hall and attic levels. These arches broke up the vertical bulk of its elevations and provided a robust visual "cap" below the cornice. Though the arches appeared facile to critics, they accentuated only the top and base stories—a limited approach that was arguably in line with Sullivan's recommendations for articulation at a skyscraper's top and base. Between these, First National's office block remained a cellular composition of pier, spandrel, mullion, and window, albeit one rendered with heavier choices in ornament and articulation.

Burnham and Anderson's use of classical forms in the service of commerce found its greatest expression yet in First National's interior. The entry from Dearborn passed through the central three bays of the facade and opened to a shallow, wide marble staircase that rose to a double-height banking hall on the second floor. The effect was "more than impressive," reported *Inland Architect* in 1905, praising it as a long-awaited "adaptation of the laws of art to the modern business structure." Later critics felt differently. "This

building," wrote Carl Condit of the First National Bank's emergent ornamental program "makes us feel that the Chicago school existed in vain."[38] Such critical focus on the building's classical atmosphere overshadowed its structural and constructional accomplishment. It was taller than all but a handful of downtown structures, and its ten thousand tons of steel were far more than in any other Chicago building. The phasing of the construction had posed significant challenges for its general contractor, John Griffiths, and its steel erector, Charles Volkmann, who set the steelwork for the final phase in an astonishing fifty days.[39]

The Commercial Bank, completed in 1908, was one story taller than First National but on a smaller footprint. Its skin—granite for the first four floors and matching semiglazed terra-cotta above—was detailed in a restrained classical style that was Burnham and Anderson's most solid facade yet. The ten-foot-tall candelabras in its banking hall suggest that it also marked the greatest reliance yet by a commercial block on electric lighting.[40] The bank was not, however, fully electrified. The banking hall, located on the second story, relied on a sixty- by one-hundred-foot skylight to supplement the candelabras, and above the skylight a light court lined in enameled brick still channeled daylight to interior offices. Its more expressive classical language at the base and top echoed Henry

7.6 Commercial Bank, corner of Adams and Clark Streets, D. H. Burnham & Co., 1907, view from southwest. (*120 Photographic Views of Chicago*, Rand McNally, 1909)

Cobb's Post Office, completed in 1905 across Adams Street.[41] Yet the Commercial Bank's office floors, too, went one step further than the balanced grids of First National Bank. While the facades on First National read largely as a classicized grid that hovered between an expressed frame and a punched block, there was no such ambiguity

to the Commercial Bank, which was clearly a mass into which windows were punched. Its corner piers of stone veneer with single punched windows at each story, further emphasized this reading at the expense of views from offices within.[42]

Burnham's office was not the only firm to experiment with the marriage of classical aesthetics and the skeletal proportions of the steel frame, but their buildings were widely considered more successful than others. E. R. Krause's 1906 Majestic Building on Monroe deployed lavish terra-cotta ornament—described charitably by *Inland* as "unusually ornate"—over its twenty stories, though these excesses were related to the large commercial theater at its base.[43] Other buildings that showed a gradual tilt away from the expressed frame and toward more solid, ornamented facades included the 1907 American Trust by Jarvis Hunt (1859–1941) at the corner of Clark and Monroe across the street from First National, and Shepley, Rutan, and Coolidge's 1908 Corn Exchange and 1911 Harris Trust.

BURNHAM'S FINAL WORKS: CLASSICISM AND THE SKYSCRAPER CITY BEAUTIFUL

Four large neoclassical office blocks designed by Burnham's office around the time of his death in 1912—People's Gas (1911), the Insurance Exchange (1912), the Conway (1913), and the Continental and Commercial Bank (1913)—rep-

resented a full deployment of Beaux-Arts aesthetics to the large commercial skyscraper, in line with the classical vision of Burnham and Bennett's 1909 Plan of Chicago. Where First National and the Commercial Bank had balanced the application of classically derived ornament with an open elevational frame, the material and illuminatory logic of the building skin had changed completely by the time of People's Gas. This building and its contemporaries show a definitive move toward thicker, deeper exterior walls, fully electrified interiors, smaller windows, and more extensive ornament on broader solid elevational planes. There is little doubt that the firm's classicism was encouraged and reinforced by the reception accorded the 1909 Plan. But even the Commercial Bank's spandrels did not permit more than light rustication on their surfaces, and earlier, more attenuated facades by the office—Merchant's Bank, say—were limited in their ornamental fields to base stories and cornices. By 1911, however, with lighting largely accomplished with more cost-effective electric fixtures, windows could be even smaller, leaving larger areas of solid stone and terracotta that allowed for a greater profusion of classical ornament.

These four late Burnham and Company buildings were all constructed to the city's height limit of two hundred and sixty feet, in either twenty or twenty-one stories. All were steel

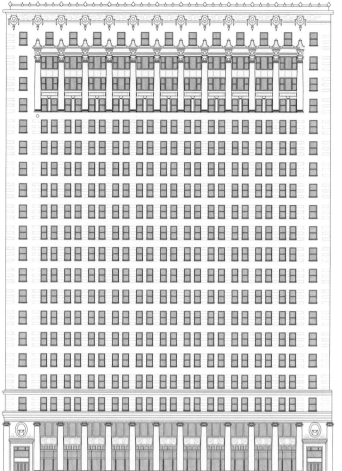

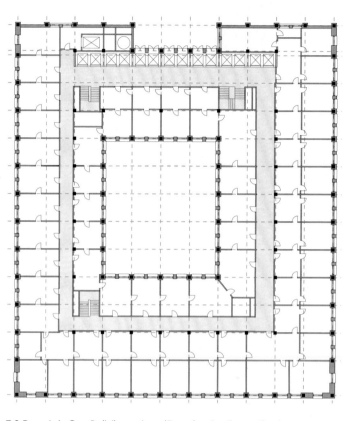

7.7 People's Gas Building, corner of Michigan Avenue and Adams Street, D. H. Burnham & Co., 1911, elevation. (Drawing by the author)

7.8 People's Gas Building, plan. (Drawing by the author)

framed, and all had approximately the same quarter-block dimensions of between one hundred and sixty and two hundred feet square, although the Continental and Commercial Bank and eventually the Insurance Exchange doubled these to a half-block. All four were built around light courts, as earlier quarter-block buildings by the firm had been. This might suggest that their reliance on electricity was incomplete, as the wasted rental volume of this strategy remained considerable. But while lighting had progressed rapidly, these buildings still relied on cross-ventilation for cooling. Light courts provided access to fresh air by leaving narrow cross sections through which air could flow through transom panels above office doors. This continued to justify the large central voids as environmental devices, though the onset of mechanical ventilation soon challenged this long-standing feature of skyscraper construction.

People's Gas, the first of these blocks to be built, represented a colossal undertaking—over 8,700,000 cubic feet, accommodating over 1500 offices at a cost of over $3,000,000 (figures 7.7–7.9).[44] Construction was phased so that an existing corner building could remain occupied while the northern two-thirds of the new building were being

7.9 People's Gas Building, view from southeast. (*120 Photographic Views of Chicago*, Rand McNally, 1909)

built, and this defined the dimensions of its office wings and light court.[45] This complexity was masked, however, by an imposing facade. Elevations were treated as monolithic blocks of glazed terra-cotta speckled gray to match the granite used for the first three floors. Windows were paired and set deeply within the thick facade. Nothing could be further from the dialogues between horizontals and verticals found in Merchant's Bank, for instance, suggesting

that the office block was now being rethought as a carved, lithic mass.

At the top and at street level, heavy stringcourses framed ranks of ten columns—granite Ionic at the street level and terra-cotta Corinthian above. The street facade's deep colonnades on Michigan and Adams Streets presented a telling conundrum for the engineer, Joachim Giaver (1856–1925). While these forty-six-inch granite columns would have been structural in an earlier generation, Giaver balked at the idea of supporting seventeen stories atop stone.[46] Thus, the walls above, and with them the edges of each floor slab, were carried on steel columns resting on story-deep cantilevers that sit atop the granite columns, transferring the floor loads above to the next lines of columns. This complex structure failed to impress engineers or critics—Peter B. Wight believed the cantilevers were wasted money, while Harriett Monroe found them a hallmark of stylistic relativism. People's Gas "lifts a well-proportioned assemblage of diapered wall and gleaming windows above its granite colonnade" that was valid, she allowed ironically, only "if one accepts the 'classic' convention of truss-supported Ionic columns."[47]

Burnham's Insurance Exchange marked a continuation of these technical and stylistic formulas but with a layout that portended important changes (figures 7.10, 7.11).[48] Burnham's initial plans for the site showed

a block of twenty stories, each of nearly thirty-five thousand square feet around a light court. The structural plan matched that of the People's Gas building, with three concentric squares of column lines: one at the light court, one at the exterior wall, and one running halfway between. While earlier buildings had a central corridor along this middle column, plans of the Insurance Exchange published in 1915 show that this arrangement was modified on some floors to provide deeper offices accessed by single-loaded corridors along the light court itself.[49] Office depths in this plan were thus much greater than those of People's Gas or the Railway Exchange—indeed they were far greater than the proportions dictated for proper daylighting in Root's "Great Architectural Problem." Although this arrangement may have represented only a variation in a more typical double-loaded plan, it provides evidence that sometime before 1915 deeper office plans had become economically viable. The "light" court, again, remained an important component of environmental strategy, and the *total* depth of the floor plate from edge to edge remained limited by the need for cross-ventilation. But the corridor's location in these plans along the court suggests that the attraction of rented space to windows no longer governed office layout. Outside, the Insurance Exchange continued the solid block ideal of the People's Gas Building but

7.10 Insurance Exchange Building, 175 W. Jackson, D. H. Burnham & Co., 1913, perspective view from northeast. (Art Institute of Chicago)

with subtler ornament that made sparing use of enameled terra-cotta. The main block's windows were contained within a grid of pronounced verticals and recessed spandrels in enameled brick, though this rhythm stopped at the bulkier corners. Colonnades at the top and base continued the framing effect of People's Gas, but their more straightforward positioning eliminated the expense of cantilevering the entire exterior wall. Chamfered corners made allusions to French precedents, but also solved a clearance problem with adjacent elevated rail tracks.

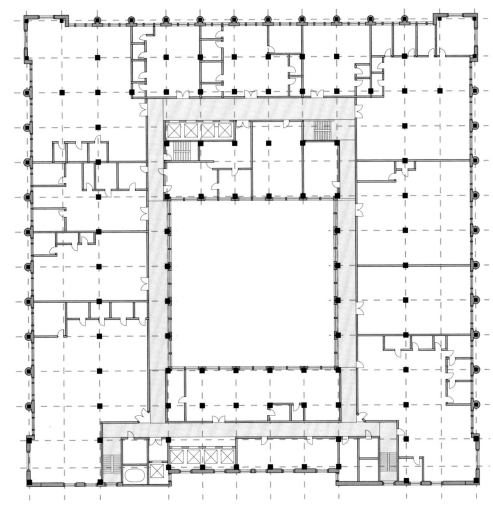

7.11 Insurance Exchange Building, plan. (Drawing by the author)

structural piers. Burnham & Co.'s commitment to a distinctly French classicism was evident at the building's corners, which were rounded as in Second Empire blocks. The facades were divided into three-story bands by light scrollwork and given a slight hierarchy by blank panels beneath and in line with each window—a two-dimensional version of the spandrel and column dialogues in earlier, expressed frame structures.

The largest Loop building by Burnham & Co. was the Continental and Commercial Bank, occupying the half block bounded by Adams, Quincy, Wells, and LaSalle streets and announced in 1911, before restrictive height limits were passed that spring. The client was a hybrid of two Burnham & Co. building tenants—the Commercial, which had moved to its headquarters a block east in 1908, and the Continental, which had occupied the old Insurance Exchange Building across LaSalle Street from the Rookery. When the two banks merged, neither building proved large enough for the combined trust and savings departments, but Rand McNally's planned move from its Burnham & Root building of 1890 opened up a block-long site along Adams. When its footprint of just under 53,400 square feet was multiplied to the code limit, the twenty planned stories offered over 25 acres of commercial space, besting First National Bank for the largest commercial building in Chicago and becoming, it

A similar approach informed the Conway Building, announced in 1912 for the corner of Clark and Washington, the site of Cobb and Frost's Opera House (figures 7.12, 7.13). Financed by the Marshall Field Estate and completed in 1913, the Conway ranked just behind the Insurance Exchange in area and, at $3,500,000, cost. It was a reiteration of the light court and racetrack corridor arrangement, with elevators grouped at the back of the site and stairs at each corner of the light court. On the exterior, however, the Conway featured two new developments. Its fenestration marked an intermediate position between the heavily ornamented People's Gas and the more plainly detailed Insurance Exchange, pairing double-hung windows between was claimed, the largest bank building in the world.[50] Burnham & Co.'s design was an expansion of its classical block type. Office floors were stretched versions of standard light-court schemes, with elevators and stairs paired in each corner and a double-loaded corridor through the middle of each leg. The prospective customer entered on the lot's short sides, between elevator cores and through a corridor lined with retail banking facilities. Marble staircases led to the second-floor banking hall—by far the largest and most elaborate in the city—where tellers and bankers faced inward and daylight streamed in from a barrel-vaulted skylight four stories above. On the exterior, the lower three stories contained granite columns hollowed out to receive not only steelwork but also fire-protective concrete, visually echoing the firm's nearby Illinois Trust building and eliminating the costly cantilevers of People's Gas.[51]

Along with a 1913–1914 annex for Marshall Field's, also by Burnham & Co., these buildings were a distillation of the light court and racetrack plan pioneered by the Rookery. Their exteriors, however, displayed a new formula of less daylighting and more classical ornament. Although window sizes, groupings, and proportions changed from project to project—large and paired in the Marshall Field Annex, for instance, but tightly delimited and individual in People's Gas—these elevations all developed curtain walls into massive

7.12 Conway Building, corner of Clark and Washington Streets, D. H. Burnham & Co., 1913, view from northeast. (Contemporary postcard, collection of the author)

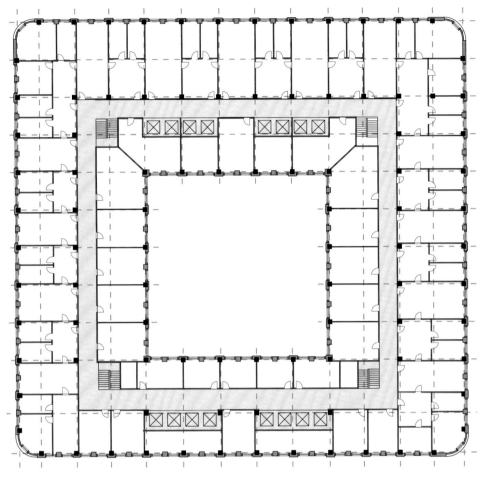

7.13 Conway Building, plan. (Drawing by the author)

blocks rather than articulated frames. Classical expression met a synergetic partner in the functionally solid facade, while the development of enameled terra-cotta could achieve stonelike effects at low cost. Material, function, and aesthetics combined to produce a repeatable, economical, and—at least according to the popular tastes of the day—aesthetically successful type. Burnham & Co. designed versions of this type not only in Chicago but also in Philadelphia, New York, and dozens of cities throughout North America.

DEATH OF DANIEL BURNHAM, JUNE 1, 1912

As crews began demolishing Burnham & Root's Rand-McNally Building to make way for the Continental and Commercial Bank in late May 1912, Burnham, who had been vacationing in Heidelberg, Germany, lay gravely ill with ulcerative colitis. He died on June 1, and the Chicago press made a quick connection between his passing and the demise of Rand-McNally, a building still among his best known achievements.[52] *Architectural Record* published a memorial to Burnham in August 1912 that included tributes from architects throughout the world, and it began work on a massive retrospective issue that was published in 1915.[53] His obituaries cemented Burnham's reputation as an administrator, a bon vivant, and a Beaux-Arts enthusiast. Cass Gilbert remarked on his "boyish and sophomoric" love of classicism, but believed that it had always been tempered by a willingness to tackle "practical problems." Peter B. Wight, Burnham's early employer, agreed.[54] Even Frank Lloyd Wright, who saw Burnham as a nemesis to Sullivan's legacy, grudgingly admitted that Burnham had "made masterful use of the methods and men of his time to produce what seemed to him the nearest thing to architecture commercially expedient." "He was not a creative architect," concluded Wright, "but he was a great man."[55]

The assessment of Burnham as a gifted administrator but a naive enthusiast for a facile, popular style has flavored history's view of his buildings. If his stylistic choices were convenient, however, and if they played to contemporary tastes while failing to further the rich tectonic expressions of Sullivan or Holabird & Roche's buildings of the day, they nevertheless presented a valid integration of technology and aesthetic refinement. Their popularity with clients, users, and the public suggests that Burnham understood aesthetics as an important function on its own. The same "branding" that had plastered hotels, banks, and clubs with classicizing or antique veneers found an economically valid expression on the larger facades of commercial offices, and Burnham worked toward reasonable accommodations between a style ratified by European tastes and the interior requirements.

It was Burnham's gift for associating with talented designers and engineers that proved to be his greatest legacy, and his firm was quickly reorganized. Heir to Burnham's administrative talents was Ernest Graham, and the office was renamed Graham, Burnham, & Co. Peirce Anderson controlled design, maintaining the company's allegiance to Beaux-Arts models; Edward Probst ran the drafting room; and H. J. White managed engineering.[56] A younger generation of draftsmen included Rebori, Thomas Tallmadge (1876–1940), and Alfred P. Shaw (1895–1970). More technically minded designers such as Sigurd Naess (1887–1970) came to prominence for their ability to continue the firm's tradition of effective problem solving. Finally, Charles Murphy

(1890–1985), who had come to the firm as Burnham's secretary, became Graham's protégé and absorbed the management skills that had distinguished the office. Burnham's two sons, Daniel H. Burnham Jr. (1886–1961) and Hubert Burnham (1885–1969), initially shared the partnership with Graham, but when a five-year agreement expired in 1917 they were forced out and opened their own firm, Burnham Brothers. After the split, Graham, Burnham, & Co. was hastily rechristened Graham, Anderson, Probst, and White. After World War I this firm continued Burnham's theme of the classically derived, white terracotta commercial block, notably in the twin porticos of the Federal Reserve and the Continental Illinois at the base of LaSalle Street and in the partially realized scheme for Union Station. The reconstituted firm would gradually expand its vocabulary and challenge Chicago's restrictive zoning envelope with more towering buildings, one of which would form the city's most iconic image at the foot of a revived and reconstructed Michigan Avenue.

CONCLUSIONS

The concealed frame was a cogent response to cultural and technical factors in skyscraper construction between 1905 and 1914. While it posed a far different—and to many, a less progressive—model than the curtain walls of the 1890s or the expressed frames of

the early 1900s, the concealed frame was as technically rigorous a response to the economics of structure, materials, daylighting, and climate control as the earlier, more heralded buildings. The introduction of Beaux-Arts styling adds confusion to the narrative—an apparently *arriere-garde* choice of ornament and expression seems to contradict the prescience of the earlier structures. But the classical skyscrapers of 1907–1914 were practical solutions first and Beaux-Arts monuments second. They relied on the same structural and cladding principles as their immediate predecessors, but the functional prerogatives of their exteriors—reduced need for daylighting and the continued concern for environmental separation—led to different window proportions and a different base on which to deploy ornament. This era saw other technical advances in elevators, construction techniques, and fire safety that challenged old assumptions about height limitations and the economics of building taller. If the pattern of development from 1892–1913 showed the refinement of a code-mandated envelope into greater and greater spatial and lighting efficiency, the major developments in the decades following returned to the quest for height that had preoccupied architects, builders, engineers, and developers before the strict limitations of the 1893 Code.

Chapter 8
Power and Height: The Electric Skyscraper, 1920–1934

For thirty years after the implementation of the 1893 Code, Chicago skyscrapers were limited by absolute height restrictions. As a result, their designs were focused on making their limited volumes as efficient as possible—first, by bringing in as much daylight as possible while maximizing floor area, and, later, by developing exteriors as environmentally effective solid skins. While structural developments were important—particularly the distillation of wind-bracing systems into efficient moment frames—Chicago's strict limits foreclosed any serious attempt to build higher than 180 or, later, 260 feet. Instead, intensive research and development into taller skyscrapers occurred in New York, where the 1913 Woolworth Building by Cass Gilbert reached an astonishing 785 feet. But after World War I, a loophole in Chicago's ordinance that permitted "Spires, Towers, and Domes" sparked a

controversy and then a race for new heights. The sudden appearance of the 556-foot Chicago Temple in the center of the Loop agitated property owners, architects, and engineers into a new quest for height—at first within the limits of the spire and tower loophole and then to the relaxed requirements of a new zoning ordinance that was tailor-made for a new, powered skyscraper era. The interwar electric skyscrapers arrived during a record-setting real estate boom, and they transformed a skyline of flat cornices into an array of ornamented towers.

POWER AND HEIGHT—
EFFECTS ON BUILDING MASSING

Electric lighting led to changes in building skins by 1912, but developments in electricity and internal combustion also influenced skyscraper design through two important developments—pneu-

matic power for construction and electric power for elevator operation (figure 8.1). These innovations, along with the almost unlimited reach promised by caisson foundations, eventually pushed the city to allow taller buildings.

Although steel components were machine cut, drilled, or riveted in shops, they were still assembled by hand on site as late as 1913. Speed increased with experience, but manual riveting dictated the pace of steelwork, which held up other tasks. By 1912, however, more efficient pneumatic tools replaced hand hammers and drills, speeding construction. Heavy compressors had to be maintained and fueled, requiring extensive space on the ground. But the hoses they pressurized could be strung across a job site, promising unlimited reach to powered tools. Pneumatic power was safer than steam, and it was cleaner and more reliable than horsepower. Most importantly, it fomented what builder C. I. Henrikson termed a "revolution" in steel construction. "To the question, 'How can I get this work or this job to the machine,'" he noted, "the pneumatic tool answers, 'bring the tool to the work.'"[1] For riveting, that tool was the pneumatic hammer, a device held by a single worker that used air pressure to power a rapidly oscillating piston. It drove rivets more quickly, accurately, and safely than manual hammers. Pneumatically powered riveting and drilling had important implications for building height, too. Mechanically riveted joints were tighter and thus more rigid, translating into higher allowable stress per rivet.[2] The Woolworth Building was among the first to use pneumatic riveting in New York, and it set records not only for building height but also for speed of steel erection, which was completed within just eight months.[3]

Faster construction, however, did not guarantee a more functional building. Here, too, power played a role in colonizing greater heights. While hydraulic elevators proved acceptable for buildings under ten stories, for taller buildings they proved problematically slow—the upper floors of Burnham & Root's 1892 Masonic Temple, for example, were entirely abandoned by 1909 because of lethargic elevator service.[4] Electric companies, however, saw markets in the provision of elevator power alongside lighting current, and they

8.1 Pneumatic riveting. (*Scientific American*)

strategically encouraged faster, electrically driven lifts. The worm gear drum made its first appearance in 1890, and over the next decade it displaced hydraulic systems in taller buildings.[5] It relied on a motor designed to haul a fully loaded car, however, and was therefore geared not for speed but power, which was wasted on a typical load of just two or three persons. The electricity needed to start and stop such large motors made these systems costly to operate and they were only marginally faster than hydraulic elevators.

In 1903, though, the Otis Company introduced a new traction system that relied not on the capacity of the motor alone but on the balance between a loaded cab and a dedicated counterweight.[6] These offsetting loads were suspended at the opposite ends of a cable that was wrapped around a rotating cylinder, or sheave, at the top of a shaft. By adjusting the size of the sheaves, a small, high-speed motor did not have to lift the *full* weight of the system (counterweight plus cab) but the *balanced* weight of the two (counterweight minus cab). By 1908, such systems were twice as efficient as traditional hydraulic elevators in terms of power consumption per pound of load, and they were also quicker. As a result, so-called "gearless traction" systems quickly overtook hydraulic and worm-gear elevators for tall building applications.[7]

New elevator systems also promised advances in safety. To arrest a car falling from skyscraper height, Otis developed electromagnetic wheels spun by auxiliary cables fixed to both cab and shaft. If a falling car reached a dangerous speed, the magnet's coil would energize, and its current would trip a contact switch, releasing a magnetically held brake. Though complex, these "governor switches" proved reliable.[8] Other safety features included circuit breakers that prevented motors from running too fast and that shut down the system if cabs became misaligned. The electrification of elevators also allowed them to be programmed through a network of magnetic switches. Cars arriving at an assigned stop could trigger accurately placed magnets that would automatically bring them to a level stop, a first step in eliminating elevator operators. The Singer Building in New York, completed in 1908, used traction elevators to service its record-breaking forty-seven floors, proving that the new system was limited only by cable length and weight. A burst of tall building construction in New York followed, but in Chicago height limitations had not kept pace with technical advances.[9]

HEIGHT LIMITS AND THE BUILDING CODE—1918–1922

Chicago developers submitted more applications for exceptions to the building ordinance in the economic boom following World War I, suggesting that height limits were politically malleable. Had architects had the *ability* to build taller buildings, these challenges might well have come far earlier. Instead, the city's limits tended to formalize heights past which construction became less economical anyway. As buildings were powered past the sixteen-story restriction of the 1890s, the Code's limits rose with them fitfully, depending on the makeup of the city council and the influence of property owners. After an increase to 260 feet, or twenty stories, in 1902, limits fell to 200 feet in 1911, and were then raised to 260 feet in the better economy of 1921.[10] Throughout these changes the exception for towers, domes, and spires allowed such elements to be built "on the roofs of buildings" provided they did not take up more than one-fourth of the building's street frontage, contain more than 3,600 square feet, take up more than 15 percent of the building's total area, or rise beyond 400 feet.[11] Architects were slow to catch on to the potential of this formula, and Richard Schmidt's 394-foot Montgomery Ward Tower (1899) remained the only downtown structure to exploit it until the early 1920s (figure 8.2).

There was, however, pent-up demand for new downtown office space after the break in construction surrounding World War I, particularly as the city began implementing key elements of Burnham & Bennett's 1909 Plan of Chicago. The construction of the Michigan Avenue Bridge in 1920 and the start of construction on a riverside esplanade promised new transportation links, new territory for commercial construction, and a fresh image for the north and west borders of the Loop. The country's postwar economic surge fueled new business growth in the city, encouraging larger and higher-class investments, contributing to a record-breaking building binge of over one hundred and forty million dollars of construction in 1922. A more efficient, data-driven approach to tall building development recognized difficulties in building higher; additional floors meant bigger steel, which meant more weight for the lower floors to support, larger foundations, and more complex elevatoring.[12] But by the 1920s calculations suggested that despite such difficulties the maximum return for buildings in the Loop would occur between fifty and sixty-five stories. With a restriction of just twenty floors, speculators in Chicago now felt cheated out of skyward territory that promised further profit.[13]

Chicago developers and builders had another, less objective reason to push for higher buildings. The city was badly "out-towered" by the Woolworth Building, which not only set a new record for height, but also a new standard for architectural expression. "By its emphasis on vertical lines," wrote Harriet Monroe, its Gothic style rendered in terra-cotta or stone "would seem to lend itself more readily to skyscraping architecture" than the just-completed classical blocks by Burnham & Co. Even critics who saw the Gothic as

decadent or unsophisticated had to admit that Chicago classicism was, as one put it, "Greece built high on Gothic steel." There were also practical considerations that doomed certain classical elements. Heavy cornices, a typical Beaux-Arts response to the strict height limit, presented serious dangers if water corroded anchors or began to pry them loose by freezing.[14] While critics such as Monroe may well have preferred the Gothic's promise of "grace and continuity of line," falling stonework contributed to the image of the classical skyscraper as an outdated trope.

The Woolworth's most direct influence on Chicago architecture came with William Wrigley Jr.'s headquarters for his chewing gum company, designed by Graham, Anderson, Probst, and White and built in 1921 at the head of the new Michigan Avenue Bridge (figure 8.3). Wrigley had purchased the unassuming site in 1918, betting on the new bridge to open the industrial area on the north side of the river to commercial interests. The north and south legs of Michigan Avenue were misaligned by roughly 60 feet, which made Wrigley's site strikingly visible from the south. GAPW's design filled the then maximum 200-foot block, but it was topped with a spire based on the Giralda Tower of the Seville Cathedral. Unoccupied save for a clock and an observation deck, the tower was the first Loop structure taller than 260 feet since Montgomery Ward, and at 398 feet it was the tallest in the

8.2 Montgomery Ward (Tower) Building, 6 N. Michigan Avenue, Richard Schmidt, 1901, view from southwest. (Contemporary postcard, collection of the author)

city. The Wrigley Building's most striking features, however, were the two hundred high-powered incandescent projectors mounted on adjacent buildings, throwing over twenty-five million candlepower onto its facades and making the building visible—indeed, unavoidable—from the riverfront and Michigan Avenue. This nighttime display was sure evidence of electricity's new dominance in skyscraper design.[15] The Lon-

8.3 Wrigley Building, 410 N. Michigan Avenue, Graham, Anderson, Probst, and White, 1921, view from southeast. (Contemporary postcard, collection of the author)

don Guarantee Insurance Company, designed by Alfred Alschuler (1876–1940) and constructed directly across the river in 1923, followed a similar approach to the Wrigley, rising to 260 feet on its irregular footprint and ending with a shorter, classically allusive ornamental tower that marked it on the riverfront skyline (figure 8.4).[16] By the time of London Guarantee's completion, however, the rules governing skyscraper composition and height had been aggressively confronted and were on the verge of being completely recast.

The most provocative challenge to the outdated height limit was the Chicago Temple, designed by Holabird & Roche. Chicago's downtown Methodist congregation occupied one of the most commercially desirable corners of the Loop at Washington and Clark, and church leadership sought ways to combine new worship facilities with a development that would share in the accelerating real estate market.[17] In March 1922, they announced an ambitious scheme to replace their 1872 church with a skyscraper that would house a twelve-hundred-seat sanctuary at street level and twenty-one stories of first-class office space above, surmounted by a spire "of ecclesiastical design" to rise to the city's absolute height limit of four hundred feet (figure 8.5). The preliminary design was strikingly Gothic and similar to Holabird & Roche's University Club on Michigan Avenue (1909), but with offices designed to "rival in modernness those of other buildings."[18]

This initial scheme stayed within the City's height restriction—barely. But a political scrape with City Hall in April 1922 had dramatic consequences for the project and for skyscraper regulation throughout the city. With ceremonies for wrecking the old church scheduled for May 1, the city's Building Commissioner, Charles Bostrom, announced on April 27 that the spire's height exceeded an overlooked restriction that based the footprint of the spire on one-quarter of the building's "frontage." Bostrom claimed that the code recognized frontage only along the elevation faced by the tower, in this case the narrow Washington Street facade, rather than by the building's entire street frontage, which had been the code's traditional interpretation. The church—and many on the city council—cried foul, suggesting a link between Bostrom's denial and the church's recent refusal to endorse Mayor William Hale Thompson in an election season.[19] Whether political harassment or general disagreement, Bostrom relented under political pressure, and demolition commenced as scheduled.[20]

Buoyed by their success, the Methodists grew more ambitious, asking Holabird & Roche to come up with a scheme for a spire of 556 feet—1 foot higher than the Washington Monument. In December, having quietly lobbied the city council, they applied for a permit that would violate the code limit by more than 150 feet. The application was cannily submitted between city council elections that dealt a serious blow to Thompson's political clout in November and the mayoral primaries in which Thompson faced internal opposition in February 1923. Council members courting the increasingly powerful Methodist vote unanimously approved the permit and Thompson reluctantly signed it on Dec. 21, 1922.[21] "The Methodists," wrote *Tribune* critic James O'Donnell Bennett, "have found a way to break through

8.4 London Guarantee Building, 360 N. Michigan Avenue, Alfred Alschuler, 1923.

the 400-foot crust which truncates Chicago architecture." The council's decision, though, set a precedent only for owners to petition for a relaxation of the limit; they were not yet actually "taking the lid off."[22]

Despite delays in construction, companies that desired the prestige of occupying the city's tallest structure and the implied endorsement that came with being housed in a church leased its space enthusiastically.[23] The success of the Temple as a spiritual home and a real estate venture was matched by its critical and public reception. A combination of commercial and Gothic styles integrated the tower with the 260-foot office block below, a unifying sleight-of-hand that Holabird & Roche would exploit in their later work, and that seemed an architectural unification of God and mammon.[24]

THE 1923 SETBACK ORDINANCE

Skyscraperville! announced the *Chicago Daily Tribune* on March 13, 1923, as the Temple neared completion and its political legacy began to transform the city's skyline. Owners and aldermen alike balked at the precedent that the controversy had set: neither politicians nor owners wanted every tall project to have to come before the Council as the Temple had done. The incoming

8.5 Chicago Temple, corner of Clark and Washington Streets, Holabird and Roche, 1923, view from northwest. (Contemporary postcard, collection of the author)

mayor, William Dever, wisely left the fracas firmly in the hands of Bostrom and a newly appointed zoning commission. While Bostrom professed skepticism that the market actually demanded action, noting that only 8 percent of the downtown district had been built even to the existing limits, he recognized that the Chicago Temple's exemption had made the current height limits untenable.[25] The zoning commission had recently been charged with drafting a new, comprehensive ordinance that limited usage based on location, and the Temple controversy spurred them to consider a progressive approach to height limits, too.[26]

The commission divided Chicago into five "volume districts" in which height, footprint, overall volume, and setback distance were each balanced with perceived demand. These ranged from the first district, which mandated single-family houses or small apartment buildings, to the fifth, intended for downtown but eventually doubled in size at the insistence of property owners north of the Loop, creating the Daily Tribune's "Skyscraperville" that extended from Halsted Street to the Lake and from 22nd Street to Chicago Avenue. The zoning commission and city council passed the final drafts of the ordinance in Spring 1923. In place of the spire and tower exception, the new ordinance based maximum allowable height in the 5th Volume District on the distance from lot lines or the street edge.[27]

While a 264-foot cornice line still regulated the bulk of rentable space, structures above this were allowed if they stayed within 25 percent of the building footprint, if their total volume was less than one-sixth of the overall building volume, and if they stayed behind a 1:10 slope struck from the top of the 264-foot street or lot line wall. The new ordinance placed no absolute restriction on height, since the old 400-foot maximum limit on spires and towers disappeared in the final weeks of debate. The "lid" that had held buildings down was finally "torn off."[28] The new code made no mention of restrictions to occupancy in these upper reaches, suggesting by its silence that this new territory could be occupied and rented.[29] The building community had not expected such a permissive outcome, and after a year of cautious—and even stunned—reaction, architects and developers responded by enthusiastically exploiting the new ordinance.

Writing in 1925, Andrew Rebori noted that the new legislation offered two strategies for pushing rental space above the 264-foot limit: a "block" and "tower" approach that filled the base volume and added a single, prismatic volume within the limits above, and a "setback" approach where the entire volume would be integrated into a tapering form.[30] This second alternative, to Rebori and others, seemed to offer a way out of the city's reputation for sterile, "dry-goods boxes," and a chance

to think of skyscraper form as "jagged beauty" or "towered symmetry."[31] Experiments in these two interpretations would define the city's skyscrapers of the 1920s.

THE TRIBUNE TOWER

The *Chicago Tribune* was an interested party in its reporting on the Temple controversy. Having outgrown its headquarters at Dearborn and Madison, the paper announced an open competition in May 1922 to design a new headquarters on the recently opened North Michigan Avenue, and it selected the international team of winners on December 2, 1922 (figure 8.6). Holabird & Roche took third place for a blocky, Gothic scheme and the jury awarded second place to Eliel Saarinen and his Chicago associates, Dwight Wallace and Bertel Grenman, whose scheme echoed the vertical nature of Holabird & Roche's entry but with a more graceful, setback top. Saarinen's scheme also won the popular vote with an astonishing 90 percent of ballots cast.[32]

The jury, however, premiated the entry of New York architects John Mead Howells (1868–1959) and his Ecole des Beaux-Arts classmate Raymond Hood (1881–1934), which was an even more explicit statement of gothic verticality. The *Tribune* stood accused of lacking the courage of its convictions in choosing an American architect, Howells, over the more popular Finnish entry. But Hood & Howells' scheme was an

efficient and clever exploitation of the building code. It included the pre-Temple code-maximum twenty-one stories in a chamfered, vertically striped block and a higher, central ornamental lantern, linking these two elements with a set of eight nonstructural flying buttresses that unified the two code-limited elements with more visual continuity than the block and tower combination of the Wrigley.[33] Save for its heavy base, the entire shaft of Hood & Howells' scheme was an essay in verticality that, if it did not match Saarinen's scheme for subtlety and abstraction, nevertheless combined aesthetic and technical principles of skyscraper construction with a unifying, recognizable theme.[34] Howells made an explicit connection between the steel frame and the scheme's Gothic style, echoing Cass Gilbert's belief that the two had a natural affinity. "Your building must express its use and its construction," he told reporters the day after their winning scheme was announced: "I believe that the type of design chosen by the *Tribune* expresses not only the American office building but the actual steel cage, with its vertical steel columns from top to bottom and its interpolated steel beams. When you have done this you have produced

8.6 Tribune Tower, 435 N. Michigan, Hood & Howells, 1925, view from southwest. (Contemporary postcard, collection of the author)

something Gothic in line, because the Gothic architecture was also one of structural expression."[35]

The *Tribune*'s critics and editors, notably James O'Donnell Bennett, propagandized heavily for their choice, but the paper was increasingly assailed for rejecting Saarinen's scheme.[36] "Saarinen's forms," Chicago architect Irving Pond wrote in the *Architectural Forum*, "are steel forms clothed in stone, and not, like those of the design placed first by the jury, stone or masonry forms stayed and stiffened to their task by steel."[37] An ailing Louis Sullivan agreed, writing that Hood & Howells' entry was "imaginary, not imaginative," and that Saarinen's more "virile" proposal "advanced the steel frame as a thesis."[38] Saarinen himself was more gracious, calling Hood & Howell's scheme "strong and whole in form and proportion."[39] He spoke at length to the *Tribune* about the philosophy behind his own design, asserting that a skyscraper should allow the eye to follow its "logical construction" from bottom to top, at close range and on the skyline. To do this, he said, required the vertical continuity that Sullivan had championed, abandoning the horizontal emphasis that had been "borrowed from the antique and the renaissance," and adopting instead the verticality of the Gothic as Hood & Howells had done.[40] The idea of "Greece raised high on Gothic steel" had clearly passed in favor of a style more carefully hewed

to the thin proportions of the framework behind, a recapitulation, in some ways, of Atwood's Gothic experiments at the Reliance and Fisher, but rendered in heavier stone and with more solid exteriors.

Hood & Howells stayed above the fray, neither complaining of their treatment in the press nor feeling compelled to defend themselves. Hood was asked, in 1924, to write a piece for *Architectural Forum* on "The Exterior of Office Buildings," but he avoided engaging his critics, claiming of the Tower that its controversial "style and surface ornament" were "a very minor and unessential part of the problem." He argued that facades were simply the resultants of internal planning, with visual composition coming late in the process.[41]

Hood & Howells had hardly proposed an unsophisticated pastiche. Like Saarinen, they developed their scheme in rhythm with its steel skeleton, emphasizing a strong vertical character throughout. The decorative top and base, with their riots of gothic stone ornament and faux-buttresses that disappointed Pond were, Howells explained, a nod to the Woolworth's lacy parapets and arguably not so far from Sullivan's suggestion that building tops and bases be intentionally attractive. But the shaft of their tower was resolutely abstract, entirely without ornament save for shallow relief on cast-iron window spandrels. "On the handsomest exteriors," Howells explained, "decora-

tion and ornament and cornices and belt courses are being eliminated, and the beauty of native stones in plain surfaces is taking their place."[42] The result was a rhythmic progression around the tower of dark and light, structure, mullion, and void, in which every detail worked to counter what the *Tribune*'s critic referred to as the stereotypical "trivial checkerboard effect" of Chicago towers to that point.[43]

The Methodist's successful application to exceed the 400-foot "absolute" height limit came just three weeks after the announcement of Hood & Howells' scheme, and the *Tribune* understandably saw the controversy as an opening to argue for the upward extension of its own building. In December 1922, it published alternate schemes by Hood & Howells for a tower of 570 and even 650 feet (figure 8.7).[44] Ultimately, the tower's design was enlarged to 462 feet. Its site—100 by 135 feet—was not large, and while its isolation had salutary effects on the building's massing and appearance, the availability of views on four sides led to offices organized around a single corridor and a central core. For the lower twenty-one stories the addition of the "bustle" to the east added eight more offices per floor, above which each floor housed only seventeen offices.[45] Such inefficiencies suggested that the tower's massing had as much to do with its presence on Chicago's skyline as on its functionality—the paper's staff mostly decamped

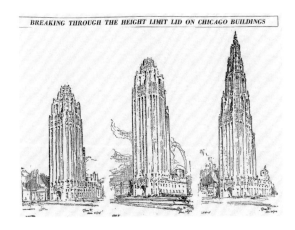

8.7 Tribune Tower, height studies, 1923.
(Hood & Howells)

into a more efficient annex several years later—and indeed the Tower's primary legacy has been as an urban object. (figures 8.8, 8.9).

STRAUS—A METICULOUS PUSH SKYWARD

Most towers built in the aftermath of the 1923 ordinance followed the pioneering example of the 1924 Straus Building, which faithfully expressed the ordinance's block and tower formula (figures 8.10, 8.11). S. W. Straus & Co. was a real estate financing firm with a reputation for diligent if uninspired development. In November 1922, Straus executives announced that they intended to "build the finest bank and office building in the world," suggesting their building would rival the First National Bank as the city's premiere commercial address. Like the *Tribune*, Straus & Co. immediately sought to exploit the

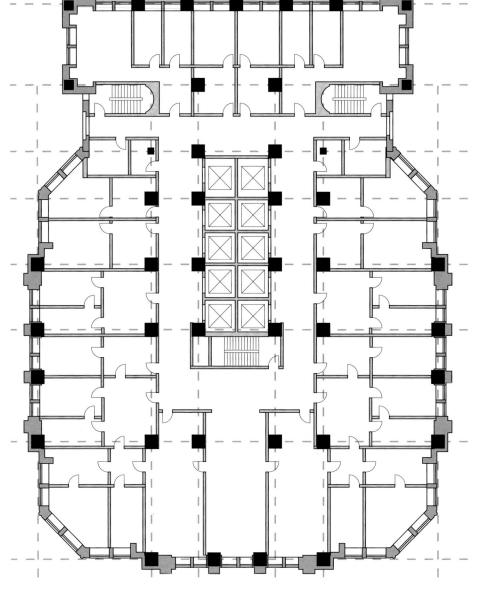

8.8 Tribune Tower, plan. (Drawing by the author)

ongoing Chicago Temple controversy. While it was then unclear exactly what the new zoning ordinance would entail, Straus wasted no time, hiring Graham, Anderson, Probst & White to draw up

plans that could be adapted to whatever the final height and setback formula might be. They also took the unusual step of hiring a consultant team to work alongside GAPW, regularly audit-

8.9 Tribune Tower, second place competition entry by Eliel Saarninen. (Art Institute of Chicago)

ing the scheme and promising a design and construction schedule of just sixteen months.[46] A perspective rendering of the planned building was published just after the new zoning ordinance was published, on April 15, 1923, with a claimed height of 400 feet.[47] Straus believed that the site would permit a tower of 565 feet, but eventually they built only to 475 feet. This still marked the first permit in the city—however tentative—for a tower over 400 feet.[48]

8.10 Straus Building, 310 S. Michigan, Graham, Anderson, Probst, and White, 1924, view from northeast. (Contemporary postcard, collection of the author)

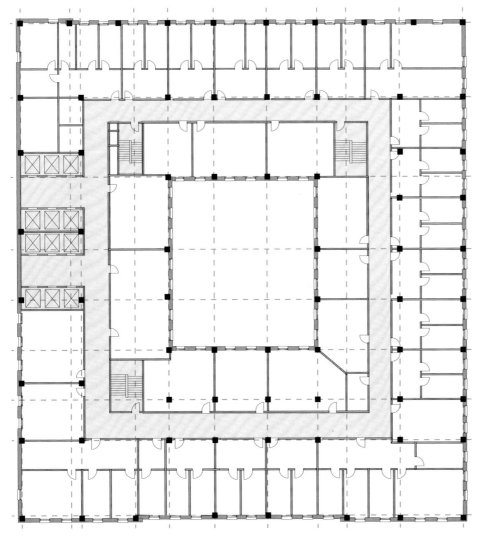

8.11 Straus Building, plan. (Drawing by the author)

on the skylight at the base of the light court. Designer Peirce Anderson placed two banks of elevators against the south party wall, zoned to serve upper and lower floors.[49] While the elevators occupied otherwise undesirable space, they presented a conundrum for the taller tower, requiring tenants to travel to the twenty-first floor and to then transfer to a separate core that served the tower alone. The tower floor plans were cramped, wrapping a twenty-foot band of rental space in a C-shaped plan around a core that consumed a third of each level. Rental spaces in the tower were valued for their unparalleled views and for being the highest offices in the city, but they hardly represented the Straus Company's ideal of large, flexible floor plates. Straus had likely figured how many of these awkward spaces the project could afford in the name of visibility; after just six levels, GAPW's plans called for a pyramidal roof that reached its advertised 475 feet with minimum investment and no further lettable space.[50]

Construction on the Straus began even before the permit was assured; Thompson-Starrett began placing foundations in March 1923, prior to the passage of the final height ordinance, though only the foundations under the tower faced uncertain loads since the 264-foot block limit was widely known by then. The contractor's condensed schedule relied on assurances that the basic layout of the building—its floor

Such a determined attack on the construction effort marked Straus's reputation for efficiency—a very different interpretation of the enlightened functionalism proffered by Sullivan and Schuyler. Architectural beauty in this case wasn't something integral to the solution, but rather a commodity, something that would earn its keep in tenant prestige and the resulting rentals. The scheme drawn up by GAPW pursued Straus's rigorous approach, offering modest improvements to the standard light-court office block while integrating structure and circulation for the tower above. First-floor retail offered pedestrian paths through the corner lot and a second-floor banking hall was centered sizes, positions of columns, and general massing—were all fixed.[51] But foremost in their calculations was minimizing the time of construction. Steelwork was ordered from seven different factories to speed production, and stone cladding was erected just behind the structural frame. This came with immense organizational complexities, since scheduling, material handling, and crane usage had to be exquisitely coordinated. Nothing could have been further from the chaotic job sites of the 1870s and 1880s, when a single architect presided over a loosely assembled group of laborers and skilled craftsmen. "We must go back to Imperial Rome," commented Rebori on the building's completion, "with its engineering skill and organized effort, to find a parallel to our own active time."[52] The Roman scale of the operation, Rebori felt, was matched by the Roman atmosphere of the completed building. Arriving tenants found "massive impressiveness, surpassing in grandeur any work of like character in Chicago" and a signature "beehive" beacon containing multicolored electric lights that capped the tower with an unmistakable signature, all expenses that were justified by the building's reputation and prestige.[53] Despite these moments, however, Rebori was unimpressed by the final result. "It does not aspire toward originality," he wrote, casting the building as a rigidly calculated exploitation of the new zoning ordinance, with a precise quantity of veneered, accountancy classicism to welcome tenants "of the right class."[54]

BLOCK AND TOWER

Like the Straus, the American Furniture Mart (Henry Raeder Associates, 1925) on Lake Shore Drive included only a 475-foot tower, even though the new ordinance would have allowed it to rise 500 feet or more. There were real concerns about the lettability of the small tower floors permitted by the new ordinance, but in later buildings the push for height was coupled with optimism that small office floors, perched well above the smoke and noise of streets below, might appeal to small, high-class tenants. The Jewelers Building was the first to confidently push lettable space above the 500-foot limit (figure 8.12). Designed as a home for the city's jewelry industry, it promised opportunities for networking between dealers, easy comparison shopping for buyers, and security for tenants, who had run the risk of being mugged while going from their cars to their shops. Project developer Earl Clemons purchased a quarter of a block at Wacker and State.[55] In April 1924, Clemons announced a design by former Burnham & Co. engineer Joachim Giaver and designer Frederick P. Dinkelberg for a twenty-three-story block surmounted by a tower reaching 502 feet, though later that year a more ambitious plan increased the tower to 547 feet.[56] The scheme filled the deep reaches of the resulting building volume with automobile parking rather than a light court, and energetically applied Dinkelberg's trademark highly wrought classicism to the resulting mass. Placing the tower directly in the center of the quarter-block site left a massive terracotta–clad block of interlaced horizontal and vertical ornament and small punched windows, all held between a solid base and a colonnaded top. The narrow band of retail shops wrapped around the garage found functional expression in larger tripartite windows around the perimeter, reflecting the importance of bright daylight to the retail jewelry trade even as the function of the light court was lost. The tower extended the base block's language for an additional sixteen floors, with setbacks punctuated by classical temple forms at their corners. At the very top, the tower narrowed to a three-story cylindrical shaft topped by a domed space that held a tiny (though eventually storied) club room. By adopting strong classical language, the project tied itself to the style and appeal of the new Wacker Drive, whose construction it paralleled. The Jewelers Building was only partly successful in luring its namesake industry from Wabash Avenue. The building's visibility appealed to large companies, however—especially the Pure Oil Company of Cleveland, for whom the building was subsequently named.

Joining the Jewelers along the eastern stretch of the river in 1928 was a unique tower/block interpretation that

8.12 Jewelers (Pure Oil) Building, 35 E. Wacker Drive, Giaver and Dinkelberg, 1926, view from northeast. (Contemporary postcard, collection of the author)

proved to be one of the most enigmatic in the Loop (figure 8.13). Alonzo Mather, an independent industrialist with a real estate hobby, purchased a narrow lot at 75 East Wacker Drive in the mid-1920s and announced plans for twin towers: one on the just-purchased site and another on the site of his three-story retail and office building at 330 N. Michigan. Together these were to form an angled arcade between Wacker and Michigan behind the London Guarantee Building, but only one tower, on Wacker, was realized.[57] Mather's architect, Herbert Hugh Riddle (1875–1939), had a distinguished career as a residential architect but had never designed a skyscraper, and at 65 by 100 feet the site presented major planning and structural complications. Mather was undeterred, directing Riddle to make the tower as tall as possible, with little concern about the lettability of such space.

Borrowing gothic elements from the Tribune Tower and white enameled terra-cotta from the Wrigley Building, Riddle designed a tower 521 feet tall, with a street-wall block set precisely to the city limit of 264 feet supporting a remarkably slender 256-foot tower. To accomplish this height the block's 5,900-square-foot floor plates were further reduced above the twenty-fifth story, where setback requirements reduced the allowable floor size first to a 42-foot square and eventually to an octagon just twenty-two feet in diameter. The top two floors measured just 350 and 280 square feet, which were too small even to accommodate an elevator shaft; tenants on these levels had to walk up a dedicated stairway from a small elevator lobby.[58]

This attenuated massing presented serious structural problems, and Lieberman and Hein, who had debuted as major engineering talents with the American Furniture Mart, were hired to design a structure for the site's unforgiving proportions. Setbacks required transfer and cantilever girders throughout, since the undersized floors had no room for additional internal columns. More serious, however, was lateral stability. No tower had been built to such slender proportions, and there were few opportunities for diagonal bracing in the tower's narrow direction because of its river views. Instead, gusset plates attached to the tops and bottoms of each spandrel girder provided moment connections in the lower block, and similar plates at each major column and girder connection braced the even slimmer tower. Finally, a thick shear slab at the interface of the tower and block transferred lateral loads between the two stacked frames. The Mather was so slender that its foundations had to be designed for uplift, and were literally screwed into bedrock.[59]

TOWER AND BLOCK VERSUS SETBACK—PITTSFIELD AND 333 N. MICHIGAN

Few developers were willing to put up with the inefficiencies that marked the Mather Tower, however, and two large skyscrapers constructed within months of each other show more fluently reconciled massing, circulation, and structure within integrated, streamlined forms.

8.13 (opposite) Mather Tower, 75 E. Wacker, Herbert Hugh Riddle, 1928, view from north. (Photograph by the author)

The Pittsfield, designed by Albert Shaw of Graham, Anderson, Probst & White, made important planning improvements on the tower and block arrangement, borrowing from the firm's signature white terra-cotta exteriors of the early part of the decade but extending this language into the neo-Gothic style popularized by the Tribune Tower. Meanwhile, Holabird & Roche looked to Eliel Saarinen's second place *Tribune* competition for 333 N. Michigan, a tower that redefined architectural approaches to the zoning ordinance.

The Pittsfield was a mix of retail and office space at the corner of Wabash and Washington (figure 8.14). Financed by the Marshall Field estate, it featured extensive retail space on lower floors. Shaw's design extended the Straus Building's massing strategy, with a tall tower set atop a light-court block and retail arcade. Shaw solved the earlier tower's circulation problems by locating the Pittsfield's elevator shafts in five-car banks along a narrow streetfront lobby. These elevators served both block and tower, eliminating the need for a transfer.[60] Shaw also further developed the Straus's massing strategy, taking the Pittsfield's setback from the rear lot line and siting the tower flush with Washington Street. This larger tower took greater advantage of the zoning

8.14 Pittsfield Building, 55 E. Washington, Graham, Anderson, Probst, and White, perspective drawing from northeast. (Chicago History Museum)

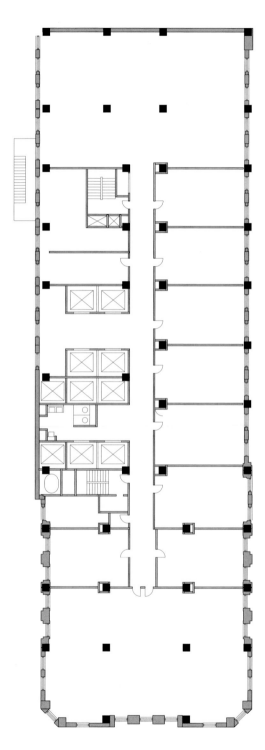

8.15 333 N. Michigan Avenue, Holabird &
Root, 1928, plan. (Drawing by the author)

8.16 333 N. Michigan Avenue, view from northeast. (*Architectural Record*)

envelope, and its thirty-eight stories and 557 feet set a record in the city. Shaw refined the Straus's blocky classicism by cladding the Pittsfield in gleaming white terra-cotta and telescoping the tower from the base block, blending the two with vertical neo-Gothic ornament.[61]

The syndicate that developed the 333 N. Michigan project in 1927 included Holabird & Roche, which designed a streamlined structure for the narrow, 60- by 200-foot lot (figures 8.15, 8.16). The building was based around a 265-foot slab clad with vertically oriented, unadorned stone strips and inset terra-cotta spandrels.[62] The northern end incorporated a 472-foot-tall pylon set back from the main block's edges at four key points, giving the sense that the entire north end of the structure was rising out of the main mass. "This handling of the exterior lines," suggested *Architectural Record*, "of the masses, and of the setbacks required by the zoning ordinance, is one more natural interpretation of present-day practical construction."[63]

The so-called "setback skyscraper" was a natural expression of the economic forces that pushed for height, and of the legislative ones that restrained it. While Holabird & Roche's design borrowed proportions and rhythms from the Beaux-Arts, it also drew upon the verticality of Gothic examples. It had a clear debt to Saarinen's *Tribune* entry, and new tropes such as chamfered corners and zigguratlike profiles echoed the art deco sensibility made popular by the 1925 Paris Exposition. Little of the design for 333 N. Michigan was entirely original, but in blending these influences Holabird & Roche presented a new alternative to the rigid massing of tower and block.

As Carol Willis discusses in *Form Follows Finance*, the setback approach that 333 adopted had possibilities for larger sites that made it more efficient than the tower/block scheme.[64] Placing a slender tower on top of a 265-foot block presented significant circulation and structural problems but left the most desirable, upper reaches of the building with small floor plates. What 333 portended was a generation of towers that featured artful tapering, forgoing volume from upper limits where views and prestige made up for small floor plates, enlarging the floors just above the 264-foot limit. At 333 the confines of the site sharply restricted the tower volume—it was no larger than the Straus's and still required a transfer at the block's top floor. The firm would thoroughly exploit this technique on later projects with larger footprints and more flexible tower massing.[65]

The efficient planning of the Pittsfield and the architectural innovations of 333 N. Michigan inspired further efforts to exploit the new ordinance. The Burnham Brothers' Carbon and Carbide Building at 230 N. Michigan was more a tribute to Hood's American Radiator Building of New York than to Saarinen's Tribune Tower, with deep black and green stone and terra-cotta with bright gold trim. But other projects maintained a stricter allegiance to the gothic appearance of both the built and unbuilt Tribune Towers. Further south on Michigan, The Willoughby Tower by Samuel Crowen (1872–1935) took many of its neo-Gothic cues from the Henry Cobb's Chicago Athletic Club next door and Holabird & Roche's University Club at the south end of its block. Even with its peaked windows and gargoyles, however, the Willoughby also made tentative gestures toward tower stepbacks, where a rooftop mechanical space was concealed by a setback turret.

Two skyscraper commissions by former Holabird & Roche employees Frederick J. Thielbar (1866–1941) and John R. Fugard (1887–1968), for the McGraw-Hill Company on Michigan Avenue north of the river and for the Trustees Systems Services at Lake and Wells, also extended the setback language.[66] The Trustees Systems Service Building combined tower and setback aesthetics to reach thirty stories, or 337 feet, despite its 85- by 150-foot site at the corner of Lake and Wells. With little spare volume, the architects pushed the tower to the Lake Street end of the site, stepping it back in small increments as it rose seven stories above the street wall to an ornamental pyramid. The building's structure was a virtual encyclopedia of techniques. Experimental hybrids of tapering cast-iron cores and concrete casings called Emperger columns were used for the building's twenty-story base, while concrete-fireproofed steel supported the taller tower and simple reinforced concrete supported a low portion under a light court in the northeast corner.[67] The tower's "receding pylons" were direct nods to 333 N. Michigan, and the pyramid top evoked the Straus Building.

Despite the commercial and aesthetic successes of the tower/block and setback skyscrapers, there were buildings of this era, notably Karl Vitzthum (1880–1967) and John J. Burns's (1886–1956) Bell Building of 1925, GAPW's Builder's Building of 1927 on Wacker Drive and LaSalle Street, and the Burnham Brothers' Engineering Building of 1928, that met their commercial programs without towers or spires above 260 feet. These clients—all building upon small sites that would have restricted any tower's volume and footprint—arrived at a different calculus than those of the taller structures; limited floor space above 260 feet was, to them, not worth the added construction cost or circulation inefficiencies.

SETBACK SKYSCRAPERS AFTER 333 N. MICHIGAN

After the opening of the Michigan Avenue Bridge and the construction of the Wrigley and Tribune Towers, retailers and commercial developers wasted little time in raising the standards of North Michigan Avenue.[68] In an ambitious attempt to "break the iron bands of the Loop," the Palmolive-Peet Company purchased a corner lot a mile north of the river that was 107 by 231 feet, and in July 1927 announced plans for a forty-two-story tower (figures 8.17, 8.18).[69] Land prices that far north were high by residential but not commercial standards, and the company saved millions by fleeing the overheated market of the Loop.

The scheme proffered by Holabird & Root—now led by William Holabird's son John A. Holabird (1886–1945) and John Wellborn Root Jr. (1887–1963)—was the most literal interpretation yet of the ordinance, with six setbacks that reduced floor plates along the 1:10 slope. The 264-foot limit occurred at the top of its twenty-first floor, above which a short four-story skirt made the transition to the remaining sixteen stories of "tower." The two setbacks below the limit reduced the size of the corner bays only, while the setbacks above eliminated whole column bays of floor space. Palmolive would occupy the lower, larger floors and individual tenants that required less space and better views could be accommodated above.[70]

These setbacks created outdoor roof terraces with unparalleled views of the city and the lake and they doubled as platforms for exterior lighting. The Palmolive's exterior skin was utterly flat between its setbacks, with no projections on its solid, Bedford stone verticals. Floodlights placed close to these

8.17 Palmolive Building, 919 N. Michigan Avenue, Holabird & Root, 1929, night view from south. (Contemporary postcard, collection of the author)

surfaces provided dramatic uplighting without casting long shadows while an aeronautical beacon emphasized the building's dominant position on the northern skyline.[71] The result was a "silver tower," a moniker enshrined in the name of the first-floor restaurant, the *Tour l'Argent*. Reporting on the building for *Architectural Forum*, critic Henry J. B. Hoskins noted that the Palmolive

8.18 Palmolive Building, construction view. (*Architectural Forum*)

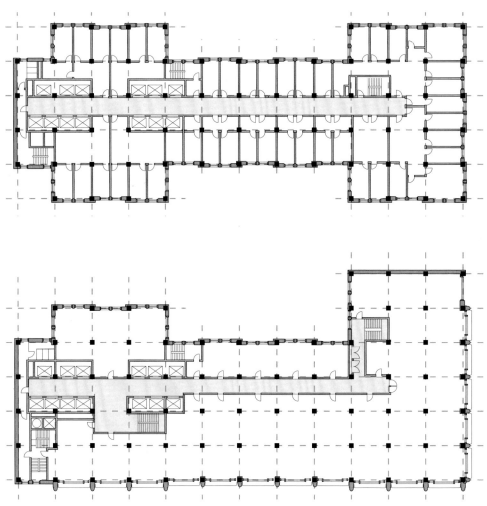

8.19 Palmolive Building, plans of lower and upper levels. (Drawings by the author)

reflected a rigor in planning and structure, but that its ornament and detail referred more to stylistic ideas. "The exterior of our modern skyscraper," he noted, "bears the same relation to the internal fabric as the hood of an automobile does to its chassis and engine" (figures 8.19, 8.20).

The Palmolive's structure was more carefully coordinated with its setback form than earlier towers; even where the exterior skin of the building shifted, column lines remained consistent, dropping off at the ends but never requiring extensive transfer structures like those at Mather Tower. Appointments and services represented the range of technologies available for a first-class commer-

cial development. Office floors featured ceiling heights of 10 feet, 7 inches, higher than average and designed to take advantage of "cooling cross breezes" off the Lake.[72] Steam heating was provided by concealed, "phantom" radiation that eased cleaning, but otherwise the Palmolive relied on operable windows, transoms, and its narrow floor plate for ventilation. Its twelve high-speed, gearless traction elevators traveled at up to 700 feet per minute, with automatic braking and leveling that reduced stopping times while providing a smoother ride, while indicators in each cab and at the first floor informed riders of cab location, and how long the wait would be—all new advances in elevator comfort and efficiency that would quickly become standard in tall commercial construction.[73]

In the wake of 333 N. Michigan's critical success, four other towers—the 1929 Medinah Athletic Club (Walter Ahlschlager [1887–1965]), the Steuben Club Building and 1 N. LaSalle (Vitzthum and Burns, 1929 and 1930), the Foreman State Bank (GAPW, 1929), and LaSalle-Wacker (Holabird & Root/Rebori, Wentworth, Dewey, & McCormick, 1930)— all matched the setback-defined height envelope of the 1923 code with streamlined art deco massing. Once a balance between base and tower volumes was fixed, the architects used dark, recessed spandrels and flush, undecorated limestone to add vertical emphasis to their compositions. Each of these buildings offered advanced elevator systems without transfers, and 1 N. LaSalle claimed for its lower floors the first mechanical air conditioning system in the Loop.[74]

GIANT PROJECTS, 1929–1934

Powered construction, advanced structural engineering, and rapid elevators found their ultimate expression in four record-breaking Chicago projects built on the brink of the Depression. The Civic Opera (GAPW, 1929), the Daily News Building (H&R, 1929), the Board of Trade (H&R, 1930), and the Merchandise Mart (GAPW, 1930) each faced complex structural and circulation problems that were solved almost entirely behind the scenes, with their heroic engineering disguised by streamlined art deco veneers.

The Civic Opera was formed in 1922 under electricity magnate Samuel Insull, who envisioned a massive home for the company on Wacker Drive's western end (figure 8.21). The planned complex would hold the Opera's theater, a smaller "Civic" theater that could be leased, and an office tower above that would bankroll production and operating costs. The Opera hired Graham, Anderson, Probst & White to tackle the complexities of combining the theaters and offices on a narrow site, and the resulting design showed Alfred Shaw's ability to solve complex functional problems behind facades that were a sophisticated blend of classical and moderne styling. Shaw's initial impulse was to match a light-court scheme with the auditorium below, but Ernest Graham is credited with suggesting that the offices be pulled together into a U-shaped office block, tapered through setbacks into a 555-foot tower and capped with a pyramidal roof. The resulting chairlike massing was often derisively referred to as "In-

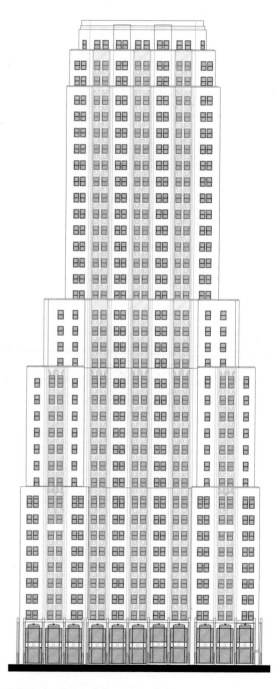

8.20 Palmolive Building, elevation. (Drawing by the author)

8.21 Civic Opera, 20 N. Wacker Drive, Graham, Anderson, Probst, and White, 1929, view from southwest. (Contemporary postcard, collection of the author)

sull's Throne," but the unintentionally allusive form allowed Shaw to push the main theater to the river's edge while maximizing street frontage. This transformation of light courts into view-oriented H-shaped plans became standard in the Loop in the late 1920s. The 878-seat Civic Theater was set at right angles to the main hall at the narrower, northern edge of the tapered site. This left space for the tower lobby, with elevator cores pressed into the interstices of the Opera theater, a grand lobby for the main auditorium that extended across the entire Madison Street front, and a smaller, separate foyer for the Civic Theater at the site's northeastern corner.

The simple massing of the Opera Building belied a complex but entirely hidden system of steel trusses and girders that supported the office tower above the wide-span theaters. Although Shaw's planning on the lower floors was masterful, even the narrow slabs of office space in the tower and end blocks did not quite leave enough room for the two theaters below. Instead, the inner edges of the office blocks had to be cantilevered over the Opera Theater and bridged entirely over the main theater lobby and the Civic Theatre. It fell to Magnus Gunderson, structural engineer for GAPW, to trace intricate pathways across, over, and around these large voids. Columns for the upper portions of the tower were recentered by transfer trusses at the twenty-third floor, and these loads were again transferred at the ceiling level of the auditorium to story-high cantilever trusses. Gunderson reinforced the tower blocks against wind through a combination of moment connections, gusset plates, and horizontal trusses.[75] The engineering was the most complex and challenging in the city to date; it would have been inconceivable without the standardization of steel sections, rapid hoists, pneumatic riveting, electric construction lifts, and truck-hauled steelwork developed in the previous twenty years.[76]

For the Opera's office tower, GAPW specified gearless traction cars in three banks, each of which served a zone of offices. The upper zones relied on electric braking to speed cabs to their respective service zones, and then to slow them down as they traveled between floors, providing a gentler ride. The cars were still manned by operators, but two of the tower elevators were designed for nighttime use, stopping at all levels and allowing passengers to select their own floors by means of push buttons—an innovation that would finally spell the end of the manual operator. The Opera's massing and its double-hung windows gave tenants "unusually liberal daylight provisions" for the time, but they also allowed the tower to be fully ventilated with outside air. Offices relied on operable windows for ventilation, tempered by radiant heat, while corridors and the attic spaces had ducted fresh air. By contrast, mechanically ducted and heated air was pro-

8.22 Chicago Daily News, 400 W. Madison Street, Holabird & Root, 1929, view from southeast. (Contemporary postcard, collection of the author)

vided to the two theaters. Although the technology was thus available to mechanically service the entire building, it remained expensive enough to make natural ventilation the preferred choice even for such prestigious offices.[77]

The Opera attracted national attention for its cultural accomplishment, but its early success faded in the face of the grim financial news of 1929 and 1930.[78] The office block became a liability and was sold to raise cash, severing the Opera from a lucrative source of rental income. Worse, the ingenious weaving of theatrical space and structure compromised the acoustics of the theater, leading to numerous retrofits and, serendipitously, a renewed appreciation for Adler & Sullivan's then-threatened Auditorium.[79] Insull himself resigned in disgrace from the Opera board after he was accused of securities fraud.

Constructed across the river from the Civic Opera, Holabird & Root's *Daily News* was a parallel experiment in setting office blocks atop long-span programs, and it shared Shaw's blend of art deco styling and Beaux-Arts massing (figure 8.22). The *News* was the city's second newspaper, and the *Tribune*'s new tower on Michigan Avenue led the paper's directors to consider a competing version. Like the *Tribune*, the *News* required rail access and space for large printing presses and newsrooms. There were few places left in the Loop large enough to accommodate such programs, but there were new legal mechanisms that allowed railroads to sell air rights over active track. Such agreements led to complex planning issues; buildings had to be inserted between rail lines that remained active during construction. But they offered enormous new areas in the Loop's "iron necklace" that could be converted into business centers with easy access to freight and passenger lines. The *Daily News* site, over freightyards shared by Chicago & Northwestern and the Illinois Central, faced the Chicago River on one side and C&NW's passenger station on the other. It offered freight access to the yards below, and placed the paper's headquarters at a key pedestrian

point in the Loop alongside a riverfront that promised continued improvement. The area over the railyards was large enough that the *News* dedicated half of it to the City's first riverfront plaza, which Holabird & Root connected to a pedestrian concourse on the building's southern edge that bridged Canal Street and connected to the C&NW passenger station to the site's west.[80]

The *News* required a complicated mix of goods handling, printing facilities, and office space. Its presses were enormously heavy, and they required access to incoming rail.[81] Above, offices had to accommodate the unique requirements of the newsroom, and roughly twenty floors of lettable office space had to provide the standards of light, access, and air competitive with other commercial blocks downtown.[82] Holabird & Root assembled these diverse components into a unified form, building on functional and aesthetic lessons of the Palmolive. The main mass of the building was pushed to Canal Street, stepping toward the river in two short wings reflecting the massing of the Opera across the river. The building's core was located at the corner of Washington and Canal Street, connecting with the interior concourse to the C&NW station. Pedestrians hurrying through this concourse remained unaware that immediately to the north the paper was being printed and that just beneath them lay a massive truck dock. All of this was so tightly woven to-

gether that *Architectural Forum* drew a biological analogy, noting its "balanced, efficient structures with bones of steel and cement, nerves of electricity, [and] lungs that breath[e] in fresh air, maintaining a constant temperature."[83] This was not, of course, the organic philosophy championed by Sullivan or Wright. Rather, Holabird & Root masked this complexity by matching zoning compliance with a symmetrical massing and streamlined ornament that marked the *Daily News* as a modernized competitor to the *Tribune*. The lower, broader floors of the office slab were devoted to the *Daily News* itself, with open plan newsrooms and business departments, and private offices for the publisher and editors. The larger floor plates were mechanically ventilated, but the upper offices narrowed to sixty feet and relied on cross-ventilation.[84]

Although shorter than the Opera, at just twenty-six stories and 302 feet, the Daily News Building was nonetheless equally complex. W. B. Gray, Engineer in Charge of Structural Design for Holabird & Root, faced similar issues to those that confronted Gunderson at the Civic Opera: offices stacked above long-span spaces, different foundation loads for tower and plaza, and foundations adjacent to the river. Even more challenging were the tracks below, which offered few uninterrupted straight lines for columns. Gray established a uniform 20-foot bay spacing from north to south, adjusting the location of columns east to west to fit between curving and merging tracks, resulting in spans ranging from 30 feet to 102 feet. The air rights agreement stipulated that construction not interfere with the workings of the yard, and the structure was thus built between and over the tracks. As a result, Gray wrote in 1930, its steel frame had "some particularly interesting features."[85]

These began with the foundations. Gray calculated that the tower would require one hundred bedrock caissons, ninety feet deep, while the plaza and wings could be supported on fifty-nine shallower hardpan caissons of about sixty feet. Contractors constructed a work platform atop the entire site, lowering digging equipment and removing excavated earth in narrow spaces between operating trains.[86] Gray's solution for supporting the heavy printing room atop a complex of switching tracks was no less ingenious—and no more visible—than Gunderson's cantilevered Opera Tower. At the fourth floor Gray specified story-high trusses, each resting on columns under the main office slab and on A-frame columns that spanned tracks on the east. Beneath these trusses, tension columns suspended the printing room's north half, leaving the space beneath free of columns. In other areas, the office planning and the setback scheme required transfer girders and cantilevers to deliver loads to columns placed between rail tracks, requiring girders up to twelve feet deep.[87] These trusses, transfer girders, and cantilevers were entirely hidden by the unifying exterior of Indiana limestone and polished black granite.

A similar combination of structural and programmatic complexity with classical-moderne massing and styling faced Holabird & Root with the new Board of Trade building, completed in 1930. The old building had long since failed to serve the scale of the exchange, which moved into temporary quarters on Clark Street in 1928.[88] Holabird & Root were asked to design a new trading floor of twenty-one thousand square feet, sixty feet high, column-free, and with over forty stories of office space above.[89] Gray handled the complex transfer bridgework using six trusses, each five stories tall, woven invisibly between offices from the fourth through ninth floors.

Above the trading floor was a fourteen-story block of offices that reached the 264-foot limit, planned in an H-shape to open the interior to light, air, and magnificent views up LaSalle Street while multiplying the number of corner offices on each floor, a strategy borrowed from the Opera. At the twentieth floor, the building set back into a single tower that rose to 575 feet, topped by a shallow hipped roof and a 33-foot tall aluminum statue of Ceres.[90] The building's electrical accommodations drew special attention. The trading floor was illuminated by an eight-ton fixture reputed to be the world's largest, and its offices were equipped with electric quotation boards that enabled brokers to keep pace with action in the pit.[91] On the exterior, Holabird & Root matched their work on the Palmolive, using setback terraces, strategically placed inset spandrel panels and flat Indiana limestone cladding to serve as an architectural canvas for extensive floodlighting, marking the base of LaSalle Street for miles to the north. Hegemann-Harris were in charge of construction, and their use of newly developed powered traveling cranes enabled a work force of over twelve hundred to complete the building by mid-1930, where it became, in the words of the *Tribune*, the "loftiest in a City of Towers," a title it held until the completion of the 601-foot Prudential Building in 1955.[92]

As impressive as the Opera, Daily News, and Board of Trade were, however, nothing challenged the scale of the Merchandise Mart, built over the tracks of the Chicago and Northwestern Railway between 1928 and 1931 (figure 8.23). By 1920, Marshall Field & Co. began maneuvering to bring all of its wholesale business to one location with the goal of replacing the 1885 H. H. Richardson building and dozens of satellite sites around the Loop. The Field Corporation's timing was fortunate. By the late 1920s, Wacker Drive on the river's south bank was well underway, and a matching promenade on the north seemed inevitable. As president of Marshall Field & Co. and head of the Chi-

8.23 Merchandise Mart, Wells and Chicago River, Graham, Anderson, Probst, and White, 1931, view from southwest. (Contemporary postcard, collection of the author)

cago Plan Commission, James Simpson saw an opportunity to extend the interests of both the city and his company to the North Loop.[93] In March 1927, the company published a scheme by GAPW for a fifteen-million-dollar structure to fill the entire block-and-a-half on the river between Franklin and the angled Orleans Street.[94] Alfred Shaw's renderings showed a massive stone-clad block 264 feet tall, filling the entire site. A stubby tower was centered on the riverfront facade, with six-hundred-foot long elevations punctuated by repeated vertical recesses. Beneath the building, barely visible in the published renderings, lay another Chicago and Northwestern freightyard.

Over the next year Field & Company expanded the project to include leased showroom space, doubling its budget to thirty million dollars and making the building the world's largest at over four million square feet. Each of its eighteen showroom floors had the area of a typical ten-story building, and like the deep floors of the Furniture Mart the building was entirely illuminated by electricity day and night. Windows brightened only a tiny percentage of the five-acre floor plates. Its showrooms alone, in fact, boasted more than twice as much plate glass as the exterior, while full mechanical ventilation eliminated the lingering need for large open courts.[95]

Construction began in August 1928, with general contractor John W. Griffiths & Sons moving a "tented city" of machinery and workers to the site to excavate 458 caissons.[96] McLintic-Marshall, known for bridge construction, fabricated sixty-one thousand steel elements designed by Magnus Gunderson. They were pneumatically riveted into subassemblies and sent to the site by truck, rail, or barge and lifted by a set of nine derricks and erected by a crew of over twenty-five hundred.[97] Careful planning, efficient scheduling, and a relentlessly standardized twenty- by twenty-foot structural grid allowed Griffiths to top out the steelwork on Dec. 31, 1929, less than sixteen months after work had commenced.[98] The Mart was the ultimate expression to date of the possibilities of modular design, managed production, and powered construction.[99]

The Field Estate made one last foray into commercial construction in the Loop before the Depression took hold. Announced on September 29, 1929, just days before the stock market crash, the Field Building was to occupy the southern half of the block bounded by Adams, LaSalle, and Clark Streets (figure 8.24). The first design by GAPW looked like the Merchandise Mart extended to an office tower, a solid block

8.24 Field Building, 135 S. LaSalle Street, Graham, Anderson, Probst, and White, 1934, view from southeast. (Contemporary postcard, collection of the author)

of vertical stripes rising to twenty-two stories and a central tower flush with the street adding twenty-one stories in three setbacks.[100] The project was planned in two phases, the first replacing the Home Insurance Building on the LaSalle Street corner, the second replacing the Merchant's Loan and Trust at Clark. Daunted by the onset of financial disaster, the Field Estate waited until March 1931 to take out permits, and massing changed from a solid block reminiscent of the Mart to a set of five interlocking rectangles: four perimeter blocks rose to twenty-three stories and a central tower rose to forty-two. This scheme provided twelve corner offices per floor.[101]

Just thirteen months later the project had been bid, foundations prepared, and the steelwork completed—the last taking just forty working days.[102] With the Depression at its depths, George Fuller & Co. had little trouble getting labor, and an estimated seventy-five hundred workers were employed on site at its busiest.[103] The exterior combined smooth Indiana limestone panels and cast aluminum spandrels, and its simplicity and regularity helped set a record construction pace of one floor per day. Tenants began to move into the first phase at the end of May 1932, and construction on the entire complex was complete by 1934. The Field Building boasted a rooftop club, fully air-conditioned lower floors, exercise rooms, and a restaurant designed by Shaw in a "re-strained Baroque style." Important technical advances matched these luxurious accommodations. Elevators were the fastest in the Loop, at one thousand feet per minute, and they comprised the largest elevator installation yet in a Chicago office building, with forty-two cabs outfitted with position indicators and programmed to automatically return to the lobby—both new features. The Field was also the first in the Loop to use aluminum for window frames. Aluminum had been a luxury material, but improvements in electrolytic refinement had reduced its cost, and the precision possible in its manufacture made it ideal for complex operable window systems, while its strength allowed thinner frames and more glass for a given opening. "There is virtually no rattle and air or dust leakage," *Architectural Record* reported, portending a shift away from iron and wood frames to a material that would become ubiquitous in the next generation.[104]

As the Depression strangled Chicago's real estate market these giant projects were the last to be built in the Loop. Nothing of great height would be built downtown for twenty years. And while the Field looked forward to this new generation in some of its details—notably its aluminum windows, its provision for air conditioning, and its fast elevators—it was also the product of generations before. The differences between it and the Home Insurance and Merchant's Loan Buildings that had stood on its site were important, but the changes that occurred between these structures were evolutionary. The Field's steel structure evolved directly from the frames that first solved problems of lateral stiffness in the 1890s with riveted connections. Its aluminum-framed windows answered a need for ventilation and light that had shaped the skin of the Merchant's Loan.

That the Field stood at a juncture between skyscraper eras was emphasized by the demolition of the Home Insurance and the debates over whether it had stood as the "first" of anything—skeleton frame, curtain wall, or even skyscraper. The committee organized by the Field Estate and led by architect Thomas Tallmadge concluded that it had; an independent group of western engineers thought not. In the intervening years, elevator technology, riveted steel, and electric lighting had fostered taller, larger buildings. The technical and legal restrictions that had limited height had given way, allowing towers that would have awed Jenney. But with the Home Insurance gone and a new public interest in its achievement and its mythology, a generation of historians, practitioners, and scholars began to look back and to ask what, exactly, had happened in Chicago over the previous sixty years.

Chapter 9
Chicago, 1934

The Field, the Merchandise Mart, the Board of Trade, and the twin riverfront monoliths of the *Chicago Daily News* and the Chicago Opera represented the end of the 1920s boom, and of three generations of Chicago construction that had pushed toward greater height, efficiency, and performance. With the onset of the Depression, the only major construction in the Loop involved corporations exploiting distressed construction costs or syndicates so broad as to be nearly public, like the Board of Trade. The Field Building went forward only after it proved less expensive than severance payments to desperate subcontractors, and it stood largely empty upon opening, a testament to the general economic paralysis. More common were demolitions and the construction of so-called "taxpayers"—one- to three-story retail buildings that brought

in enough rent to cover maintenance and property taxes.

The gravity of the Depression can be understood by what was *not* built. Early 1929 witnessed one of the city's ugliest zoning controversies, over plans by financier John F. Cuneo to develop the corner of Michigan and Randolph with a forty-story tower rising straight from its lot lines. Reporters and other developers were shocked to find that Cuneo, through a friendly alderman, had benefited from a provision secretly introduced in the city council that May that lifted the height of the street wall in the Loop from 264 feet to 440 feet for lots that faced a public park—a clause that applied to Cuneo's lot and few others.[1] The issue ended up in circuit court by November of that year, where it was struck down, but Cuneo's plan was shelved even as

the case went to trial in the dark, early days of the economic crisis.[2]

An even more dramatic indication of the real estate market's sudden collapse was the ill-fated plan drawn up by Walter Ahlschlager for a massive complex of office towers, showrooms, lodging, and leisure facilities known variously as Crane Tower, Chicago tower, and the Apparel Mart. Announced by a group of apparel executives in June 1928, the scheme proposed a seventy-five-story setback tower—taller than the Woolworth—atop a base that was to span railyards between the extended Randolph Street and Wacker Drive. The Apparel Mart project was more ambitious than the Merchandise Mart; visiting buyers would have all of their showrooms as well as hotel and club facilities in one place. The project commenced the next month with the purchase of Illinois Central's air rights but soon ran up against an overbuilt market. Ahlschlager reconceived the complex as an office tower only and put together a new group led by the Crane railroad company in May 1929, but nothing more was heard of the project after the October crash.[3] The idea of a city rising above the Illinois Central yards attracted other schemes but no serious investment until after 1950.[4]

The cessation of architectural and construction work in Chicago was matched by the passing of the city's post-fire generation of designers and engineers. Louis Sullivan's death from alcoholism in April 1924 merited only a brief mention in the *Tribune*. Andrew Rebori lamented that "as far as the material world is concerned, he ceased to exist some fifteen years ago," though Sullivan's impassioned critique of Hood & Howells's tower and the publication of his *System of Architectural Ornament* had cast him back into architectural discussions.[5] In death his reputation grew, and a community that had largely forgotten the man memorialized his philosophy. Sullivan's obscure death nearly a quarter-century after his last major Chicago commission contrasted with the sudden loss of Peirce Anderson in 1924, from cancer, in the prime of his career. This deprived Graham, Anderson, Probst, and White of their leading designer, and advanced the career of Alfred Shaw.[6] Edward Clapp Shankland, Burnham's engineer through the 1890s,

died in 1924; John Holabird died in 1923 and Martin Roche in 1927. Perhaps most poignant was the death of Peter Bonnett Wight in 1925 at the age of eighty-seven. Wight's career spanned the 1871 fire, a partnership with Asher Carter, a consulting engineering position that figured in the first grillage foundations, a fireproofing company that made crucial advances in protecting early steel buildings and a late career as writer and critic. By the end of the 1930s, Ernest Graham and Howard White had died, too; Shaw was subsequently forced out of GAPW along with engineer Sigurd Naess and architect Charles Murphy.[7] These three formed a new firm—Shaw, Naess, and Murphy—that captured some of Graham, Anderson, Probst, and White's clientele. Other young architects scrambled to open their own offices in the stressful atmosphere of the Depression, including Louis Skidmore (1897–1962) and Nathaniel Owings (1903–1985), who leveraged connections made during their work on the 1933 Century of Progress Exhibition into valuable commercial contracts during the ensuing dry years. These younger firms formed links with a new generation of contractors after the War but, until better times came, work for Shaw, Naess, and Murphy and for Skidmore and Owings (joined by John Merrill [1896–1975] in 1937) was piecemeal and mostly away from the business district.

While Sullivan and Frank Lloyd Wright had self-consciously consid-

ered their places in history, most Chicago firms avoided talk of a movement or influence. Burnham had no hesitation in designing projects that involved the demolition of his firm's earlier buildings; Continental and Commercial Bank occupied the site of Burnham & Root's Rand McNally and old Insurance Exchange buildings, and First National Bank demolished the Montauk on Burnham's suggestion. But the city's remaining skyscrapers formed an archive of architectural and constructive techniques that came to be globally appreciated. Erich Mendelsohn's influential *Amerika*, published in 1928, featured images of the city's skyscrapers and contrasted those of the nineteenth century with contemporary, revivalist structures such as the Federal Reserve Bank: "Greece," Mendelsohn remarked of the latter, "has become a burden for the steel frame." The city's grain elevators (some of which were actually Montreal's) and the El reflected what he saw as the city's true character, but in the Tribune Tower and along Michigan Avenue, Mendelsohn lamented, "Chicago wants to become New York."

Others saw the city's development in more nuanced terms. Francisco Mujica, a South American architect, published a comprehensive and polemical *History of the Skyscraper* in Paris in 1929, outlining the type's manifestations in various American cities and recognizing the evolutionary nature of its technical achievement. Mujica believed that the elevator was the true motive cause of the tall building, that the steel frame followed its lead, and that skyscrapers could be divided into "simple prisms," "isolated towers" of neoclassical or gothic style, and "set-back pyramids" which he felt were truly American because they offered "a striking resemblance with many of our [Meso-] American pyramids."[8] Although his theory of origin was never widely accepted, Mujica's skyscraper history was impressive and influential. The elevator, he felt, allowed "pre-skyscrapers" of ten to twelve stories, but only when combined with the steel frame did it enable true "skyscrapers." Hydraulic technology limited these buildings to eighteen to twenty stories, but with the advent of high-speed electric elevators, he believed height was now "technically unlimited." Steel framing had also, in his view, allowed skyscrapers to take better advantage of daylight, where apertures could "go right up to the line of the steel columns without impairing the resistance of walls." Mujica acknowledged the confusion over the skyscraper's "invention," constructing a carefully parsed summary of its many-fathered birth:

> [T]he honor of having invented the skyscraper must be divided. To Jenney and Post falls the honor of having invented and executed the first metal frames; Jenney has the honor of having built the first embryo skyscraper; Hola-

bird & Roche have somewhat improved this embryo skyscraper; Baumann has the honor of having the first complete vision of the skeleton skyscraper. Buffington has designed the first building with all-steel frame and the first skyscraper of great height, Burnham & Root have the honor of having constructed the first all-steel frame skyscraper and the honor which falls to all of them together as inventors and initiators of the steel skeleton skyscraper belongs to the United States of America.[9]

Mujica left no doubt that Chicago enjoyed the strongest claim on the earliest skyscraper, even if one could not parse exactly which building this was. His understanding of the Home Insurance's structure was particularly subtle, recognizing that its frame was not self-supporting against lateral loads. After 1899, however, Chicago's height restrictions meant that, for him, the skyscraper had "acclimatized" in New York. That city's zoning codes had encouraged the setback ziggurat form that for him recalled preconquest pyramids and monuments.

Other histories followed that were less ambitious than Mujica's. Locals and historians branded the Home Insurance Building as an important historical work even if its precise achievement was open to debate. Thomas Tallmadge produced an anecdotal history of Chicago architecture, published in incomplete form after his death in 1940, but it did little to assess the larger patterns of development that had characterized the era. Sigfried Giedion's 1941 *Space, Time, and Architecture*, on the other hand, made grandiose claims, institutionalizing Frank Lloyd Wright's lament that the 1893 Columbian Exposition had effectively killed off the "Chicago School," an ill-defined term that Giedion took to include both the solid masonry structures of the 1880s and the frame structures that were built after the Fair.[10] Giedion conflated technical and functional innovation with aesthetics, suggesting that the two great achievements of the School, in his view, were making "the first expressive use of the new technical potentialities in buildings" while striving for "pure forms."[11] Giedion believed that these two factors were necessarily related, a slippery claim that shaded much of the city's architectural history in decades to come. In 1949, Frank Randall, a former Chicago engineer turned University of Illinois professor, published his sure-footed *History of the Development of Building Construction in Chicago*, a list of major structures in and around the Loop that aimed at documentation rather than argument.[12] Randall's annotations, however, stressed the importance of foundations, fireproofing, and steel framing, providing evidence of the vast number of experiments in these areas that went on nearly simultaneously. Unlike Giedion, he made no architectural or aesthetic assessment, implicitly arguing that these buildings could be understood solely as engineering accomplishments.

The 1950s saw more academic debate, including arguments over just what constituted a "skyscraper," and which one might be the "first" of the type. Winston Weisman published an intentionally provocative paper in the *Journal of Architectural Historians* in 1952 titled "New York and the Problem of the First Skyscraper," in which he argued that the Western Union Telegraph Building by George B. Post and the *New York Tribune* Building by Richard M. Hunt, both of 1875, deserved recognition as the first "skyscrapers." He made a pointed argument against the "technological" requirement of a skeleton framed structure to qualify, noting that the term "skyscraper" had always referred to tall or high objects—the topsail on a full-rigged ship, for instance.[13] It thus made sense to him that a "visual" argument, rather than a "technological" one, be deployed in assessing claims to primacy. Further objections to the technological basis, Weisman argued, were that it ignored the complex sociocultural *milieu* that had helped to shape skyscraper form and style, reducing buildings with rich urban meaning to mere "gadgets." He felt that focusing on technical criteria alone led to inevitable exclusions—for instance, the Monadnock Block, which relied on a hybrid of masonry and iron rather than pure skeletal construction. If the Montauk were to be considered a skyscraper, he concluded, then surely the two earlier structures by Post and Hunt, which were as tall but nearly a decade earlier, trumped any claims of Chicago to have built the first of the type.[14]

J. Carson Webster, a professor of art history at Northwestern, refuted Weisman's argument in 1959, suggesting that it relied on a false duality between technological and visual arguments, noting favorably Mujica's hybrid definition of a skyscraper as "a building of great height constructed on a steel skeleton and provided with high-speed electric elevators." Webster proposed three factors that defined the skyscraper type: "essential characteristics," "necessary means," and "favoring conditions." These related to function, construction, and sociocultural influences—a broader and more thorough consideration than Weisman's duality. "Essential characteristics" translated as number of stories, and Webster rather arbitrarily suggested that fifteen stories be treated as the cutoff for inclusion. "Necessary means" suggested skeletal framing, and here, too, Webster proposed a frustratingly loose definition, namely that any incorporation of metal framing ought to merit consideration, even if only for a street front. The interaction of these two, rather than the existence of one or the other, was for Webster the key factor: "The rela-

tion between the skyscraper and skeleton construction is as follows: in what we call a skyscraper skeleton construction is used in the service of height, light, and space, that is, so as to permit greater height with a greater amount of light (if desired) with a greater amount of usable space on every floor."[15]

The application of this principle to light excluded so-called "cage" construction in which the outer wall was a masonry bearing wall while the interior was of metal framing, thus eliminating Weisman's New York examples but also the Montauk. The Monadnock would not have fit this definition either, as its hybrid of masonry and iron certainly failed to meet the spirit of Webster's definition, even if it met some of its specific requirements. Webster instead turned to the local press, noting that the *Tribune* had first used the term in an article of January 13, 1889, and suggesting that the buildings therein described—the Owings, the Tacoma, and the Chamber of Commerce—might well deserve the title of Chicago's first skyscrapers, while New York's contenders "were apparently not sufficient to call forth the new name, although the word in its extended sense was ready at hand."[16]

Webster had a powerful influence on Carl Condit, whose 1952 *Rise of the Skyscraper* entered into this academic fray without really taking a position on the definition of a skyscraper or on which building might make claim to being first. Condit added an aesthetic argument to the debate, however, making ornament and style, or lack thereof, a key factor in assessing the historic importance of individual structures. This further clouded the topic. The book's expansion into the 1964 *Chicago School of Architecture* proposed that its titular phrase also be applied to works by Mies van der Rohe, Perkins and Will, and other postwar architects—along with the Prairie School architects whose inclusion Weisman found so problematic. This raised the historiographical stakes by suggesting a conceptual continuity between "First" Chicago School architects such as Sullivan and "Second" Chicago School architects such as Mies and Skidmore, Owings, and Merrill (SOM). The "Technico-Aesthetic Synthesis" that Condit had posited as an essential characteristic of the "First" School certainly seemed to describe much of the "Second" School's work as well, but the use of this term at the expense of New York examples rankled many, and cast the history of the city's architecture as a parlor game over various "firsts." This debate occurred in the reviews of Condit's books (noted in chapter 1) and in a heated exchange of letters in the *Journal of the Society of Architectural Historians* between Weisman and Donald Hoffman in 1973. The subject was treated more expansively in a symposium held in 1972 (and transcribed for the *Prairie School Review*)

that featured Condit and Weisman presenting dueling cases for Chicago and New York.[17] Condit, facing a heavy barrage of precedents from Weisman, argued that the articulated wall and its expression of the modernist tenet of "diagrammatic architecture" marked Chicago's work as both progressive and influential in ways that merely technical precedents were not.[18]

Efforts to identify the "first" skyscraper or its city of origin, while entertaining, were ultimately futile, and a subsequent generation saw Condit in particular as a convenient straw man to argue against technological vectors as the primary means of understanding these structures. Robert Bruegmann in particular deflated the "Myth of the Chicago School" in Katerina Ruedi Ray and Charles Waldheim's provocative collection *Chicago Architecture: Histories, Revisions, Alternatives*. Condit, Bruegmann wrote, "laid particular stress on the development of structure, especially the invention of skeletal framing. And, perhaps because he was an American living in the Chicago area, he was very ready to credit a Chicago architect, Jenney, with the creation of the first metal skeleton office building despite what had already become a considerable weight of opposing evidence."[19]

Bruegmann further argued that alternative readings in the intervening generation showed discrepancies in the thinking of major "Chicago School" figures and a consistent interest in dec-

oration and ornament that belied Giedion's stylistic narrative. "The modernist vision of the 'Chicago school' as a group of architects interested in creating a new, ahistorical architecture primarily based on the expression of structure is too reductivist," he concluded, suggesting that the link between technology and aesthetics was naive and misleading.[20] Other essays in Ruedi Ray and Waldheim's book argued for understanding the city's architecture not as canonical works of modernism and premodernism but as socially and culturally constructed artifacts, a "soft" understanding designed to compete with the traditional "hard" understanding of the city's buildings as technological monuments.

These two poles of "soft" interpretation and "hard" explanation, however, have left a vast territory in between; surely no critic today would see the city's early skyscrapers as "pure" or "determined" statements of technology or economics, but it seems equally narrow to intentionally dismiss these as factors in understanding how and why these buildings were built, and why, a century later, we still find them compelling. What did happen in Chicago, and why do we recognize elements of its early architecture as influential or meaningful even today? The answer may lie between Condit and Bruegmann, in understanding technological or "hard" memes as factors among the thousands of decisions that occurred within a typical building's design and construction in a broader but less immediate milieu of other, "softer," factors. The resolution between these two spheres brings with it inevitable questions of agency and cause, as discussed in the Preface of this book, but it is precisely these questions that may shed light on the affinity we feel for these buildings today. Process, integration, and collaboration played vital roles in the conception and execution of these structures.

It is thus worth recapping the history outlined in this book in an attempt to understand the economic, material, performance, and sociocultural vectors influencing Weisman's "patterns of development." Builders after the Fire, faced with informal pressure to build better but without means to do so, constructed buildings that improved incrementally on the traditional methods of masonry, timber, and cast iron. The Fire, however, spurred entrepreneurs from both Chicago and New York to develop new fireproofing techniques. Pressed brick, metal beams and columns, and improved elevators changed the economics that had limited developers to five to seven stories, and buildings such as the Montauk proved that higher floors were both possible and desirable. Terra-cotta and metal then offered possibilities for lightweight construction, which architects, engineers, and builders explored in the early 1880s. The pressing need for daylighting led to experiments in combining brick and iron,

and the foundation technique of isolated piers encouraged architects and engineers to understand buildings as systems of point loads rather than continuous walls. These factors all led to experiments in masonry and iron hybrids, ranging from Jenney's First Leiter Store to Burnham & Root's Rookery, while Holabird & Roche showed the benefits of decoupling structure and cladding with the glass-filled wall of the Tacoma.

The lightweight skin of the Tacoma found a structural complement in the slightly later development of wind-braced frames. Steel played an important role in allowing metal frames to resist lateral loads. Brick, a material with a history of labor complications and inherent spatial inefficiencies, began to fall from favor with architects and engineers, who instead combined internally braced steel frames with lighter terra-cotta and glass skins to achieve greater transparency, more efficient plans, and speedier construction.

Designers used these new materials and techniques to create buildings that offered aesthetic opportunities as well as larger financial returns. The skeletization of building structures allowed increased apertures that could be filled with affordable plate glass. This combination suggested that heavy masonry could be replaced with exteriors that emphasized delicacy and verticality. Code changes forced designers to abandon cantilevered bays and terra-cotta jackets in favor of flat ele-

vations and brick piers, however, and they again responded with schemes that exploited large windows and slightly bulkier piers, at the same time fashioning ornamental programs that could tease visual coherence from the resulting grids. The trabeated nature of these elevations was a fertile matrix for light Beaux-Arts ornament, and as glass prices rose and electricity offered a more convenient method of lighting, architects responded with more solid elevations, which in turn allowed more robust classical ornament. Meanwhile the development of caissons, pneumatically powered construction, and electrically powered and controlled elevators put pressure on the city to allow taller buildings, leading to code changes that ushered in a generation of spires, towers, and setback skyscrapers. Architects and engineers again assembled schemes based on economical arrangements of pneumatically assembled steelwork, traction elevators, and electrically illuminated office interiors. Building exteriors were once again faced with density that called for new ornamental rhetoric, emphasizing first the relationship between block and tower and then the stepping of setback skyscrapers in unified compositions.

Although others have been tempted to parse these buildings into "firsts," it is clear from this overview that Jenney's 1872 Portland Block and Graham, Anderson, Probst, and White's 1934 Field Building stood at the ends of a continuum of iteration and entrepreneurial experiment in which architects, engineers, contractors, and speculators constantly examined the state of the art and sought ways to leverage their own advantage in whatever project came next. This was fueled by the need to outdo other developers and, by extension, other architects and engineers in efficiency, provision, or market appeal. But it was also an enterprise in which competitors subjected their designs to one another's scrutiny and shared their knowledge in public forums. *Inland Architect* was only the most obvious example of Chicago's architects and engineers willingly revealing their secrets; regular meetings of the Western Society of Architects, the Western Society of Engineers, and the Illinois Society of Architects sponsored technical lectures in which all benefited from the acquired knowledge of fellow professionals.[21]

Some combination of these factors also existed in New York, Boston, and Philadelphia. So what happened in Chicago that was distinct from these other cities? Chicago's poor soil was cited by many as a motivation for both lighter construction and skeletal design. Here, the most telling evidence comes from Jenney, whose description of the Home Insurance for *Engineering Record* in 1891 focused almost entirely on the building's foundations and the reduced weight they had to bear. Even his title: "The Chicago Construction, or Tall Buildings on a Compressible Soil," focused

on the connection between footings and superstructure. While lighting was offered as one reason for reducing pier sizes using iron, Jenney also cited the magnitude of the building's foundation loads as an equally impelling cause: "The piers must be narrow in order that proper space might be left for windows, the walls must not be as heavy as the old construction would demand, or there would not be sufficient space on the ground for the foundations. A column in each pier was the natural solution of the problem."[22]

Gerald Larson has noted that both P. B. Wight and Henry Ericsson understood the "intimate relationship between Chicago's foundations and the need for fireproof . . . iron construction" based on weight alone, and Baumann's system of isolated piers suggested condensing superstructures into skeletal systems.[23] Wight traced the tendency of Chicago skyscrapers to resemble in mass and material those of New York to the introduction of caisson foundations.[24] But until these caissons were tried and tested by Sooy Smith and Adler in 1895, the city had to focus on light weight and point loading, a point made by the *Tribune*'s John Howland in 1904: "There are in Chicago today buildings that rise above fifteen stories which, if put into a scales, would weigh much less than the four-story houses of the same ground area that were built and admired twenty years ago. To rear buildings as tall as the modern office

buildings of Chicago out of the same quantity and quality of material used twenty years ago would be an engineering impossibility."[25] New York and Boston designers, in this argument, did not have the impetus toward dissolving the structural wall into a series of point supports, nor were they under pressure to reduce the weight of their structures.

Somewhat more difficult to trace is the influence of Chicago's intense economy on the technical development of the skyscraper. The fixed boundaries of the Loop encouraged greater height, this argument asserts, and thus also influenced architects to design buildings that could provide more floor space per construction dollar. Reflecting on the construction of its own new building in 1901, the *Tribune* hailed Holabird & Roche's design as exemplifying the local tradition of lightweight, spacious, well-illuminated structures: "This 'Chicago construction,' of which the *Tribune* Building is to be one of the newest and best examples, has overturned the old ideas of builders, who worked from heavy foundations, building old-fashioned, solid-masonry piers, exterior walls, and partition walls together from the bottom up. It has given more floor space, more strength, and more light."[26]

Squeezing every inch out of a lot was hardly unique to Chicago, but the confines of the Loop contrasted with the spread of New York's financial district northward along Manhattan Island, and the existence of a second major commercial district in Midtown. Barr Ferree, among others, believed that the "concentration" of Chicago's business in an area of "relatively small dimension" accounted in part for the greater fidelity to regular, easily divisible floors that in turn influenced a more repetitious facade.[27] Of perhaps even greater importance, most of Chicago's early skyscrapers were speculative projects, whereas most large New York projects were built for a major tenant. Owners such as Peter and Shepard Brooks, whatever their attitudes toward building appearance, wanted the flexibility to rent to tenants of all sizes, from one-person operations to large corporations that might require multiple floors or a banking hall. Masonry bearing or shear walls in these plans presented real challenges. Architects thus took every opportunity to clear floor plans of masonry walls. W. G. Williamson, a longtime architect with W. W. Boyington's office, reflected on the changes that his office had seen in commercial work: "[M]assive walls and brick piers were a bar to transformations. It was easier and cheaper to tear down an old building than to try to make it over. The Royal Insurance and Columbus Memorial, designed by this firm, are two prominent buildings whose construction is entirely dissimilar and represents the changes of some fifteen years. The former has heavy brick partitions from basement

to roof, a building in which changes in the way of enlarging rooms are practically impossible."[28]

The explosive escalation in land values that occurred with Chicago's four great real estate booms—in the mid-1880s, the early 1890s, around 1910 and in the mid-1920s—also made speculation an all-or-nothing proposition. Developers did not hesitate to wreck an existing building and construct anew, because the promise of short-term profits and the unwillingness of tenants to settle for obsolete accommodations made even the largest demolition job a profitable proposition. Steel construction allowed speculators to get in and out of projects quickly, before markets reversed course. Speculators came to depend on a regular one-year timetable from the beginning of design to the end of construction, and this encouraged repetitive job site tasks and the use of mass-produced rather than custom-made components.

Keen attention to budget, performance, and schedule meant that Chicago architects also adopted a style of practice that contrasted with the patrician image of the eastern architect. Jenney and Burnham echoed Sullivan's dictum that a tall office building was first a problem to be solved, and only then a composition to be refined. Speaking to the Chicago Architectural Sketch Club in 1889, Jenney foreshadowed the modernist obsession with the

plan as generator, though his intention was more purely economic: "In designing a building it is best to confine oneself, as far as practicable, solely to the plan, with little or no regard for an elevation until a satisfactory plan is obtained. Then design the best elevation the plan will admit of, modifying the plan, if desirable, wherever this can be done without injury, but never sacrifice any part of the plan to the elevation. If you cannot make your elevation what you wish, without injury to the plan, *tant pis* for the elevation."[29]

More evidence for the importance of the plan in skyscraper design can be found in Burnham's letters to his clients, notably to Chicagoan Lyman J. Gage regarding a bank project in New York in 1902, in which he outlined a dogged process of iterative work: "This means that first of all [the client's] architect should show him on paper every one of the different kinds of plans that can be devised for such a building. Having these exhaustive documents before them, [the client] and his architect would, by exclusion, be able to come to a definite conclusion. The same sort of process should follow in the artistic work."[30]

If there was a reductive nature to Chicago's architecture, it came in this scenario from an empirical process of experimentation and ruling out, rather than from a singular, germinal ideal developed through levels of scale and detail as the Beaux-Arts methodology proposed. Each change of scale, for Jenney and Burnham, presented a new problem, and with it possibilities that could be assessed and developed or rejected based on analysis—even, Burnham noted, as the project moved into choices that were purely stylistic. Here, the elevations of Chicago's more expressive frames are manifestations of this approach at a detailed level. Building cladding, according to J. W. Yost, could be broken down into components, which could then be treated as individual design problems: "There seem," he wrote in his paper on steel construction and plate glass in 1896, "to be four parts to be disposed of in the design for a modern steel building. First, the continuous posts; second, the lintels between stories; third, the panel of brick or other material which fills the space between the posts and lintels; and fourth, the windows."[31]

This articulated approach defined the majority of Chicago's skyscrapers and it reflects the empirical approach of Burnham and Jenney. The facade was treated in "Chicago construction" as an assemblage of *components*, each of which had an inherent logic that was balanced within functional, material, and compositional dialogues that established or emphasized the facade's hierarchies. This interplay could be surprisingly rich; the narrow terracotta column covers that pass in front of the spandrels on the Fisher Building, for instance, create a far different impression than the thicker piers and spandrels that are set flush at Sullivan's Schlesinger & Mayer.

At some point, this distilled, articulated problem solving became a shorthand for the city's aversion to academic pretensions or facadism. As Chicago's reputation for architectural innovation grew, the development of integrated solutions and their expression went from studio necessity to architectural philosophy. Often discussed but never fully codified, this included such tenets as the alignment of structural, programmatic, and elevational grids; the layering of facade elements to reflect visual and structural orders; and the sparing use of ornament to punctuate, rather than conceal, elevational rhythms and hierarchies. Chicago architects—especially Jenney—took pride in this largely unspoken but clearly legible utilitarian theory. "You are not pictorial artists," he told the Architectural Sketch Club in 1889, "but architects, and . . . your art is of little value unless you are practical." Art had its place in commercial practice, but it was limited to articulating an otherwise legible and composed scheme:

First, the construction, i.e., the engineering, which, it goes without saying, must be substantial and economical; then the application of art, the adjusting of the proportions, so that the construction is pleasing in its appearance; and then, for further ornamentation, the details of the construction are accented by moldings and carving that is ornamented. The practical is at the bottom of the whole and underlies all that makes claim to architecture. The plan and the entire construction, from turret to foundation stone, is purely practical science, leaving but a small and superficial area for the application of art.[32]

Jenney believed that this process must be scientifically rigorous, and he began this talk by citing Darwin and noting that the "same law of 'survival of the fittest' is just as true of the order *Primates*, genus *Homo*, species *member of the Chicago Architectural Sketch Club*, as of any other animal."[33] Sullivan, of course, also echoed Darwin in his claim that form followed function, and Root argued that the economic pressures of Chicago led to evolutionary pressures: "To other and older types of architecture these new problems are related as the poetry of Darwin's evolution is to other poetry. They destroy indeed much of the most admirable and inspiring of architectural forms, but they create forms adapted to the expression of new ideas and new aspects of life."[34]

Even critics who were not convinced by the evolutionary argument admitted that in the "course of grimness and bare utility" evidenced by Chicago's commercial buildings there was a frank admission that the "heart of Chicago 'looks like business.'" "A commercial building should simply answer its purpose," Montgomery Schuyler relented, "Anything beyond that is irrelevant, incompetent, and impertinent."[35] Others found radical simplicity and repetitive facades unbearably plain, and argued that strict adherence to the functional diagram was simply the "statement of the problem" rather than a "solution."[36] G. Twose, for example, wrote of Adler & Sullivan's Stock Exchange that it "certainly satisfies that reasoning which insists that similar function be expressed by similar forms, but the repression of all character in the windows leaves unsatisfied that part of us which cries for beauty . . . these beautiful traditions receive no recognition whatever, the character of the openings being purely arbitrary, expressive of neither construction, nor anything else, bad in proportion, and utterly lacking in interest or beauty, and indicative only of a desire to suppress and deny them."[37] In shunning traditions of beauty, Twose felt, the Stock Exchange told only "half the truth," failing to reconcile the expressed functional diagram with established precedent.

Adler also felt that Sullivan had told only "half the truth," though his con-cerns had to do not with traditions of beauty but with the importance of material and construction in influencing or inspiring form. The "prosaic output of furnace and mill," Adler felt, could also be transformed into "the language of poetry and art," but only through the "genius of man."[38] Function, he argued, changed little during the genesis and evolution of tall commercial structures—it consisted, in the main, of stacking floor upon floor of well-illuminated, easily accessed lettable space and arranging columns, walls, and elevators so as to gain the most rental income from the least expenditure and site area. If Sullivan were correct, Adler reasoned, there would be none of the variety in building massing or elevations that had occurred in their lifetimes. Instead, Adler argued for an expansion of Sullivan's aphorism, to read "function and environment determine form," bringing the whole milieux of industrial, financial, cultural, and material environments to bear on any single project. A material environment of steel and plate glass, for example, led to far different compositions than one of brick and stone. Adler was influenced by Viollet-le-Duc, who had been published widely and serialized in 1894 in *American Architect and Building News.*[39] But Adler also recalled Gottfried Semper's foundational theories from decades before. Indeed, the articulated wall, which both Schuyler and Barr Ferree believed to be the essential feature of Chicago's skyscrapers, was a concise summary of Semperian theory, which regarded building as woven structure and ornament as an accent designating "the proper relation of parts." Semper's writings had been translated and published by John Root in *Inland Architect* in 1889. Semper's taxonomy of hearth, roof, "circumvallation" and "substruction" and his proposal that "style" was based on the "harmony of a building with the conditions of its coming into existence" found a keen audience in Chicago, where German natives such as Adler and Frederick Baumann held influential positions.[40]

But neither Semper's essentialism nor Viollet-le-Duc's empiricism generated Chicago's distinctive skyscraper style. Rather, these theories seemed to describe the city's approach. Chicago formed a laboratory free from the pretensions of the east. Its position on the fringe of the nation's culture and settlement and its mercenary economy presented architects and clients with a slate that, if not completely free of tradition and manners, was at least well scrubbed. Many reporters noted that Chicago architects felt themselves free of East Coast influence during the 1890s and early 1900s, and the arrival of mercantile classicism with the heavy frames of 1900–1910 came only with technical changes and more established banks and corporations as clients. Even then, the city served as a site for technical and compositional experiments. Novelty was not only accepted in Chicago, it was practically required for potential tenants. The race to build the most advanced, most commodious, and most appealing skyscraper brought with it pressure to innovate and to respond to the innovations of others. Writing in 1894, Barr Ferree summed up the Chicago attitude and style in terms of these pressures: "The progressive spirit of the West has no place for precedent where it does not rest on reason and is not superior to something new. The exigencies of Chicago life having caused the evolution of the high building, Chicago architects have been quick to recognize the impossibility of following ordinary methods of design in it, and have attacked the problem in a new way, as it properly demanded."[41]

This, more than many similar quotes, reflects the nature of practice in Chicago as an active affair. Rather than *passively* applying stylistic precedent to the skyscraper, the city's architects were *actively* engaged in developing new aesthetic norms from the new problems it posed. Neither technology, society, nor culture designed or constructed these buildings. Rather, clients, architects, engineers, and builders collaborated to conceive, organize, and produce structures with clear agendas and little time for willful excursions. These structures' legacies as architectural objects are open to endless debate—were they protomodern? which was the first skyscraper? and would the

"second Chicago School" have existed without the "first"? But their most powerful influences may have been in the ways their designers and builders collaborated, and the way they sought to integrate their knowledge and responsibilities not only in practice but also in the fabrics of the buildings themselves. These years in Chicago saw general contracting replace the individual builder-craftsman, the rise of the drafting office as a site of machinelike production, the beginnings of scientifically rigorous estimating and scheduling, and the establishment of consulting engineers as key designers. Architectural practice in Chicago went, in these sixty-three years, from a provincial guild of carpenters and builders to a community of specialists organized into efficient, professional teams. While Sullivan and his biographers have cast the story of these buildings in heroic, individualist terms, the reality is that they were only achievable through collaborations of astonishing intensity and complexity. Evidence for these collaborations exists in correspondence, in professional journals, and in the lavish toasts that these practitioners gave to one another at conventions. But it also exists in the buildings themselves and in records of practice and tenancy.

Ultimately, this transition from sole practitioners to corporate entities is the most important change in Chicago's architecture during this period. Loop buildings were no longer simple enough

to be carried in the mind of one person. While it was often commercially desirable for one or two designers to serve as figureheads—Burnham or Holabird & Roche, for instance—later firms built offices, corporate cultures, and design methodologies around groups of specialists. Burnham's skill at administration, organization, and office management meant that Burnham & Co.'s practice became as much about collaboration and integration as about singular works of architecture or singular figures responsible for design. The challenge for firms at the end of this era was to forge cogent, legible statements out of the tremendous complexity of a building like the Palmolive and the Opera and the matching complexity of their design and construction teams.

The combination of knowledge, iterative process, collaboration, and testing was summarized by Dankmar Adler, writing for *Cassier's Magazine* in 1897. After explaining the "engineering problems" involved in the "tall business building," Adler closed by noting that these many systems could be organized into a successful piece of skyscraper architecture only by a dedicated, collaborative team, all willing to "subordinate themselves to an important and difficult task, to harmonize their views and efforts with those of their co-labourers." Adler's closing paragraph can serve not only as a summary of Chicago's tacit architectural philosophy, but as a reminder that the study of any reasonably complex building must place itself at the desks of designers and in the shoes of builders:

The writer will have accomplished his object if he has succeeded in demonstrating that to attain the highest possible degree of commercial success in the erection of a tall business building, it is necessary to rear a structure which is at once a work of art and a realization of the best in the science and practice of structural, mechanical, electric and sanitary engineering; that this many-sided perfection can be reached only by the co-operative action of the many minds whose work is made tributary to the purposes of the enterprise, and unless there is, from the very first, a comprehensive grasp of all the requirements of the situation and of all the contributing forces and elements, and a consequent adaptation and co-ordination of all to one central purpose, the result will be chaos, and partial, if not total, failure.[42]

Appendix
Chicago Skyscrapers, 1871–1934

Information compiled from contemporary sources and from Frank Randall, *History of Building Construction in Chicago*

Date	Building	Architect	Location	Demolished	Façade Type	Height (stories)	Foundation
1871	Central Union Block	F. and E. Baumann	Market (Wacker) & Madison	1889	Bearing Masonry	3	NA
1871	Nixon	Otto H. Matz	LaSalle & Monroe	1889	Bearing Masonry	6	NA
1872	Bay State	Carter, Drake, & Wight	State & Randolph		Bearing Masonry	6	spread
1872	Berghoff	NA	17 W. Adams		Cast-Iron Façade	NA	NA
1872	Bowen	W. W. Boyington	62–74 E. Randolph		Bearing Masonry	5	NA
1872	City Hall	John van Osdel	LaSalle & Adams	1885	Bearing Masonry	2	spread
1872	Honore	C. M. Palmer	Dearborn & Adams	1894	Bearing Masonry	6	NA
1872	McCarthy	John van Osdel	Dearborn & Washington	1990	Cast-Iron Façade	4	NA
1872	Portland	William Le Baron Jenney	Dearborn & Washington	1933	Bearing Masonry	7	spread
1873	American Express	H. H. Richardson & Peter B. Wight	21–29 W. Monroe	1896	Bearing Masonry	5	spread
1873	Chicago Real Estate Exchange	John van Osdel	40 N. Dearborn	1940	Bearing Masonry	8	spread
1873	Grand Pacific Hotel	W. W. Boyington	LaSalle & Jackson	1895	Bearing Masonry	6	spread
1873	Page	NA	177–191 N. State		Cast Iron Façade	6	spread
1874	Delaware	Wheelock & Thomas	36 W. Randolph		Cast-Iron Façade	8	spread
1875	Palmer House I	John van Osdel	State & Monroe	1925	Bearing Masonry	7	NA
1875	Walsh	NA	Franklin & Lake	1990	NA	6	NA
1879	Central Music Hall	Burling & Adler	State & Randolph	1901	Bearing Masonry	6	NA
1879	Chicago Post Office & Custom House	John van Osdel	Dearborn & Adams	1896	Bearing Masonry	4	mat
1879	First Leiter	William L. Jenney	Wells & Monroe	1970	Masonry Piers	5	NA
1880	Borden	Dankmar Adler	50–56 W. Randolph	1916	Masonry Piers	6	NA
1881	Brunswick and Baike Factory	Adler & Sullivan	Orleans & Huron	1989	Bearing Masonry	NA	NA
1881	First National Bank (1)	Monroe Burling & Whitehouse	Dearborn & Monroe	1902	Bearing Masonry	6	spread
1881	Grannis Block	Burnham & Root	21–29 N. Dearborn	1885	Bearing Masonry	7	spread
1881	Rothschild	Adler & Sullivan	210–212 W. Monroe	1972	Masonry Piers/Cast Iron	5	NA

Date	Building	Architect	Location	Demolished	Façade Type	Height (stories)	Foundation
1882	Jewelers	Adler & Sullivan	15–19 S. Wabash		Masonry Piers	5	NA
1882	Montauk	Burnham & Root	64–70 W. Monroe	1902	Bearing Masonry	10	pyramidal/grillage
1883	Chicago, Burlington, and Quincy Railroad	Burnham & Root	Franklin & Adams	1926	Bearing Masonry	6	spread
1883	Donohue	J. Speyer	701–721 S. Dearborn		Masonry Piers	8	NA
1883	Hiram Sibley Warehouse	George Edbrooke	315–331 N. Clark	1980	Masonry Piers	9	spread/pier
1883	Revell	Adler & Sullivan	Wabash & Adams	1968	Masonry Piers	6	NA
1884	Calumet	Burnham & Root	111–117 S. LaSalle	1913	Bearing Masonry	9	spread
1884	Counselman	Burnham & Root	238–240 W. LaSalle	1920	Bearing Masonry	9	spread
1884	Gaff	Stephen V. Shipman	230 S. LaSalle	1920	Bearing Masonry	9	spread
1884	Mallers	John J. Flanders	LaSalle & Quincy	1920	Masonry Piers	12	spread
1884	Pullman	S. S. Beman	Adams & Michigan	1956	Bearing Masonry	10	NA
1884	Ryerson	Adler & Sullivan	16–20 E. Randolph	1939	Masonry Piers	6	NA
1884	Troescher	Adler & Sullivan	15 S. Wacker	1978	Masonry Piers	6	NA
1885	Board of Trade	W. W. Boyington	141 W. Jackson	1929	Bearing Masonry	10	spread
1885	Cook County Courthouse	James Egan	LaSalle & Randolph	1906	Bearing Masonry	5	piles
1885	Home Insurance	William L. Jenney	LaSalle & Adams	1931	Bearing Masonry/Skeleton Frame	9	pyramidal
1885	Insurance Exchange (1)	Burnham & Root	LaSalle & Adams	1912	Masonry Piers	9	spread
1885	Opera House	Cobb & Frost	Clark & Washington	1912	Masonry Piers	10	spread
1885	Royal Insurance	W. W. Boyington	160 W. Jackson	1920	Masonry Piers	13	pyramidal spread
1885	Ward	Beers, Clay & Dutton	14 N. Michigan		Masonry Piers	8	pile
1886	Forman & Kohn	Bauer & Hill	305 W. Adams	1970	NA	8	spread
1886	Mergenthaler Linotype	Richard E. Schmidt, Garden & Martin	531–537 S. Plymouth Court		Masonry Piers	NA	NA
1886	Rialto	Burnham & Root	LaSalle & Van Buren	1940	Masonry Piers	9	spread grillage
1886	Richardson	Treat & Foltz	Congress & Wabash		Masonry Piers	7	NA
1886	Studebaker/Fine Arts	S. S. Beman	410 S. Michigan		Masonry Piers	8	spread
1887	Conkey/Franklin	Baumann & Lotz	519–531 S. Dearborn		Masonry Piers	7	NA
1887	Marshall Field Wholesale Store	H. H. Richardson	Adams bet. Wells & Franklin	1930	Bearing Masonry	NA	NA
1887	Phoenix	Burnham & Root	111 W. Jackson St.	1957	Masonry Piers	11	spread
1887	Willoughby Building	George H. Edbrooke	Jackson & Franklin	1927	Masonry Piers	8	spread
1887	Wirt Dexter	Adler & Sullivan	624–630 S. Wabash	2007	Masonry Piers	6	spread
1888	Phelps, Dodge, and Palmer	Burling & Whitehouse	200 W. Adams	1985	NA	6	NA
1888	Rookery	Burnham & Root	LaSalle & Adams		Masonry Piers	11	spread grillage
1889	Auditorium	Adler & Sullivan	Michigan & Congress		Bearing Masonry	18	grillage (modified)
1889	Tacoma	Holabird & Roche	LaSalle & Madison	1929	Curtain Wall	12	spread grillage
1889	Walker Warehouse	Adler & Sullivan	200–214 S. Market	1953	Masonry Piers	6	NA
1890	Caxton	Holabird & Roche	508 S. Dearborn	1947	Veneered	12	spread grillage
1890	Chamber of Commerce	Baumann & Huehl	LaSalle & Washington	1928	Skeleton Frame	13	spread
1890	Manhattan	William L. Jenney	431 S. Dearborn		Veneered	16	spread grillage and cantilever
1890	Monon	John van Osdel	436–444 S. Dearborn	1947	Veneered	13	spread
1890	Owings	Cobb & Frost	Dearborn & Adams	1940	Veneered	14	mat
1890	Second Rand McNally	Burnham & Root	LaSalle & Adams	1911	Skeleton Frame	10	spread grillage
1891	Ludington	William L. Jenney	Wabash & 11th		Skeleton Frame	8	spread
1891	Monadnock	Burnham & Root	Dearborn & Jackson		Bearing Wall	16	NA
1891	Pontiac	Holabird & Roche	Dearborn & Harrison		Veneered	14	spread grillage
1891	Second Leiter/Sears	William L. Jenney	State & Van Buren		Skeleton Frame	8	spread grillage

Date	Building	Architect	Location	Demolished	Façade Type	Height (stories)	Foundation
1891	Western Bank Note/Willoughby	Charles S. Frost	8 S. Michigan	1927	NA	8	NA
1892	30 N. Dearborn	Henry Cobb	30 N. Dearborn	1962	NA	12	spread
1892	Ashland	Burnham & Root	Clark & Randolph	1949	Veneered	16	spread
1892	Chicago Title & Trust	Henry Cobb	69 W. Washington	1962	NA	17	spread
1892	Criminal Courts	Otto H. Matz	54 W. Hubbard	(altered)	Bearing Masonry	6	NA
1892	Fair	William L. Jenney	State & Adams	1986	Skeleton Frame	9	spread grillage
1892	Great Northern Hotel	Burnham & Root	Dearborn & Jackson	1940	Veneered	16	spread grillage
1892	Isabella	William L. Jenney	21 E. Van Buren.	2003?	Skeleton Frame	11	spread grillage
1892	Marshall Field Annex	D. H. Burnham	Wabash & Washington		Veneered	9	spread
1892	Masonic Temple/Capitol	Burnham & Root	State & Randolph	1939	Veneered	21	spread grillage
1892	Schiller/Garrick	Adler & Sullivan	64 W. Randolph	1961	Veneered	17	piles
1892	Unity	C. J. Warren	127 N. Dearborn	1990	Veneered	16	spread
1892	Venetian	Holabird & Roche	15 E. Washington	1957	Expressed Frame	13	NA
1892	Woman's Temple	Burnham & Root	LaSalle & Monroe	1926	Bearing Masonry	13	spread grillage
1892	Yondorf	NA	225 S. Wacker	1968	Curtain Wall	NA	NA
1893	Brewster Apartments	Enoch Hill Turnock	2800 N. Pine Grove		NA	NA	NA
1893	Central YMCA	Jenney & Mundie	19 S. LaSalle		Solid Curtain Wall	16	spread grillage
1893	Chicago Athletic Club	Henry Cobb	12 S. Michigan		Veneered	10	spread
1893	Columbus Memorial Building	W. W. Boyington	Washington & State	1959	Veneered	14	spread
1893	Congress Hotel	C. J. Warren	Michigan & Congress		Curtain Wall	10	spread
1893	Hartford	Henry Cobb	8 S. Dearborn	ca. 1960	NA	14	spread
1893	Majestic Hotel	D. H. Burnham	29 W. Quincy	1961	Curtain Wall	17	NA
1893	Maller's Warehouse	Flanders & Zimmerman	225 S. Market	1950	Curtain Wall	NA	NA
1893	Monadnock South Block	Holabird & Roche	Dearborn & Van Buren		Expressed Frame	17	NA
1893	Teutonic	Handy & Cady	179 W. Washington	(altered)	Veneered	10	spread
1893	Van Buren	Flanders & Zimmerman	210–214 W. Van Buren		Curtain Wall	NA	NA
1894	Champlain I	Holabird & Roche	State & Madison	1916	Expressed Frame	15	spread
1894	New York Life	William L. Jenney	37–43 S. LaSalle		Solid Curtain Wall	12	spread grillage
1894	Old Colony	Holabird & Roche	Dearborn & Van Buren		Curtain Wall	17	spread grillage
1894	Stock Exchange	Adler & Sullivan	30 N. LaSalle	1972	Expressed Frame/Curtain Wall	13	pile/caisson
1895	Fort Dearborn	Jenney & Mundie	105 W. Monroe	ca. 1960	Veneered	16	spread grillage
1895	Marquette	Holabird & Roche	Dearborn & Adams		Expressed Frame	17	spread grillage
1895	Reliance	D. H. Burnham	State & Washington		Curtain Wall	16	spread grillage
1895	Studebaker	S. S. Beman	629 S. Wabash	(altered)	Curtain Wall	10	spread
1896	Atwood	Holabird & Roche	Clark & Madison	1941	Curtain Wall	10	grillage
1896	Fisher	D. H. Burnham	Dearborn & Van Buren		Curtain Wall	18	piles/spread
1896	Great Northern Hotel Addition	D. H. Burnham	Dearborn bet. Quincy & Jackson	ca. 1960	Curtain Wall	16	NA
1896	Morton	William L. Jenney	538 S. Dearborn		Curtain Wall	11	NA
1897	R. R. Donnelley/731 South Plymouth	Howard Van Doren Shaw	731 S. Plymouth		Expressed Frame	7	NA
1897	Silversmith	D. H. Burnham	10 S. Wabash		Expressed Frame	10	pile
1897	Stewart	D. H. Burnham	State & Washington		Solid Curtain Wall	12	NA
1897	Trude	Jenney & Mundie	Wabash & Randolph	1913	NA	16	spread
1898	Bailey	Holabird & Roche	529 S. Franklin	1953	Expressed Frame	10	piles
1898	Williams	Holabird & Roche	205 W. Monroe'		Expressed Frame	10	spread
1899	Cable	Holabird & Roche	Wabash & Jackson	1961	Expressed Frame	10	pile/caisson

Date	Building	Architect	Location	Demolished	Façade Type	Height (stories)	Foundation
1899	Schlesinger & Mayer/Carson Pirie Scott	Louis Sullivan	State & Madison		Expressed Frame	12	pile
1899	Gage Group	Holabird & Roche	18–30 S. Michigan		Expressed Frame	7	NA
1899	Gage Group	Louis Sullivan	18 S. Michigan		Expressed Frame	8	NA
1899	Methodist Book Concern	Harry B. Wheelock	12–14 W. Washington	1990	Expressed Frame	11	caissons
1899	Montgomery Ward/Tower	Richard Schmidt	6 N. Michigan	(altered)	Expressed Frame	12	pile
1899	Plymouth	Simeon B. Eisendrath	417 S. Dearborn		Expressed Frame	11	spread
1900	Ayer/McClurg	Holabird & Roche	218 S. Wabash		Expressed Frame	9	pile/caisson
1900	Mandel Brothers	Holabird & Roche	Wabash & Madison		Expressed Frame	9	pile/caisson
1901	Grommes & Ulrich	Richard Schmidt	108–114 W. Illinois		Expressed Frame	4	NA
1901	Merchants Loan and Trust Bank	D. H. Burnham	Clark & Adams	1933	Expressed Frame	12	piles
1902	Congress Hotel Addition	Holabird & Roche	Michigan & Congress		Curtain Wall	14	caissons/piles
1902	Marshall Field	D. H. Burnham	State & Randolph		Expressed Frame	12	caissons
1902	National Life/Equitable	Jenney & Mundie	29 S. LaSalle		Expressed Frame	12	spread
1902	Tribune	Holabird & Roche	Dearborn & Madison	2000	Expressed Frame	17	caissons
1903	Brock & Rankin	Holabird & Roche	615–627 S. LaSalle		Expressed Frame	7	NA
1903	Champlain	Holabird & Roche	Wabash & Monroe		Expressed Frame	13	piles/caissons
1903	First National Bank (3)	D. H. Burnham	Monroe & Dearborn	1969	Expressed Frame	17	caissons
1904	Chapin & Gore	Richard Schmidt	63 E. Adams		Expressed Frame	8	wood piles
1904	Chicago & Northwestern Offices	Frost & Granger	226 W. Jackson		Expressed Frame	14	caissons
1904	Foundation Hall	E. R. Krause	1006 S. Michigan		Expressed Frame	8	NA
1904	McNeil	Holabird & Roche	Wacker & Jackson	1990	Expressed Frame	10	piles/caissons
1904	Railway Exchange	D. H. Burnham	Michigan & Jackson		Curtain Wall	17	caissons
1904	Winton	James Gamble Rogers	S. Michigan & 13th	ca. 1990?	Expressed Frame	3	NA
1905	Boston	Holabird & Roche	Dearborn & Madison		Expressed Frame	17	caissons
1905	Chicago	Holabird & Roche	State & Madison		Expressed Frame/Curtain Wall	15	caissons
1905	Garment Center	Jenney, Mundie & Jensen	Franklin & Van Buren	1975	Expressed Frame	10	pile
1905	Heyworth	D. H. Burnham	Wabash & Madison		Expressed Frame	18	caissons
1905	Kresge	Holabird & Roche	10–14 S. State	2000	Expressed Frame	6	NA
1905	Majestic	E. R. Krause	16 W. Monroe		Expressed Frame/Beaux-Arts	20	caissons
1905	Northern Trust	Frost & Granger	LaSalle & Monroe		Solid Curtain Wall	4	caissons
1905	Orchestra Hall	D. H. Burnham	220 S. Michigan		Solid Curtain Wall	10	piles
1905	Patten	C. A. Eckstorm	161 W. Harrison		Expressed Frame	12	pile/caisson
1905	Republic	Holabird & Roche	209 S. State	1961	Expressed Frame	12	NA
1906	Fairbanks, Morse, & Co.	Holabird & Roche	Wabash & 9th		Expressed Frame	7	pile
1906	Lakeview	Jenney, Mundie & Jensen	116 S. Michigan		Expressed Frame	12	caissons
1906	Mentor	Howard Van Doren Shaw	Monroe & State		Expressed Frame	17	caissons
1906	Plamondon	Leon E. Stanhope	Clinton & Monroe	ca. 1980	NA	7	spread
1906	Rector	Jarvis Hunt	79 W. Monroe		Expressed Frame	13	piles/caissons
1907	Commercial Bank/Edison	D. H. Burnham	Clark & Adams		Solid Curtain Wall	18	caissons
1907	Montgomery Ward Warehouse	Schmidt Garden & Martin	618 W. Chicago		Expressed Frame	8	piles
1908	Born	Holabird & Roche	540 S. Wells	1953	Expressed Frame	12	piles
1908	Corn Exchange	Shepley Rutan & Coolidge	122–136 S. LaSalle	1985	Solid Curtain Wall	17	caissons
1908	Hunter	Christian Eckstrom	Madison & Wacker	1978	Expressed Frame	12	NA
1908	Oliver	Holabird & Roche	159–167 N. Dearborn		Expressed Frame	7	piles
1909	Blackstone Hotel	Marshall & Fox	Michigan & Balbo		Solid Curtain Wall	22	caissons

Date	Building	Architect	Location	Demolished	Façade Type	Height (stories)	Foundation
1909	LaSalle Hotel	Holabird & Roche	LaSalle & Madison	1977	Solid Curtain Wall	22	caissons
1909	University Club	Holabird & Roche	Michigan & Monroe		Solid Curtain Wall	14	pile
1910	Brooks	Holabird & Roche	Franklin & Jackson		Expressed Frame	12	pile
1910	Chicago Business College	D. H. Burnham	Adams & Wabash	1995	Expressed Frame	8	caissons
1910	Hart, Schaffner, & Marx	Holabird & Roche	36 S. Franklin	1983	NA	12	piles/caissons
1910	Kesner	Mundie & Jensen	Madison & Wabash		Expressed Frame	17	caissons
1910	McCormick	Holabird & Roche	332 S. Michigan		Solid Curtain Wall	20	caissons
1910	Studebaker III	William E. Walker	S. Michigan & E. 21st		Expressed Frame	7	caissons
1911	City Hall	Holabird & Roche	Clark & Washington		NA	12	caissons
1911	Dwight	Richard Schmidt	626 S. Clark		Expressed Frame	10	caissons
1911	Harris Trust and Savings Bank	Shepley Rutan & Coolidge	111 W. Monroe		Solid Curtain Wall	20	caissons
1911	Hearst	James C. Green	326 W. Madison	1990	Solid Curtain Wall	11	caissons
1911	Karpen/Standard Oil	Marshall & Fox	910 S. Michigan		Solid Curtain Wall	13	caissons
1911	People's Gas	D. H. Burnham	Michigan & Adams		Solid Curtain Wall	20	caissons
1911	Transportation	F. V. Prather	Dearborn & Harrison		Solid Curtain Wall	22	caissons
1911	Winston	Paul Gerhardt Sr.	341–349 E. Ohio	ca. 1990?	Expressed Frame	6	NA
1912	1550 N. State	Marshall & Fox	1550 N. State		Solid Curtain Wall	NA	NA
1912	Boyce	D. H. Burnham	510 N. Dearborn		Expressed Frame	10	caissons/spread
1912	Franklin	George Nimmons	720–736 S. Dearborn		Expressed Frame	13	caissons
1912	Goldblatt's	Holabird & Roche	State & Van Buren		Expressed Frame	10	caissons
1912	Insurance Exchange	D. H. Burnham	175 W. Jackson		Solid Curtain Wall	21	caissons
1912	Mallers	Christian Eckstrom	67 E. Madison		Expressed Frame	21	caissons
1912	Medinah Temple	Huehl & Schmid	Ontario & Wabash		Solid Curtain Wall	4	spread
1912	Monroe Building	Holabird & Roche	26 E. Monroe		Expressed Frame	16	caissons
1912	North American	Holabird & Roche	36 S. State		Expressed Frame	19	caissons
1912	Otis	Holabird & Roche	10 S. LaSalle		Solid Curtain Wall	16	caissons
1912	Polk-Wells	D. H. Burnham	801 S. Wells		Expressed Frame	10	caissons
1912	Rand McNally III	Holabird & Roche	538 S. Clark		Expressed Frame	10	piles/caissons
1912	Stevens Store	D. H. Burnham	17 N. State		Solid Curtain Wall	19	caissons
1913	Butler Brothers	D. H. Burnham	Canal & Randolph	(altered)	Expressed Frame	14	caissons
1913	Consumers	Mundie & Jensen	220 S. State		Expressed Frame	21	caissons
1913	Conway	D. H. Burnham	Clark & Washington		Solid Curtain Wall	21	caissons
1913	Reid Murdoch	George Nimmons	320 N. Clark		Expressed Frame	10	pile
1913	Society Brand Building	Graham Burnham & Co.	416 S. Franklin	1950	Expressed Frame	13	pile/caisson
1914	Annex	D. H. Burnham	Wabash & Washington		Expressed Frame	20	NA
1914	Continental National Bank	D. H. Burnham	208 S. LaSalle		Solid Curtain Wall	20	caissons
1914	Fort Dearborn Hotel	Holabird & Roche	410 S. LaSalle		Solid Curtain Wall	17	caissons
1914	LeMoyne Building	Mundie, Jensen & McClurg	180 N. Wabash		Expressed Frame	8	NA
1914	Morrison Hotel	Marshall & Fox	71–89 W. Madison	1966	Solid Curtain Wall	23	caissons
1914	People's Trust	Jarvis Hunt	30 N. Michigan		Solid Curtain Wall	15	caissons
1915	Century	Holabird & Roche	State & Adams		Expressed Frame	16	caissons
1915	Garland	C. A. Eckstorm	58 E. Washington		Expressed Frame	21	caissons
1915	Lumber Exchange	Holabird & Roche	11 S. LaSalle		Expressed Frame	16	caissons
1915	YMCA Hotel	Robert Berlin	826 S. Wabash		Solid Curtain Wall	19	caissons
1917	State-Lake	Rapp & Rapp	State & Lake		Expressed Frame	12	caissons

Date	Building	Architect	Location	Demolished	Façade Type	Height (stories)	Foundation
1920	Crerar Library	Holabird & Roche	Michigan & Randolph	1981	Solid Curtain Wall	16	caissons
1920	Drake Hotel	Marshall & Fox	Lake Shore Drive & Walton		Solid Curtain Wall	13	piles
1921	Wrigley	Graham Anderson Probst & White	410 N. Michigan		Solid Curtain Wall	28	caissons
1922	Federal Reserve Bank	Graham Anderson Probst & White	230 S. LaSalle		Solid Curtain Wall	14	caissons
1923	Chicago Temple	Holabird & Roche	77 W. Washington		Solid Curtain Wall	21	caissons
1923	Hartman	A. S. Alschuler	30 E. Adams		Solid Curtain Wall	12	pile
1923	London Guarantee	Alfred Alschuler	360 N. Michigan		Solid Curtain Wall	21	caissons
1924	Allerton House	Murgatroyd & Ogden	701 N. Michigan		Solid Curtain Wall	25	caissons
1924	Burnham	Burnham Brothers	160 N. LaSalle		Solid Curtain Wall	20	caissons
1924	Continental Illinois	Graham Anderson Probst & White	231 S. LaSalle		Solid Curtain Wall	19	caissons
1924	Lake Shore Club	Jarvis Hunt	850 N. Lake Shore Drive		Solid Curtain Wall	18	pile
1924	Straus	Graham Anderson Probst & White	310 S. Michigan		Solid Curtain Wall	21	piles
1925	American Furniture Mart	Henry Raeder Associates	680 N. Lake Shore Drive		Solid Curtain Wall	16	pile
1925	Bell Building	Vitzhum & Burns	307 N. Michigan		Solid Curtain Wall	24	caissons
1925	Morrison Hotel Tower	Holabird & Roche	15–29 S. Clark	1966	Solid Curtain Wall	45	caissons
1925	Tribune Tower	Hood & Howell	435 N. Michigan		Solid Curtain Wall	36	caissons
1925	Union Station	Graham Anderson Probst & White	Canal & Adams		Solid Curtain Wall	5	caissons
1926	32 W. Randolph/Oriental	Rapp & Rapp	32 W. Randolph		Solid Curtain Wall	22	caissons
1926	Pure Oil	Giaver & Dinkelberg	35 E. Wacker		Solid Curtain Wall	41	caissons
1926	Singer	Mundie & Jensen	120 S. State		Expressed Frame	10	caissons
1927	Adams-Franklin	A. S. Alschuler	222 W. Adams		Solid Curtain Wall	16	pile
1927	Builders Building	Graham Anderson Probst & White	222 N. LaSalle	(altered)	Solid Curtain Wall	22	caissons
1927	Palmer House	Holabird & Roche	101–129 S. State		Solid Curtain Wall	25	caissons
1927	Pittsfield	Graham Anderson Probst & White	55 E. Washington		Solid Curtain Wall	38	caissons
1927	Stevens Hotel	Holabird & Roche	720 S. Michigan		Solid Curtain Wall	29	caissons
1928	333 N. Michigan	Holabird & Root	333 N. Michigan		Solid Curtain Wall	35	caissons
1928	Chicago Motor Club	Holabird & Root	68 E. Wacker		Solid Curtain Wall	17	caissons
1928	Dearborn State Bank	Rapp & Rapp	203 N. Wabash		Solid Curtain Wall	22	caissons
1928	Engineering Building	Burnham Brothers	205 W. Wacker		Solid Curtain Wall	23	caissons
1928	Mather Tower	Herbert Hugh Riddle	75 E. Wacker		Solid Curtain Wall	42	caissons
1928	Women's Athletic Club	Philip B. Maher	626 N. Michigan		Solid Curtain Wall	9	pile
1928	Woolworth	Walter Ahlschlager	20–30 N. State		Solid Curtain Wall	10	caissons
1929	105 W. Madison	Burnham Brothers	105 W. Madison		Solid Curtain Wall	23	caissons
1929	Carbide & Carbon	Burnham Brothers	230 N. Michigan		Solid Curtain Wall	40	caissons
1929	Chicago Daily News	Holabird & Root	400 W. Madison		Solid Curtain Wall	26	caissons
1929	Civic Opera	Graham Anderson Probst & White	20 N. Wacker		Solid Curtain Wall	45	caissons
1929	McGraw-Hill	Thielbar & Fugard	520 N. Michigan		Solid Curtain Wall	17	piles
1929	Medinah Athletic Club	Walter Ahlschlager	505 N. Michigan		Solid Curtain Wall	45	caissons
1929	Palmolive	Holabird & Root	919 N. Michigan		Solid Curtain Wall	36	caissons
1929	Steuben Club Building	Vitzhum & Burns	188 W. Randolph		Solid Curtain Wall	42	caissons
1929	Willoughby Tower	Samuel N. Crowen	8 S. Michigan		Solid Curtain Wall	36	caissons
1930	1 North LaSalle	Vitzhum & Burns	1 N. LaSalle		Solid Curtain Wall	49	caissons
1930	Board of Trade	Holabird & Root	141 W. Jackson		Solid Curtain Wall	45	caissons
1930	Buckingham	Holabird & Root	59–67 E. Van Buren		Solid Curtain Wall	27	caissons
1930	Foreman State National Bank	Graham Anderson Probst & White	33 N. LaSalle		Solid Curtain Wall	38	caissons

Date	Building	Architect	Location	Demolished	Façade Type	Height (stories)	Foundation
1930	LaSalle Wacker	Holabird & Root	221 N. LaSalle		Solid Curtain Wall	41	caissons
1930	Trustees Systems Service Building	Thielbar & Fugard	201 N. Wells		Solid Curtain Wall	28	caissons
1931	Lawson YMCA	Chatten & Hammond	30 W. Chicago		Solid Curtain Wall	24	mat/piles/caissons
1931	Merchandise Mart	Graham Anderson Probst & White	Chicago River & Wells		Solid Curtain Wall	25	caissons
1934	Field Building	Graham Anderson Probst & White	135 S. LaSalle		Solid Curtain Wall	42	caissons

Notes

PREFACE

1. Carl Condit, *The Rise of the Sky-scraper: The Genius of Chicago Architecture from the Great Fire to Louis Sullivan* (Chicago: University of Chicago Press, 1952).

2. Condit, "Modern Architecture," 45–54.

3. Sherman, review of *Chicago School of Architecture*, 507–508.

4. Kann, review of "*Chicago School of Architecture*," 472–475.

5. Hitchcock, review of *Rise of the Sky-scraper*, 351–359.

6. Ibid.

7. Weisman, review of *Chicago School of Architecture*, 312–314.

8. Thomas Leslie, "Dankmar Adler's Response to Louis Sullivan's 'The Tall Office Building Artistically Considered': Architecture and the 'Four Causes,'" *Journal of Architectural Education*, Vol. 64, no. 1, Sept. 2010, 86–96. I am grateful to Kevin Alter for discussing with me the genesis of his very fine aphorism.

9. "Chicago's Sky-Scrapers," *Chicago Daily Tribune*, Jan. 13, 1889, 2. This article holds the distinction of being the earliest mention in the *Tribune*'s pages of tall buildings as "skyscrapers."

10. "Its Big Buildings," *Chicago Daily Tribune*, Oct. 16, 1892, 35.

11. Schuyler, "Glimpses of Western Architecture: Chicago—II," 561.

12. Ibid., 560.

13. "Two Types of Office Building," *Chicago Daily Tribune*, Nov. 29, 1891, 28.

14. "[T]o other and older types of architecture these new problems are related as the poetry of Darwin's evolution is to other poetry." Root, "Great Architectural Problem," 71. For other references to Darwin, see Kimball, "Louis Sullivan—An Old Master," 296; and W. L. B. Jenney, "A Few Practical Hints [paper read before the Chicago Architectural Sketch Club, January 28, 1889]," *Inland Architect and News Record*, Vol. XIII, no. 1, Feb. 1889, 7.

15. Misa, *Nation of Steel*, 69.

16. Winkler [Schuyler], "Some Chicago Buildings," 313.

17. Ferree, "Modern Office Building [Part III, May 1986],"35.

18. "Office-Building Projects," *Chicago Daily Tribune*, Aug. 9, 1891, 14.

19. Head, "Heart of Chicago," 559–560.

20. "Office Buildings of Two Cities," *Chicago Daily Tribune*, Dec. 6, 1891, 28.

21. Misa, *Nation of Steel*, 69.

22. "Chicago Shocks British Writer," *Chicago Daily*, Oct. 17, 1902, 4; and Stone, "Chicago: Before the Fire," 679.

23. "Its Big Buildings," 35. See, for instance, "Two Types of Office Buildings," 28; or Head, "Heart of Chicago," 561.

24. Fitzpatrick, "Chicago," 46.

25. Montgomery Schuyler, "The Economics of Steel Frame Construction," 1895, rep. in Lewis Mumford, *Roots of Contemporary American Architecture* (New York: Reinhold, 1952).

26. Schuyler, "'Sky-Scraper' Up to Date," 255.

27. Fitzpatrick, "Chicago," 46. See also "Chicago Architects in Lead," *Chicago Daily Tribune*, Oct. 11, 1903, 18.

28. Ferree, "High Building and Its Art," 310.

29. Henry Van Brunt, "Architecture in the West," *Inland Architect and News Record*, Vol. XIV, no. 7, Dec. 1889, 79.

CHAPTER 1. OCTOBER 1871

1. Landau, *P. B. Wight*, 30.

2. Peter B. Wight, "Daniel Hudson Burnham: An Appreciation," *Architectural Record*, Vol. XXXII, no. 167, Aug. 1912, 184.

3. Cronon, *Nature's Metropolis*.

4. See Susan E. Hirsch, "Economic Geography," in James R. Grossman, Ann Durkin Keating, and Janice L. Reiff, eds., *The Encyclopedia of Chicago* (Chicago: University of Chicago Press, 2004), 254–260.

5. Cronon's thesis was foreseen by Franklin Head in 1892: "A city originates no wealth, but lives by adding new value, either in labor or transportation, to the products of the fields, forests, and mines." Head, "Heart of Chicago," 556–557. See also Lewis, "Chicago—The Evolution,"1558.

6. H. Roger Grant, "Transportation," in Grossman, Keating, and Reiff, *Encyclopedia*, 826–832.

7. "More Cloud Supporters," 9.

8. Ibid. See also Stone, "Chicago: Before the Fire," 670.

9. "A Year's Building," *Chicago Tribune*, Dec. 28, 1884, 10:1.

10. "Anniversary of the Great Fire," *Chicago*, Oct. 9, 1872, 5.

11. "Practical Quality of Granite," 3. See also table published in *Industrial Chicago*, 446.

12. Ibid.

13. "Lifetime of Building Stones," 44.

14. "Mosaics," *Inland Architect and News Record*, Vol. IX, no. 8, June 1887, 84.

15. "Practical Quality of Granite," 3.

16. *Industrial Chicago*, 453; and Jenney, "Building Stones of Chicago," 1–2.

17. "Greatest of All in Building," *Chicago Daily Tribune*, Mar. 4, 1907, 20.

18. Larson, "Fire, Earth, and Wind," 31.

19. *Industrial Chicago*, 445; and Larson, "Fire, Earth, and Wind," 31.

20. *Industrial Chicago*, 455.

21. Ibid., 454. Editorial, *Inland Architect and Builder*, Vol. 1, no. 3, Apr. 1883, 32–33.

22. *Industrial Chicago*, 460.

23. Ibid., 452.

24. Ibid., 451; see also "Fire-Proof Buildings," *Chicago Tribune*, Mar. 12, 1872, 2; and Freitag, *Architectural Engineering*, 152.

25. Beaumont, "Brickwork," 61.

26. Ibid.

27. *Industrial Chicago*, 386.

28. Ibid.

29. "The Chicago Brick and Lumber Market," *Engineering News and American Contract Journal*, May 20, 1882, 162–163.

30. Editorial, *Inland Architect and Builder*, 32.

31. The following capsule history of cast iron in Chicago is based on *Industrial Chicago*, 384–476.

32. Ewen, "Foundations," 687. For notes on Chicago's bedrock, see also Shankland, "Foundations," in Britten and Jones, *Half-Century*, 109.

33. William Le Baron Jenney, "The Construction of a Heavy Fire Proof Building on a Compressible Soil," *Sanitary Engineer*, Vol. XIII, Dec. 10, 1885, 32.

34. Shankland, "Foundations," in Britten and Jones, 111. For other descriptions of the hardpan layer and its depth, see "Office Buildings of Two Cities," *Chicago Daily Tribune*, Dec. 6, 1891, 28; Harry Lawrie, "Chicago Foundations," *Inland Architect and Builder*, Vol. VI, no. 7, 111; and "Chicago's Building Foundations," *Chicago Daily Tribune*, Oct. 11, 1891, 12. William Sooy-Smith is quoted in "Safe High Buildings," *Chicago Daily*, Apr. 1, 1892, 9. For other estimates of soil-bearing capacity, see Henry Ives Cobb quoted in "High Building Problem," *Chicago Daily*, Nov. 11, 1891, 9; and Jenney, quoted in "Chicago's Big Buildings," *Chicago Daily Tribune*, Sept. 13, 1891, 25. Shankland, "Steel Skeleton"; and *Industrial Chicago*, 169–170.

35. Shankland, "Steel Skeleton," 1–2.

36. "Safe High Buildings," 9. See also W. L. B. Jenney, "Chicago Construction, or Tall Buildings on a Compressible Soil," *Engineering Record*, Nov. 14, 1891, 390; and "High Building Plans," *Chicago Daily*, Apr. 4, 1892, 9.

37. Purdy, "Evolution of High Building," 203–204.

38. "How Firm a Foundation," *Chicago Daily Tribune*, Aug. 2, 1891, 26. See also Ewen, "Foundations."

39. Shankland, "Steel Skeleton," 2. See also Shankland, "Foundations," in Britten and Jones, 111.

40. "Chicago's Building Foundations," *Chicago Daily Tribune*, Oct. 11, 1891, 12. Fitz-Simons's comments were republished with great relish by the *Times* a week later: see "The Crust at Chicago," *New York Times*, Oct. 18, 1891, 4.

41. *Industrial Chicago*, 169–170. "High Building Problem," 9.

42. "Anniversary of the Great Fire," *Chicago*, Oct. 9, 1872, 5. See also Stone, "Chicago: Before the Fire," 670–674.

43. The iron boulder was not moved when it was rediscovered during excavations for the Masonic Temple in 1891. "Four Big Buildings," *Chicago Daily*, Jan. 22, 1893, 34.

44. "Anniversary of the Great Fire," 5.

45. "The secret of the building's imperviousness to the flames lay in the fact that all the iron beams were coated over with heavy layers of plaster of paris. . . . The building also had brick arches throughout covered with ordinary plaster. The old Postoffice Building and the Illinois Central office building also had brick arches, but the beams were not covered with plaster, so that the beams exposed directly to the heat bent and allowed the walls to fall." "Only Building Saved," *Chicago Daily*, June 4, 1893, 36. See also letters from John Corlies, the Nixon's contractor, "Fire-Proof Buildings [Letter to the Editor]," *Chicago Tribune*, Nov. 26, 1871, 2.

46. "Only Building Saved," 36. "Miscellaneous Items," *Chicago*, Oct. 12, 1871, 3.

47. Kirkland and Moses, *History of Chicago*, 219–220.

48. Ibid., 231.

49. Root, "Great Architectural Problem," 68. Adler, "Tall Business Building," 193–210. Similar overviews of the skyscraper as a functional and constructive type can be found in G. Hill, "Office Building," 11–18; Ferree, "Modern Office Building, Part I," 4–5 and subsequent nos.; and two invaluable textbooks: Birkmire, *Planning and Construction*, and Freitag, *Architectural Engineering*. Among all of these, of course, lay Sullivan's "Tall Office Building," 32–34.

50. Adler, "Tall Business Building," 193.

51. Ibid.

52. Root, "Great Architectural Problem," 67–68.

53. Adler, "Tall Business Building," 198–199.

54. Root, "Great Architectural Problem," 71. Quotation from Adler, "Tall Business Building," 193–194.

55. "Commercial Architecture," in *Industrial Chicago*, 168. See also "Central Music Hall," *Chicago Daily Tribune*, Mar. 11, 1879, 6; "New Central Music Hall," 150–151; "The Music Hall," *Chicago Daily Tribune*, Dec. 5, 1879, 7; and "The New Music Hall," *Chicago Daily Tribune*, Dec. 7, 1879, 4.

CHAPTER 2. "BUILT MOSTLY OF ITSELF"

1. "Greatest of All in Building," *Chicago Daily Tribune*, Mar. 4, 1907, 20. For the transition from handmade to machine-pressed brick in Chicago, see Thomas Leslie, "'Built Mostly of Itself': The Chicago Brick Industry and the Masonry Skyscraper in the Late 19th Century," *Construction History*, 25, 2010.

2. "Architectural and Building Notes," *Inland Architect and Builder*, Vol. 1, no. 1, Feb. 1883, 11.

3. The history of fireproofing in America is superbly covered in Sara Wermiel, *The Fireproof Building* (Baltimore: Johns Hopkins Press, 2000).

4. Freitag, *Architectural Engineering*, 4.

5. Thomas Bellamy, "Fire-Proof Construction," *Manufacturer and Builder*, Vol. 5, no. 4, Apr. 1873, 85.

6. William J. Fryer, "Skeleton Construction," *Architectural Record*, Vol. 1, 1895, 235.

7. Purdy, "Evolution of High Building," 203. See also Larson, "Fire, Earth," 27. Frederick A. Peterson was credited with installing the floor pots and has often been credited with patenting the system in the United States; however, there is no such patent bearing his name.

8. George H. Johnson and Balthasar Kreischer, U.S. Patent no. 112,926, issued Mar. 21, 1871.

9. Balthasar Kreischer, U.S. Patent no. 112,930, issued Mar. 21, 1871.

10. Fryer, "Skeleton Construction," 30.

11. George H. Johnson and William Freeborn, U.S. Patent No. 132,292, issued Oct. 15, 1872.

12. "[W]e enter upon a new age—an age of steel and burnt clay." Jenney, "Age of Steel and Clay, 77. See also "Fire-Proof Buildings," 43.

13. Quoting Dankmar Adler, Editorial, "The Combustibility of Modern 'Fireproof' Buildings," *Engineering Record*, Vol. 33, no. 15, Mar. 14, 1896, 15.

14. *Industrial Chicago*, 412.

15. "Fire-proof Buildings," 190.

16. Freitag, *Architectural Engineering*, 96.

17. "Fireproofing Tests of Building Materials," *Engineering Record*, Vol. XXXIV, no. 10., Aug. 8, 1896, 179.

18. "In all the advance which has taken place in the fire-proof construction of the country . . . Chicago has kept the lead," "Building Construction Details, No. XVI," 72.

19. Wight, "Recent Fireproof Building in Chicago," 52.

20. "New Publications," *Inland Architect and Builder*, Vol. V, no. 5, July 1885, 94.

21. Birkmire, *Planning and Construction*, 196.

22. Editorial, *Brickbuilder*, Vol. 2, no. 9, Sept. 1893, 83.

23. L. O. Danse, quoted in "Fire-proof Buildings," *Manufacturer and Builder*, Vol. 19, no. 8, Aug., 1887, 190–191; and Freitag, *Architectural Engineering*, 190.

24. *Industrial Chicago*, 388–390.

25. "Hydraulic Pressed Brick," *Inland Architect and Builder*, Vol. 1, no. 6, July 1883, 85; and "Synopsis of Building News," *Inland Architect and Builder*, Vol. V, no. 1, Feb. 1885, 14.

26. "Chicago Anderson Pressed Brick," *Inland Architect and Builder*, Vol. VII, no. 9, June 1886, 84.

27. "Trade Notes," *Brickbuilder*, Vol. III, no. 3, Mar. 1893, 48.

28. "The Grannis Block: A Triumph of Architectural and Building Enterprise," *Chicago Daily*. May 1, 1881, 5.

29. "Synopsis of Building News," *Inland Architect and Builder*, Vol. IV, no. 8, Mar. 1885, 27.

30. "Grannis Block."

31. "The Chicago Fire: Further Facts as to the Burning of the Grannis Block," *New York Times*, Feb. 21, 1885, 2.

32. "The Origin [Grannis Block fire]," *Chicago Daily Tribune*, Feb. 21, 1885, 2.

33. P. B. Wight, "The Fire-Proofing of High Office Buildings," *Brickbuilder*, Vol. XI, 1902, 147.

34. "Chicago Fire"; and "Synopsis of Building News," Mar. 1885, 27.

35. In 1896, reflecting on the development of tall building construction, the *Chicago Daily* opined that the Montauk's achievement "was little more than increasing the height" of typical bearing masonry construction "from the former six or seven stories to nine stories above basement." "Old and New Chicago," *Chicago Daily*, May 24, 1896, 43.

36. This correspondence has apparently been lost with the folding, in the 1960s, of Owen Aldis's successor firm. It is quoted, selectively though at length, in Condit, *Chicago School of Architecture*.

37. "Ten Stories," *Chicago Daily Tribune*, Oct. 15, 1882, 6.

38. "This marked the era of very light floor construction." P. B. Wight, quoted in D. Everett Waid, "Skeleton Construction," *Brickbuilder*, Vol. III, no. 1, Jan. 1894, 13.

39. Wight, "Development of the Fireproofing," 9–10.

40. D. Everett Waid, "Skeleton Construction," 13.

41. Harriett Monroe, quoted in Thomas H. Hines, *Burnham of Chicago* (Chicago: University of Chicago Press, 1979), 53–54.

42. "Ten Stories," *Chicago Daily Tribune*, Oct. 15, 1882, 6.

43. Condit, *Chicago School of Architecture*, 52.

44. Hines, *Burnham of Chicago*, 52.

45. "Ten Stories," 6.

46. "Fires," Chicago, Dec. 31, 1883, 1.

47. Donald Hoffmann, *The Architecture of John Wellborn Root* (Paperback ed., Chicago: University of Chicago Press, 1988), 24.

48. "The Burlington," *Chicago Daily Tribune*, July 9, 1881, 8.

49. Hoffman, *Architecture of John Wellborn Root*, 40–41.

50. "The Agitation for an Opera-House," *Chicago Daily Tribune*, Feb. 3, 1880, 4.

51. "Opera-House for Chicago," *Chicago Daily Tribune*, Jan. 24, 1884, 1.

52. "Real Estate," *Chicago Daily*, May 20, 1883, 15. "The Union Club," *Chicago Daily Tribune*, Dec. 18, 1881, 13. Biographical information on Cobb and Frost from "Henry I. Cobb, Widely Known Architect, Dies," *Chicago Daily Tribune*, Mar. 28, 1931, 14; and "Charles S. Frost, Architect Here since 1882, Dies," *Chicago Daily Tribune*, Dec. 12, 1931, 18.

53. "The Great Opera-House Building," *Chicago*, May 10, 1885, 15.

54. "For Business Purposes," *Chicago Daily Tribune*, Dec. 28, 1884, 10.

55. "Synopsis of Building News," *Inland Architect and Builder*, Vol. IV, no. 5, Dec. 1884, 70.

56. "Great Opera-House Building," 15.

57. "Real Estate," *Chicago Tribune*, Jan. 18, 1885, 3:3–6.

58. "The Studebaker Building," *Chicago Daily Tribune*, Mar. 26, 1887, 7.

59. O'Gorman, "Marshall Field Wholesale Store," 175–194.

60. "Real Estate," *Chicago*, Oct. 25, 1885, 28.

61. O'Gorman, "Marshall Field," 188. Harriett Monroe recalled Richardson visiting John Wellborn Root and inquiring about local techniques for building on Chicago's soil. H. Monroe, *John Wellborn Root*, 119–120.

62. *Industrial Chicago*, 186.

63. O'Gorman, "Marshall Field," 188.

64. Ferree, "High Building and Its Art," 306. See also the enticingly titled *Chicago by Day and Night: The Pleasure Seeker's Guide to the Paris of America* (Chicago: Thomson and Zimmerman, 1892), 25.

65. "The Design of Steel-Skeleton Buildings" (selection of letters), *Engineering Record*, Vol. XXXIV, no. 6, July 11, 1896, 103.

66. Misa, *Nation of Steel*, 47–48.

67. Shankland, "Steel Skeleton [Paper]," 58.

68. See "More Cloud Supporters."

69. Given that the approximate square footage of the building was around 300,000 square feet, this figure—one light for every 60 square feet of space—presents a good indication of lighting's limited application in commercial structures at the time. The building also contained over 60,000 square feet of plate glass. "The Auditorium Building," *Chicago Daily Tribune*, Dec. 15, 1889, 6.

70. "Completion of the Chicago Auditorium," *Inland Architect and News Record*, Vol. XIV, no. 8, Jan. 1890, 87–88.

71. Ferree, "High Building and Its Art," 306.

72. Schuyler, "Glimpses of Western Architecture: Chicago—I," 401.

73. "It was not a real steel-frame building and did not involve any new feature of construction." Purdy, "Evolution of High Building," 206.

74. The most complete summary of the Monadnock's design history is found in Hoffman, *Architecture of John Wellborn Root*, 155–176.

75. "Real Estate," *Chicago Tribune*, Jan. 11, 1885, 16. Drawings in the collection of the Canadian Centre for Architecture date as far back as 1885.

76. Hoffmann, "John Root's Monadnock Building," 272; and "More Cloud Supporters." A plan of this scheme survives; see Burnham & Root, "Monadnock Building, Chicago: First and second floor plans for the sixteen-storey steel frame project," 1889. Drawing No. DR1986:0767:134, Collection of the Canadian Centre for Architecture.

77. Hoffmann, "John Root's Monadnock Building," 275.

78. Editorial, *Brickbuilder*, Vol. 2, no. 6, June. 1893, 59.

79. Condit, "Chicago School of Architecture: A Symposium—Part II, 12.

80. Ferree, "High Building and Its Art," 312; and "Its Big Buildings," 35.

81. "Shut from the Sun," *Chicago Daily*, Jan. 31, 1897, 25.

82. The bearing construction of the Woman's Temple was cited as a major reason for its early obsolescence in the late 1920s. "Obsolescence Study of an Office Building in Chicago," 137.

83. Purdy, "Evolution of High Building," 204–205.

84. For the Monadnock's electrical

system, see Platt, *Electric City*, 38. The building's gas and electric fixtures are documented in Burnham & Root, "Monadnock Building, Chicago: Elevations for electric and gas lighting fixtures," 1891–1892. Drawing No. DR1986:0767:190, Collection of the Canadian Centre for Architecture.

85. Condit, *Chicago School of Architecture*, 67. D. H. Burnham & Co.[?], "Monadnock Building, Chicago: Partial plan showing settlement of piers and columns," 1895. Drawing No. DR1986:0767:192, Collection of the Canadian Centre for Architecture.

86. Tallmadge, *Architecture in Old Chicago*, 153.

CHAPTER 3. IRON AND LIGHT

1. Root, "Great Architectural Problem," 68.

2. Kidder, *Architect's and Builder's Pocket-Book*, 1295.

3. "Synopsis of Building News," *Inland Architect and Builder*, Vol. IV, no. 3, Oct. 1884, 44.

4. Bell, *Art of Illumination*, 86; *Industrial Chicago*, 270; Grosser, "Gas and Electric," 202; and "Synopsis of Building News," *Inland Architect and Builder*, Vol. V, no. 2, Mar. 1885, 27.

5. "Decadence of the Use of Gas as an Illuminant," *Inland Architect and News Record*, Vol. XX, no. 6, Jan. 1893, 60; and Editorial, *Inland Architect and Builder*, Vol. III, no. 5, June 1884, 60.

6. Platt, *Electric City*, 3; and "Electric Light in Chicago," 30. Grosser, "Gas and Electric," 204.

7. Hayward, "Electricity in the Province," 4–5.

8. Platt, *Electric City*, 30, 33.

9. This was the case as late as 1907, when the Illuminating Engineer published the following comparative costs:

Type	Candle-power	Cost/cp/Month
Flat Flame		
Oil Lamp	10.2	2.90
Rochester Lamp		
(kerosene)	33.2	1.89
High Pressure		
Kerosene		
w/Mantle*	112	0.87
Gasoline with		
Mantle	30	1.67
Open Burner		
Gas Flame	20	2.20
Welsbach Burner	6	0.94
High Pressure		
Gas Lamps	42	0.45
Incandescent		
Electric	16	2.80
Nernst (Electric)		
($.10 per kw/h)	165	1.52
Electric Arc	200	1.35

* "[R]equires a good deal of attention and the average man cannot keep it in proper working order."

For contemporary assessment, see R. H. Thurston, quoted in *Sanitary Engineer*, Nov. 8, 1882, 486.

10. "Notes," *Inland Architect and Builder*, Vol. 1, no. 1, Feb. 1883, 11.

11. W. Monroe, "Electric Lighting," 113.

12. H. S. Treherne, "Windows," *Inland Architect and Builder*, Vol. IV, no. 2, Sept. 1884, 22.

13. Ibid., 69–70.

14. "Crust at Chicago," 4.

15. "How a Skyscraper Is Lifted," E5.

16. Shankland, "Steel Skeleton," 15–16. See Letter, D. H. Burnham to Dion Geraldine, July 6, 1891, D. H. Burnham Letterpress Copybooks, Microfilm 1972.4, reel 1, Ryerson & Burnham Library, Art Institute of Chicago.

17. Birkmire, *Planning and Construction*, 52–54.

18. Ewen, "Foundations," 690.

19. "How Firm a Foundation," *Chicago Daily Tribune*, Aug. 2, 1891, 26.

20. Baumann, *Art of Preparing Foundations*.

21. *Industrial Chicago*, 473.

22. Schuyler, "Glimpses of Western Architecture: Chicago—I," 396. See also Jenney, "Construction of a Heavy Fire Proof Building," [*Sanitary Engineer*] 32–33.

23. "How Firm a Foundation," 26.

24. *Industrial Chicago*, 466.

25. For a different claim, see H. Monroe, *John Wellborn Root*, 114–115.

26. Waid, "Skeleton Construction," 13. See also Freitag, *Architectural Engineering*; and Shankland, "Steel Skeleton," 2.

27. Waid, "Skeleton Construction," 13. See also Wight, "Development of the Fireproofing," 8–12.

28. G. Twose, "Steel and Terra-Cotta Buildings in Chicago, and Some Deductions," *Brickbuilder*, Vol. III, no. 1, Jan. 1894, 1.

29. Hastings, "High Buildings and Good Architecture," *American Architect and Building News*, Vol. XLVI, no. 986, Nov. 17, 1894, 67–68.

30. "Of the many fallacies anent the high building and its art that enjoy a sort of vogue in even good circles, none is more absurd than the notion that, because . . . the walls and piers are only curtains or external inclosures of the inner frame, that does the work, therefore the design must express this construction in order to be truthful." Ferree, "High Building and Its Art," 316–317.

31. *Industrial Chicago*, 170.

32. "[M]any of the lofty buildings are as unpicturesque as a dry-goods box pierced with holes for windows." Head, "Heart of Chicago," 561. In like manner, the Tribune praised the ornamental profusion of the Women's Temple in 1891 by noting "it appeals to the eye in a manner wholly unlike any of the 'dry-goods box' giants which are becoming so common." "Two Types of Office Buildings," *Chicago Daily Tribune*, Nov. 29, 1891, 28.

33. Wight, "Additions to Chicago's Skyline," 19.

34. "Its Big Buildings," *Chicago Daily*, Oct. 16, 1892, 35.

35. Schuyler, "Glimpses of Western Architecture: Chicago—II," 559–561.

36. Ibid., 559.

37. Baumann, *Improvement in the Construction* (Chicago: J. M. Wing and Co.[?], 1884).

38. Ibid.

39. "Our Illustrations," *Inland Architect and Builder*, Vol. IV, no. 2, Sept. 1884, 24.

40. "Synopsis of Building News," *Inland Architect and Builder*, Vol. III, no. 3, Apr. 1884, 42. See also "Architectural and Building Notes," *Inland Architect and Builder*, Vol. III, no. 2, Mar. 1884, 23.

41. W. L. B. Jenney, one of a selection of letters in "Design of Steel-Skeleton Buildings," 103.

42. Jenney, "Chicago Construction," 389.

43. Hugh S. Fullerton, "How the First Skyscraper Came to Be Built," *Chicago Daily Tribune*, June 23, 1907, E1.

44. Jenney, "Design of Steel-Skeleton Buildings." It is notable that Jenney published this concern only in later essays.

45. Jenney, "Construction of a Heavy Fire Proof Building," [*Sanitary Engineer*] 33. Jenney would later note that "a column in each pier was the natural solution of the problem," again an unclear formulation that retained the structural term *pier* for the brickwork, implying that it, too, bore some of the load ("Design of Steel-Skeleton Buildings").

46. Jenney claimed only that "lintels between columns, forming heads of windows, carried the street walls story by story," while Joseph Freitag noted in 1904 that "the exterior piers were made self supporting, but the spandrel portions, between the top of one window and the bottom of the window above, were carried on iron girders placed in the exterior walls and extending from column to column." Jenney, "Chicago Construction," 389–390; and Freitag, *Architectural Engineering*, 6. Forensic work done by Sanderson et al. during the demolition of the Home Insurance confirmed that the brick elements surrounding the iron columns "were of sufficient thickness to be self-sustaining without the use of columns in the pilasters." Sanderson, McConnell, and Thielbar, "Home Insurance Building," 8.

47. These lintels were notched toward their front to avoid interfering with the brick piers; Gerald Larson and Roula Mouroudellis Geraniotis noted in 1987 that this detail alone demonstrates that the structure relied on both iron and masonry to support its own weight: "While the iron lintels carried the weight of the masonry spandrels to the iron mullions and columns, the structure created by the lintel pans, mullions, and columns was far from being a rigid-self supporting iron skeleton that independently carried its masonry envelope at each floor, which the Home Insurance Building was later claimed to have been." Larson and Geraniotis, "Toward a Better Understanding," 43.

48. Jenney, "Chicago Construction," 389. It may be objected that Jenney was here talking about the construction of the party walls, rather than the masonry piers. The depth of the party walls, however, was legislated by code, and Jenney makes no note of any appeal on these walls' depth. See also Larson and Geraniotis, "Toward a Better Understanding," 44, who concur that Jenney was here describing the brickwork of the piers.

49. C. L. Strobel, "The Design of Steel Skeleton Buildings," *Engineering Record*, Vol. XXXIV, no. 8, July 25, 1896.

50. Jenney, "Chicago Construction," 390; and Sanderson, McConnell, and Thielbar, "Home Insurance Building."

51. "As the bolts do not accurately fit the holes, a clamp was introduced to pull the beams close together, so that the least movement is felt at once over the whole beam." W. L. B. Jenney, "The Construction of Heavy, Fireproof Building on a Compressible Soil," *Inland Architect and Builder*, Vol. VI, no. 6, Dec. 1885, 100.

52. Larson and Geraniotis, "Toward a Better Understanding,"41–43.

53. Jenney, "Chicago Construction," 389.

54. Jenney, "Construction of a Heavy Fire Proof Building," [*Sanitary Engineer*] 33. George Fuller suggested that steel had been used in Cobb & Frost's Opera House, constructed at the same time, but this is not substantiated elsewhere. "Like a City of Steel," *Chicago Daily*, June 25, 1891, 8.

55. Thomas Tallmadge, ed., *The Origin of the Skyscraper: Report of the Committee Appointed by the Trustees of the Estate of Marshall Field for the Examination of the Structure of the Home Insurance Building* (rep. Chicago: Alderbrink Press, 1939), 17.

56. Sanderson, McConnell, and Thielbar, "Home Insurance Building," 8–9.

57. Subsequent scholarship has been less measured in its criticism of Jenney, in particular Gerald Larson and Roula Geraniotis, whose previously cited work suggests that Jenney was influenced by Frederick Baumann's article on iron framing and that Baumann's conception was more advanced than Jenney's system . They also suggest that Jenney may well have been influenced by W. W. Boyington's use of Phoenix columns in the Board of Trade Tower, but these iron columns were not integrated into the masonry fabric of the tower; rather, they appear to have been used within the main space of the exchange floor to prop up the back edge of the tower itself.

58. Sullivan, *Autobiography*, 258.

59. "When piles and masses of stone were exclusively used the foundations for

non-resisting soils was practically one solid mass, but when concrete and steel girders came into vogue, or even before, isolated piers and buttresses became the rule." Sullivan, "Architecture and Building," 36.

60. See Tallmadge, *Architecture in Old Chicago*, 254.

61. D. Davis, quoted in David Van Zanten, *Sullivan's City: The Meaning of Ornament for Louis Sullivan* (New York: W. W. Norton, 2000), 15.

62. Hugh Morrison, *Louis Sullivan, Prophet of Modern Architecture* (rep. New York: Norton, 1998), 35.

63. Sullivan's claims that it was the first to follow Baumann's prescription are refuted by the probable use of isolated piers under buildings by Carter, Drake, and Wight, and by John Van Osdel in the 1870s. Louis Sullivan, "Development of Construction," in Twombly, *Louis Sullivan*, 10.

64. "A Notable Event," *Chicago Daily Tribune*, Mar. 29, 1883, 8.

65. Van Zanten, *Sullivan's City*, 19.

66. Tallmadge, *Architecture in Old Chicago*, 187.

67. "The Insurance Exchange Building" [Advertising Supplement], *Inland Architect and Builder*, Vol. V, no. 6, July 1885, 2.

68. Blackall, "Notes of Travel," 313–315.

69. *Bird's Eye Views and Guide to Chicago* (Chicago: Rand McNally, 1892). Reprinted in Randall and Randall, *History*, 205.

70. P. B. Wight: "[T]he Home Insurance Building is not an example of skeleton construction as now understood." Quoted in D. Everett Waid, "Skeleton Construction," 13.

71. But see *Industrial Chicago*, 188–189.

72. Hoffman, "John Root's Monadnock Building," 269–277.

73. "Real Estate," *Chicago Tribune*, Jan. 11, 1885, 16:1–3.

74. Head, "Heart of Chicago," 556.

75. "A Great Office Building [Rookery]."

76. Ibid.; and *Industrial Chicago*, 168.

77. Suggestions of iron in the Rookery's columns can be found in Fullerton, "How the First Skyscraper," E1; and D. Everett Waid, "A History of Steel Skeleton Construction," *Brickbuilder*, Vol. III, no. 8, Aug. 1894, 159.

78. "Building Construction Details: No. XIII," 272–274.

79. "Chicago's Great Office Building [Rookery]," *Chicago Daily Tribune*, Jun. 17, 1888, 3; and "Building Construction Details: No. XIII."

80. Building Construction Details: No. XIII," 273.

81. "Great Office Building [Rookery]," 80.

CHAPTER 4. STEEL AND WIND

1. A version of this chapter originally appeared as "Built like Bridges: Iron, Steel, and the Importance of Riveted Steel to the Nineteenth Century Skyscraper," *Journal of the Society of Architectural Historians*, Vol. 69, no.2, June 2010. I am profoundly indebted to David Brownlee and to two anonymous readers who provided guidance and editorial advice in refining these arguments.

2. "Cast-Iron Columns for Buildings," 308.

3. Quimby, "Wind Bracing," Nov. 1892, 394.

4. "Tay Bridge Disaster," 70–71.

5. Shankland, "Steel Skeleton," 6–8; and Birkmire, *Planning and Construction*, 205–206.

6. Quimby, "Wind Bracing," 298.

7. D. Everett Waid, "History of Steel Skeleton Construction," 158. Waid also noted that Jenney's frame for the Home Insurance had been described at the time as a "railroad bridge standing on end."

8. "Chicago Building That Stopped Clocks," *American Architect and Building News*, Vol. XLIV, no. 959, May 12, 1894, 68.

9. "Some Phenomena," *Engineering Record*, Vol. XXXIV, no. 3, Jun. 20, 1896; and Editorial, *American Architect and Building News*, Vol. XLVII, no. 1002, Mar. 9, 1895, 97–98.

10. "Stability and Security," 149.

11. Birkmire, *Planning and Construction*, 20.

12. "Maximum Wind Pressure," *Engineering Record and American Contract Journal*, Oct. 10, 1885, 235.

13. Quimby, "Wind Bracing," 260; and Shankland, "Steel Skeleton," 9. For comparison's sake, code-mandated loads in the United States today vary by geography, with those in hurricane-prone regions requiring between 44 and 55 psf.

14. Freitag, *Architectural Engineering*, 82.

15. Ibid., 258.

16. Shankland, "Steel Skeleton," 7–8.

17. "Illustrations: New York Life Insurance Company's Building, Northeast Corner La Salle and Monroe Streets, Chicago, Ill.," *American Architect and Building News*, Vol. XLII, no. 933, Nov. 11, 1893, 79.

18. See Purdy, "Steel Skeleton[II]," 560–561; and Freitag, *Architectural Engineering*, 264–268. The Venetian's wind bracing system was designed to absorb 70 percent of the assumed load, with the other 30 percent to be taken up by the inherent stiffness of the building's partitions.

19. Shankland, "Steel Skeleton," 6–8; and Freitag, *Architectural Engineering*, 263–264.

20. Historic American Buildings Survey No. ILL 1053, "Old Colony Building, 407 South Dearborn Street, Chicago, Illinois," Chicago Project II, 1964, Sheet 3 of 3, West Elevation.

21. Bruegmann, *Holabird & Roche/Holabird & Root*, 131.

22. Freitag, *Architectural Engineering*, 272. A similar system braced Holabird

& Roche's extension to the Monadnock Building, 1892.

23. Jenney, "Chicago Construction," 390.

24. Freitag, *Architectural Engineering*, 259.

25. Shankland, "Steel Skeleton," 8–9.

26. Jenney, "Chicago Construction," 390.

27. Quimby, "Wind Bracing," Nov. 1892, 395.

28. Quimby, "Wind Bracing," Dec. 1892, 99.

29. Foster Milliken, in Quimby, "Wind Bracing," Jan. 1893, 162.

30. H. W. Brinckerhoff, in Quimby, "Wind Bracing," Jan. 1893, 180.

31. F. E. Kidder, "Safe Loads for H-Shaped Cast-Iron Columns," *American Architect and Building News*, Vol. XLV, no. 969, Jul. 21, 1894, 27–28.

32. "Field riveting has now entirely superseded the use of bolts in skeleton or cage construction, or indeed in any character of high-class building work." Freitag, *Architectural Engineering*, 68.

33. Oversized boltholes were cited as a major contributing factor to the Tay Bridge's collapse. A. V. Gravelle, "Riveted versus Bolted Field Connections [Letter]," *Engineering News*, Vol. 35, no. 4, Dec. 26, 1896, 75; "Cast-Iron Columns in Buildings," *Engineering News*, Vol. 36, no. 5, July 3, 1897; and "Report on the Tay Bridge Disaster," 268.

34. Freitag, *Architectural Engineering*, 68, 138; see also Gravelle, "Riveted Versus Bolted."

35. William Le Baron Jenney, quoted in "Chicago's Big Buildings," *Chicago Daily Tribune*, sec. 1, Sept. 13, 1891.

36. "Cast-Iron Columns in Buildings." See also Waid, "History of Steel Skeleton Construction," 158–159; and Strobel, one of a selection of letters in "Design of Steel Skeleton Buildings."

37. Freitag, *Architectural Engineering*, 68, 77.

38. W. H. Breithaupt, "On Iron Skeletons for Buildings," *Engineering Record*, Mar. 5, 1892, 226.

39. Freitag, *Architectural Engineering*, 214.

40. "Design of Steel-Skeleton Buildings [selection of letters]," 103.

41. Freitag, *Architectural Engineering*, 40, 58, 68, 192 .

42. Ibid., 56–57.

43. Breithaupt, "On Iron Skeletons," 226.

44. Birkmire, *Planning and Construction*, 194.

45. Shankland, "Steel Skeleton," 6.

46. Freitag, *Architectural Engineering*, 209.

47. Wermiel, "Introduction of Steel Columns in American Buildings, 1862–1920"; Sara E. Wermiel, "Introduction of Steel Columns in American Buildings, 1862–1920," *Engineering History and Heritage*, Vol. 162, no. 1, Feb. 2009, 19–27.

CHAPTER 5. GLASS AND LIGHT

1. Portions of this chapter originally appeared as "'As Large as the Situation of the Columns Will Allow': Building Cladding and Plate Glass in the Chicago Skyscraper, 1885–1905," *Technology and Culture*, Vol. 49, no. 2, Apr. 2008; and "Glass and Light: The Role of Interior Illumination in the Chicago School," *Journal of Architectural Education*, Volume 58, no. 1, Sept. 2004. Funding for much of the on-site research in Indiana was provided by the National Endowment for the Humanities in 2006. I am particularly grateful to Ted Cavanagh, editor of the *JAE* theme issue in which this appeared, for his constructive advice and encouragement in pursuing this topic further.

2. Birkmire, *Planning and Construction*, 103–104.

3. "Chicago's Big Buildings," 25.

4. Winston Weisman, "The Chicago School Issue," in Webster, "Forward," 12.

5. Quimby, "Wind Bracing," Mar. 1893, 299.

6. Freitag, *Architectural Engineering*, 179–180.

7. Birkmire, *Planning and Construction*, 103.

8. Ibid.

9. "Chicago's Veneered Buildings," 4.

10. While in common use in the technical press since around 1895, the first use of the phrase "curtain wall" in the Chicago press occurred in 1904. "News of the Insurance World," *Chicago Daily Tribune*, May 24, 1904, 13.

11. Bruegmann, *Holabird & Roche/Holabird & Root*, 12.

12. Holabird & Roche contract drawing #10, H&R Project NC37 in Chicago History Museum, Holabird & Roche collection.

13. Holabird & Roche contract drawing #58b, H&R Project NC37 in Chicago History Museum, Holabird & Roche collection.

14. "Chicago's Sky-Scrapers," *Chicago Daily Tribune*, Jan. 13, 1889, 2.

15. *Industrial Chicago*, 192.

16. "Chicago Building Obsolescent after 40 Years," 1003–1004.

17. "Chicago's Sky-Scrapers."

18. *Chicago Economist*, Jan. 31, 1891, 167, cited in Bruegmann, *Holabird & Roche/Holabird & Root*, 1, 44.

19. "Architectural and Building Notes," *Inland Architect and Builder*, Vol. 1, no. 2, Mar. 1883, 26; and Vol. II, no. 3, Oct. 1883, 122. See also "Mosaics," *Inland Architect and Builder*, Vol. IV, no. 6, Jan. 1885, 81.

20. "Mosaics," *Inland Architect and Builder*, Vol. III, no. 2, Mar. 1884, 26. See "Architectural and Building Notes," *Inland Architect and Builder*, Vol. III, no. 4, May 1884, 51, for a list of Northwestern's clients.

21. E. V. Johnson, "The Structural Value," 13.

22. "J. J. Rockwell, "Fireproofing Chicago's Buildings," in Britten and Jones, eds., *Half-Century*, 117.

23. "Fire-Resisting Construction," *Inland Architect and Builder*, Vol. III, no. 4, May 1884, 50–51. See Tunick, "Evolution of Terra Cotta," 5.

24. Ibid. See also "Terra Cotta and Stone," *Brickbuilder*, Vol. 1, No. 4, Apr. 1892, 30–31. Tunick reports that terra-cotta could be had for one-tenth the cost of stone. See also E. V. Johnson, "The Structural Value," 14–15.

25. Twose, "Steel and Terra-Cotta," 1.

26. Kidder, *Architect's and Builder's Pocket-Book*,1416. See also Fay V. Tooley, *Handbook of Glass Manufacture* (New York: Ogden, 1960), esp. section XX, "Flat Glass Manufacturing Processes," 227; and F. J. Terence Maloney, *Glass in the Modern World: A Study in Materials Development* (Garden City: Doubleday, 1968).

27. A. U. Howard, "Plate versus Cylinder Glass" [Letter read at the Nashville Convention of the American Institute of Architects]. Reprinted in *Inland Architect and News-Record*, Vol. XXVIII, no. 4, Nov. 1896.

28. "Manufacture of Plate Glass," *Scientific American*, Vol. 84, no. 20, May 18, 1901, 304, 311.

29. Scoville, *Studies in Economic History*, 20–21; Weeks, "Glass," 316.

30. Austin, "Glass," 962; and "Pittsburgh Plate Glass Company (1120 East Vaile Avenue). Study of Kokomo, ref. # 977.285 Mi, leaflet in flat file of Howard County Local History Collection, Kokomo Public Library, Local History Department.

31. "Natural Gas for Glass-Making," *Engineering Record and American Contract Journal*, Vol. XIV, Nov. 28, 1885, 344.

32. News Item, Kokomo Daily Dispatch, Apr. 25, 1891, 5:5–6. See also "The Pan Handle Pins It," *Kokomo Gazette Tribune*, May 25, 1888, 2:2.

33. News Item, *Kokomo Gazette Tribune*, Feb. 25, 1888, 2:2. Seiberling would go on to negotiate direct rights to 2500 acres of "the choicest gas-bearing land in Howard County" in 1889. See News Item, *Kokomo Gazette Tribune*, July 18, 1889, 4:2.

34. See "All the Wheels Go Round," *Kokomo Gazette Tribune*, Nov. 15, 1890, 2, cols. 3–4.

35. "Why It Is a Success," *Kokomo Gazette Tribune*, Nov. 18, 1890, 2:3. For a less biased, but equally impressive, assessment of Diamond Plate Glass quality, see H. C. Hovey, "Manufacture of Plate Glass at Kokomo, Indiana," *Scientific American*, Vol. 63, no. 16, Oct. 18, 1890, 241.

36. [Oscar Austill], *Souvenir of Elwood, the Buckle of the Indiana Natural Gas Belt* (n.p., 1893). In folder marked "Elwood History File—Glass History," Local History Collection, Elwood, Indiana, Public Library.

37. "Industrial Notes," *Kokomo Dispatch*, Mar. 27, 1890, 1:1.

38. *Kokomo Daily Dispatch*, June 13, 1891, 4:5; and John L. Forkner, *History of Madison County, Indiana: A Narrative Account of Its Historical Progress, Its People and Its Principal Interests* (Chicago: Lewis Publishing Company, 1914), 155–156.

39. "A Short Strike," *Kokomo Dispatch*, July 24, 1890, 5, col. 2.

40. "A Glass Trades Paper Reviews the Situation," *Kokomo Dispatch*, June 15, 1893, 9:2. See also "All Are Closed," *Kokomo Dispatch*, June 22, 1893, 1:4.

41. "A Plate Glass War," *Kokomo Daily Dispatch*, Jan. 2, 1895, 1:1. See also "Prices in Plate Glass Trade," *Chicago Daily Tribune*, Jan. 4, 1895, 3; and "The Plate Glass Trust's Organization: Every Factory in the Country Is in the New Combination," *New York Times*, Apr. 6, 1895, 10. See also Scoville, *Studies in Economic History*, 239. See also "Pittsburgh Plate Glass Company, Kokomo Public Library Local History Department.

42. Dankmar Adler, "The Influence of Steel Construction and Plate-Glass upon Style," *American Architect and Building News*, Vol. LIV, no. 1088, Oct. 31, 1896, 39.

43. "Old and New Chicago," *Chicago Daily*, May 24, 1896, 43.

44. Twose, "Steel and Terra-Cotta," 2.

45. Head, "Heart of Chicago," 559.

46. Ferree, "High Building and Its Art," 316. Confronted with the architectural realities of the new skins only two years later, Ferree would have a much less enthusiastic reaction; see his comments on the Reliance, below.

47. Twose, "Steel and Terra-Cotta," 3.

48. Ibid., 46.

49. Dankmar Adler, response to Yost, "Influence of Steel Construction and of Plate Glass upon the Development of the Modern Style," *Inland Architect and News-Record*, Vol. XXVIII, no. 4, Nov. 1896, 36.

50. Ibid.

51. "Springs Up by Magic," *Chicago Daily*, Aug. 26, 1894, 34.

52. "Informal Opening of the Reliance," *Chicago Daily Tribune*, 16 Mar., 1895, 8.

53. "Springs Up by Magic."

54. "Reliance Building, Chicago," 17.

55. Jenkins, "White Enameled Building," 299.

56. Rebori, "Work of Burnham & Root," 66.

57. Shankland, "Steel Skeleton," 18.

58. "Technical Review, The Fisher Building, Chicago."

59. "Chicago," *American Architect and Building News*, Vol. LI, no. 1057, Mar. 28, 1896, 145.

60. "Shut from the Sun," *Chicago Daily*, Jan. 31, 1897, 25.

61. "Building of the Year 1895," *Chicago Daily Tribune*, Dec. 29, 1895, 29.

CHAPTER 6. STEEL, CLAY, AND GLASS

1. "Change in Building Ordinance," *Chicago Daily Tribune*, Jan. 12, 1896, 35; "The Height of Offices," *Chicago Daily Tribune*, June 16, 1901, 29; and "Cost per Cubic Foot of Buildings," *Inland Architect and News Record*, Vol. XXXIX, no. 2, Mar. 1902, 12–13. For the 1902 revision, see "Council Lifts Building Limit," *Chicago Daily*, Feb. 4, 1902, 1. See also Letter, D. H. Burnham to Alderman E. F. Cullerton, Chicago, Jan. 8, 1902, D. H. Burnham Letterpress Copybooks, Microfilm 1972.4, reel 4, Ryerson & Burnham Library, Art Institute of Chicago.

2. *Ordinance Relating to the Department of Buildings*, Sections 94, 117, 135.

3. "New Stock Exchange," *Chicago Daily*, Feb. 25, 1893, 6.

4. Desmond, "Rationalizing the Skyscraper," 422.

5. Bensman and Wilson, "Iron and Steel"; "Opens New Era in Iron," *Chicago Daily*, Dec. 20, 1899, 7, 425; and *Inland Steel at 100: Beginning a Second Century of Progress* (Chicago[?]: Jack H. Morris/Inland Steel Industries, 1993).

6. "Indiana's Great Trusts," *Fort Wayne Weekly Sentinel*, Dec. 27, 1899; Austin, "Glass," 962; and "Will Control Plate Glass Trade," *Chicago Daily Tribune*, May 9, 1896, 5.

7. "The Pittsburgh Plate Glass Company," leaflet in flat file, Kokomo Public Library Local History Department, marked "This information was provided by PPG Industries by mail, May 17, 1979"; and "Elwood Glass Plant to Quit," [Elwood, Indiana?] *Herald*, Jan. 18, n.d, in folder marked "Elwood History—Glass Factories" in the Local History Room of the Elwood, Indiana, Public Library. See also "Pittsburgh Plate Glass Company (1120 East Vaile Avenue), Study of Kokomo 977.285 Mi Howard County Local History Misc, leaflet in flat file, Kokomo Public Library Local History Department.

8. Kidder, *Architect's and Builder's Pocket-Book*, 1416.

9. Adler, "Slow-Burning and Fireproof," 60–61.

10. "Fireproofing Tests of Building Materials," *Engineering Record*, Vol. XXXIV, no. 10, Aug. 8, 1896, 179. See also "Asbestos and Its Uses," *Inland Architect and News Record*, Vol. XXVIII, no. 1, Jan. 1897.

11. Freitag, *Architectural Engineering*, 103–104.

12. Turner, "Reinforced Concrete," 16–18.

13. Newman, "Before the Second," E1.

14. Adler, quoted in *Industrial Chicago*.

15. Jenney, "A Few Practical Hints," 8.

16. "How Chicago Has Grown Skywards," *Chicago Daily Tribune*, Oct. 6, 1901, 37.

17. Adler, quoted in *Industrial Chicago*, 473.

18. Shankland, "Steel Skeleton," 18.

19. *Industrial Chicago*, 473.

20. Ibid., 476–477.

21. "Safe High Buildings," *Chicago Daily*, Apr. 1, 1892, 9.

22. *Industrial Chicago*, 473–477.

23. "Safe High Buildings," 9.

24. *Industrial Chicago*, 478–479.

25. Purdy, "Evolution of High Building," 206. Such systems were not foolproof, however; see Williams, "What Steel Did," 16.

26. Tratman, "Shallow and Deep."

27. "New Building of the Tribune," *Chicago Tribune*, Jan. 1, 1901, 1.

28. *Inland Architect Supplement*.

29. Birkmire, *Planning and Construction*; and *Skeleton Construction in Buildings with Numerous Practical Illustrations of High Buildings* (New York: John Wiley and Sons, 1894).

30. Freitag, *Architectural Engineering*; Freitag, *Fireproofing of Steel Buildings*.

31. Merwood-Salisbury, *Chicago 1890*. Skyscrapers began to appear in popular literature of the day by the late 1890s;

Henry B. Fuller's *The Cliff Dwellers* appeared in 1893 and stood as the first skyscraper novel. But serialization in Chicago papers also reflected fascination with the type. See "Sky Scraper Sketches," *Chicago Daily Tribune*, Aug. 15, 1900, 6; and O. Henry [William Sydney Porter], "psyche and the Pskyscraper," *Chicago Daily* [Originally Copyright Press Publishing Company, *New York World*, 1905], Jan. 15, 1905, E7.

32. "How Will Chicago Buildings Look Fifty Years from Now?" *Chicago Daily Tribune*, Feb. 16, 1902, 49.

33. "Limit of Ten Stories," *Chicago Daily*, Mar. 9, 1893, 3; "Shut from the Sun," *Chicago Daily*, Jan. 31, 1897, 25; and Willett, "Skeleton Structures," 48. See also "Problem of the Sky-Scrapers," *Chicago Daily Tribune*, Oct. 15, 1891, 9; and "Alps of a City," *Chicago Daily Tribune*, May 29, 1898, 34.

34. As one example, "many of the lofty buildings are as unpicturesque as a drygoods box pierced with holes for windows." Head, "Heart of Chicago," 561. *American Architect and Building News* weighed in with a more damning assessment in 1895: "There seems to be a hopeless settling down to the idea that a large office-building must be a huge box pierced with holes at regular intervals." "Chicago," *American Architect and Building News*, Vol. XLVII, no. 996, Jan. 26, 1895, 42–43.

35. Twose, "Steel and Terra-Cotta," 3.

36. "Its Big Buildings," 35.

37. "How Will Chicago Buildings Look?"

38. Sullivan, "Tall Office Building," 33.

39. Ibid.

40. Ibid.

41. Dankmar Adler, untitled response to J. W. Yost, "Influence of Steel Construction and of Plate Glass upon the Development of the Modern Style," *Inland Architect and News-Record*, Vol. XXVIII, no. 4, Nov. 1896, 36–37.

42. Siry, "Adler and Sullivan's Guaranty Building," 19.

43. See Stuart Cohen, quoted in Bruegmann, *Holabird & Roche/Holabird & Root*, 95.

44. "Recent Chicago Tall Buildings," 250.

45. "Chicago," 43. See also Waid, "Recent Brick and Terra-Cotta Work," 132–133. "Fourteen Story Structure to be Known as the Marquette Building," *Chicago Daily Tribune*, Nov. 19, 1893, 10. See also "Some Facts about the Marquette," 44.

46. "Chicago," 118. The Marquette was seen by others as a hallmark of the city's labor troubles at the time. A strike over nonunion electrical workers halted work on the site in September 1894, and subsequent violence culminated in the shooting death of a union plumber. See "Delay on Marquette Building," *Chicago Daily Tribune*, Sept. 9, 1894, 6; and "Ends with a Murder," *Chicago Daily*, Nov. 11, 1894, 1.

47. "Old and New Chicago," 43.

48. Waid, "Recent Brick and Terra-Cotta Work," 132.

49. Quoted in Bruegmann, *Holabird & Roche/Holabird & Root*, 142.

50. Winkler, "Some Chicago Buildings," 318.

51. Ibid., 318, 322.

52. Sheets 1036–1072, Folder D-4, Project NC119 ("Williams"), Drawing Collection of the Chicago History Museum.

53. "Ayer Building Now to Go Ahead," *Chicago Daily Tribune*, Oct. 2, 1898, 34.

54. Wight, "Recent Improvements in Fire-Proof Construction," 34. "Lease to M'Clurg Firm," *Chicago Daily*, Mar. 23, 1899, 10.

55. *Ornamental Iron and Bronze Executed by the Winslow Bros. Company, Chicago* (Chicago: Winslow Bros., 1910).

56. Louis H. Sullivan, "Sub-structure at the New Schlesinger," 194–196.

57. A drawing published in a contemporary Rand McNally view book shows this lower scheme. Bracing of the structure came from existing party walls, later incorporated as structural elements as the building again expanded in 1908.

58. "Architecture in the Shopping District," 46–47.

59. H. Monroe, "Show Reveals Architectural Art," B5.

60. "Two New Skyscrapers," *Chicago Daily Tribune.*, July 5, 1896, 18.

61. "Stewarts Win Building Fight," *Chicago Daily Tribune*, July 13, 1912, 3; and Al Chase, "Stewart Building in Loop Purchased by Loan Association," *Chicago Daily Tribune*, Jan. 31, 1951, B5.

CHAPTER 7. STEEL, LIGHT, AND STYLE

1. "Building Boom Means New City," *Chicago*, Nov. 16, 1910, B13. See also "Chicago Is Busy with Buildings," *Chicago Daily Tribune.*, Nov. 23, 1910, A6.

2. "Building Boom Means New City," B13.

3. "Natural Gas Supply Decreasing," *Chicago Daily Tribune*, June 20, 1897, 15; Austin, "Glass," 949–967; and Ned Booker, *Kokomo: A Pictorial History* (St. Louis: G. Bradley, 1989), See also "Pittsburg Plate Glass Company (1120 East Vaile Avenue), Study of Kokomo 977.285 Mi Howard County Local History Misc. Leaflet in flat file, Kokomo Public Library Local History Department, which describes ongoing technical innovations at the Kokomo plant as late as 1910 and the departure of plate glass-making to Crystal City in 1929.

4. Robert M. Knight, "Facelift for a Loop Landmark," *Chicago Tribune*, June 5, 1983, I38–141.

5. "It is always the case," the chief librarian told the *Tribune*, "that something has to be sacrificed for the sake of something else. In this case coolness has suffered a little at the expense of light." "Suffer in the Library," *Chicago Daily*, July 21, 1898, 7.

6. Al Chase, "Architects Do Bit O' Throwing at Glass Homes," *Chicago Daily Tribune*, Sept. 13, 1931, 26.

7. Although the Hallidie Building in San Francisco produced a striking example of an all-glass facade in 1918, the predictable problems with intense heat gain in the summer meant that this experiment was not repeated in American commercial architecture for many years. Macdonald W. Scott, "Notes and Comment: A Glass-Front Building [Hallidie, San Francisco]," *Architectural Record*, Vol. XLIV, no. 4, Oct. 1918, 381–384.

8. "Plan Windowless Factory in East for Simonds Saw & Steel," *Chicago Daily Tribune*, Oct. 14, 1930, 29. See also Kocher and Frey, "Windows," Feb. 1931, 127–137; and "Windowless Buildings Next," *Chicago Daily Tribune*, Mar. 13, 1898, 37.

9. Doane, "Electric Light," 2–26, 5–6; Arthur Vaughn Abbot, "Electrical Engineering for Architects," *Inland Architect Supplement: Technical Review of the Interesting Development of the Building Arts*, Supplement to Vol. XXXIV, no. 6, Jan. 1900, 19. Lighting costs taken from Platt, *Electric City*, 148.

10. "Chicago Second in Electricity," *Chicago Daily Tribune*, Nov. 16, 1910, A21.

11. Kocher and Frey, "Windows," *Architectural Record*, Feb. 1931, 136.

12. Luckiesh, *Light and Work*, 80.

13. Siegfried Giedion, *Space, Time, and Architecture: The Growth of a New Tradition* (3rd ed., Cambridge: Harvard University Press, 1954), 380.

14. Winkler [Schuyler], "Some Chicago Buildings," 331.

15. Pietsch, "What the Beaux Arts Training Means," 54.

16. Frederick Baumann, quoted by Eugen Seeger, *Chicago, the Wonder City* (Chicago: The Geo. Gregory Printing Company, 1893), 202–204.

17. Quoted in William H. Jordy, ed., *Montgomery Schuyler: American Architecture and Other Writings* (New York: Atheneum, 1964), 47.

18. Fitzpatrick, "Chicago," 48.

19. Hyde, "New Era," *Harper's Weekly*, Sept. 7, 1901, 893.

20. Rebori, "Work of Burnham & Root," 66.

21. Ibid., 69.

22. Jenkins, "A White Enameled Building," 299.

23. Peter B. Wight, "Daniel Hudson Burnham: An Appreciation," *Architectural Record*, Vol. XXXII, no. 167, Aug. 1912, 183.

24. "E. R. Graham, Architect, Dies," *Chicago Daily Tribune*, Nov. 22, 1936, 1.

25. Burnham's sons, Hubert and D. H. Jr., were also made partners in 1910. Wight, "Daniel Hudson Burnham and His Associates," 1.

26. Ibid., 4. The best biographies of these four associates are found in Sally A. Kitt Chappell, *Architecture and Planning of Graham, Anderson, Probst and White, 1912–1936: Transforming Tradition* (Chicago: University of Chicago Press, 1992), 259–281.

27. "Famed Designer of Skyscrapers Dies in Poverty," *Chicago Daily Tribune*, Feb. 11, 1935, 3.

28. Dinkelberg, "Thoughts on Architecture," 39–40.

29. Ibid. See also Zukowsky and Saliga, "Late Works by Burnham and Sullivan," 70–79, for attribution of these works.

30. Plans originally called for a shorter, ten-story structure. "Will Erect New Bank Building," *Chicago Daily Tribune*, Feb. 1, 1899, 1. For further details, see Clark, "Chicago's Most Modern," 2.

31. Clark, "Chicago's Most Modern," 2–3.

32. Ibid., 1, 3.

33. Rebori, "Work of Burnham & Root," 68.

34. "Will Build Unique Store," *Chicago Daily Tribune*, Jan. 22, 1905, B6.

35. "Center of Chicago History," *Chicago*, Dec. 28, 1901, 1.

36. "Bank to Build $3,000,000 Block," *Chicago*, Dec. 28, 1901, 1.

37. A plan of the building can be found in Rebori, "Work of Burnham & Root."

38. Condit, *The Chicago School of Architecture*, 112.

39. "Chicago's Most Massive and Costly," 2–3.

40. "Commercial Bank Building," 6–7.

41. See Thomas Leslie, "Henry Ives Cobb and the Chicago Post Office 'Botch,'" *Journal of Illinois History*, Vol. 13, no. 2, Summer 2010, 82–106, for a history of this remarkably ill-fated building.

42. Interestingly, the Commercial Bank Building was bought by Commonwealth Edison in 1912. "Edison Company Buys Bank Block: Gives $2,860,000," *Chicago Daily Tribune*, Jan. 10, 1912, 1.

43. "Majestic Theater Building," iii–iv.

44. "Highest Office Building in Chicago Planned by the Peoples Gaslight Co," *Chicago Daily Tribune*, Sept. 13, 1908, 4.

45. A plan of the building can be found in the memorial issue of *Architectural Record* devoted to Burnham's work: Rebori, "Work of Burnham & Root, 11–168.

46. Wight, "Additions to Chicago's Skyline," 23–24.

47. H. Monroe, "Margin of Safety in Skyscrapers," A2.

48. "'Corner' a Block; Plan Skyscraper," *Chicago Daily Tribune*, Oct. 6, 1910, 1.

49. Rebori, "Work of Burnham & Root," 11–168.

50. All statistics from "Bank Will Erect $10,000,000 Block," *Chicago Daily Tribune*, Jan. 15, 1911, 7.

51. Rebori, "Work of Burnham & Root," 166–167.

52. "Daniel Burnham, Architect, Dead," *Chicago Daily Tribune*, June 2, 1912, 2.

53. Wight, "Daniel Hudson Burnham: An Appreciation," 175–176; and Rebori, "Work of Burnham & Root."

54. "Daniel Burnham, Architect, Dead," 2.

55. All quotes from Wight, "Daniel Hudson Burnham," 175–176.

56. Thomas Tallmadge would later recall Anderson saying that he preferred "a building beautiful and dumb to ugly and interesting." Thomas E. Tallmadge, "Peirce Anderson (1870–1924)," *Architectural Record*, Vol. 55, no. 5, May 1924.

CHAPTER 8. POWER AND HEIGHT

1. C. I. Henrikson, "Pneumatic Tool Help to Builder," *Chicago Daily Tribune*, June 22, 1913, J5. See also "Some Novel Uses of Compressed Air," 8–9, 21; "Pneumatic Tools Follow the Job," *Chicago Daily Tribune*, June 28, 1914, G10; and Oney Fred Sweet, "Cowboys of the Sky," *Chicago Daily Tribune*, Oct. 8, 1916, G4.

2. See Friedman, *Historical Building Construction*, 236–248, for a comprehensive listing of these and other allowable values.

3. Gail Fenske, *The Skyscraper and the City: The Woolworth Building and the Making of Modern New York* (Chicago: University of Chicago Press, 2008), 193. See also "Tallest Office Building," 224–225, 233.

4. Al Chase, "One Time World's Tallest Office Building—Masonic Temple—May Be Razed," *Chicago Daily Tribune*, Dec. 25, 1938, 8.

5. Ihlder, "Electric Elevators," 353.

6. Elliott, *Technics and Architecture*.

7. Ihlder, "Electric Elevators," 353–354, 366–367.

8. Ibid., 362.

9. Ibid., 366–367. See also Platt, *Electric City*, 104–105, 213.

10. "Finds 20 Flaws in Building Code," *Chicago Daily Tribune*, Mar. 11, 1910, 11; "Aldermen Vote 16 Story Limit on Skyscrapers," *Chicago Daily Tribune*, Dec. 2, 1910, 1.

11. "Building Ordinance of the City of Chicago," in *Illinois Society of Architects, Handbook for Architects and Builders* (Chicago: Hildmann, 1914), 129 [Code Section 592].

12. R. H. Shreve, "The Economic Design of Office Buildings," *Architectural Record*, Vol. 67, no. 4, Apr. 1930, 359.

13. Clark and Kingston, *Skyscraper*, 24.

14. Schuyler, "Towers of Manhattan," 104, 108; H. Monroe, "Task Confronts Architect," B2; "Vertical Classicism," *Chicago Daily Tribune*, Jun. 8, 1924, 8; "Falling Stone Kills Woman in State Street," *Chicago Daily Tribune*, Feb. 12, 1921, 1; "Girl Killed, 50 Hurt as Gale Sweeps City," *Chicago Daily Tribune*, Apr. 20, 1922, 1. John Holabird noted the role of the cornice and its potential lethality in the change in style from the corniced Beaux-Arts to the Gothic. Philip Hampson, "Cornice Called Serious Peril to Loop Crowds," *Chicago Daily Tribune*, Apr. 15, 1928, B1. See also "Making Terra-Cotta Cornices," 511.

15. "Architecture and Illumination," 135.

16. See "London Guarantee," 100, Plates 38–40. The building's unusual floorplate is explained in "Playing a $4,000,000 Joke," *Chicago Daily Tribune*, Oct. 20, 1921, 3.

17. W. B. Norton, "Old First M. E. Is Being Razed for Skyscraper," *Chicago Daily Tribune*, May 1, 1922, 19; and "The Chicago Temple, Holabird & Roche, Architects," *Architecture*, Vol. L, no. 5, Nov. 1924, 391.

18. W. B. Norton, "Methodists See Dream Realized in Loop Temple," *Chicago Daily Tribune*, Mar. 26, 1922, 6.

19. "New First M. E. Church Permit Tangle Bared," *Chicago Daily Tribune*, Apr. 28, 1922, 7.

20. "Permit to Be Issued for $3,500,000 Loop Temple," *Chicago Daily Tribune*, Apr. 29, 1922, 1; Norton, "Old First M. E.," 19.

21. W. B. Norton, "Chicago Temple Gets Permit for Tower, Highest in Chicago," *Chicago Daily Tribune*, Dec. 21, 1922, 17.

22. James O'Donnell Bennett, "M. E. Building Opens New Era of Skyscrapers," Chicago Daily Tribune, Dec., 27, 1922, 1.

23. W. B. Norton, "Methodists to Dedicate Loop Temple," *Chicago Daily Tribune*, Sept. 26, 1924, 21.

24. Croly, "Notes and Comments," 203.

25. "Skyline of New Jagged Beauty Visioned Here," *Chicago Daily Tribune*, Dec. 28, 1922, 5.

26. "Zone Ordinance Hearings Open in Early January," *Chicago Daily Tribune*, Dec. 10, 1922, 19.

27. "Skyscraperville!" *Chicago Daily Tribune*, Mar. 13, 1923, 7; R. F. Schuchardt, "Peril to Climate in Lake Shore Skyscrapers," *Chicago Daily Tribune*, Mar. 19, 1923, 8. See also Last Zone Draft Gives Boul Mich Skyscraper Line," *Chicago Daily Tribune*, Mar. 13, 1923, 7; City Council and City of Chicago, *Chicago Zoning*.

28. Al Chase, "Zoning Tears Lid off City's Height Limit," *Chicago Daily Tribune*, Jan. 2, 1924, 26.

29. "Al Chase, "Real Estate News: Straus Building to Top Wrigley Spire by 75 Feet," *Chicago Daily Tribune*, Sept. 16, 1923, 30.

30. Rebori, "Notes and Comments," 89.

31. "Skyline of New Jagged," 5. See also "Saarinen Likens City to Beauty Doffing Her Rags," *Chicago Daily Tribune*, Mar. 26, 1923, 7.

32. See Robert Bruegmann, "When Worlds Collided: European and American Entries to the Chicago Tribune Competition of 1922," in Zukowsky, *Chicago Architecture, 1872–1922*, 303–318.

33. "James O'Donnell Bennett, "Tribune Tower Opens Its Doors to Public Today," *Chicago Daily Tribune*, Jul. 6, 1925, 1.

34. James O'Donnell Bennett, "Howells Wins in Contest for Tribune Tower," *Chicago Daily Tribune*, Dec. 3, 1922, 1.

35. James O'Donnell Bennett, "Howells Tells of Ideal Sought in Tribune Tower," *Chicago Daily Tribune*, Dec. 4, 1922, 5; Bennett, "Howells Wins," 1; and Bennett, "Tribune Tower Opens," 1.

36. Bennett, "Howells Wins."

37. Irving K. Pond, "High Buildings and Beauty, Part I," *Architectural Forum*, Vol. XXXVIII, no. 2, Feb. 1923, 42; and Sullivan, "Chicago Tribune Competition," 156.

38. Sullivan, "Chicago Tribune Competition."

39. Eliel Saarinen, "Europe Wakes Up to Need of U. S. Skyscraper," *Chicago Daily Tribune*, Jan. 23, 1923, 7.

40. Ibid. See also "Noted Architect from Finland is Chicago Visitor," *Chicago Daily Tribune*, Mar. 18, 1923, 5.

41. Hood, "Exterior Architecture," 97, 98.

42. "Calls Tribune Tower Latest Building Art," *Chicago Daily Tribune*, Jun. 23, 1923, 13.

43. Bennett, "Tribune Tower Opens," 1.

44. Bennett, "M. E. Building Opens," 1.

45. "Tribune Tower Building," 100.

46. "The Straus Building, Chicago," *Architectural Forum*, Vol. XLII, no. 4, Apr. 1925, 227.

47. "For Michigan Avenue," *Chicago Daily Tribune*, Apr. 15, 1923, 16.

48. Chase, "Real Estate News," 30.

49. The most thorough set of published floor plans of the Straus Building is in Rebori, "Straus Building," 385–394, 418–424.

50. Sheridan, "Economic Factors," 128.

51. "Rapid Progress Made,"541.

52. Rebori, "Straus Building," 385.

53. Ibid., 385. Sheridan and Clark, "Straus Building, Chicago," 225–229.

54. Rebori, "Straus Building, Chicago," 385. The Straus was among the last works to benefit from the design input of Peirce Anderson, who died on Feb. 10, 1924, just four days before the building was topped out.

55. Al Chase, "Jewelers' New $10,000,000 Bldg. Partly Garage," *Chicago Daily Tribune*, Apr. 16, 1924, 1.

56. I am grateful to Len Koroski of Goettsch Partnership for providing some enlightening biographical material on Giaver.

57. "Lincoln Tower Success Defies Modern Concepts," *Chicago Tribune*, Jul. 16, 1967, D1.

58. Ibid.

59. "Tower 256 Ft. High," 824.

60. Chappell, *Architecture and Planning*, 184–187.

61. Jane H. Clarke, "Pittsfield Building, Michigan Boulevard Building, Willoughby Tower," in Saliga and Clarke, *The Sky's the Limit*.

62. Al Chase, "Work to Start June 1st on Newest of Boul Mich Tower Group," *Chicago Daily Tribune*, May 1, 1927, B1.

63. "333 North Michigan Avenue," 158.

64. Willis, *Form Follows Finance*, 71–73.

65. "333 North Michigan Avenue," 157. See also Chase, "Work to Start June 1st"; and Reed, "Some Recent Work," 1.

66. Thielbar had been superintendent of construction at Holabird & Roche until 1918 and lead designer of the Chicago Temple. His partnership with John Reed Fugard, a native of Newton, Iowa, and twenty years his junior, came about as a result of both men's affiliation with the Methodist Church. As associated architects, they worked with Giaver and Dinkelberg on the Jewelers Building, but quickly found work of their own. "F. J. Thielbar, Architect Here 49 Years, Dies," *Chicago Daily Tribune*, Nov. 16, 1941, 16.

67. "Cast-Iron Cores Used," 129. Al Chase, "Trustees System Service Plans 32 Story Tower in Loop," *Chicago Daily Tribune*, June 9, 1929, B1.

68. Hoskins, "Palmolive Building," 655.

69. "Tenants of New Building Hold Open House," *Chicago Daily Tribune*, June 12, 1929, 12.

70. Ibid.

71. Hoskins, "Palmolive Building"; "Palmolive Company to Make Boul Mich Home 37 Stories," *Chicago Daily Tribune*, July 15, 1928, B1.

72. "Tenants of New Building," 12.

73. Hoskins, "Structure and Equipment," 736.

74. Al Chase, "Forty-Seven Story Tower to Replace Tacoma Building," *Chicago Daily Tribune*, Aug. 5, 1928, B1.

75. Gundersen, "Structural Design," 595–598.

76. "Beauty of New Opera Home to Show on Nov. 4," *Chicago Daily Tribune*, Sept. 13, 1929, 1. Frazier, "Mechanical Equipment," 613.

77. Lee, "Chicago Civic Opera," 495; Frazier, "Mechanical Equipment," 610–611.

78. Lee, "Chicago Civic Opera," 491. The Opera opened on Nov. 4, 1929, less than two weeks after Wall Street's "Black Thursday."

79. James O'Donnell Bennett, "Old Auditorium Is Restored to Former Glory," *Chicago Daily Tribune*, Dec. 11, 1932, 8.

80. Lee, "Chicago Daily News Building," 21. See also F. Brown, "Chicago Daily News Building," *Journal of the Western Society of Engineers*, Vol. XXXIV, no. 1, Jan. 1929, 19.

81. Lee, "Chicago Daily News Building," 32.

82. Stowell, "Structure and Equipment," 107.

83. Ibid., 107.

84. Lee, "Chicago Daily News Building," 28, 32; Stowell, "Structure and Equipment," 112.

85. Gray, "Engineering Features," 60–61, 100–102.

86. Lee, "Chicago Daily News Building," 21.

87. Stowell, "Structure and Equipment," 108–109. See also Lee, "Chicago Daily News Building," 21–22.

88. H. Monroe, "Margin of Safety," A2. Philip Hampson, "Chicago's Pit Will Rise 600 Feet over City," *Chicago Daily Tribune*, Nov. 18, 1928, B1.

89. "Board of Trade Trusses Weigh 222 Tons Each," *Chicago Daily Tribune*, July 14, 1929, B3.

90. "New Chicago Board of Trade Building—The Mid-West's Commercial Capitol—Rapidly Nears Completion," *Chicago Daily Tribune*, Jan. 27, 1930, 28.

91. "Notable Architectural, Engineering, and Electrical Achievements Distinguish New Chicago Board of Trade Building," *Chicago Daily Tribune*, Feb. 25, 1930, 28.

92. "Thousands Employed in Finishing New Board of Trade Building—Ready for Influx of Tenants May 1st," *Chicago Daily Tribune*, Mar. 24, 1930, 30.

93. Al Chase, "Merchandise Mart to Be World's Largest Business Building," *Chicago Daily Tribune*, May 6, 1928, B1.

94. "Two Salits Gangsters Slain—Three Slayers Escape Prison—Marshall Field & Co. Plan $15,000,000 Building," *Chicago Daily Tribune*, Mar. 12, 1927, 34.

95. Two small light courts for riverfront offices on its upper floors offered daylight and fresh air, however.

96. "Construction of Merchandise Mart Started," *Chicago Daily Tribune*, Aug. 14, 1928, 26.

97. Philip Hampson, "61,000 Members Used in Giant Mart," *Chicago Daily Tribune*, Sept. 22, 1929, B7.

98. "Merchandise Mart Steel Work Finished," *Chicago Daily Tribune*, Dec. 31, 1929, 4.

99. "Some 'World's Greatest Dope' for Fact Fiends [Merchandise Mart]," *Chicago Daily Tribune*, Dec. 9, 1928, B5. See

also print advertisement from American Steel & Wire Fabric, *Architectural Record*, Oct. 1932, 29; and "Freight Station with Air-Rights Warehouse at Chicago," *Engineering News-Record*, Aug. 19, 1929, 325–326.

100. Al Chase, "Marshall Field Estate Plans $15,000,000 Office Building," *Chicago Daily Tribune*, Sept. 29, 1929, E7.

101. Al Chase, "Issue Permit for Chicago's Largest Office Building," *Chicago Daily Tribune*, Mar. 26, 1931, 31.

102. "Money Lane's Biggest Cloud Tickler," *Chicago Daily Tribune*, Apr. 24, 1932, A6. The structural steel contract, calling for 25,000 tons of fabricated elements, was second only to the Merchandise Mart in Chicago construction. Al Chase, "Jobs for 7,500 as Fuller Gets Field Contract," *Chicago Daily Tribune*, Jul. 18, 1931, 5.

103. Chase, "Jobs for 7,500," 5. C. F. Murphy recalls that labor and material prices were so depressed that it was cheaper to actually construct the building rather than pay the contract's cancellation clauses: Manny, *Chicago Architects Oral History Project*, 20.

104. "Field Building: Chicago's Newest Skyscraper," 120. It is often claimed that the Field was the earliest Chicago skyscraper to be mechanically air-conditioned, but Murphy recalls this installation happening after WWII: "Oral History of Charles F. Murphy," in Manny, *Chicago Architects Oral History Project*.

CHAPTER 9. CHICAGO, 1934

1. Oscar Hewitt, "Start Inquiry into New High Building Law," *Chicago Daily Tribune*, Jul. 14, 1929, 1. See also Al Chase, "Architects Make Protest on New Skyscraper Law," *Chicago Daily Tribune*, Jul. 12, 1929, 14.

2. "Judge Gives His Ideas in Debate on Cuneo Permit," *Chicago Daily Tribune*, Nov. 7, 1929, 6.

3. Al Chase, "World's Tallest Structure for New Randolph Boulevard [Crane Tower]," *Chicago Daily Tribune*, May 5, 1929, B1.

4. William Clark, "Plans for Rail Air Rights May Have Revival," *Chicago Daily Tribune*, May 19, 1950, C5.

5. "Architect to Be Buried Today in Graceland," *Chicago Daily Tribune*, Apr. 16, 1924, 10; Rebori, "Louis H. Sullivan (1856–1924)," 587. Sullivan's final years have been the subject of rumor and speculation. He divorced in 1916, alleging that his wife had deserted him. He died in the Warner Hotel, a notorious gambling and drinking den.

6. Manny, *Chicago Architects Oral History Project*, 39.

7. Al Chase, "Famed Architectural Firm Takes In Second Generation," *Chicago Daily Tribune*, Jan. 2, 1937, 18; "Three Form a New Firm of Architects," *Chicago Daily Tribune*, Dec. 13, 1936, B6; and "3 Architects Quit Old Firm; Form New Unit," *Chicago Daily Tribune*, June 28, 1936, 18.

8. Mujica, *History of the Skyscraper*, 18–19.

9. Ibid., 28.

10. The problems associated with the term "Chicago School" are most brilliantly elucidated in H. Brooks, "Chicago School," 115–118.

11. Giedion, *Space, Time, and Architecture*, 381.

12. Frank Alfred Randall and John D. Randall, *History of the Development of Building Construction in Chicago* (rep., expanded version, Champaign: University of Illinois Press, 1999).

13. The term was also often used by sportswriters to describe a high fly ball in baseball. "The only item that counted was a tremendous sky-scraper by Pike, which scaled the west fence and gave an easy home-run." "Sporting Events," *Chicago Daily Tribune*, Oct. 3, 1877, 2.

14. Weisman, "New York and the Problem," 13–21.

15. Webster, "Skyscraper," 129.

16. Ibid., 126–139.

17. Webster, guest ed., "Chicago School Issue," *Prairie School Review*, Vol. IX, no. 1, First Quarter 1972 ["The Chicago School of Architecture, A Symposium, Part I"], 6–30; cont., in Condit, "Chicago School of Architecture: A Symposium—Part II," 5–37. Donald Hoffman and Winston Weisman, Letters to the Editor, in *Journal of Architectural Historians*, Vol. 32, no. 3, Oct. 1973, 264.

18. Condit, "Chicago School of Architecture: A Symposium—Part II," 9.

19. Bruegmann, "Myth of the Chicago School," 15–29.

20. Ibid., 21.

21. Wells, "Modern Office Building," 84.

22. Jenney, "Chicago Construction," 389–390.

23. Larson, "Fire, Earth, and Wind," 20–37.

24. Wight, "Additions to Chicago's Skyline," 15.

25. John A. Howland, "Modern Skyscraper," *Chicago Daily Tribune*, Oct. 10, 1904, B5.

26. "How Structural Iron Work Is Done on the Tribune's New Building," *Chicago Daily Tribune*, Oct. 27, 1901, 45.

27. Ferree, "Modern Office Building, Part I," 4–5.

28. "Old and New Chicago," *Chicago Daily*, May 24, 1896, 43.

29. Jenney, "A Few Practical Hints," 7.

30. Letter, D. H. Burnham to Lyman J. Gage, Pres., U.S. Trust, New York, May 15, 1902, D. H. Burnham Letterpress Copybooks, Microfilm 1972.4, reel 5, Ryerson & Burnham Library, Art Institute of Chicago. See also Letter, D. H. Burnham to E. W. Hopkins, San Francisco, Dec. 12, 1901, D. H. Burnham Letterpress Copybooks, Microfilm 1972.4, reel 4, Ryerson & Burnham Library, Art Institute of Chicago.

31. J. W. Yost, "Influence of Steel Construction and of Plate glass upon the

Development of Modern Style [Series of papers read at the Thirtieth Annual Convention of the American Institute of Architects, Nashville, Tennessee, Oct. 29, 1896]," *Inland Architect and News Record*, Vol. XXVIII, no. 4, Nov. 1896, 34.

32. Jenney, "A Few Practical Hints," 7.

33. Ibid.

34. Root, "A Great Architectural Problem," 71.

35. Winkler [Schuyler], "Some Chicago Buildings, " 314.

36. Rebori, "Work of Burnham & Root, " 62.

37. Twose, "Steel and Terra-Cotta," 5.

38. Adler, Response to J. W. Yost, "Influence of Steel Construction," 36.

39. *American Architect and Building News*, Vol. XLIV, no. 961 and subsequent, May 26, 1894 forward.

40. See, for instance, Baumann's citation of Semper in "Thoughts on Architecture [Lecture delivered before the American Institute of Architects, Washington D.C., Oct. 23, 1889]," *Inland Architect and News Record*, Vol. XVI, no. 5, Nov. 1890, 59. The impact of German culture and theory on Chicago architecture is fully covered by Roula Mouroudellis Geraniotis, "German Architectural Theory and Practice in Chicago, 1850–1900," *Winterthur Portfolio*, Vol. 21, no. 4, Winter 1986, 293–306.

41. Ferree, "High Building," 310.

42. Adler, "Tall Business Building," 210.

Bibliography

"333 North Michigan Avenue, Chicago: Holabird & Root, Architects." *Architectural Record.* Vol. 65, no. 2. Feb. 1929. 157–159.

Bill Addis. *Building: 3000 Years of Design, Engineering, and Construction* (London: Phaidon Press Limited, 2007).

Dankmar Adler. "The Auditorium Tower [Letter]." *American Architect and Building News.* Vol. XXXII, no. 797. Apr. 4, 1891. 15–16.

———. "Chicago Building Ordinance Revision." *Inland Architect and News Record.* Vol. XXI, no. 2. Mar. 1893. 27.

———. "Criticism on Builders' Code." *Inland Architect and News Record.* Vol. XXIX, no. 1. Feb. 1897. 2.

———. "The General Contractor from the Standpoint of the Architect." *Inland Architect and News Record.* Vol. XXXIII, no. 5. June 1899. 38–39.

———. "Light in Tall Office Buildings." *Engineering Magazine.* Vol. IV, no. 2. Nov. 1892. 171–186.

———. "Municipal Building Laws." *Inland Architect and News Record.* Vol. XXV, no. 4. May 1895. 36–38.

———. "Slow-Burning and Fireproof Construction." *Inland Architect and News Record.* Vol. XXVI, no. 6. Jan. 1896. 60–61.

———. "The Tall Business Building: Some of Its Engineering Problems." *Cassier's Magazine.* Vol. XII, no. 3. July 1897. 193–210.

———. "Tall Office Buildings—Past and Future." *Engineering Magazine.* Vol. III, no. 6. Sept. 1892. 765–773.

"Advantages of Fireproof Building." *Inland Architect and News Record.* Vol. XLVIII, no. 2. Sept. 1906. 14.

Arthur T. Aldis. "Modern Office Buildings as Investments." *Chicago Daily Tribune.* June 9, 1901. 29.

"Architecture and Illumination: A Notable Example in the Wrigley Building, Chicago." *Architectural Forum.* Vol. XXXV, no. 4. Oct. 1921. 135.

"Architecture in the Shopping District." *Inland Architect and News Record.* Vol. XXXIV, no. 6. Jan. 1900. 46–47.

"The Architecture of Chicago." *American Architect and Building News.* Vol. XLII, no. 933. n.d. 75–76.

"Arraignment of the Skyscraper." *Inland Architect and News Record.* Vol. L, no. 4. Oct.1907. 37.

A. S. Atkinson. "The Commercial Value of Fireproof Buildings." *Inland Architect and News Record.* Vol. XLVI, no. 6. Jan. 1906. 75.

———. "Electric Elevators." *Inland Architect and News-Record.* Vol. XLVIII, no. 4. Nov. 1906. 40–41.

Shirley P. Austin. "Glass." *Twelfth Census of the United States of America.* 1900. 949–967.

Julius Baier. "High Buildings [From 'Wind Pressure in the St. Louis Tornado]." *Journal of the Western Society of Engineers.* Vol. II, Jan./Dec. 1897. 509–512.

Turpin C. Bannister. "Bogardus Revisited: Part II: The Iron Towers." *Journal of the Society of Architectural Historians.* Vol. 16, no. 1. Mar. 1957. 11–19.

G. H. Barbour. "Wind Bracing in High Buildings [Letter to the Editor]." *Engineering Record.* Jan. 14, 1893. 138.

Frederick Baumann. "About Fireproof Buildings." *Inland Architect and News Record.* Vol. XLIII, no. 3. Apr. 1904. 18–19.

———. *The Art of Preparing Foundations for All Kinds of Buildings with Particular Illustrations of the 'Method of Isolated Piers' as Followed in Chicago* (Chicago: J. M. Wing and Co., 1873).

———. "The Art of Preparing Foundations, with Particular Illustration of the 'Method of Isolated Piers,' as Followed in Chicago." Supplement to George T. Powell, *Foundations and Foundation Walls for All Classes of Buildings* (New York: William T. Comstock, 1889). 146–166.

———. "Foundations." *Inland Architect and News Record.* Vol. XXXII, no. 5. Dec. 1898. 42–44.

———. *Improvement in the Construction of Tall Buildings* (Chicago: J. M. Wing and Co.[?], 1884), attached to a copy of Baumann 1873 Foundations pamphlet in UIUC Library.

———. "Notes on the Art of Building." *Inland Architect and News Record.* Vol. LI, no. 2. Feb. 1908. 4.

G. M. Beattie. *History of the Peoples Gas Building Construction: Its Progress from Foundation to Flag Pole* (Chicago: D. H. Burnham & Co., Architects, 1911).

George Beaumont. "Brickwork." *Inland Architect and Builder.* Vol. VII, no. 7. May 1886. 61.

Louis Bell. *The Art of Illumination* (New York: McGraw-Hill, 1912).

David Bensman and Mark R. Wilson. "Iron and Steel," in James R. Grossman, Ann Durkin Keating, and Janice L. Reiff, eds. *The Encyclopedia of Chicago* (Chicago: University of Chicago Press, 2004). 425–427.

Better Elevator Service (New York: Otis Elevator Company, 1916).

William H. Birkmire. *The Planning and Construction of High Office Buildings* (2nd ed., New York: John Wiley and Sons, 1900).

C. H. Blackall. "Notes of Travel. Chicago." *American Architect and Building News.* Vol. XXII, no. 626. Dec. 24, 1887. 299–300; Vol. XXII, no. 627. Dec. 31, 1887. 313–315; Vol. XXIII, no. 635. Feb. 25, 1888. 88–91; Vol. XXIII, no. 639. Mar. 24, 1888. 140–142.

Daniel Bluestone. *Constructing Chicago* (New Haven: Yale University Press, 1993).

H. Morton Bodfish. "Real Estate Activity in Chicago Accompanying the World's Fair of 1893." *Journal of Land and Public Utility Economics.* Vol. 4, no. 4. Nov. 1928. 405–416.

W. W. Boyington. "Architecture at the Present Time as Compared with That of Fifty Years Ago." *Inland Architect and News Record.* Vol. X, no. 5. Oct. 1887. 51.

"A Bright, Clean and Brilliant City." *Inland Architect and News Record.* Vol. XXXI, no. 4. May 1898. 38.

Fred A. Britten and John H. Jones, eds. *A Half-Century of Chicago Building* (Chicago: n.p., 1910).

H. Allen Brooks. "'Chicago School': Metamorphosis of a Term." *Journal of the Society of Architectural Historians.* Vol. 25, no. 2. May 1966. 115–118.

———. "Review of Carl Condit, *The Chicago School of Architecture*." *Art Bulletin.* Vol. 47, no. 2. June 1965. 304–305.

Morgan Brooks. "The Relation of Lighting to Architectural Interiors." *Scientific American.* Supplement no. 2161. June 2, 1917. 347.

Frank E. Brown. "Chicago Daily News Building." *Journal of the Western Society of Engineers.* Vol. XXXIV, no. 1. Jan. 1929. 19.

Thomas Brown. "Passenger Elevators." *American Architect and Building News.* Vol. LXXXVI, no. 1507. Nov. 12, 1904. 51–54.

Robert Bruegmann. *Holabird & Roche/ Holabird & Root: An Illustrated Catalogue of Works, 1880–1940* (New York: Garland, 1991).

———. "Myth of the Chicago School," in Ruedi Ray, Katerina Waldheim, and Charles Waldheim, eds. *Chicago Architecture: Histories, Revisions, Alternatives* (Chicago: University of Chicago Press, 2005). 15–29.

"Building Construction Details: no. XIII: The Rookery Building, Chicago." *Engineering and Building Record.* Vol. XVIII, no. 23. Nov. 3, 1888. 272–274.

"Building Construction Details, no. XVI: Fireproof Construction in Chicago." *Engineering and Building Record.* Vol. XIX. Jan. 5, 1888[?]. 71–72.

"Building Construction Details, No. XLVIII: The Rand and McNally Building, Chicago. Part I—General Plan and Details of Foundations." *Engineering Record.* Dec. 12, 1891. 25.

"Building Construction Details. The Masonic Temple, Chicago." *Engineering Record.* Jan. 21, 1893. 160–161; May 13, 1893. 478–479; May 27, 1893. 514; Sept. 2, 1893. 222; Oct. 28, 1893. 349.

Building Floodlighting and Its Possibilities with Terra Cotta (New York: National Terra Cotta Society, 1927[?]).

D. H. Burnham. "Increasing Usage of Glass in Construction." Speech delivered June 5, year (note—Burnham & Root Architects, 115 Monroe St., 188[?]). Delivered to Architectural Association of Illinois. Box FF 63.12, Daniel H. Burnham Collection.

D. H. Burnham & Co. " Letterpress Copybooks 1890–1912," v. 7–10 (1894–1902) reel 4 in The Burnham Library and Archives, Art Institute of Chicago.

H. J. Burt. "Growth of Steel Frame Buildings: Origin and Some Problems of the Skyscraper." *Engineering News Record—Fiftieth Anniversary Number.* Vol. 92, No. 16. n.d. 680–684.

J. M. Camp and C. B. Francis. *The Making, Shaping, and Treating of Steel* (2nd ed., Pittsburgh: Carnegie Steel Company, 1920).

"Cast-Iron Columns for Buildings." *Engineering Record*. Vol. XXXII, no. 18. Sept. 28, 1895. 308.

"Cast-Iron Cores Used in Columns of 16-Story Concrete Building [McGraw-Hill]." *Engineering News-Record*. July 25, 1929. 129–131.

"Cheapening Fire-Proof Buildings." *Manufacturer and Builder*. Vol. 11, no. 5. May 1879. 101.

Paul Chesterton. "Concrete as a Fireproofer." *Cement World*. Nov. 1912. 26–33.

"Chicago Building Obsolescent after 40 Years." *Engineering News-Record*. Vol. 103. Dec. 26, 1929. 1003–1004.

"Chicago Foundations." *Chicago Daily Tribune*. Apr. 3, 1892. 28.

Chicago of Today: The Metropolis of the West (Chicago: ACME Publishing and Engraving Co., 1891).

"The Chicago School of Architecture." *Brickbuilder*. Vol. 2, no. 7. July 1893. 71.

"Chicago's Latest Steel Frame Building." *Inland Architect and News Record*. Vol. XXVIII, no. 1. Aug. 1896. 7.

"Chicago's Most Massive and Costly Office Building [First National Bank]." Supplement to *Inland Architect and News Record*. Vol. XLVI, no. 4. Nov. 1905. 1–7.

"Chicago's Veneered Buildings." *New York Times*. Nov. 30, 1891. 4.

"The Chicago Temple: Holabird & Roche, Architects." *Architecture*. Vol. L, no. 5. Nov. 1924. 369–370, 391.

City Council and City of Chicago. *Chicago Zoning Ordinance*. Passed Apr. 5, 1923.

E. C. Clark. "Chicago's Most Modern Banking and Office Building," in "Technical Review, The Merchants' Loan and Trust Co. Bank Building, Chicago." *Inland Architect and News Record*. Special Supplement. Vol. XXXVII, no. 3. Apr. 1901. 1–7.

———. "Latest Developments in Building Design and Arrangements." *Inland Architect and News Record*. Vol. XXXI, no. 3. Apr. 1898. 29.

T. M. Clark. "Recent Improvements in Building." *Inland Architect and News Record*. Vol. XLV, no. 6. July 1905. 61–62; Vol. XLVI, no. 1. Aug. 1905. 3–4; Vol. XLVI, no. 2. Sept. 1905. 19–20.

W. C. Clark and J. L. Kingston. *The Skyscraper: A Study in the Economic Height of Modern Office Buildings* (New York: American Institute of Steel Construction, 1930).

Meredith L. Clausen. "Frank Lloyd Wright, Vertical Space, and the Chicago School's Quest for Light." *Journal of the Society of Architectural Historians*. Vol. 44, no. 1. Mar. 1985. 66–74.

F. Collingwood. "Fire-Proof Construction." *Sanitary Engineer*. Sept. 16, 1886. 371–372.

"The Commercial Bank Building: A Splendid Business Structure of the Best Modern American Type. D. H. Burnham & Company, Architects." *Inland Architect and News Record*. Vol. LI, no. 2. Feb. 1908. 6–7.

"Concrete in Building Construction." *Inland Architect and News Record*. Vol. XLVII, no. 2. Mar. 1906. 22.

Carl W. Condit. *The Chicago School of Architecture: A History of Commercial and Public Building in the Chicago Area 1875–1925* (Chicago: University of Chicago Press, 1964).

———. "The Chicago School of Architecture: A Symposium—Part II. Structural Development." *Prairie School Review*. Vol. IX, no. 2. Second Quarter 1972. 5–37.

———. "The First Reinforced-Concrete Skyscraper: The Ingalls Building in Cincinnati and Its Place in Structural History." *Technology and Culture*. Vol. 9, no. 1. Jan. 1968. 1–33.

———. "Modern Architecture: A New Technical-Aesthetic Synthesis." *Journal of Aesthetics and Art Criticism*. Vol. 6, no. 1. Sept. 1947. 45–54.

———. "Review of Francisco Mujica, *History of the Skyscraper*." *Technology and Culture*. Vol. 19, no. 3. July 1978. 533–534.

———. "The Structural System of Adler and Sullivan's Garrick Theater Building." *Technology and Culture*. Vol. 5, no. 4. Autumn 1964. 523–540.

———. "The Wind Bracing of Buildings." *Scientific American*. Vol. 230, no. 2. Feb. 1974. 92–105.

Theodore L. Condron. "A Unique Type of Reinforced Concrete Construction." *Journal of the Western Society of Engineers*. Vol. XIV, no. 6. Dec. 1909. 824–864.

"The Construction in Detail," in "Technical Review, The Merchants' Loan and Trust Co. Bank Building, Chicago." *Inland Architect and News Record*. Special Supplement. Vol. XXXVII, no. 3. Apr. 1901. 7–22.

Harvey Wiley Corbett. "The Future of the Tall Building." *Engineering News-Record*. Vol. 106, no. 8. Feb. 19, 1931. 307–310.

———. "The Planning of Office Buildings." *Architectural Forum*. Vol. XLI, no. 3. Sept. 1924. 89–93.

"Correspondence: Brick-Making in Chicago and Vicinity." *American Architect and Building News*. Sept. 8, 1877. 289–290.

Herbert D. Croly. "Notes and Comments: The Skyscraper in the Service of Religion." *Architectural Record*. Vol. 55, no. 2. Feb. 1924. 203–204.

William Cronon. *Nature's Metropolis: Chicago and the Great West* (New York: Norton, 1992).

"Cut Building Cost and Increase Floor Space by Study of Plans." *Engineering News-Record*. Vol. 91, no. 3. Aug. 30, 1923. 343.

Raymond C. Daly. *75 Years of Construc-*

tion Pioneering: George A. Fuller Company (1882–1957) (New York: The Newcomen Society in North America, 1957).

Thaddeus S. Dayton. "Miracles in Iron and Steel." *Harper's*. Mar. 23, 1912. 9.

"Design of the Champlain Office Building, N. W. Corner State and Madison Streets, Chicago." *Inland Architect and News-Record*. Vol. XXI, no. 4. May 1893.

Harry W. Desmond. "Rationalizing the Skyscraper." *Architectural Record*. Vol. 17. May 1905. 422–425.

"Developments of Architectural Construction." *Engineering Record*. Vol. XXXVIII, no. 6. July 2, 1898. 99; Vol. XXXVIII, no. 8. July 23, 1898. 166; Vol. XXXVIII, no. 9. July 30, 1898. 190–191; Vol. XXXVIII, no. 11. Aug. 6, 1898. 209–210; Vol. XXXVIII, no. 11. Aug. 13, 1898. 233; Vol. XXXVIII, no. 14. Sept. 3, 1898. 299–300; Vol. XXXVIII, no. 16. Sept. 17, 1898. 343–345; Vol. XXXVIII, no. 18. Oct. 1, 1898. 383.

"Diamond Plate Glass Works." *Kokomo Daily Dispatch*. Apr. 12, 1892. Special Ed. 2:3. Clipping in file marked "VF-1, Local Business File. Diamond Plate Glass Co (Kokomo)." Stan Mohr Local History Library, Kokomo, Indiana.

H. E. Dickson. "Review of *The Chicago School of Architecture: A History of Commercial and Public Building in the Chicago Area, 1875–1925*." *Journal of American History*. Vol. 52, no. 1. June 1965. 180–181.

Frederick P. Dinkelberg. "Thoughts on Architecture." *Inland Architect and News Record*. Vol. LI, no. 5. May 1908. 39–40.

S. E. Doane. "Electric Light—A Factor in Civilization." *Journal of the Western Society of Engineers*. Vol. XX, no. 1. Jan. 1915. 2–26.

"Early Skeleton Construction." *Engineering Record*. Vol. 40, no. 11. Aug. 12, 1899. 237–238.

"Electricity in Chicago." *Scientific American*. Vol. CVI, no. 10. Mar. 9, 1912.

"Electric Lamps in the United States." *Scientific American*. Vol. CXII, no. 8. Feb. 20, 1915. 173.

"Electric Light in Chicago." *Engineering News and American Contract Journal*. Vol. XIII. Jan. 10, 1885. 30.

"Elevators." *Inland Architect and Builder*. Vol. V, no. 3. Apr. 1885. 3.

Cecil Elliott. *Technics and Architecture: The Development of Materials and Systems for Buildings* (Cambridge: MIT Press, 1994).

"Enameled Bricks for the Fronts of Buildings." *Inland Architect and News Record*. Vol. XXX, no. 1. Aug. 1897. 5–6.

"Essential Features of Steel Building Construction [Reply to Letter]." *Engineering Record*. Feb. 11, 1893. 219.

John M. Ewen. "Foundations for Chicago Buildings." *Journal of the Western Society of Engineers*. Vol. X, no. 6. Dec. 1905. 687–704.

"An Experiment in Economic Floor Construction." *Inland Architect and News Record*. Vol. XXVII, no. 6. July 1896. 58.

Sir William Fairbairn. *On the Application of Cast and Wrought Iron to Building Purposes* (4th ed., London: Longmans, Green and Co., 1870).

———. "On the Durability and Preservation of Iron Ships, and on Riveted Joints [Abstract]." *Proceedings of the Royal Society of London*. Vol. 21. 1872–1873. 259–263.

"The Father of All Skyscrapers." *Scientific American*. May 1932. 290–291.

Barr Ferree. "Architecture." *Engineering Magazine*. Vol. III, no. 4. July 1892. 570–572.

———. "The High Building and Its Art." *Scribner's Magazine*. Vol. 15, no. 3. Mar. 1894. 297–318.

———. "The Modern Office Building [Lecture Delivered to the Franklin Institute, Nov. 15, 1895]." *Inland Architect*

and *News Record*. Vol. XXVII, no. 1. Feb. 1896. 4–5; Vol. XXVII, no. 2. Mar. 1896. 12–14; Vol. XXVII, no. 4. May 1896. 34–35; Vol. XXVII, no. 5. June 1896. 45–47.

"The Field Building: Chicago's Newest Skyscraper." *Architectural Record*. Aug. 1934. 120–128.

"Financial Returns on Fireproof Buildings." *Inland Architect and News-Record*. Vol. XLVI, no. 3. Oct. 1905. 26.

"Fire-proof Buildings." *Manufacturer and Builder*. Vol. 19, no. 8. Aug. 1887. 190–191.

"Fires Due to Combustible Construction." *Inland Architect and News Record*. Vol. XXXI, no. 3. Apr. 1898.

"Fire Tests on Iron Columns." *Inland Architect and News Record*. Vol. XXVIII, no. 2. Sept. 1896. 11–12.

F. W. Fitzpatrick. "Chicago." *Inland Architect and News Record*. Vol. XLV, no. 5. June 1905. 46–48.

———. "Fifty Years of Architectural Evolution." *American Architect*. Vol. CXXXIV, no. 2553. Sept. 20, 1928. 357–360.

"Foes of the Skyscraper Vanquished." *Inland Architect and News Record*. Vol. XLV, no. 6. July 1905. 58.

C. A. Frazier. "Mechanical Equipment of the Chicago Civic Opera Building." *Architectural Forum*. Vol. LII, no. 4. Apr. 1930. 610–614.

Geo. A. Frederick. "Municipal Building Laws." *Inland Architect and News Record*. Vol. XII, no. 4. Oct. 1888.

Joseph Kendall Freitag. *Architectural Engineering. With Especial Reference to High Building Construction, Including Many Examples of Prominent Office Buildings* (2nd ed., New York: Wiley and Sons, 1904).

———. *The Fireproofing of Steel Buildings* (New York: Wiley, 1899).

Donald Friedman. "Anchoring Systems for Architectural Terra Cotta in Curtain-

Wall Construction." *APT Bulletin*. Vol. 32, no. 4. 2001. 17–21.

———. *Historical Building Construction* (2nd ed., New York: W. W. Norton, 2010).

"The Furniture Mart Building, Chicago." *Architecture*. Vol. LI, no. 3. Mar. 1925. 85–88.

"The Future of Steel and Iron." *Engineering News*. Jan. 8, 1881. 13.

William D. Gates. "Clay Material as Used in the Best Modern Buildings." *The Inland Architect Supplement: Technical Review of the Interesting Development of the Building Arts*. Vol. XXXIV, no. 6. Jan. 1900. 15–17.

"General Contracting a Menace to Architects." *Inland Architect and News Record*. Vol. XXXIII, no. 4. May 1899. 29–30.

"Getting Daylight into a Skyscraper." *Architectural Record*. Vol. XXXIII, no. 3. Mar. 1913. 279.

Cass Gilbert. "Daniel Hudson Burnham: An Appreciation." *Architectural Record*. Vol. XXXII, no. 167. Aug. 1912. 175–176.

R. W. Gleson. "Observations on Heavy Buildings." *Inland Architect and News Record*. Vol. XII, no. 4. Oct. 1888. 32.

"Good Fire-Proof Construction." *Brickbuilder*. Vol. 1, no. 9. Sept. 1892. 71–72.

Ernest R. Graham. Foreword to *The Architectural Work of Graham Anderson Probst & White Chicago and Their Predecessors, D. H. Burnham & Co., and Graham, Burnham, & Co.* (2 vol., London: B. T. Batsford, Ltd., 1933).

W. B. Gray. "Engineering Features of the Daily News Building, Chicago. Holabird & Root, Architects." *American Architect*. Vol. CXXXVII, no. 2579. Jan. 1930. 60–61, 100–102.

The Gray Column: Tables of Safe Loads (4th ed., New York: Gray and Gronau, 1896).

"Great American Industries: VIII—A Piece of Glass." *Harper's New Monthly Magazine*. Vol. 79, no. 470. July 1889. 245–265.

"The Great Northern Hotel, Chicago: Burnham and Root, Architects." *Inland Architect and News Record*. Vol. XXI, no. 3. n.d.

"A Great Office Building [Rookery]." *Inland Architect and Builder*. Vol. VII, no. 9. June 1886. 80.

Hugo Grosser. "Gas and Electric Light Service: Chicago." *Annals of the American Academy of Political and Social Science*. Vol. 27. Jan. 1906. 202–206.

Magnus Gunderson. "The Structural Design of the Chicago Civic Opera Building." *Architectural Forum*. Vol. LII, no. 4. Apr. 1930. 595–598.

Thomas Hastings. "High Buildings and Good Architecture: What Principles Should Govern Their Design?" *American Architect and Building News*. Vol. XLVI, no. 986. Nov. 17, 1894. 67–68.

Albert W. Hayward. "Electricity in the Province of the Architect [Paper Read before the Cincinnati Chapter of the American Institute of Architects, Jan. 25, 1898]." *Inland Architect and News Record*. Vol. XXXI, no. 1. Feb. 1898. 4–5.

Franklin H. Head. "The Heart of Chicago." *New England Magazine*. Vol. VI, no. 5. July 1892. 551–567.

R. E. Heine. "The Electric Lighting of Buildings [Part I]." *Inland Architect and News Record*. Vol. XLVII, no. 3. Apr. 1906. 43; Vol. XLVII, no. 4. May 1906. 56; Vol. XLVII, no. 5. June 1906. 68; Vol. XLVII, no. 6. July 1906. 88.

"The High Building Not without Friends." *Inland Architect and News Record*. Vol. L, no. 4. Oct. 1907. 37–38.

Albert F. Hill. "Riveted Girders." *Engineering News*. Apr. 8, 1882. 109.

———. "Steel Specifications." *Engineering News and Contract Journal*. June 17, 1882. 202–203.

George Hill. "Office Building," in Russell Sturgis, ed. *A Dictionary of Architecture and Building, Biographical, Historical and Descriptive* (New York: The MacMillan Company, 1902). Vol. II, 11–18.

———. "Some Practical Limitations in the Design of Office Buildings." *Architectural Record*. Volume II. n.d. 445–467.

A. L. A. Himmelwright. "High Buildings." *North American Review*. Vol. 163, no. 480. Nov. 1896. 580–586.

Henry Russell Hitchcock. "Review of Carl Condit, *The Rise of the Skyscraper*." *American Quarterly*. Vol. 4, no. 4. Winter 1952. 351–359.

Donald Hoffman. "John Root's Monadnock Building." *Journal of the Society of Architectural Historians*. Vol. 26, no. 4. Dec. 1967. 269–277.

———. "Pioneer Building Foundations: 1890." *Journal of the Society of Architectural Historians*. Vol. 25, no. 1. Mar. 1966. 68–71.

———. "The Setback Skyscraper City of 1891: An Unknown Essay by Louis H. Sullivan." *Journal of the Society of Architectural Historians*. Vol. 29, no. 2. May 1970. 181–187.

"Hollow Tile versus Concrete Construction." *Inland Architect and News Record*. Vol. LXI, no. 6. July 1903. 50.

Raymond M. Hood. "Exterior Architecture of Office Buildings." *Architectural Forum*. Vol. XLI, no. 3. Sept. 1924. 97–99.

Henry J. B. Hoskins. "The Palmolive Building, Chicago." *Architectural Forum*. Vol. LII, no. 5. May 1930. 655–688.

———. "Structure and Equipment of the Palmolive Building." *Architectural Forum*. Vol. LII, no. 5. May 1930. 731–736.

A. U. Howard. "Plate versus Cylinder Glass [Letter Read at the Nashville Convention of the American Institute of Architects]." Reprinted in *Inland Architect and News-Record*. Vol. XXVIII, no. 4. Nov. 1896.

"How a Skyscraper Is Lifted; Magic of Modern Engineer." *Chicago Daily Tribune.* Mar. 3, 1907. E5.

"How Hollow Steel Piles, Compressed Air and Concrete Are Employed to Make a Foundation." *Scientific American.* Vol. CIX, no. 26. Dec. 27, 1913. 494–495.

Charles L. Hubbard. "The Question of Heat and Ventilation." *Architectural Record.* Vol. XXXIII, no. 5. May 1913. 444–456.

Henry M. Hyde. "A New Era of Building in Chicago." *Harper's Weekly.* Sept. 7, 1901. 893.

John D. Ihlder. "Electric Elevators for High Buildings." *Journal of the Western Society of Engineers.* Vol. XIII, no. 3. June 1908. 353–375.

The Importance of Quality in Incandescent Lamps: Information of Importance and Interest to Users of Incandescent Lamps (Harrison, N.J.: General Electric Company, 1898).

Industrial Chicago: The Building Interests (Chicago: The Goodspeed Publishing Co., 1891).

"Influence of Lighting on Design." *Inland Architect and News Record.* Vol. XLIX, no. 2. Feb. 1907. 24.

The Inland Architect Supplement: Technical Review of the Interesting Development of the Building Arts. Supplement to Vol. XXXIV, no. 6. Jan. 1900.

"The Insurance Exchange Building [Advertising Supplement]." *Inland Architect and Builder.* Vol. V, no. 6. July 1885. 2.

"The Invention of Steel Skeleton Construction up Again." *Inland Architect and News Record.* Vol. XLIV, no. 2. Sept. 1904.

"Iron Castings." *American Architect and Building News.* July 15, 1876. 229–230.

C. Henry Irwin. "Relative Cost of Light from Different Sources." *Illuminating Engineer.* Vol. 2, no. 8. Oct. 1907. 623–624.

J. H. Jallings. "Elevators," in *Cyclopedia of Architecture, Carpentry and Building* (Chicago: American School of Correspondence/American Technical Society, 1907). Vol. V, 315–366.

Chas. E. Jenkins. "A White Enameled Building [Reliance]." *Architectural Record.* Vol. IV, no. 3. Jan.–Mar. 1895. 299–307.

W. L. B. Jenney. "An Age of Steel and Clay [Paper Read before the Chicago Architectural Sketch Club, Oct. 6, 1890]." *Inland Architect and News Record.* Vol. XVI, no. 7. Dec. 1890. 75–77.

———. "The Best Fireproof Construction for Buildings Occupied for Mercantile Purposes." *Inland Architect and News Record.* Vol. XXX, no. 3. Oct. 1897. 22–26.

———. "The Building Stones of Chicago [Reprint of Paper Read before the Chicago Academy of Sciences, Nov. 1883]." *Engineering News and American Contract Journal.* Jan. 5, 1884. 1–3.

———. "Chicago Construction, or Tall Buildings on a Compressible Soil." *Engineering Record.* Nov. 14, 1891. 389–390. Also rep. in *Inland Architect and News Record.* Vol. XVIII, no. 4. Nov. 1891. 41.

———. "The Construction of a Heavy Fire Proof Building on a Compressible Soil." *Sanitary Engineer.* Vol. XIII. Dec. 10, 1885. 32–33.

———. "The Construction of Heavy, Fireproof Building on a Compressible Soil." *Inland Architect and Builder.* Vol. VI, no. 6. Dec. 1885. 100.

———. "The Dangers of Tall Steel Structures." *Cassier's Magazine.* Vol. XIII, no. 5. Mar. 1898. 413–422.

———. "Economy in the Use of Steel in Building Construction." *Inland Architect and News-Record.* Vol. XIV, no. 8. Jan. 1890. 94.

———. "A Few Practical Hints [Paper Read before the Chicago Architectural Sketch Club, Jan. 28, 1889]." *Inland Architect and News Record.* Vol. XIII, no. 1. Feb. 1889. 7.

———. "Steel Skeleton Building Construction [Letter to the Editor]." *Engineering Record.* Jan 6, 1894. 90.

———. "The Steel Skeleton, or the Modern Skyscrapers—The Engineering Principles." *The Inland Architect Supplement: Technical Review of the Interesting Development of the Building Arts.* Vol. XXXIV, no. 6. Jan. 1900. 2–8.

———. "Terra-Cotta Cornices for Steel Skeleton Buildings." *Brickbuilder.* Vol. VI, no. 6. June 1897. 115.

———. "The Use and Abuse of the Lemont Limestone." *Chicago Daily Tribune.* June 9, 1878. 11.

Jenney & Mundie. "The Constructive Methods Used in the New York Life Building, Chicago." *American Architect and Building News.* Vol. XLIII, no. 946. Feb. 10, 1894. 71–72.

Robert A. Jewett. "Structural Antecedents of the I-Beam, 1800–1850." *Technology and Culture.* Vol. 8, no. 3. July 1967. 346–362.

E. V. Johnson. "Correspondence: The Facts in Regard to Fire Losses at Baltimore." *Inland Architect and News Record.* Vol. XLIII, no. 6. July 1904. 47.

———. "Standard Floor Arch Construction." *Journal of the Western Society of Engineers.* Vol. IX, no. 5. Oct. 1904. 458–473.

———. "The Structural Value of Hollow Tile for Buildings." *The Inland Architect and News Record,* Vol. XLV, no. 2. Mar. 1905. 13.

Henry Robert Kann. "The Chicago School of Architecture [Review of Carl Condit]." *Technology and Culture.* Vol. 6, no. 3. Summer 1965. 472–475.

F. H. Kidder. *The Architect's and Builder's Pocket-Book. A Handbook for Architects, Structural Engineers, Build-*

ers, and Draughtsmen (14th ed., New York: Wiley and Sons, 1905).

Fiske Kimball. "The Classic in the Skyscraper." *Architectural Record*. Vol. 57, no. 2. Feb. 1925. 189–190.

———. "Louis Sullivan—An Old Master." *Architectural Record*. Vol. 57, no. 4. Apr. 1925. 289–304.

F. H. Kindl. "Iron and Steel Skeleton-Frames." *American Architect and Building News*. Vol. XXXIV, no. 833. Dec. 12, 1891. 170–171.

———, ed. *Pocket Companion Containing Useful Information and Tables Appertaining to the Use of Steel, as Manufactured by the Carnegie Steel Company, Limited, Pittsburgh, Pa* (Pittsburgh: Carnegie Steel Company, 1893).

Joseph Kirkland and John Moses. *The History of Chicago, Illinois* (Chicago: Munsell and Co., 1895).

A. Lawrence Kocher and Albert Frey. "Windows." *Architectural Record*. Feb. 1931. 127–137.

"Lack of Care in the Details of Iron-Work." *Engineering News*. Apr. 29, 1882. 135.

Sarah Bradford Landau. *P. B. Wight: Architect, Contractor, and Critic, 1838–1925* (Chicago: Art Institute of Chicago, 1981).

M. A. Lane. "High Buildings in Chicago." *Harper's Weekly*. Oct. 31, 1891. 853–857.

Gerald R. Larson. "Fire, Earth, and Wind: Technical Sources of the Chicago Skyscraper." *Inland Architect*. Sept. 1981. 20–37.

Gerald R. Larson and Roula Mouroudellis Geraniotis. "Toward a Better Understanding of the Evolution of the Iron Skeleton Frame in Chicago." *Journal of the Society of Architectural Historians*. Vol. 46, no. 1. Mar. 1987. 39–48.

Anne Lee. "The Chicago Civic Opera Building." *Architectural Forum*. Vol. LII, no. 4. Apr. 1930. 491–500.

———. "The Chicago Daily News Build-ing. Holabird & Root, Architects." *Architectural Forum*. Vol. LII, no. 1. Jan. 1930. 21–32.

Henry Harrison Lewis. "Chicago—The Evolution of a Great City." *Harper's*. Oct. 28, 1905. 1558–1564.

"The Lifetime of Building Stones." *Inland Architect and Builder*. Vol. IV, no. 3. Oct. 1884. 44.

Light: Its Use and Misuse. A Primer of Illumination Prepared under the Direction of the Illuminating Engineering Society (New York: Illuminating Engineering Society, 1912).

"London Guarantee and Accident Building, Chicago." *Architectural Forum*. Vol. XLI, no. 3. Sept. 1924. 100, plates 38–40.

"Low Percentage of Loss in Fireproofed Buildings." *Inland Architect and News Record*. Vol. XLIII, no. 6. July 1904.

M. Luckiesh. *Light and Work: A Discussion of Quality and Quantity of Light in Relation to Effective Vision and Efficient Work* (New York: D. Van Nostrand Company, 1924).

"The Majestic Theater Building, Chicago. Edmund R. Krause, Architect." *Inland Architect and News Record*. Vol. XLVII, no. 2. Mar. 1906. iii–iv.

"Making Terra-Cotta Cornices and Parapets Practically Safe." *Engineering News-Record*. Vol. 93, no. 13. Sept. 25, 1924. 511.

"The Mallers Building [Advertising Supplement]." *Inland Architect and Builder*. Vol. V, no. 6. July 1885. 2.

"A Mammoth Opera House." *Inland Architect and Builder*. Vol. IV, no. 8. Mar. 1885. 25.

Carter H. Manny. *Chicago Architects Oral History Project: Oral History of Charles F. Murphy* (Chicago: The Art Institute of Chicago, 1995).

"The Manufacture of Terra-Cotta in Chicago." *American Architect and Building News*. Dec. 30, 1876. 420–421.

"Merchandise Mart Building, Chicago, Ill." *American Architect*. Vol. CXXXIII, no. 2547. June 20, 1928. 846.

Joanna Merwood-Salisbury. *Chicago 1890: The Skyscraper and the Modern City* (Chicago: University of Chicago Press, 2009).

Donald L. Miller. *City of the Century: The Epic of Chicago and the Making of America* (New York: Simon and Schuster, 1997).

Thomas J. Misa. *A Nation of Steel: The Making of Modern America, 1865–1925* (Paperback ed., Baltimore: Johns Hopkins University Press, 1999).

Robert Craik M'Lean. "Dankmar Adler." *Inland Architect and News Record*. Vol. XXXV, no. 4. May 1900. 26–27.

"Modern Architecture—Antique Clothes." *Inland Architect and News Record*. Vol. LII, no. 4. Oct. 1908. 43–44.

Harriett Monroe. *John Wellborn Root: A Study of His Life and Work* (Cambridge: Riverside Press, 1896).

———. "Margin of Safety in Skyscrapers; Some Cases Dangerously Small." *Chicago Daily Tribune*. June 16, 1912. A2.

———. "Show Reveals Architectural Art Slighted in Favor of Shoddiness." *Chicago Daily Tribune*. May 11, 1913. B5.

———. "Task Confronts Architect to Meet Modern Era." *Chicago Daily Tribune*. Apr. 14, 1912. B2.

William S. Monroe. "Electric Lighting of Modern Office Buildings." *Architectural Record*. Volume VI. 1896. 105–113.

J. T. Montgomery. "Fireproof Floor Construction." *Journal of the Western Society of Engineers*. Vol. IX, no. 5. Oct. 1904. 451–457.

"The Montgomery Ward & Company Building, Chicago." *Engineering Record*. May 25, 1901. 491–493.

"More Cloud Supporters." *Chicago Daily Tribune*. July 7, 1889. 9.

Francisco Mujica. *History of the Skyscraper*

(Paris: Archaeology and Architecture Press, 1929).

Lewis Mumford. "The Sky Line—Fresh Start." *New Yorker.* Mar. 8, 1952. 72–78.

"Natural Gas Phenomenon in Indiana." *Scientific American.* Vol. 63, no. 10. Sept. 6, 1890. 145.

"The Necessity for Abolishing General Contracting." *Inland Architect and News Record.* Vol. XXXIII, no. 4. May 1899. 29.

"New Building Ordinance for Chicago." *Engineering Record.* Vol. 27, no. 17. Mar. 25, 1893. 1–2.

"The New Central Music Hall." *American Architect and Building News.* Vol. VI, no. 202. Nov. 8, 1879. 150–151.

"The New Chicago Tribune Building." *Inland Architect and News Record.* Vol. XL, no. 2. Sept. 1902. 12–14.

Oscar Newman. "Before the Second 'Age of Stone' the 'Iron Age' Trembles." *Chicago Daily Tribune.* June 12, 1910. E1.

"The New Schlesinger and Mayer Building, Chicago." *Brickbuilder.* Vol. 12, no. 5. May 1903. 101–104.

"The New York Life Building at Chicago." *Inland Architect and News Record.* Vol. XXIV, no. 3. Oct. 1894. 30.

"New York Life Insurance Company's Building, Northeast Corner La Salle and Monroe Streets, Chicago, Ill." *American Architect and Building News.* Vol. XLII, no. 933. Nov. 11, 1893. 78–79, plus plates.

W. K. Nixon. "Fire-Proof Buildings [Letter to the Editor]." *Chicago Tribune.* Nov. 26, 1871. 2.

"The North American Building, Chicago, Ill." *Brickbuilder.* Vol. XXII, no. 1. Jan. 1913. 21–24.

"Notable Fireproof Buildings Now Being Erected at Chicago." *Brickbuilder.* Vol. 13. no. 9. Sept. 1904. 191–192.

"Not Building Laws but Fireproofed Structures." *Inland Architect and News Record.* Vol. XLIII, no. 1. Feb. 1904. 6.

"Notes and Clippings: The Chicago Auditorium." *American Architect and Building News.* Vol. XXVI, no. 724. Nov. 9, 1889. 223–224.

"Notes and Comment." *Engineering Record.* Vol. 50, no. 17. Oct. 22, 1904. 470. [Incandescent Lamp Replacement]

"Obituary: W. L. B. Jenney." *Inland Architect and News Record.* Vol. L, no. 1. July 1907. 1.

"Obsolescence Study of an Office Building in Chicago [Woman's Temple]." *Engineering News-Record.* Vol. 99, no. 4. July 28, 1927. 136–137.

"Obsolete Methods of Fireproofing Condemned." *Inland Architect and News Record.* Vol. XLI, no. 3. Apr. 1903. 20.

James F. O'Gorman. "The Marshall Field Wholesale Store: Materials toward a Monograph." *Journal of the Society of Architectural Historians.* Vol. 37, no. 3. Oct. 1978. 175–194.

———. *Three American Architects* (Chicago: University of Chicago Press, 1991).

"Old and New Patents on Tungsten Incandescent Lamps." *Scientific American.* Vol. CVI, no. 16. Apr. 20, 1912. 364.

Harold Bennett Olin. "A Brief History of the Chicago Building Code." Typescript in the Chicago Municipal Reference Library. Nov. 1997.

"On Iron Skeletons for Buildings." *Engineering Record.* Mar. 5, 1892. 226.

"The Opera House Office Building." *Inland Architect and Builder.* Supplement. Vol. V, no. 3. Apr. 1885. 3.

An Ordinance Relating to the Department of Buildings and Governing the Erection of Buildings, etc., in the City of Chicago (Chicago: Moorman and Geller, 1903).

Otis Brothers & Co. Established 1856. Hydraulic, Electric, Steam and Belt Elevators [Trade Catalogue] (New York: Otis Brothers and Co., 1893).

Otis Electric Elevators (New York: Otis Elevator Company, 1905).

Otis Elevator Company: Offices in All Principal Cities of the World [Trade Catalogue] (New York: Otis Elevator Company, 1922[?]).

"Our Illustrations [Gaff, Opera House]." *Inland Architect and Builder.* Vol. V, no. 3. Apr. 1885. 39.

"Our Illustrations [Troescher Store]." *Inland Architect and Builder.* Vol. IV, no. 5. Dec. 1885.

"Our Illustrations [Majestic]." *Inland Architect and News Record.* Vol. XLVII, no. 2. Mar. 1906. 32.

"Our Illustrations: The Manhattan Office Building." *Inland Architect and News Record.* Vol. XIII, no. 8. July 1889. 104.

Dominic A. Pacyga. *Chicago: A Biography* (Chicago: University of Chicago Press, 2010).

P. B. Wight's Combination Fire and Water Resisting Columns, of Cast or Wrought Iron: Protected by Gore-Shaped Blocks of Fire Proof Concrete or Porous Terra Cotta Plastered and Polished (Chicago: P. B. Wight and H. B. Merrell, ca. 1880).

Ralph B. Peck. "History of Building Foundations in Chicago." *University of Illinois Bulletin.* Vol. 45, no. 29. Jan. 2, 1948.

Tom Peters *Building the Nineteenth Century* (Cambridge: MIT Press, 1996).

Harry Pickhardt. "The New Lighting." *Architectural Record.* Vol. XXXIII, no. 11. Feb. 1913. 152–155.

Theodore Wells Pietsch. "What the Beaux Arts Training Means to American Architects." *Inland Architect and News Record.* Vol. XXXII, no. 6. Jan. 1899. 53–54.

"Plate Glass Manufacture." *Manufacturer and Builder.* Vol. 15, no. 9. Sept. 1884.

Harold L. Platt. *The Electric City: Energy and the Growth of the Chicago Area, 1880–1930* (Chicago: University of Chicago Press, 1991).

Irving K. Pond. "Concrete Architecture [Report Submitted at the Chicago Convention of the AIA, Nov. 19, 1907]." *Inland Architect and News Record.* Vol. L, no. 5. Nov. 1907. 50–51.

"The Practical Quality of Granite." *Inland Architect and Builder.*" Vol. V, no. 3. Apr. 1885. 3.

Prominent Buildings Erected by the George A. Fuller Company, General Contractors (New York[?]: George A. Fuller Co., 1893[?]).

"Proposed Tests of Structural Materials." *Inland Architect and News Record.* Vol. XLVI, no. 4. Nov. 1905. xiii.

Corydon T. Purdy. "The Evolution of High Building Construction." *Journal of the Western Society of Engineers.* Vol. XXXVII, no. 4. Aug. 1932. 201–211.

———. "Iron and Steel Tall Building Construction," in J. B. Johnson, C W. Bryan, and F. E. Turneaure. *The Theory and Practice of Modern Framed Structures* (New York: Wiley, 1895). 439–459.

———. "The Relation of the Engineer to the Architect [Paper Read at the 38th Annual Convention of the American Institute of Architects, Washington, D.C.]." *Inland Architect and News Record.* Vol. XLIV, no. 6. Jan. 1905. 43–45; Vol. XLV, no. 7 [1?]. Feb. 1905. 4–6.

———. "The Steel Construction of Buildings." *Bulletin of the University of Wisconsin, Engineering Series.* Vol. 1, no. 3. Oct. 1894. 41–67.

———. "The Steel Skeleton Type of High Buildings—I." *Engineering News.* Dec. 5, 1891. 534–536.

———. "The Steel Skeleton Type of High Buildings—II." *Engineering News.* Dec. 12, 1891. 560–561.

H. H. Quimby. "Wind Bracing in High Buildings." *Engineering Record.* Nov. 19, 1892. 394–395; Dec. 31, 1892. 99; Jan. 28, 1893. 180; Feb. 25, 1893. 260; Mar. 11, 1893. 298–99; Mar. 18, 1893. 320.

"The Railway Exchange Building." *Inland Architect and News Record.* Vol. XLIV, no. 3. Oct. 1904. 24.

Frank A. Randall and John Randall, *History of the Development of Building Construction in Chicago* (Champaign: University of Illinois Press, 1999).

"Rapid Progress Made on 32-Story Office Building at Chicago [Straus]." *Engineering News-Record.* Vol. 92, no. 13. Mar. 27, 1924. 541.

A. N. Rebori. "Louis H. Sullivan (1856–1924)." *Architectural Record.* Vol. 55, no. 6. June 1924. 586–587.

———. "Notes and Comments: Zoning Skyscrapers in Chicago." *Architectural Record.* Vol. 58, no. 1. July 1925. 88–90.

———. "The Straus Building, Chicago: Graham, Anderson, Probst & White, Architects." *Architectural Record.* Vol. 57, no. 5. May 1925. 385–394, 418–424.

———. "The Work of Burnham & Root, D. H. Burnham, D. H. Burnham & Co., and Graham, Burnham, & Co." *Architectural Record.* Vol. XXXVIII, no. 1. July 1915. 11–168.

"Recent Brick and Terra-Cotta Work in American Cities." *Brickbuilder.* Vol. V, no. 2. Feb. 1896. 16.

"Recent Chicago Tall Buildings." *Engineering News.* Vol. XXXIV, no. 16. Oct. 17, 1895. 250–252.

Earl H. Reed Jr. "Some Recent Work of Holabird & Root, Architects." *Architecture.* Vol. LXI, no. 1. Jan. 1930. 1–40.

"Reinforced Concrete as a Fire-Proofing Material." *Inland Architect and News Record.* Vol. XLII, no. 6. Jan. 1904. 47.

"A Reinforced Concrete Building in Chicago." *Engineering Record.* Vol. 49, no. 23. June 4, 1904. 713–715.

"Reinforced Concrete Considered." *Inland Architect and News Record.* Vol. XLVIII, no. 1. Aug. 1906. 2.

"The Reliance Building, Chicago." *Scientific American, Building Edition.* Jan. 1895. 17.

"A Remarkable Advance in Fireproofing Methods." *Inland Architect and News Record.* Vol. XXXIX, no. 2. Mar. 1902.

"Report on the Tay Bridge Disaster." *Manufacturer and Builder.* Vol. 12, no. 12. Dec. 1880. 268.

"The Republic Building." *Inland Architect and News Record.* Vol. XLV, no. 2. Mar. 1905. 20.

"Revision of Chicago Building Ordinance." *Inland Architect and News Record.* Vol. XLV, no. 3. Apr. 1905. 22–23.

John W. Root. "A Great Architectural Problem [Paper Read before the Architectural Class of the Art Institute, Chicago]." *Inland Architect and News Record.* Vol. XV, no. 5. June 1890. 67–71.

Fred Ruchti. "Comparative Designs of Office Buildings." *Journal of the Western Society of Engineers.* Vol. XXI, no. 8. Oct. 1916. 640–696.

"Safe Loads on Iron Columns." *Scientific American.* Mar. 14, 1884. 164.

Pauline Saliga and Jane Clarke. *The Sky's The Limit: A Century of Chicago Skyscrapers* (New York: Rizzoli, 1998).

J. C. Sanderson, J. L. McConnell, and F. J. Thielbar. "Home Insurance Building—A Report on Types of Construction Used." *Journal of the Western Society of Engineers.* Vol. XXXVII, no. 1. Feb. 1932. 7–9.

"Saved by Its Fireproofing." *Inland Architect and News Record.* Vol. XXXIX, no. 2. Mar. 1902. 18–19.

Henry Schroeder. "The Incandescent Lamp—Its History." *Lighting Data: Edison Lamp Works of General Electric Company.* Index 7, Bulletin L. D 118A. Jan. 1923.

Montgomery Schuyler. "D. H. Burnham & Co." *Architectural Record*. Vol. V, no. 2. Dec. 1895. 56.

———. "Glimpses of Western Architecture: Chicago—I." *Harper's New Monthly*. Vol. 83, no. 495. Aug. 1891. 395–406.

———. "Glimpses of Western Architecture: Chicago—II." *Harper's New Monthly*. Vol. 83, no. 495. Aug. 1891. 559–580.

———. "The 'Sky-Scraper' up to Date." *Architectural Record*. Vol. VIII, no. 3. Jan.–Mar. 1899. 231–257.

———. "'The Towers of Manhattan' and Notes on the Woolworth Building." *Architectural Record*. Vol. XXXIII, no. 2. Feb. 1913. 99–117.

Warren Candler Scoville. *Studies in Economic History: Revolution in Glassmaking* (Cambridge: Harvard University Printing Office, 1948).

"Seven Plants Fabricate Steel for Chicago Building [Straus]." *Engineering News-Record*. Vol. 91, no. 20. Nov. 15, 1923. 794–795.

E. C. Shankland. "Chicago Foundations [Reprinted from *The Technograph* of the Engineering Societies at the University of Illinois]." *Engineering Record*. Vol. 52, no. 5. July 29, 1905. 131–132.

———. "Modern Constructive Methods." *Inland Architect and News Record*. Vol. XL, no. 6. Jan. 1903. 46–47.

———. "Steel Skeleton Construction in Chicago." *Journal of the Institution of Civil Engineers*. Vol. CXXVIII, Session 1896–7, Part II. 1–27.

———. "Steel Skeleton Construction in Chicago [Paper Read before the Institution of Civil Engineers of England, Dec. 22, 1896]." *Inland Architect and News Record*. Vol. XXX, no. 6. Jan. 1898. 56–58.

Leo J. Sheridan. "Economic Factors of the Office Building Project." *Architectural Forum*. Vol. XLI, no. 3. Sept. 1924. 121–132.

Leo J. Sheridan and W. C. Clark. "The Straus Building, Chicago." *Architectural Forum*. Vol. XLII, no. 4. Apr. 1925. 225–229.

Paul Sherman. "Review of *The Chicago School of Architecture: A History of Commercial and Public Building in the Chicago Area, 1875–1925*." *American Quarterly*. Vol. 16, no. 3. Autumn 1964. 507–508.

Earle Shultz. "The Office Building and the City." *Architectural Forum*. Vol. XLI, no. 3. Sept. 1924. 141–142.

Alice Sinkevitch, American Institute of Architects. Chicago Chapter, Chicago Architecture Foundation, and the Landmarks Preservation Council of Illinois, eds. *AIA Guide to Chicago* (2d ed., New York: Houghton Mifflin Harcourt, 2004).

Joseph Siry. "Adler and Sullivan's Guaranty Building in Buffalo." *Journal of the Society of Architectural Historians*. Vol. 55, no. 1. Mar. 1996. 6–37.

———. *Carson Pirie Scott: Louis Sullivan and the Chicago Department Store* (Chicago: University of Chicago Press, 1988).

———. *The Chicago Auditorium Building: Adler and Sullivan's Architecture and the City* (Chicago: University of Chicago Press, 2004).

"Skeleton Construction." *New York Times*. Aug. 16, 1899. 1.

Maurice M. Sloan. "Architectural and Structural Engineering." *Inland Architect and News Record*. Vol. XLIX, no. 2. Feb. 1907. 27–28; Vol. XLIX, no. 3. Mar. 1907. 43; Vol. XLIX, no. 4. Apr. 1907. 55; Vol. XLIX, no. 5. May 1907. 61; Vol. XLIX, no. 6. June 1907. 77–78; Vol. L., no. 3. Sept. 1907. 28; Vol. LI, no. 1. Jan. 1908. 86.

"Some Facts about the Marquette Building, Chicago." *Inland Architect and News Record*. Vol. XXVI, no. 4. Nov. 1895. 44.

"Some Novel Uses of Compressed Air." *Scientific American*. Vol. CIX, no. 1. July 5, 1913. 8–9, 21.

"Some Tall Chicago Buildings." *Engineering Record*. Nov. 7, 1891[?].

Henry V. Spurr. *Wind Bracing: The Importance of Rigidity in High Towers* (New York: McGraw-Hill, 1930).

"The Stability and Security of Skeleton Buildings." *Engineering Record*. Vol. 27, no. 8. Jan. 21, 1893. 149.

"Stability of High Buildings [Reprint of Engineering Record article]." *Chicago Daily Tribune*. Oct. 16, 1892. 26.

"Steel and Concrete Framing in Tall Chicago Building [Trustees System Building]." *Engineering News-Record*. Dec. 19, 1929. 969.

"Steel vs. Iron Girders." *Engineering News and American Contract Journal*. June 28, 1884. 322.

Charles P. Steinmetz. "Light and Illumination." *Journal of the Western Society of Engineers*. Vol. XX, no. 9. Nov. 1915. 737–751.

Melville E. Stone. "Chicago: Before the Fire, After the Fire, and To-Day." *Scribner's Magazine*. Vol. XVII, no. 6. [year?]. 663–679.

Kenneth Kingley Stowell. "The Structure and Equipment of the Chicago Daily News Building: Holabird & Root, Architects." *Architectural Forum*. Vol. LII, no. 1. Jan. 1930. 107–114.

Russell Sturgis. "Lighting," in Russell Sturgis, ed. *A Dictionary of Architecture and Building, Biographical, Historical and Descriptive* (New York: The MacMillan Company, 1902). 765–768.

Louis H. Sullivan. "Architecture and Building." *Chicago Daily Tribune*. Apr. 27, 1890. 36.

———. "The Chicago Tribune Competition." *Architectural Record*. Vol. LIII, no. 2. Feb. 1923. 151–157.

———. "Reality in the Architectural Art." *Chicago Daily Tribune*. Aug. 5, 1900. 39.

———. "Sub-structure at the New Schlesinger & Mayer Store Building, Chicago." *Engineering Record*. Vol. 47, no. 8. Feb. 21, 1903. 194–196.

———. "The Tall Office Building Artistically Considered [Reprint from *Lippincott's*, Mar. 1896]." *Inland Architect and News Record*. Vol. XXVII, no. 4. May 1896. 32–34.

The Superiority of the Electric Light as an Illuminant (Published ca. 1895).

"The S. W. Straus Building, Chicago. Graham, Anderson, Probst and White, Architects." *Architectural Forum*. Vol. XLI, no. 3. Sept. 1924. 100, plate 44.

"Synopsis of Building News [Grannis Fire]." *Inland Architect and Builder*. Vol. IV, no. 8. Mar. 1885. 27.

"The Tallest Building in Chicago [Montgomery Ward Tower]." *Inland Architect and News Record*. Vol. XXXVI, no. 5. Dec. 1900. 36–38.

"The Tallest Office Building in the World." *Scientific American*. Vol. CVIII, no. 10. Mar. 8, 1913. 224–225, 233.

Thomas E. Tallmadge. *Architecture in Old Chicago* (Reprint, Chicago: University of Chicago Press, 1975).

———. "The Development of the Office Building Since 1924." *Architectural Forum*. Vol. LII, no. 6. June 1930. 780–781.

"The Tay Bridge Disaster." *Science*. Vol. 1, no. 6. Aug. 7, 1880. 70–71.

"Technical Review, Great Northern Theater and Hotel Building, Chicago." *Inland Architect and News Record*. Special Supplement. Vol. XXVIII, no. 2. Sept. 1896.

"Technical Review, The Fisher Building, Chicago—A Building without Walls." *Inland Architect and News Record*. Special Supplement. Vol. XXVII, no. 4. May 1896.

Charles U. Thrall. "Terra Cotta: Its Character and Construction—I." *Brickbuilder*. Vol. XVIII, no. 10. Oct. 1909. 204–207.

"To Light Interiors." *New York Times*. Mar. 19, 1893. 2.

"Tower 256 Ft. High Tops 24-Story Building." *Engineering News-Record*. Vol. 99, no. 21. Nov. 24, 1927. 824–827. [Mather]

E. E. R. Tratman. "Shallow and Deep Foundations in Chicago." Typescript, copy in Burnham Archives, Microfilm. ca. 1904.

"The Tribune Tower Building, Chicago: John M. Howells, Raymond M. Hood, Associated Architects." *Architectural Forum*. Vol. XLI, no. 3. Sept. 1924. 100.

Dmitris Tselos. "The Enigma of Buffington's Skyscraper." *Art Bulletin*. Vol. XXVI, no. 1. Mar. 1944.

Susan Tunick. "The Evolution of Terra Cotta: 'Glazing New Trails.'" *APT Bulletin*. Vol. 32, no. 4. 2001. 3–8.

Theodore Turak. "Remembrances of the Home Insurance Building." *Journal of the Society of Architectural Historians*. Vol. 44, no. 1. Mar. 1985. 60–65.

C. A. P. Turner. "Concrete in the Northwest." *Cement Age*. Vol. 5, no. 5. Nov. 1907. 303–309.

———. "Reinforced Concrete [Paper Read before the Northwest Concrete Products Convention, Minneapolis, Jan. 24, 1905]." *Inland Architect and News Record*. Vol. XLV, no. 2. Mar. 1905. 16–18.

"The University Club. Holabird & Roche, Architects." *Inland Architect and News Record*. Vol. LI, no. 4. Apr. 1908. 29–30.

"The Use of Electric Lights." *Engineering News*. Nov. 5, 1881. 453.

"V. F. Local Business File." *Kokomo Daily Dispatch*. Dec. 14, 1891. 3:4–5. Stan Mohr Local History Library, Kokomo, Indiana.

F. Wagner. "Hints on Design in Terra-Cotta." *Brickbuilder*. Vol. 12, no. 6. June 1903. 119–124.

D. Everett Waid. "Recent Brick and Terra-Cotta Work in American Cities." *Brickbuilder*. Vol. IV, no. 6. June, 1895. 132–133.

George Ethelbert Walsh. "Modern Building Organizations." *Inland Architect and News Record*. Vol. XLVIII, no. 2. Sept. 1906. 18–19.

J. Carson Webster. "Forward." *Prairie School Review*. Vol. IX, no. 1. First Quarter 1972 [*The Chicago School of Architecture, A Symposium, Part I*]. 4–5.

———. "The Skyscraper: Logical and Historical Considerations." *Journal of the Society of Architectural Historians*. Vol. 18, no. 4. Dec. 1959. 126–139.

Joseph D. Weeks. "Glass." *The Eleventh Census of the United States of America*. 1900. 311–340.

Harry Weese & Associates. *Four Landmark Buildings in Chicago's Loop: A Study of Historic Conservation Options* (Chicago: Harry Weese & Associates, 1978).

Winston R. Weisman. "The Chicago School of Architecture: Symposium." *Prairie School Review*. Vol. IX, no. 1. First Quarter 1972; Vol. IX, no. 2. Second Quarter whole issue.

———. "The Commercial Architecture of George B. Post." *Journal of the Society of Architectural Historians*. Vol. 31, no. 3. Oct. 1972. 176–203.

———. "New York and the Problem of the First Skyscraper." *Journal of the Society of Architectural Historians*. Vol. 12, no. 1. Mar. 1953. 13–21.

———. "Review of Carl Condit, *The Chicago School of Architecture*." *Journal of the Society of Architectural Historians*. Vol. 26, no. 4. Dec. 1967. 312–314.

———. "Review of Carl Condit, *The Rise of the Skyscraper*." *Journal of the Society of Architectural Historians*. Vol. 12, no. 3. Oct. 1953. 30–31.

J. Hollis Wells. "The Modern Office Building." *Brickbuilder*. Vol. IV, no. 4. Apr. 1895. 84–85.

Sara E. Wermiel. "Introduction of Steel Columns in American Buildings, 1862–1920." *Engineering History and Heritage*. Vol. 162, no. 1. Feb. 2009. 19–27.

Langdon White. "Geography's Part in the Plant Cost of Iron and Steel Production at Pittsburgh, Chicago, and Birmingham." *Economic Geography*. Vol. 5, no. 4. Oct. 1929. 327–334.

Peter B. Wight. "Additions to Chicago's Skyline: A Few Recent Skyscrapers." *Architectural Record*. Vol. XXVIII, no. 1. July 1910. 15–24.

———. "Daniel Hudson Burnham and His Associates." *Architectural Record*. Vol. XXXVIII, no. 1. July 1915. 1–10.

———. "Development of the Fireproofing of Buildings." *The Inland Architect Supplement: Technical Review of the Interesting Development of the Building Arts*. Vol. XXXIV, no. 6. Jan. 1900. 8–12.

———. "Fire-Proofing Department: The Present Condition of the Art of Fire-Proofing." *Brickbuilder*. Vol. VI, no. 10. n.d. 250.

———. "The Foundations." *Chicago Daily Tribune*. May 9, 1875. 1.

———. "Passenger Elevators." *Chicago Daily Tribune*. June 19, 1881. 16.

———. "Recent Fireproof Building in Chicago." *Inland Architect and Builder*. Vol. V, Extra No. Apr. 1885. 52.

———. "Recent Fireproof Building in Chicago." *Inland Architect and News-Record*. Vol. XIX. Mar. 1892. 21–22.

———. "Recent Improvements in Fire-Proof Construction at Chicago: The Ayer Building." *Brickbuilder*. Vol. VIII, no. 2. Feb. 1899. 33–34.

———. Remarks in the *Proceedings of the Fifth Annual Convention of the American Institute of Architects Held in Boston, November 14th and 15th, 1871* (New York: American Institute of Architects, 1872). 45–52.

———. *Remarks on Fire-Proof Construction: A Paper Read before the New York Chapter of the American Institute of Architects, April 8th, 1869* (New York: The Committee on Library and Publications, AIA, 1869).

———. "Soap and Water in Relation to Architecture." *Inland Architect and News Record*. Vol. XXV, no. 4. May 1895. 38–39.

James R. Willett. "Skeleton Structures in Building." *Inland Architect and News Record*. Vol. XXVI, no. 5. Dec. 1895. 47–48.

"William Le Baron Jenney." *Inland Architect and News Record*. Vol. L, no. 1. July 1907. 8–9.

Charlton Williams. "What Steel Did for a Great City." *Harper's*. Dec. 28, 1912. 16.

Carol Willis. *Form Follows Finance* (New York: Princeton Architectural Press, 1995).

Franz Winkler [Montgomery Schuyler]. "Some Chicago Buildings Represented by the Work of Holabird & Roche." *Architectural Record*. Vol. XXXI, no. 4. Apr. 1912. 313–370.

"The Work of Holabird & Roche, Architects." *American Architect*. Vol. CXVIII, no. 2331. Aug. 25, 1920. 231–242.

Frank Lloyd Wright. "Louis H. Sullivan—His Work." *Architectural Record*. Vol. 56, no. 1. July 1924. 28–32.

David Yeomans. "The Origins of the Modern Curtain Wall." *APT Bulletin*. Vol. 32, no. 1. 2001. 13–18.

J. W. Yost. "Influence of Steel Construction, and of Plate Glass upon the Development of Modern Style." *American Architect and Building News*. Vol. LIV, no. 1089. Nov. 7, 1896. 45–46.

John Zukowsky, ed. *Chicago Architecture, 1872–1922: Birth of a Metropolis* (Berlin: Prestel, 2000).

———, ed. *Chicago Architecture and Design, 1923–1993: Reconfiguration of an American Metropolis* (Berlin: Prestel, 2000).

John Zukowsky and Pauline Saliga. "Late Works by Burnham and Sullivan." *Art Institute of Chicago Museum Studies*. Vol. 11, no. 1. Autumn 1984. 70–79.

Index

glass, influence of manufacture on, 60, 89, 110; Home Insurance (1885), use in, 43; illumination, most economical source of, 36; iron structure, enabling of, 11, 48, 61; Jewelers Building (1926), use in, 157; light courts, provision for, 18, 22, 55; masonry construction, conflicts with, 33, 37, 52, 57, 60; Merchandise Mart (1931), use in, 206n95; Merchant's Loan and Trust (1901), use in, 131; Monadnock (1891), use in, 33; office dimensions, influence upon, 138; Opera House (1885), use in, 23; pre-fire buildings, benefits to, 8; Reliance Building (1895), use in, 91; Rookery (1888), use in, 55–58; Root, John Wellborn, opinions on, 13, 35, 36; Ryerson Building (1884), use in, 52; skeletal frame, influence upon, xvi, 34, 43, 48, 57, 130, 144, 178; skylights, provision by, 141; speculative development, importance to, 8; steel construction, enabling of, 90, 175; Sullivan, Louis H., opinions on, 48

demolition, 37, 149, 172–173, 174, 180, 198n46

Depression, Great, xv, 165, 171–172, 173–174

Depression of 1873–1879, 2, 11, 14

Depression of 1893–1897, 91, 100, 134

Des Plaines River, 1, 4

Dever, William, 151

Diamond Plate Glass, 87–89, 126, 201n35

Dinkelberg, Frederick, 130, 157–158, 206n66

Drake, William H., 1, 199n63

"dry-goods boxes," critique of Chicago buildings as, 23, 108, 151, 197n32

Edison, Thomas A., 36

Egan, James, Cook County Courthouse (1885), 37

electricity: Auditorium (1889), provision in, 29; Board of Trade (1930), provision in, 169; building skins, influence upon, 144; Chicago, availability and price in, 36, 98, 127; construction, use in, 167, 178; dangers of, 36; demon-strations of, early, 36; elevators, use in, 144–146, 167, 175, 176; First National Bank (1903), provision in, 135; illumination, 126–127, 133, 135–136, 147, 157, 178; Marshall Field & Co. Store, 1902, provision in, 133; Merchandise Mart (1931), provision in, 170; Monadnock (1891), provision in 33, 196n84; Montauk Block (1882), provision in, 21–22; nerves, analogous to, 168; New York City, installation in, 36; Royal Insurance (1885), provision in, 26; Straus (1924), provision in, 157

electric power, xvi, 109, 127, 144–146, 165, 169, 171, 178

elevators: Civic Opera (1929), installation in, 166–167; Continental and Commercial Bank (1913), installation in, 141; Conway Building (1912), installation in, 140; electrically powered, 144–146, 176; Field Building (1934), installation in, 172; fireproofing, conflicts with, 17, 19–20; First National Bank (1903), 134; gearless traction, 146; Grannis Block (1881), installation in, 18; improvements in, 11, 143; influence on skyscraper height, xiii-xiv, 172, 174–175, 178; Leiter Store (1879), installation in, 41; Masonic Temple (1892), poor performance in, 145; Mather Tower (1928), installation in, 158; Montauk Block (1882), installation in, 22; obsolescence, slow performance as cause, 125; Phoenix Building (1887), installation in, 54; Pittsfield Building (1927), installation in, 160; planning for, 182; problems with early installations, 3; programmed, 146; shafts, fireproofing of, 105; Singer Building, New York City (1908), installation in, 146; space requirements for, 37; Straus Building (1924), installation in, 156; Tacoma Building (1889), installation in 80; 333 N. Michigan Ave. (1928), installation in, 165

Elwood, IN, 87–89, 126

Emperger columns, 163

Ericsson, Henry, 179

Evolution, xv, 89, 96, 124, 172–174, 181–183, 193n14

Fairbairn, William, 73

Ferree, Barr: articulated wall, as essential feature, 182; Auditorium (1889), criticism of, 29; Chicago skyscrapers, praise for, xx; concealment of structure, preference for, 39–40, 90; concentration of business as influence on skyscraper design, 180; Monadnock (1891), praise for, 32; New York lot sizes, comment on, xvii; progressive spirit of Chicago, praise for, 183; Reliance (1895), criticism of, 92

Field, Marshall, 26, 131, 133; estate of, 140, 160, 171–172

Field & Co., Marshall, 169–170

fire districts, 3, 11

fireproof construction: Auditorium (1889), use of, 29; brick, xiv, 4, 11, 15–16, 43, 61; cast-iron, 6; columns, problems with, 74, 76; companies, 16, 174; concrete, 104–105, 141, 163; Continental and Commercial Bank (1914), use in, 140; costs, 17; curtain walls, 93; development after 1871 Fire, 178; early skyscrapers, importance to, xvi; exterior walls, influence on, 35; failure in 1871 Fire, 8–9; Field Warehouse (1887), use in, 26; Grannis Block (1881), failure of, 19–20; Home Insurance (1885), use in, 44; insurance, requirements for, 15; Insurance Exchange (1885), use in, 53; masonry jackets in post-1893 code buildings, xvi, 101, 103, 122; Merchant's Loan and Trust (1901), use in, 131; mill construction, 3; Montauk Block (1882), use in, 20, 22; Nixon Block (1872), success of, 10–11, 16; party walls, 18; performance requirement of skyscrapers, xiv; plaster, 10, 17; reliability, 103, 108; Revell Building (1883), use in, 51; Rookery (1888), use in, 56, 58; shafts, vertical, 17, 105; standardization, 103, 107; stone, 3, 4; terra cotta, 4, 15–17, 79, 85–86, 91, 103, 117, 131;

ence on 'ziggurat' form, 175; 1923 Ordinance, basis on, 150–151; Palmolive
Building (1929), sophisticated integration of, 163; Pittsfield Building (1927),
approach to building massing, 160;
"setback skyscraper," influence on,
162, 163, 178; Straus Building (1924),
impact on massing, 154; structural design, integration with, 158; 164; 333 N.
Michigan Ave. (1927), integrated massing of, 162; Tribune Tower competition,
influence on, 151; Trustees Systems Services Building (1930), effect on, 162;
Willoughby Tower (1929), integration
with Gothic massing, 162

Shankland, E. C.: building footprint, proportions of to resist wind, opinions
on, 63; death of, 1924; Fisher Building
(1896), engineering of, 91, 93; lattice
girders, design of, 91; moment frame,
development of, 70; Reliance Building
(1895), engineering of, 91; retirement
of, 130; soil bearing pressure, allowable, opinions on, 7; sway rods, comparison to railway viaduct, 68; "table
leg principle," coining of term, 70; wind
loads, opinions on, 64; wind velocities,
measurements of, 64

Shaw, Alfred P.: Civic Opera (1929), design of, 165–166, 168; Field Building
(1934), design of, 172; Graham, Anderson, Probst, and White, career with,
143, 174; Merchandise Mart (1931), design of, 170; Pittsfield Building (1927),
design of, 160, 162; Shaw, Naess, and
Murphy, formation of, 174

Shaw, Naess, and Murphy, 174

Shepley, Rutan, and Coolidge: Art Institute (1893), 129; Corn Exchange
(1908), 136, 188; Harris Trust (1911), 136,
189; Public Library (1897), 105, 127

Sherman, Paul, xii

Shipman, Steven V.: Gaff Building (1885),
17, 26, 186

Simonds Saw and Steel Building, Fitchburg, MA, 127

Singer Building, NYC, 146
skeletal frames: Adler and Sullivan, interest and early experiments in, 47–52;
architectural expression of, 38–39, 45,
47–48, 60, 86, 89–90; Baumann, Frederick, 1884 pamphlet promoting, 43,
175; Burnham, D. H. & Co., attempts
to meld with classical aesthetics, 136;
cast iron storefronts, precursor to, 35;
Chamber of Commerce (1890), structure of, 43; Condit, Carl, stress on as
element of skyscraper definition, 177;
Conkey (1887), structure of, 43; connections in, 200n32; curtain wall, enabling of, 34, 47; daylighting, enabling
of, 34, 35, 43, 60, 89, 178; facades, hierarchy of based on, 48–49, 60; foundations, influence on, xviii, 38, 179;
height, building, effect on, 13; Holabird
& Roche, recapitulation of, 111; Home
Insurance Building, structure of and un-
certainty regarding, 43–46, 172, 177,
198n47, 199n70; Hood & Howells, expression of underlying, 153; hybrid with
masonry, 18, 26, 45–46, 52, 60, 82, 176;
internal, in "cage" construction, 35, 38;
Isabella (1892), structure of, 85; Leiter
Store (1879), structure of, 41; Ludington
(1891), structure of, 85; masonry walls,
replacement for, 8, 34, 55, 178; "modern construction," definition of based
on, 47; Monadnock Block (1891), early
scheme as, 30, internal, 34; Mujica,
Francisco, history of, 174–175, 176; mythology of post-fire construction, 9;
Phoenix Building (1887), early example
of, 53; Republic (1905), expression of,
118; Root, John Wellborn, interest and
experiments in, 54; Royal Insurance
(1885), precursor to, 26; steel, importance to, 62; Studebaker (1886), precursor to, 34; Tacoma Building (1889),
incomplete conception of, 82; Troescher Block (1884), thorough expression of, 52; typology, xvi, 89; Webster, J.
Carson, argument for as requirement

for label 'skyscraper,' 176; weight, savings due to, 43, 62, 178; Weisman, Winston, argument against as requirement
for label 'skyscraper,' 176; wind bracing, need for, 47, 60, 71, 78

Skidmore, Louis, 174

Skidmore, Owings, and Merrill, xiii, 174, 177

Snow, J. P., 71

soil, Chicago: bearing, allowable, 37, 43,
79, 194n34; brickmaking, used for locally, 4–5; cage construction, difficulties presented by, 26, 59, 196n61;
caissons, ideal for, 106; compressible,
effect on massing, xviii, 8, 43; conditions unique to Chicago, xvii, 179; failures due to, 37; foundations, designed
for, 8, 29, 37–38, 199n59; limits to building height due to, 3, 7, 106; piles, well
suited for, 37, 106; poor bearing quality
of Chicago, xvii-xviii; skeletal frame, influence on, 12, 15, 43, 79, 179; testing,
29; weight, influence on building, 8, 43

Sooy Smith, William, 7, 106, 179

spandrel panels: art deco skyscrapers,
use in, 165; Board of Trade (1930), use
in, 169; Burnham, D. H. & Co., incorporation into monolithic elevations, 130,
134; Champlain Building (1894), use in,
112; Commercial Bank (1907), use in,
136; Conway Building (1913), use in,
140; curtain wall, structural role within,
89; façade hierarchy, role in, xiv, 13,
43, 49, 52, 55, 81, 90, 111, 114, 116, 127,
181; Field Building (1934), use in, 172;
First National Bank (1903), use in, 135;
Fisher Building (1896), use in, 93, 181;
Gaff Building (1884), use in, 26; Holabird and Roche, importance of to façade designs, 81, 110–111, 114–116,
118; Insurance Exchange (1912), use in,
139; Jenney, William Le Baron, importance of to façade designs, 58; Leiter
Building (1879), use in, 43, 49; Ludington Building (1891), use in, 59; Marquette Building (1895), use in, 111; Merchant's Loan and Trust (1901), use in,

132; Montauk Block (1883), use in, 20; Republic (1905), use in, 118–119; Revell Block (1883), use in, 51–52; Rookery (1888), structural role in, 56; Root, John Wellborn, importance of to façade designs, 52; Schlesinger and Mayer (1899), use in, 181; suitability for ornament, xiv, 13; Sullivan, Louis H., importance of to façade designs, 50, 52, 110; 333 N. Michigan Ave. (1927), use in, 162; Tribune Tower (1925), use in, 153; Venetian (1892), use in, 111; Williams Building (1898), use in, 116

speculation, real estate: Brooks, Peter and Sheppard, 18; Chicago, explosive nature of, xvii–xviii, 2, 180; construction speed, importance of, 180; creator of distinct building types, 8, 39; economy, problems with, 11; engine of local building industry, 3, 179; First National Bank, 134; height restrictions, frustration with, 147; Indiana gas belt, 87; investment from other cities, 2; neighborhood-specific, 2; river trade, basis in, 1–2; steel construction, importance of, 180; Ryerson, Martin, 51

steel: Bessemer process, 45, 62, 82; Chicago industry, 4; fireproofing of, xvi; foundations, use in, 32; influence on sksycraper height, xiii–xiv; masonry, replacement of, 33; Monadnock Block (1891), use in, 30–33; Monadnock Extension (1893), use in, 34; novelty of, xiv; separation of building frame from skin, role in, xvi; weight compared to masonry, 8; wind bracing, importance to, xvi; window frames, use in, xv

St. Louis, MO, 15, 85, 87, 109

St. Louis Hydraulic Pressed Brick Company, 18, 21–22, 53

stone. See granite; limestone; sandstone

storefronts: cast-iron, xvi, 6, 8, 25, 35; code requirements for, 11; Marshall Field Store (1902), use in existing building, 133; Opera House (1885), use of, 14, 25; polished plate glass, use in, 86; Republic Building (1905), use in, 118; Schles-

inger and Mayer Store (1899, 1902), use in, 120; subgrade, difficulties of, 37; Sullivan, Louis H., opinions on, 109–110

Straus, S. W. & Co., 154–156

strikes, 5, 6, 77, 78, 89, 203n46

Strobel, Charles, 45

structural brick. See brick, pressed (structural)

Sullivan, Louis H.: Adler, Dankmar, critiqued by, 182; Adler, Dankmar, hired by, 14; architectural philosophy of, general, 12, 40, 49, 52, 108–109, 156, 168, 180; Baumann, Frederick, early use of foundation proposal, 199n63; Bayard Building (New York, 1899), xx; Condit, Carl, assessment of, xii, 177; Darwin, Charles, influence of, 181; daylight, importance of, comments on, 48; death of, 174, 207n5; divorce of, 207n5; early life and career, 14; façade designs of, 48–52, 55, 101, 109–110, 119, 134, 181; "form follows function" (1896), xiv, 108–109; foundations, influence on designs of, 50; Gage Building (1899), 110, 118–119, 188; historical assessment of, xxi; legacy of, 142, 174, 183; ornamental designs of, 29, 50, 55, 120; posthumous reputation of, 174; Schlesinger and Mayer (Carson, Pirie, Scott) (1899, 1902), xii, xiii, xxi, 106, 110, 119–122, 181, 188; "A System of Architectural Ornament," (1922–1923), 174; "The Tall Office Building Artistically Reconsidered," (1896), 119; Tribune Tower (1925), critique of, 153; verticality in skyscraper design, champion of, 153. See also Adler and Sullivan

sway-bracing. See wind bracing

"table leg" principle, 70

Tallmadge, Thomas: Adler and Sullivan, critical assessment of, 52; Anderson, Peirce, quoting, 204; history of early Chicago architecture, 175; leadership of Field Estate committee on Home Insurance Building, 46, 172; position in Graham, Anderson, Probst, and White, 143

terra cotta: advantages of, 16, 86; Atwood, Charles, use by, 99; Auditorium (1889), use in, 29; Ayer/McClurg Building (1900), use in, 116–117; Boston Store (1905), use in, 115; brick, backup for, 81; building codes, requirements for, 17, 110, 117; Carbon and Carbide Building (1929), use in, 162; Champlain Building (1894), use in, 112, 114; Chicago, early use in, 17; classical ornament, use for, 125, 130, 138, 142; column protection, 17; Commercial Bank (1908), use in, 135; comparisons with, 15–16, 38, concrete, replacement by, 105; costs, 86, 201n24; curtain wall, role in, xii–xiii, xvi, 78, 80, 84, 91, 96; enameled, 78, 85–86, 89, 92, 99, 130, 138, 142; fireproofing, general, 4, 16, 22, 44, 79, 89, 117, 178; fires, performance in, 23, 103–104; Fisher Building (1896), use in, 91, 93, 96; floor arches, 16–17, 19–20, 56; Gaff Building (1884), use in, 26; Gothic ornament, use for, 90, 92, 99, 147; Great Northern Hotel Office Building (1896), 96; hollow tile, partitions, 17; Holabird & Roche, use by, 85, 111, 114, 116–119; Home Insurance (1885), use in, 44; improvements in, 17, 85, 130; Insurance Exchange (1885), use in, 53; Insurance Exchange (1913), use in, 139; iron, paired with, 14, 35, 39, 178; Jenney, William Le Baron, use by, 59; local industry, 16, 17, 21, 85; "lumber," 17; Majestic Building (1906), use in, 136; manufacture, 15, 116; Marquette Building (1895), use in, 111; Mather Tower (1928), use in, 158; Montauk (1883), use in, 20–22, 38; Opera House (1885), use in, 25; ornamental, 8, 13, 21, 39, 79, 85; People's Gas Building (1911), use in, 138; Pittsfield Building (1927), use in, 160, 162; plate glass, combination with and aesthetics of, 86, 89; proportions of, 38, 81, 85–86; Railway Exchange (1904), use in, 102; Reliance Building (1895), use in, 91–92; replacement for, 85; Revell Building (1883),

Thomas Leslie, AIA, is the Pickard Chilton Professor of Architecture at Iowa State University and the author of *Louis I. Kahn: Building Art, Building Science.*

The University of Illinois Press
is a founding member of the
Association of American University Presses.

————————————————————

Designed by Dustin J. Hubbart
Composed in 9/15 Century Gothic
with Myriad display
by Jim Proefrock
at the University of Illinois Press
Manufactured by Bang Printing

University of Illinois Press
1325 South Oak Street
Champaign, IL 61820-6903
www.press.uillinois.edu